RECOGNIZING PUBLIC VALUE

June, 2015

RECOGNIZING PUBLIC VALUE

MARK H. MOORE

To James,
keep Creating
Public Value!

Mark M

HARVARD UNIVERSITY PRESS
Cambridge, Massachusetts
London, England
2013

Library of Congress Cataloging-in-Publication Data

Moore, Mark Harrison.
Recognizing public value / Mark H. Moore.
p.   cm.
Includes bibliographical references and index.
ISBN 978-0-674-06695-3 (alk. paper)
1. Public administration—Moral and ethical aspects—United States—Case studies.
2. Government executives—Professional ethics—United States—Case studies.
I. Title.
JF1525.E8M68 2013
172'.2—dc23   2012022228

*To Richard E. Neustadt and Graham T. Allison.
They gave me a worthy assignment
and kept me at it over a long career.*

Contents

Figures and Tables

Tables

I wouldn't give a fig for the simplicity on this side of complexity;
I would give my right arm for the simplicity on the far side of complexity.

—Oliver Wendell Holmes Jr.

Introduction

In 1995 I published a book entitled *Creating Public Value*. The book offered practical advice to public managers who sought to make the best use of the public assets that were (temporarily, and with significant restrictions and oversight) entrusted to them. The ideas in *Creating Public Value* were developed at a time when many private management concepts were being applied to the public sector. They included

- a sharper focus on *customers* of government agencies;
- a more extensive use of *performance measurement systems* to recognize the value that public agencies were creating and to call both managers and employees to account for producing it;
- a wider, more intensive use of the methods of *total quality management* and *continuous improvement* to create productivity gains in government operations; and
- a greater reliance on *pay for performance* for both managers and frontline workers in government.

These ideas have had mixed success in government. The promise of a more efficient, effective, and "customer-friendly" public sector drove public managers to experiment with new methods and models for service delivery, production, performance measurement, and human resource management. But each of the aforementioned ideas also posed challenges, not only because they were somewhat novel in government but because the processes and practices of democratic government did not always adapt particularly well to private-sector paradigms.

Customer-Oriented Government?

The idea of focusing attention on customers did succeed in making many public agencies more attentive to the experience that individual citizens had in their individual encounters with government agencies. But many public managers and organizations remained uncertain about who their customers were, how they might best be satisfied, and how important customer satisfaction was in their overall mission. After all, public managers and agencies had spent a long time thinking that their goal was to pursue the mission that had been set for their organization, or achieving particular social outcomes. Exactly where the idea of customer satisfaction fit into these older conceptions of public value creation was unclear.

While those individuals who transacted with government agencies as service recipients and beneficiaries resembled private-sector customers in the sense that they engaged in individual transactions from which they *benefited,* they generally did not pay directly for the particular services they received at the point of service. Nor, typically, could they decide as individuals how much of the government services they would like to purchase. Moreover, these "service encounters" between government agencies and their beneficiaries represented only one kind of transaction between individuals and government. For many individuals, transactions with government resulted not in services but in *obligations.* Taxpayers, regulated economic enterprises, and alleged criminals encountered government agencies not as service recipients but as "obligatees." While it might be prudent and just for government agencies to treat those receiving obligations with decency and respect for their rights, it did not seem self-evident that the main purpose of these encounters should be to satisfy them. If the goal were to satisfy these customers, most of them would have been happy to dispense with the encounter altogether!

Finally, it seemed clear that there were many stakeholders beyond the individuals receiving services and obligations who might also be considered "customers" of public agencies, including the citizens and voters who authorized the public effort, the taxpayers who paid for government operations, the judicial system, and the officials elected to represent the interests and aspirations of citizens. Insofar as these stakeholders had the philosophical, legal, and practical basis to decide what was worth doing with public assets and to sustain government operations, they seemed to share fundamental traits with private-sector customers.

The question facing public managers, then, was how to satisfy all these various kinds of "customers" and stakeholders. What should happen when the values and interests of the citizens, taxpayers, and/or elected representatives conflicted with the values and interests of the individuals receiving services and obligations from government?

As an answer to these questions, many have pointed out that what citizens, taxpayers, and their representatives really want from government is the efficient and effective achievement of mandated social outcomes. They want fair and efficient tax collection, equal access to high-quality public education, a natural environment that is at least safe (maybe clean, ideally beautiful), and so on. But the idea that government creates value by producing these social outcomes is not quite the same as the idea that government creates value by satisfying "customers"—whether beneficiaries or obligatees. Social outcomes are a measure of aggregate social conditions—not of the subjective satisfactions of individuals who transact with government. In the end, what makes social outcomes valuable is not simply that particular individuals value them, but that the wider "public" that has tacitly agreed to be taxed and regulated to produce the desired social result values them. This suggests that in the public sector, the relevant "customer" is a collective public (local, regional, or national) acting through the imperfect processes of representative democracy rather than an individual consumer making choices about what to buy for personal benefit.

Better Performance Measurement Systems?

The idea that government agencies should develop and use stronger performance measurement systems has created somewhat less conceptual confusion. It seems fairly straightforward that developing and using relatively objective measures to recognize good and bad performance would make public managers and public agencies more accountable and drive them to perform better. Presumably, such measures might also enhance the legitimacy of government operations not only through the commitment to transparency but also to a wider understanding and recognition of what the government actually does with public money and authority. Indeed, if the principal value that government produces is collectively desired social outcomes, then all that would be necessary to create a better measurement system would be to name the desired outcomes and find methods for measuring progress made toward them.[1]

Thus at the outset the problem seemed to be mostly technical: how to develop measures that reliably captured the success of public organizations in altering social conditions in collectively desired directions—that is, in creating public value. But there was also a managerial problem: What would motivate public managers to face the significant hazards of developing and using performance measures in organizations unaccustomed to being called to account for their performance? This, in turn, exposed a political problem: while elected officials were all for increased government accountability, they found it hard to identify precisely what values they wanted particular public agencies to pursue, and they generally refused to commit to any set of ideas long enough for a public agency to develop a corresponding performance measurement system that would allow it to meet the demand for improved performance. In the background lurked a larger philosophical problem about how the public and its elected representatives ought to think about the values they wanted public agencies to produce and reflect in their operations.

Among those advocating increased use of performance measurement, there seemed to be a consensus that public managers should shift away from the input and process measures on which they had long relied and strive to develop outcome measures that could measure the ultimate value that public agencies were trying to produce for citizens. But the drive to measure ultimate outcomes soon ran into a practical problem: it was costly and difficult to gather data about social conditions that were far removed from today's transactions with a government organization. It was hard to attribute observed changes in social conditions to particular government actions. And the feedback came in too late, with too little verifiable connection to government activities to make the performance measures useful in guiding day-to-day operations. Finally, for those who wanted the government to reveal the "bottom-line" value of its activities, efforts to "monetize" the value being produced by public agencies and set it against costs incurred proved particularly problematic.

As we will see, all these practical challenges have slowed the rate at which the drive to measure government performance has been able to progress. This book aims to help government overcome many of these difficulties, at least in part by recognizing that the work that needs to be done is not simply technical but also philosophical, political, and managerial. But so far, at least, the public sector's commitment to developing and using performance measurement systems has been mostly shallow and sporadic.

Total Quality Management?

The effort to make use of private-sector practices also called attention to the processes that public agencies used to encourage and implement innovation in their operations. Many public agencies began experimenting with "total quality management," "process improvement," and "process reengineering" to find and exploit productivity-increasing innovations in their core operational procedures.[2] Agencies throughout government created productivity teams to determine whether particular steps in overly complex bureaucratic procedures could be eliminated without jeopardizing accountability or performance.[3] Following the example of General Electric, public managers convened "workout sessions" in which top managers could hear suggestions for improving performance directly from those working on the "shop floor" and act on them on the spot.

These efforts yielded some positive results—particularly in agencies that had become mired in red tape and had taken so much discretion out of the hands of workers that they no longer felt either able or motivated to do their work well. But much of this work focused on small process innovations.[4] The mechanisms of total quality improvement could not grapple with larger strategic questions about useful innovations in core operating methods, or the series of innovations necessary to guide an organization toward a new position and a new mission in a changing world. These larger changes required different kinds of political authorization.

While the interest in total quality management pushed innovation and productivity gains toward the forefront of managerial action in the public sector, the basic forces that tended to discourage innovation in government—the demand for consistency and reliability in government operations, and the consequences attached to losing a "gamble" made with public assets—remained very strong.[5]

Pay for Performance?

The idea that public agencies should rely more heavily on pay-for-performance systems has made some inroads—particularly at the senior management level in the federal government and at the worker levels of some public organizations, most notably public schoolteachers.[6] But the idea of paying for performance stumbles over the challenge of accurately defining performance in quantitative terms and then collapses in a heap before the challenge of reliably attributing observed changes in performance to the actions of individual government managers or employees. One can insist on having such a system, and make some measurements that can ostensibly support it, but it is not at all clear that such a system usefully animates and guides the performance of either managers or workers on the front line.

A Missing Idea: Strategic Management

Significantly, there was one basic tenet of private-sector management that did not draw much interest in the public sector: the concept of "strategic management" as it had been developed in the business world to guide the decision making and leadership of chief executive officers (CEOs) entrusted with the assets of private-sector firms. This was a bit ironic, since it was largely this idea that held pride of place in the business world, and to which much of the success of modern business had been attributed.[7] In the private sector, developing an organizational strategy remains the first and most important step in giving purpose and direction to one's organization. Without a strategy, how would a firm know what products and services it needed to produce, which customers to pursue, or what measures would monitor the performance of the organization as a whole or its individual members?

Of course many public managers believed they had been doing strategic management for a long time. They had strategic planning staffs who guided complex strategic planning processes in their organizations. But in the public sector, strategic management seemed to mean: (1) focusing on the long run over the short, (2) attending to large issues with a big impact on performance rather than on small issues with more minor effects on production; and (3) concentrating on ultimate ends rather than perfecting means. What strategic management meant in the private sector, however, was *finding a fit between one's organization and the external environment in which that organization was operating.* Any calculations about the long versus the short run, threats and opportunities around value production, and desired ultimate ends had to be made in light of what the external environment made possible. Figuring that out was no easy task, for the environment was understood to be both complex and dynamic—*complex* in the sense that there were many different market niches one could find and exploit, and *dynamic* in the sense that opportunities were opening and closing frequently as conditions changed in society.

It followed, then, that a critical strategic task was for private-sector managers to *diagnose the external environments they faced.* The concepts of strategic management directed managerial attention to two key features of their operating environments: (1) the customers whose wants and needs they were trying to satisfy with particular products and services, and (2) other producers of goods and services with whom they were competing. Other stakeholders—investors, employees, suppliers, and government regulators—were also important parts of the environment to be noted and accommodated or exploited in the execution of a competitive market strategy. But the overwhelming focus was on customers and competitors.[8]

Creating Public Value explicitly sought to bring the idea that a value-creating strategy for a public organization had to be as focused on the external environment of the organization as those developed in the private sector. It assumed that public managers, like their private-sector counterparts, faced a basic leadership task of imagining high-value uses of the assets that had been entrusted to them. To do so, public managers also had to look outward from their organization toward the environment that was telling them what was valuable and possible to do, providing them with resources, and posing operational challenges. The book urged public managers to look *upward* toward the *political authorizing environment* that both provided resources and judged the value of what they were producing and *outward* toward the *task environment* where their efforts to produce public value would find success or failure.

Once the focus shifted from refining internal operations to diagnosing external environments, it became obvious that the environments that public managers faced were at least as complex and dynamic as those that private-sector managers faced. Looking to their political environments for legitimacy and support, public managers saw both heterogeneous demands and rapid changes in expectations. Looking out to the operational challenges they faced in spheres such as national defense, public health, education, and child welfare, they could see that their task environment was similarly heterogeneous and dynamic. They faced many different tasks, and the tasks changed frequently—sometimes creating challenges that had never been seen before (e.g., terrorism, AIDS, etc.) and sometimes dramatically shifting the relative weight of a particular burden on the organization (e.g., responding to foreign language students, or accommodating culturally different practices of child rearing).

Consequently, public managers had to learn to think in terms of *positioning their organizations in complex, dynamic environments,* just as private-sector mangers did. Just as CEOs and business managers have to learn to respond to heterogeneous and dynamic market environments with flexibility, creativity, and innovation, so public managers would have to learn to respond to diverse and volatile political and social environments with equally restless, value-seeking imaginations.

In the years since its publication, many have found *Creating Public Value* a helpful guide in confronting and adapting to the many challenges of public management (volatile partisan politics, budget shortfalls, entrenched public employees, media outrage, unhappy government clients, "wicked" public problems, etc.). For citizens and overseers, as well as for public managers, it has emphasized the degree to which we are all dependent on the value-creating managers of public as well as private organizations. But there was much that *Creating Public Value* left unresolved.

Recognizing Public Value as a Key Step in Creating Public Value

The most obvious issue was the difficulty of giving a clear, objective definition of what constituted public value. At a time when social politics cast government as (at best) a kind of referee rather than a producing entity or (at worst) "the problem" rather than the solution, the claim that government was producing something of value—something that would improve the quality of individual and collective life for citizens—was startling and ideologically contentious.

To some degree, the claim had to be true. Why else would a citizenry with the power to control a government give up some of its money and liberty to a government if not to produce something that it valued over the costs of production? But it begged the question of exactly how public value should be defined and recognized.

The question of how public value should be defined and recognized, in turn, raised two other critical questions. The first was the procedural question of what particular social actors were the proper arbiters of public value: the clients of government services or the citizens and tax-payers in whose name the government acted? If the answer was citizens and taxpayers rather than clients, how could a large number of individuals become articulate and clear about their views on which values and outcomes were worth taxing and regulating themselves to produce in pursuit of a good and just society?[9] The second question was the substantive issue of which particular effects or dimensions of government performance those who were the proper arbiters of public value would embrace. Reducing costs? Increasing the quantity and quality of organizational outputs? Satisfying clients? Achieving desired social outcomes? Would their concerns focus only on the substantive ends of government action, or would they also be concerned about the means used? What standing would they give to concerns that individuals be treated fairly and their rights be protected when addressing those concerns affected the costs of achieving particular results? What standing would they give to the idea that government should help produce a society that was not only prosperous but also fair and just?

Taken together, the procedural question of what actors (working through what processes) could legitimize a particular concept of public value and the substantive question of which particular values this legitimate arbiter of value would choose constitute the core problem of creating accountability for government performance. Without answers to these questions, one could not really have a theory of public value creation.

As I struggled with these questions, it started to seem increasingly plausible that something that appeared to be a simple technical and managerial problem—the task of measuring the performance of government agencies—might actually be a vital solution to the general problem of strategic, value-oriented management in government. Perhaps becoming serious about performance measurement and skilled in methods for recognizing public value would facilitate more specific, concrete, and rigorous tests of whether public agency strategies were valuable, legitimate, and doable. Perhaps strong public-sector performance measurement systems would support a public discussion about what was both possible and desirable to do with the authority and money of the state. Perhaps they could help us drive the performance of individual public agencies, not only by creating accountability but also by helping the organizations learn how to improve their performance. Perhaps pressure to develop sound measures of public value creation could generate a serious political and philosophical exploration of what values "we the people" wanted to see achieved by and expressed in the operations of public-sector agencies.

The more I thought about this, the more important it seemed to develop a concept of performance measurement that was strategic, not just technical. I thought that the path to effective strategic management in government ran through the sustained, intelligent development of improved methods for recognizing public value creation. That is the pathway I have tried to stake out in this "sequel" to *Creating Public Value.*

A Brief Summary and Outline of Recognizing Public Value

Like *Creating Public Value,* this book relies on the detailed examination of case studies to highlight the many angles and intricacies of the problem of recognizing and measuring public value. I can only answer the difficult questions facing public managers through the filter of my own (more or less idiosyncratic) reasoning and experience. But I hope that in my efforts to answer them for myself, I have managed to shed some light on these issues for academic readers, for practicing public managers, and, perhaps most importantly, for all those who can hold public managers accountable—we the people. At the risk of deflating dramatic suspense, I will set out the basic argument that follows by describing the structure of the book.

In Chapter 1, I take a critical look at the landmark case of William Bratton and Compstat, a case that many have interpreted as a triumph of the application of the private sector's "bottom-line" discipline in the public sector. I use Bratton's own assertion that he was running the New York City Police Department (NYPD) as though it were a private, for-profit enterprise as the basis for exploring the critical differences in context between the private and public sectors. I look for the rudimentary elements of a "public value account" that could help define a comprehensive and accurate picture of a given public agency's performance.

Getting that picture means taking into account not only the satisfaction of individual clients of the police department (both those who call for services and those who are the objects of enforcement action) but also the capacity of the police department to achieve the outcomes that citizens desire at a cost that is tolerable to taxpayers. It means taking into account that the police department uses the authority of the state as well as tax dollars to serve its mission, and that, all other things being equal, citizens would like the police department to be able to achieve its goals with less rather than more use of authority. It means accounting for the fact that citizens and those who represent their interests are interested in the fairness of police action, and the degree to which police are effective in maintaining sociable and just relationships in their communities. And it means recognizing that while the most important job of the police might be to catch offenders and reduce criminal victimization, the police can produce many other valuable results for society, and that doing these other things well might actually help rather than hurt their crime control efforts. The goal of this chapter is to establish the core idea that public agencies should be called to account for producing value by developing a clear, explicit, and measurable public value account that names the important dimensions of public value to be pursued by and reflected in the operations of a government organization and enumerates the social and financial costs incurred along the way. That public value account emerges as a concept much larger than a dollars-and-cents "bottom line" or "customer satisfaction."

In Chapter 2, I examine the efforts by former D.C. mayor Anthony Williams to accomplish two important goals regarding government performance in Washington, D.C. On one hand, he sought to make government services more responsive and reliable for the citizens who transacted with city agencies—a goal closely aligned with the idea of improving government services to customers. On the other hand, much more ambitiously, he sought to orchestrate a political process that would "create an identity of interests" between the citizens' aspirations and their government's activities and efforts—a goal more closely aligned with creating a citizenry that could become articulate about and active in pursuing collectively desired social outcomes.

I use Williams's initiatives to sketch out the relationship between the idea of strategic management developed in *Creating Public Value* and ideas about performance measurement and performance management in government. Following the lead of Robert Kaplan and David Norton, who invented a "balanced scorecard" for private-sector performance measurement and management, I argue that one cannot effectively drive public organizations toward increased value creation with only the "public value account" developed in Chapter 1 to guide them. Even a strong public value account delivers only some of the information needed to execute a strategy designed to improve the organization's future performance.

Using the concepts of strategic management developed in *Creating Public Value,* I suggest that it would be possible to create a "public value scorecard" for government agencies that would include the public-sector equivalent of a financial bottom line (the public value account), *as well as* a set of measures designed to capture an organization's standing with all those individual and collective actors who provide it with the social legitimacy, public authority, and public funding necessary to sustain itself (the legitimacy and support perspective) and a set of measures designed to capture the organization's ability to engage in the activities and produce the outputs that are thought to be consistent with achieving desired social outcomes (the operational capacity perspective).

Embracing the idea of a public value scorecard makes performance measurement in the public sector a strategic activity in two key senses. First, it forces managers to make integrated calculations that encompass the three key points in the "strategic triangle": the concept of public value to be pursued, the bases of legitimacy and support that can justify and sustain the enterprise over time, and the development and deployment of the operational capacity to achieve the desired result. This is strategy as an integrated view of an opportunity to create public value at a particular moment in time. Second, it imagines that both the strategy of the organization and the measures used to guide its execution will develop over time as learning occurs at each point of the triangle. Over time, managers and their overseers can learn what constitutes public value—often through painful omissions. The political process that creates legitimacy and structures accountability for managers can change, and ideally improve, in both procedural and substantive ways. The operational capacity of public agencies can absorb productivity-improving innovations and reduce the costs, enhance the valued results, and increase the fairness of government operations. The measures developed to support the execution of a given strategy will not only help identify the work to be done at each point of the triangle but also capture the effects of that work. Because strategy itself is dynamic, the performance measurement system necessary to support strategy execution must be dynamic as well. At the outset there is never a firm political agreement on value or a perfect technical means for measuring it or an obvious way to use data internally to improve performance. Once a performance measurement system is established, it is always possible that it will have to be altered to reflect changing external ideas of what is valuable, or to improve its usefulness within the organization. This gives us the basic framework for taking a strategic view of performance measurement rather than a merely technical view.

In Chapter 3, I discuss the former Minnesota Department of Revenue (DOR) Commissioner John James's sustained commitment to securing legitimacy and support for his agency. I observe his dogged efforts to build trust with a key legislative oversight committee in order to negotiate mutually acceptable terms of accountability for the DOR. I frame these efforts as an initiative to build a strong public value account that the commissioner, the legislature, and DOR staff could use to determine whether the agency's performance is improving or not.

The mixed success of James's endeavor highlights the fundamental ambiguities of public-sector accountability relationships and illustrates how those difficulties might be resolved through negotiations about the shape and character of a measurement system for recognizing the public value that public agency overseers want realized by and reflected in public agency operations. I confront the gap between the ideal and real accountability relationships and make the case for developing practices that can outperform the existing institutional structures of accountability. I suggest that efforts to construct a mutually agreed-upon public value account can play an important role in strengthening accountability relationships.

In Chapter 4, I delve a bit deeper into the potential uses of different kinds of performance measures, and take up the important question of the degree to which we should rely on *outcome* versus *process* measures of performance. I examine this question in the context of a public contracting system, where the substantive issue is how best to structure contractual relationships in order to guarantee and improve performance. I look at the issue of performance contracting from the point of view of both the head of a contracting agency (Jeannette Tamayo at Project Chance, a welfare-to-work initiative of the Illinois Department of Public Aid) and one of her contractors (Toby Herr at Project Match, a program that provides support and referrals to one particular community of welfare clients).

This case, like all the cases, raises important questions about how best to define the public value to be produced by the organization. But it also focuses us on the question of how performance measurement can help managers build operational capacity—in a single organization, or in a wider network of public contractors. I present in this chapter a public-sector "value chain" as an analytic concept that informs data-gathering needs for the public value scorecard's operational capacity perspective by pointing to different points in the public value production process where information about performance could be collected.

I also make a strong case for the use of process measures as well as outcome measures in any effective system for recognizing public value creation. Process measures are vital in part because certain features of process have value in the public sector apart from their instrumental value in producing desired result, but also because if the goal is to improve performance over time, information has to be available about what the agency did as well as what results it produced.

In Chapter 5, I look at former Seattle Solid Waste Utility Commissioner Diana Gale's efforts to shepherd the citizens of Seattle through sweeping changes in solid waste management. This case focuses on two special challenges in public-sector management and the ways in which performance measurement and accountability systems can help deal with these problems. The first is the difficulty of managing a large-scale innovation in which significant performance problems are almost certain to arise and not only damage the reputation of a manager and an agency but also undermine the future success of the innovation. The second is the challenge that arises when the success of an innovation depends heavily on *coproduction*—in this case, on the willingness of large numbers of individual citizens to assume new burdens and tasks. I show how the development and use of performance data in a form that the public can understand and use to make judgments—about both the overall success of the project and its particular role in it—can help keep the project on course. This case expands our view of what might need to be included in both the legitimacy and support perspective and the operational capacity perspective of a public value scorecard.

In Chapter 6, I explore how Duncan Wyse and Jeff Tryens, as directors of the Oregon Progress Board, navigated shifting political tides as they worked to create, sustain, and make effective use of an elaborately designed structure of goals and objectives for the entire state of Oregon. The performance measurement system they created seeks to keep track of the accomplishments of not only government agencies but also the private and voluntary sectors of Oregon as they try to manage themselves self-consciously into a future that seems attractive to the entire polity. I look at the roles that *partisan politics and political ideologies* play in the definition and recognition of public value for a state political economy and how these forces shape ideas about how performance measurement systems should be constructed.

Special attention is given to the problem of creating a "hierarchy" of values, goals, and objectives to be pursued in a volatile political context. While it would be nice to settle on a simple, steady public value account, those who wish to use public value accounts to animate, guide, and coordinate action often have to create more flexible goal hierarchies that can accommodate and reflect changing political pressures and conflicts.

Finally, in Chapter 7, I follow Massachusetts Department of Social Services Commissioner Harry Spence down the "expert slope" of public management as he sought a system of accountability that could meet the public's "zero tolerance" for errors while also engaging the professional commitment of caseworkers whose work seemed to inevitably lead to bad outcomes in at least a few cases a year. The solution seemed to be neither a hard-edged system of accountability that demanded rigorous compliance with policies and procedures nor a lax system that left all the discretion to the caseworkers but one that sought to make caseworkers accountable for conscientiously developing and deploying their professional skills in every situation. This form of accountability treated a bad outcome not as the punishable result of caseworker negligence but instead as an occasion for investigating the processes of the organization and developing improved methods for handling cases similar to the one that went wrong. To create such a system, Spence had to set out some core principles that defined the basic values the agency should try to achieve and reflect in its operations. He then had to create forums throughout the organization where these principles could be used to diagnose and resolve specific issues in the practice of casework. He also had to develop and refine information systems that included both outcome and process measures and quantitative and qualitative information to support the use of the principles. Finally, he had to do political work to explain to legislative overseers and the wider public why this method of accountability was superior to the more familiar systems that held caseworkers strictly accountable for performance and defined performance solely in terms of compliance with established policies and procedures.

The book concludes with answers to basic questions about how, when, and why public agencies can and should use performance measurement and management systems to enhance organizational performance, strengthen public accountability, and create the conditions that will allow citizens, elected overseers, and public managers to align and pursue a clear vision of public value creation.

In its march through the cases, the book unfolds and develops along three quite distinct dimensions. First, it moves across many different fields within the public sector, including policing, tax collection, welfare-to-work assistance, solid waste management, political economy, and child protection. In moving across this surface, we discover that there are some differences between government organizations that primarily provide services and benefits and those that primarily impose duties, but also that the line between the two kinds of organizations might be much blurrier than we think.

Second, the book moves across different kinds of public managers in different institutional positions, with various different purposes and degrees of authority over those who can produce the desired results. All of the protagonists in our cases (except for Wyse and Tryens in Chapter 6) are line managers who have executive authority over government assets and are accountable for achieving collectively desired outcomes. Some have come to their office through direct election, some through political appointment, and some through civil service promotion. Some have very broad substantive purposes; others have far more limited purposes. Some have very little direct authority over those whom they seek to manage; others have relatively tight control.

To some degree the differences among these individual positions offer a glimpse into the way that the institutional structures of government have been changing over time, and how those changes affect the use of performance measurement systems. In the days when government both defined what was publicly valuable and produced valuable outcomes through government agencies (what David Osborne and Ted Gaebler described as doing both the "steering" and the "rowing"), performance measurement systems were constructed primarily to direct and control government employees in particular agencies.[10] As soon as government began trying to achieve its aims through more complex production systems—by contracting out to private producers, or mobilizing large numbers of citizens to be coproducers, or taking responsibility for calling a public into existence that could find and pursue its purposes through both government and civic action—performance measurement systems had to be torn out of their organizational control groove and brought in line with much different forms of governmental and collective action.

One might assume that the shift from "direct government" to "government by network" might reduce the importance of performance measurement in government because of a historical understanding of performance measurement systems as features of organizational control systems rooted in the central authority of organizational leadership. Yet it is quite possible that the importance of performance measurement will (and should) *increase* rather than decrease within the looser networks of capacity that distribute responsibility for producing desired results across different agencies and agents. The usual problem with managing performance in such networks is that the absence of central authority makes it very difficult for those trying to use and direct the network to get reliable performance out of their partners. The important working relationships are among independent peers from different sectors and organizations who are often enmeshed in different accountability systems that require them to act in particular ways, regardless of the aims of the problem-solving network. For networks seeking to solve problems through cooperative action, simple information about the state of the problem and what each member of the collaborative team has done and is now doing can become a vital substitute for hierarchical authority in creating accountability and ensuring effective and efficient cooperation.

Third, and most important, the book cumulatively develops an analytic framework that can help public managers (as well as those who would like to call them to account) find the best way to use data and performance measurement systems to improve the performance of different kinds of government agencies. Very little in this analytic framework is wholly new. But there is a great deal that is designed to challenge the particular ways in which this subject has been addressed in the past.

Indeed, one of the biggest challenges in writing this book has been to take concepts that are firmly rooted in our current thought and dialogue and give them a more particular meaning in a larger, more coherent, and useful framework. In doing this I have had to invent and develop some concepts that might seem awkward at first but that might reveal and help managers cope with parts of their world that have previously been ignored in theory if not in practice.

To find these concepts, I have shopped among many different academic disciplines and brought them to the particular practical task of recognizing public value creation when it occurs. Those disciplines include philosophy, political science, law, economics, public finance, operations research, statistics, program evaluation, benefit-cost analysis, strategic management, management control, financial management, and accounting. These fields had many useful concepts, but many also needed to be adapted a bit for the particular task of recognizing public value creation. Whether all this is helpful or not the reader will have to decide.

Ideally, at the end of the book, public managers, the citizens and elected representatives who call them to account, and the clients they meet in day-to-day encounters will have a better understanding of why it is important for public agencies to develop and use public value scorecards. Used prospectively, developing such scorecards could help organize a more productive political dialogue about the public values that we the people want our public agencies to pursue. Used retrospectively to accumulate real performance data, such scorecards could not only enhance government accountability but also promote government innovation and learning. In short, the development and use of public value scorecards may help bring us all closer to understanding the purposes we want to accomplish together, and how we might be able to push the frontier of what seems possible in our pursuit of a good and just society.

1

William Bratton and the New York City Police Department

The Challenge of Defining and Recognizing Public Value

William Bratton and the Origin of Compstat

In November 1993 New York City's citizens went to the polls to elect a mayor.[1] The incumbent, David Dinkins, touted his record in reducing crime, citing Federal Bureau of Investigation (FBI) crime reports showing a 15 percent decrease in major crimes. His opponent, Rudolph Giuliani, expressed skepticism, asserting that citizens were simply too demoralized to report crime. Giuliani believed the police were demoralized as well. Experts acknowledged that Dinkins had enjoyed at least a small decrease in crime during his run as mayor but played down the significance of short-term trends and noted that drug-related crime remained as problematic as it had been before Dinkins's election, at the height of the crack epidemic in 1989.[2] In polls, more than half of the city's citizens found the city less safe than they had four years earlier, and 50 percent had seen people selling drugs in their neighborhood, up from 38 percent in June 1990.[3]

Giuliani's stance on crime helped secure him a narrow victory, and soon after his transition team invited William Bratton to interview for the post of police commissioner. Bratton, the former head of the New York City Transit Police and the Boston Police Department, carefully pitched his presentation to appeal to the mayor-elect: he expounded upon his belief in the "broken windows" theory of crime control, which held that "disorder and crime are usually inextricably linked" and encouraged police to enforce laws against petty crimes like aggressive panhandling and public drinking in order to minimize conditions thought to foster more serious crimes.[4] He also outlined his plan to "motivate, equip, and energize" the New York City Police Department (NYPD). Audaciously, Bratton predicted his plan would reduce violent crime in New York by 40 percent in three years, with a 10 percent reduction in crime in the first year alone. On December 2, 1993, Giuliani selected Bratton to be New York City's next police commissioner.

Getting Started

Upon his appointment, Bratton set up a transition team to evaluate the condition of the department and develop a game plan for reinvigorating it. Jack Maple, who had worked with Bratton at the New York City Transit Police and in Boston (and who would soon become Bratton's deputy commissioner for crime control strategies), met with a small group of police officers, consultants, and other longtime Bratton advisers to vet the department for talent. Bratton wanted to appoint people who shared his focus on meeting ambitious crime reduction goals. He and his team asked all job candidates how much they believed the NYPD could reduce the crime rate. Those who envisioned a "two or three percent" reduction were summarily dropped from consideration.[5] "Nowhere was [the department] prepared to deal with the idea that you could literally manage the crime problem rather than just respond to it," said Bratton. The department that Bratton and his transition team found was more focused on avoiding major corruption scandals than on reducing crime, disorder, and fear by policing the streets and enforcing civilized norms of public behavior.[6]

When Bratton arrived in 1994, the NYPD had approximately thirty thousand officers. Over the next four years, the department grew substantially, in part due to a "Safe Streets, Safe City" law that imposed a small, citywide income-tax surcharge to pay for some six thousand new police officers.

Each precinct commander supervised between two hundred and four hundred officers, responsible for policing a hundred thousand-person segment of the city. But these "commanders" had relatively limited discretionary authority to go with their responsibility. Headquarters (HQ) determined staffing and deployment; detectives who worked out of precinct houses reported to the detective bureau at HQ; vice and narcotics operations required authorization from the Organized Crime Control Bureau (OCCB). In addition, an organizational layer of "divisional commanders" separated precinct commanders from the eight patrol borough commanders, from the commissioner, and from one another.[7]

In early 1994 John Linder, another former colleague of Bratton's from the New York City Transit Police, carried out a "cultural diagnostic" of the NYPD to identify institutional values and to ascertain the extent to which the department's priorities matched Bratton's.[8] Detailed surveys asked officers to rank which of their functions their superiors valued most. The officers listed "writing summonses" as the activity they believed their superiors valued most, followed by "holding down overtime," "staying out of trouble," "clearing backlog of radio runs," "reporting police corruption," and "treating bosses with deference." The function that officers believed their superiors valued least was "reducing crime, disorder, and fear."

When asked which activities officers *themselves* considered most important, they cited, in order: "reducing crime, disorder, and fear"; "making gun arrests"; "providing police services to people who requested them"; "gaining public confidence in police integrity"; "arresting drug dealers"; "correcting quality-of-life conditions"; and "staying out of trouble." The rank and file appeared to share Bratton's and Giuliani's goals, but the department's hierarchy seemed disorganized and paralyzed by a fear of corruption.

Bratton made John Timoney—a one-star chief who had headed up the office of management, analysis, and planning under former police commissioner Ray Kelly—chief of department, the NYPD's highest uniformed officer, passing over sixteen higher-ranking officers. Timoney was seen, in the words of John Miller, Bratton's deputy commissioner for public information, as someone "with a hotline to the cops' mentality," as well as encyclopedic knowledge of the NYPD. Louis Anemone, Kelly's head of the disorders control unit, was made chief of patrol. "Anemone was clearly a field general," said Miller. "He would be our Patton." On January 24, 1994, just four days after Bratton had made Timoney the chief of department, at Timoney's recommendation (and with City Hall's support), Bratton replaced four of the NYPD's five "superchiefs," the four-star officers who run the department's various operational units. The event was dubbed "Bloody Friday."

Though overall goals and strategy would be set at headquarters, Bratton gave precinct commanders significantly more discretion over ground operations so that they could devise and implement their own crime-reduction strategies. In the past these personnel had been prohibited from engaging in a number of initiatives (such as decoy and plainclothes vice operations, and other activities believed to be susceptible to corruption) and limited in the degree to which they could assign personnel to special units. Bratton lifted a number of these restrictions and gave commanding officers unprecedented authority to direct precinct-level operations.

Jack Maple stressed the need to go after guns and gun dealers.[9] All officers were encouraged to ask *everyone* they arrested if they knew where guns could be acquired. To add more muscle to the antigun initiative, NYPD leadership nearly doubled the number of officers assigned to the street crime unit (known for its aggressive tactics and its effectiveness) and directed the unit to focus its considerable energies on taking guns off the street.

The NYPD also moved quickly to crack down on the quality-of-life offenses that Giuliani had promised to take on in his mayoral campaign.[10] Police strategy gave precinct commanders new tools to combat "street prostitution, aggressive panhandlers, sales of alcohol to minors, graffiti vandalism, public urination, unlicensed peddlers, reckless bicyclists, ear-splitting noise churned out by 'boom box' cars, loud motorcycles, clubs, and spontaneous street parties." Officers were instructed to treat every arrest as a potential opportunity to make a bigger arrest and take a firearm off the streets.

The new administration also attended to rank-and-file psychology. Bratton requested and received a handgun upgrade for the NYPD, as well as new uniforms and improved bulletproof vests. Additional mobile digital terminals were provided after special operations lieutenants complained of inadequate equipment.

Bratton and Giuliani made it clear that they would not turn their backs on police officers involved in confrontations with the public without clear evidence of police wrongdoing. But Bratton also wanted to send a clear signal that corrupt cops would not be tolerated. When he learned that a dozen officers in the 30th Precinct in Harlem would be arrested for dealing drugs, he arranged to have officers in highly visible NYPD blazers participate in the arrests. The day after the arrests, Bratton appeared at the precinct to address the remaining officers and gave an impassioned speech denouncing corruption and vowing to seek out and prosecute any other corrupt officers standing before him. Bratton then assembled every precinct commander in the NYPD to announce that he was permanently retiring the badge numbers of the indicted officers and to let it be known that in the future he expected every precinct commander to take an active role in preventing corruption.

Over the course of his first year Bratton would replace more than two-thirds of the city's precinct commanders, bringing in officers who were known for their proactive approaches to crime reduction. These changes and Bratton's high-level appointments sent a clear signal that promotions would be based on performance rather than longevity and gave hope to dedicated officers among the rank and file. He eliminated the divisional command level and gave precinct commanders unprecedented authority to deploy their officers as they wished.

The "Yalta" of the NYPD: A Leadership Moment

In late March 1994 the NYPD's senior brass and a select group of outside academics, consultants, and observers went to Wave Hill, a city-owned estate on the edge of the Bronx, to discuss Bratton's plans for the department. There, for the first time, Bratton publicly announced that the department's goal for the year was to reduce crime by 10 percent.[11] Bratton's inner circle and City Hall were already familiar with Bratton's goal (though City Hall discouraged him from publicly articulating it, lest the goal not be met). However, to the assembled group, Bratton's announcement came like a thunderbolt. "If I could put it in one direct visual, jaws dropped," said Peter LaPorte, Bratton's chief of staff. "Literally, mouths opened."

Bratton, however, believed that articulating such bold goals was an important aspect of motivating the organization to perform.[12] "You needed to set the tone, and you needed to set stretch goals that would inspire people," he explained. "Ten percent the first year was really based on the idea of doing in our first year more than had been done in the previous four years." Because of the Safe Streets law, Bratton had several thousand more police officers to work with than his predecessor. With an aggressive new management team and a reenergized force, Bratton felt confident that a 10 percent reduction in crime was a feasible goal.

Institutionalizing Change and Ensuring Accountability:
The Birth of Compstat

While employed with the New York City Transit Police, Bratton had gotten a daily report on the crime that occurred in the system. In his first days on the job, Bratton slipped into a similar routine, receiving a morning briefing on the previous twenty-four hours, including reports of major incidents of crime, utility failures, and so on. After several days, Bratton expressed to Maple his astonishment that not very much seemed to be going on. Maple responded, "Are you jerking me or what, commissioner?" There was plenty happening; Bratton was just not being told about it.

Maple went after the numbers, but when he asked the detective bureau for the current crime statistics, he learned that there were no current crime statistics: the NYPD compiled crime statistics only on a quarterly basis.[13] Maple wanted weekly figures; the detective bureau's staff responded that they might be able to get him monthly figures. That was unacceptable to Maple. With Bratton's support, Maple managed to set a requirement for the detective bureau to provide crime figures on a weekly basis.

The first week the crime figures arrived "written in fucking crayon," according to Maple. Soon thereafter, every precinct was instructed to deliver a computer disk with its crime statistics for the week to borough headquarters. Each borough then sent a disk with all the crime figures for its precincts to headquarters at One Police Plaza. By the end of February, the top command staff was receiving weekly crime reports.

Maple wanted precinct and borough commanders to start looking at the crime figures too. He noticed that the precincts' pin maps of criminal incidents had very few holes in them—an indication that the pins were rarely moved. "We've got a war on crime; how do you go to war without a map?" Maple asked. At a meeting that spring, Maple informed the precincts that he wanted every precinct to keep up-to-date pin maps marking the time and location of every crime reported in their precinct. This request was met by a collective groan. "Do you know how much time it's going to take to keep up-to-date maps?" Maple was asked. "Yes," he responded, "eighteen minutes a day." (He had asked the 75th Precinct in East New York, the city's busiest precinct, to keep track of how long it took to do this for a week in order to answer just this

question.) Maple also insisted that henceforth when borough commanders came to headquarters for executive staff meetings, they should bring
up-to-date maps of the criminal activity taking place in their precincts.

These maps, though often primitive, proved exceedingly useful.
Once mapped, patterns of crime became obvious. "The beauty of the
map is that you can ask, 'Why is this happening?'" said Maple. "What
is the underlying cause? Is it that there's a school there? . . . Is there a
shopping center there, is that why there's a lot of pickpockets there?"
Maple said before the use of crime mapping, "when detectives took narcotics complaints, they filed them with Intelligence and Investigations.
Nobody was held accountable." After several executive staff meetings, it
became apparent that the borough commanders were not prepared for
the kind of detailed discussions that Maple and Anemone, chief of patrol, had in mind. Maple and Anemone were not content to hear that
an area had a heroin problem and that the police were addressing it;
they wanted to know what brand of heroin was involved, who was supplying it, and how the police were trying to break into the ring. When
it became clear that these were questions the borough commanders
could not answer, Bratton instructed them to meet every two weeks
with their precinct commanders so that they could answer detailed
questions.

To ensure that these meetings between borough and precinct commanders were in fact taking place and that the precinct commanders
were being questioned with sufficient zeal and in sufficient detail, Maple
and Anemone decided to hold one of these meetings in the third-floor
press room of One Police Plaza and to sit in on the session themselves.
By April 1994, Anemone and Maple were chairing these meetings with
rotating groups of precinct and borough commanders twice a week and
grilling them for up to three hours at a time.[14]

"This was a way to ensure that the strategies were being carried
out. It was also a way to assess these strategies," said Maple.

Representatives from every borough began to attend even when
they themselves were not presenting. Early that summer, the meetings
moved to the Command and Control Center, with seating for 115. Even
then the sessions were often standing room only. Bratton often sat in.

Maple insisted on having maps of every major category of crime.
By the end of the year, the department had upgraded to computerized
maps that could be projected onto three eight-by-eight-foot screens

mounted on the walls of the Command and Control Center. The process of analyzing these computerized crime statistics became known as "Compstat."

As a result of Compstat, by the early summer of 1994, precinct commanders were routinely interacting with the department's top brass for the first time in their careers and providing more information to One Police Plaza than ever before.[15] Every week, each of the NYPD's seventy-six precincts compiled a statistical summary of complaint, arrest, and summons activity, as well as written accounts of significant cases, crime patterns, and police activities. Precincts were required to include the exact time and location of both crimes and enforcement activities.

A newly created Compstat unit collated and entered this information into a citywide database and generated weekly reports for each precinct.[16] The reports tracked seven of the eight major crimes reported in the FBI's yearly Uniform Crime Report.[17] They also tracked shooting incidents, shooting victims, gun arrests, and summons activity. These measures were designed to capture a precinct's engagement in proactive, quality-of-life policing.[18] Data were presented on a week-to-date, month-to-date, and year-to-date basis, with comparisons to the previous year. Each precinct was also ranked for each complaint and arrest category.

At each meeting all precinct and operational unit commanders within a given patrol borough would gather from roughly 7:00 to 10:00 a.m. at the Command and Control Center. Individual commanders who were expected to answer questions at Compstat meetings were typically given a thirty-six-hour notice to prepare. When a precinct commander appeared for a Compstat presentation, the commander, his or her executive officer, and the head detective for the precinct stood behind the Command and Control Center lectern, facing the assembled crowd. Anemone, Maple, and other top brass sat in the front row of the audience. The three large screens loomed behind the precinct officers. Commander profiles, including years in rank, education, specialized training received, most recent performance evaluation, and the units the commander had previously commanded, as well as information on the precinct in question, were distributed in briefing books. The briefing books also included information intended to capture the commander's performance—personnel assigned, personnel absence rates, unfounded radio runs, radio car accidents, overtime expenditures, and summons activity. According to Bratton, these books meant that "in fifteen minutes, I could get all the information I needed."

The atmosphere at Compstat sessions was tense. Maple was particularly unforgiving with commanders he believed were not providing sustained attention to a problem and, if dissatisfied with a response, would continue to pepper them with pointed questions about what they were trying. If a problem identified at a Compstat session continued and Maple thought the commanding officer responsible for the problem was not responding, Maple, according to Bratton, "would explode."

Discussion of which tactics worked played a prominent part in Compstat sessions. Innovative and effective tactics came to light and were immediately communicated to everyone attending, just as failed tactics were quickly exposed. As Compstat took root, representatives from the various district attorneys' offices, the U.S. Attorney's Office, probation, and parole began regularly attending Compstat meetings.

Other parts of the department started their own Compstat-like meetings, to Bratton's and Maple's delight. "The detective boroughs were doing mini-Compstats with all the squad commanders to prepare the chief and his people for the real Compstat," said John Miller. "It became a trickle-down process of thinking because nobody wanted to be embarrassed at the big show."

According to Maple, about one-third of precinct commanders "clearly couldn't cut it" and were moved to less demanding assignments. Another third were transferred in more lateral career moves. Many younger officers who performed well moved up, driving down the average age of precinct commanders from the sixties to the forties.[19]

The Impact of Compstat: Short-Term Outcomes

By the end of 1994 it was clear that the NYPD had come through a remarkable year. From 1993 to 1994, New Yorkers saw a 12 percent decline in "index" crimes (those reported in the FBI's Uniform Crime Reports). Nationwide, index crimes had fallen just 1.1 percent.[20] Homicides in New York City were down 19.8 percent, rape 5.4 percent, robberies 15.6 percent, aggravated assaults 4.8 percent, burglary 10.9 percent, grand larceny 10.7 percent, and motor vehicle theft 15.2 percent. The decline in crime from 1993 to 1994 meant that 385 fewer people died, 13,461 fewer people were robbed, and 3,023 fewer people were assaulted.

The remarkable decline that began in 1994 intensified in 1995, when Bratton upped his crime reduction goal to 15 percent; by the end of 1995, crime was down by 16 percent. Crime in the rest of the country had declined by less than half of 1 percent.[21]

There was also evidence that the NYPD's focus on guns was producing results. By the end of 1994, deaths caused by gunshot wounds had dropped 23 percent. Shooting incidents had fallen 16.4 percent. The percentage of gun-related homicides had fallen from 77 percent in 1993 to 72 percent in 1994.[22]

Some worried that these statistical results were not real. Allegations that some precinct captains, eager to show progress in reducing crime, manipulated criteria for classifying crimes so that some serious crimes would be downgraded to a less serious crime (e.g., an event that would have previously been recorded as a robbery was downgraded to a larceny) became increasingly common.[23] Others argued that while the changes in reported crime might be real, they could not be causally attributed to the actions of the NYPD. Perhaps crime had fallen due to some other changes that had occurred in the environment. But to many, the statistics told a clear story. The police commissioner had promised to reinvigorate his department and make dramatic reductions in crime, and the statistics seemed to indicate an unqualified success for the commissioner and the mayor.

There was one prominent blemish on these remarkably positive statistics, however: a rise in civilian complaints about police misconduct. The celebrated results of Bratton's leadership were due at least in part to the police becoming much more aggressive in their tactics. Total arrests were up 21.5 percent. But only a small portion of these arrests were for major crimes: felony arrests rose only 5 percent. The major increases in arrests were for drug arrests (up 27.5 percent) and misdemeanor arrests (up 53.8 percent).[24] Of course, such arrests might well have been legally justified and morally deserved. And, consistent with the broken windows theory, the crackdown on minor offenses might have produced a significant impact on more serious crimes.

But the increased arrests pointed to an increase in the police force's use of public authority. The upshot of this was that civilian complaints about police misconduct had risen even faster than arrests. A small but

vocal group of critics argued that the NYPD was reducing crime by in-
discriminately stopping and frisking young black and Hispanic men in
the city's toughest neighborhoods, often roughing them up in the process. According to the case law, officers could legally stop and frisk a
person behaving suspiciously if they had a reasonable concern that the
person might be armed and dangerous.[25] In practice, some officers
were quick to spot "suspicious" behavior and the "bulge" of what might
be a handgun in order to justify a stop and frisk. Just how many officers overstepped legal boundaries was a contentious subject. "We only
teach above-board tactics," said Maple. "When a cop makes a stop, they
have to be able to make an explanation for why they made the stop. I'm
not saying the NYPD doesn't make some bad stops, but there is no wink
and nod."

At the end of 1994, the Civilian Complaint Review Board (CCRB),
a city agency created in 1993 to investigate civilian complaints against
the police, noted a 36 percent increase from the previous year.[26] The
4,877 complaints received contained 8,060 specific allegations of police
misconduct; 3,107 allegations charged police officers with the use of excessive force. And while complaints were rising, it seemed to at least
some observers that disciplinary standards were falling: an Amnesty
International investigation of the NYPD noted that while in 1992 63
percent of the cases of police misconduct brought to administrative trial
resulted in convictions, in 1994 only three of the thirty-two cases that
went to administrative trial resulted in guilty verdicts.[27]

Complaints of misconduct were not randomly distributed across
New York's diverse population. Although African Americans constituted
only about a quarter of the population of New York City, half of the
people lodging complaints were African American.[28] The trend continued in 1995, with the number of complaints rising to 5,618. In Bratton's
first two years as commissioner, overall complaints had risen almost 50
percent. Allegations of illegal searches had risen 135 percent; excessive
force allegations were up 61.9 percent.[29]

For much of this period, the data on complaints against the police
were not part of the Compstat system. The CCRB existed outside the
police department. The numbers were reported less frequently than
the crime numbers and were not disaggregated to the precinct level.
Consequently, although the information was available to the police, it
did not become part of the internal system of accountability. Overtime

payments got regular scrutiny as something that could and should be managed, but complaints against the police did not.

In fact, the police saw the increasing number of formal complaints not as an indication that misconduct was on the rise but as a statistical artifact reflecting both the recent creation of the Civilian Complaint Review Board and the increased size of the police force. The CCRB had only been established in 1993, and its well-publicized existence probably encouraged more people to make complaints. Moreover, the number of NYPD officers on the street was higher than ever before. The department pointed out that of the 2,152 investigations launched by the CCRB in 1994, just over 5 percent had been substantiated.[30] Given that in 1994 police officers responded to 4 million calls for service, wrote 5.4 million summonses, and made 227,453 arrests, these numbers did not strike police officials as particularly bad. The fact that a higher percentage of minorities filed complaints was not surprising given that most arrestees (and crime victims) were also minorities.

The End of an Era

While Bratton's team continued to experience well-publicized success in its efforts to turn around the NYPD, relations between City Hall and NYPD brass grew increasingly strained. The department was instructed to lower Bratton's press profile and reduce its public information staff. When Bratton struck a $350,000 book deal for his memoirs, City Hall let the press know it would investigate. Bratton's term expired in February 1996, his reappointment was put on hold pending a review of the book deal, and on March 29 he announced his resignation. The majority of his deputies soon followed suit.

Bratton resigned to a shower of accolades. In his twenty-seven months as police commissioner, crime in New York City had fallen to levels not seen since the 1960s. Homicides had declined by roughly 44 percent during Bratton's term; serious crime (as measured by the FBI Index) was down roughly 29 percent. An Empire State Survey poll found that 73 percent of the population had a positive view of the police, up from just 37 percent in June 1992.[31]

Developing a Public Value Account:
A "Bottom Line" for Public Agencies?

Bratton's apparent success in managing the NYPD to reduce crime, fear, and disorder stands out as a compelling example of value-creating public management—an achievement whose lessons should be thoughtfully interpreted and widely shared to improve the overall performance of public managers and public-sector agencies.[32] Perhaps the most common interpretation is that public-sector managers should adopt the perspectives and techniques of private-sector managers, specifically by committing themselves and their organizations to a "bottom line" that defines the value their organizations produce in terms of concrete goals (ideally expressed in hard numbers) and continuously measuring their achievement with respect to those goals.[33]

A Compelling Private-Sector Metaphor

Indeed, in a 1996 lecture at the Heritage Foundation in Washington, D.C., Bratton explicitly invoked a metaphor of private-sector, bottom-line management. "We began to run the NYPD as a private, profit-oriented business," he said. "What was the profit I wanted? Crime reduction. I wanted to beat my competitors—the criminals—who were out there seven days a week, 24 hours a day. I wanted to serve my customers—the public—better, and the profit I wanted to deliver to them was reduced crime."[34]

In a few short sentences, Bratton pulled the NYPD's operations into the normative and technical context of private-sector management. Casually yet consequentially, he imported three major concepts from the private into the public sector:

- *Profit* (as the goal, measure, and reward for superior organizational performance)
- *Customers* (as the individuals whose satisfactions should be taken as the final arbiter of the organization's value creation)
- *Competitors* (as those who challenge the organization to adapt and improve)

As this metaphor of private-sector management passes to the public sector, one might well observe that private-sector managers seem to be more focused on managing *outward* to the achievement of *results* (earning revenues to generate profits), while their public-sector counterparts manage *upward* to a system of accountability that pays more attention to *compliance* with policies and procedures than to the achievement of desired social outcomes. Or one might observe that the amount of information about organizational activity and accomplishment immediately available and accessible is much greater and used much more systematically in the private sector than in the public—and so on. This is the value of the metaphor; it directs attention to some possible shortcomings in the standard public-sector approach.

On the other hand, because the concepts are taken out of one context and used in another, there is a possibility that the metaphor will lead us astray. For example, the private-sector metaphor might obscure the fact that the police use the authority of the state on a daily basis, and that one police strategy might use it a lot more often, and more recklessly, than another. Further, it might cause the police to forget that there are hard-to-quantify values that attach to the use of public authority—that citizens demand justice and fairness in the use of force. And, since the money used to sustain police forces comes from tax revenues generated through coercive authority, concerns about justice and fairness might attach to the use of those dollars as well.

The private-sector metaphor might also confuse us about which stakeholders society privileges to be the arbiters of the value produced by a particular organization. In the private sector, the important arbiters of value are generally taken to be the customers, on one hand, and the shareholders, on the other. But who is the appropriate arbiter of the value produced by the NYPD? Is it the individual who calls the police for service, the taxpayer who provides the financial wherewithal for the organization to operate, the elected representative of the people, or some abstract notion of a community of citizens? It is often hard to tell whether a metaphor is helping or hurting, but warning flags should go up whenever a metaphor seems strained.

Conceptual Confusions

Bratton's metaphor, although commonly offered and widely accepted, strains mightily upon close examination. A detailed look at these chinks in the metaphorical armor helps reveal some of the conceptual challenges

that have to be overcome to make good use of private-sector management ideas in the very different context of public agencies.

Financial Profit versus Reduced Crime. Bratton's first claim was that he
wanted to run the NYPD as though it were a profit-oriented company. He
did not mean this literally, of course. He was not planning to bill those
who called the police for service and set a price for police services that
would maximize the difference between the costs of supplying them
and the revenues earned by selling them. NYPD's finest would still be
available to individuals for the price of a phone call. What he probably
did mean was that he wanted the NYPD to be dedicated to and accountable for achieving a valuable, measurable goal: crime reduction.

Surely crime reduction is an important goal of the police. But even
Bratton would agree that reducing disorder and fear was an important
goal.[35] Others might say that the goal of the NYPD was to enforce laws
fairly and impartially, or to ensure just and civil relationships among
the citizens of New York City. And the individual citizens of New York
routinely nominate many other potentially valuable uses of police forces
by dialing 911 for services—only some of which are associated with
crime they experience or witness.[36] If those in positions to define and
judge the value the NYPD produces disagree about its purposes or want
the NYPD to pursue purposes beyond reducing crime, then the single
goal of reducing crime can do neither the conceptual work of fully capturing the value produced by the NYPD nor the practical work of focusing the NYPD wholeheartedly on this single goal. As a bottom line for
the department's performance, crime reduction lacks the philosophical
and practical power that financial profit has in business.[37]

But Bratton's declaration that crime reduction was the profit that
the NYPD earned for the citizens of New York contained a more important conceptual error. The problem was not just that the NYPD produced many benefits other than crime reduction; it was that the value
called "crime reduction" did not account for the *costs* of producing that
effect. The idea of profit in the private sector captures not only the financial value produced by an organization (the revenues earned by the
sale of products and services) but also the costs of producing that value.
Profit describes a *relationship* between the revenues earned and the *costs*
of producing and selling those goods and services. Bratton's "bottom

line" of reduced crime described only one valued result of policing and seemed to ignore the costs of producing that effect.

Assuming that what gets measured is what gets prioritized, the failure to consider the *costs* of crime reduction is a serious omission. There *are* costs associated with the NYPD's efforts to control crime that need to be recognized.[38] The most obvious costs are financial—the tax dollars that pay the wages and pensions of officers, buy the cars, radios, and guns, and support the information systems that track reported crimes, cases made against offenders, and criminal records.

A less obvious but equally important cost is the burden associated with police use of public authority.[39] When the police use their authority to stop and question, to search, and to arrest and control, they place burdens on individuals. The inconvenience of being stopped may be a small price to pay for the benefit of reduced crime, and those arrested may well be guilty, but it is nonetheless true that the use of state authority creates an unwelcome burden on individuals—a burden that falls particularly heavily and painfully if it is misplaced.

If the NYPD relies on an accounting system that recognizes crime reduction but not the financial and social costs of police department operations, then citizens will not have a clear picture of the *net value* the NYPD creates. Even worse, the NYPD will be motivated to produce a distorted kind of value; in all likelihood, it will spend more of the unmonitored resources (public authority) to achieve the monitored results (crime reduction). To look at the value of crime reduction without accounting for the various costs of producing that result is as foolish as looking at the revenues earned by selling cars and ignoring the costs of producing them.

Customers versus the Public. Bratton's second claim was that his "customers" were the public, and that he wanted to return the "profit" of reduced crime to those "customers." This too revealed a fundamental confusion. In the private sector, customers are individuals who buy products and services; profits, on the other hand, are delivered to *owners, shareholders,* and *investors.*

In public agencies, those who receive services (and benefit directly from them)—the kids going to school, the elderly enjoying the public library's collection and quiet, the disabled person who takes advantage of a paratransit public transportation program—bear the most obvious resemblance to private-sector customers.

The customers of the police who most resemble customers in the private sector are those who call the police for assistance. These individuals closely resemble customers in the private sector in three respects:

1. They are "downstream" in the production process.
2. They want particular bits and pieces of service from the police and may be indifferent to everything about the organization other than what it is doing for them as individuals.
3. They benefit as individuals if they can get the services they want from the police.

Yet satisfying these individual "customers" of the police is less important than it would be in the private sector. One reason is simply that such customers do not pay directly for the service—or, more precisely, they do not pay for the service when they decide to use it for their own immediate purposes. The costs of police services are paid wholesale by taxpayers, not retail by customers. Individuals who call the police can claim thousands of dollars in public resources for their own private use with a (free) phone call. In the private sector, it is the customer's decision to spend her or his own money on products or services that allow an organization to presume it is producing something valuable. If one can have a service without paying for it, then using that service does not necessarily show that one values it, let alone how much one values it compared to the costs of production.

There is a further problem in using the private-sector concept of a customer in the context of policing. Those who call the police for services are not the only individuals who have transactions with the police that are "downstream" in the production process. The police also carry out individual transactions with those they stop to make inquiries, those they cite for minor offenses, and those they arrest for more significant offenses. In these transactions, police often use force or the threat of force to interrupt the daily lives of citizens, despite the individual desires of those citizens.

Such transactions are actually quite common in the public sector. Tax collection agencies oblige individuals to pay taxes. Environmental protection agencies require companies to refrain from dumping toxic waste into the air and water. The Securities and Exchange Commission requires private corporations to provide investors with accurate representations of their financial position and activities. Indeed, many public agencies that seem to be providing services to individuals are, in fact, providing complex blends of services and obligations: public education is a service to children (and their parents) but also is an obligation, disability services come with obligations to report personal details that prove need, and so on.

Individuals to whom public agencies deliver obligations look like customers only in the sense that they are "downstream" and engaged in an individual transaction with the agency. They are certainly not volunteering to pay for the service. (Indeed, some would volunteer to pay to *avoid* the "service"—a transaction that is ordinarily called a bribe!) And it is certainly not the aim of the public agency to make such individuals, who are not so much beneficiaries as "obligatees," happy (though it may have a responsibility to protect the rights of the "obligatees" and practical interests in treating them well enough that they will reconcile themselves to the duty being imposed).

So the individuals who are standing in the position of "customers" in the public sector—those whose individual transactions with the agency involve the delivery of services or obligations, or both—do not pay directly for the services they receive, and their satisfaction with the service does not seem to constitute its principal value. It is some other social entity that pays for the enterprise, values the results it produces, and warrants the continuation of the effort. To avoid confusion, we will refer to the individuals who transact individually with public agencies as "clients" (for lack of a better term) rather than "customers."

Bratton equated the "public" with the "customers" of the NYPD. But the "public" is a larger and different entity than those individual beneficiaries or "obligatees" described earlier. The public is made up of individuals—individual citizens, voters, and taxpayers—and of collective bodies and institutions such as the voting constituencies of elected public executives, the legislatures elected to guide and oversee the government's executive branch, the courts responsible for protecting the rights of individuals, and those who influence the actions and decisions of these institutions (such as interest groups and the media). But the public also exists in the complex *processes* of democratic government that combine individuals and aggregate institutions into an imperfectly formed and somewhat inarticulate collective that expresses what it would like to produce with the assets of government. It is this sprawling and amorphous public—the body politic as it is organized and convened to decide which purposes are worth taxing and regulating itself for—that provides the assets the NYPD uses in its operations and has the right and the responsibility to define the public value the NYPD is supposed to produce.

While the "public" provides the resources to sustain operations and defines the value of what is being produced, it looks very different from a private-sector customer. It is an aggregate, collective group rather than an individual. And it seems to stand *above* the public agency, providing it with resources according to the degree to which the organization can produce a collectively desired aggregate social result, or social outcome, which may or may not include the satisfaction of individual beneficiaries or obligatees.

Competition versus Criminal Offenders. Finally, extending the private-sector metaphor, Bratton claimed that the criminals who generated crime were the "competition" that he faced. That metaphor works in the sense that what is functionally important about competitors in the private sector is that they threaten the performance of the company and force it to adapt and innovate. One can use the metaphor to imagine, for example, that the police are engaged in a strategic game with criminal offenders, and that in order to produce the "profit" of reduced crime, they are under pressure, as Bratton suggested, to stay one step ahead of the competition.

But using the private-sector metaphor, one could also say that it is the criminals who create the market niche in which the police operate—the need or the value-creating opportunity—that the police are trying to fill. Without criminal offenders, who would be willing to pay for the services provided by a police department? One could even say that the criminals and the crimes they commit constitute the material conditions in society that the police are trying to transform. If the police produce value by reducing crime, then the material substance of their work is to find ways to understand and transform the conduct of criminal offenders (along with the social conditions that create criminal offenders and occasions for offending). As such, criminals and their crimes are more like the raw material of police work than competitors of the police.

In the private sector, competitors are not those who create the market or constitute the raw material a company transforms to create value; rather, they are alternative suppliers of the goods or services that form the heart of the business. By this logic, the competitors of the police would be others who could meet citizens' demands for security against criminal victimization—private security companies, sellers of burglar alarms, guns, and dogs, or even neighborhood watch groups.[40] But the public might be better served if one thought of these other suppliers as important partners who could help leverage the ultimate impact of the NYPD in trying to reduce crime or enhance security.[41]

The Philosophical and Practical Power of the Private Sector's
Financial Bottom Line
The fact that the ill-fitting private-sector concepts of profit, customer, and competition are both familiar and commonly accepted in public discourse about public management suggests that there is something very powerful at work in the use of this metaphor. The cynical view might be that using this language engages the support and commitment of the business community—a politically vital constituency, particularly in New York City. The business community—relieved to find public managers prepared to be accountable for performance, and to focus their organizations on reaching a simple, objectively measured goal—throws its support behind managers who play by the same rules they do.

But the wide use of the metaphor probably comes from a much broader public desire for a simple, noncontroversial bottom line to judge the performance of government agencies. Citizens want to know that the tax dollars and freedoms given to public agencies are well spent. Moreover, the public also wants to use that bottom line to hold public managers and public agencies accountable. They want the representation of value to be simple, concrete, and objective—not vague, uncertain, or intangible. It is likely that this public longing for verifiable results caused Bratton and many others before and after to reach out so aggressively for an equivalent to the private sector's bottom line.

To understand the philosophical and practical appeal of the private sector's bottom line, one has to understand what it is and why it works reasonably well in the private sector. It begins as a simple technical idea—an accounting concept.[42] Any first-year business student can set out the basic concept:

$$\text{Profit} = \text{Total Revenues} - \text{Total Costs}^{43}$$

This simple concept has the power to shape social judgments about whether a complex enterprise that used scarce resources to produce some result is, on balance, worth the effort. If the revenues earned by the sale of products and services more than covered the costs of production, one might reasonably conclude not only that the owners of the producing company could make some money but also that some net social value was being created for society as a whole.[44]

Equally important, the bottom-line equation can be easily filled with empirical, real-time information about conditions in the world. Well-established accounting practices allow private-sector enterprises to collect meaningful performance data about costs and revenues cheaply and easily, within the boundary of the organization, in real time.

But the main thing that makes the bottom line so appealing is that this simple equation packs a powerful philosophical wallop. It shows whether customers are content to pay more for goods and services than it costs to produce them, whether the company can afford to pay its employees, and whether owners and shareholders are getting a return on their investment. In a free-market social system made up chiefly of consumers, workers, entrepreneurs, and investors, a bottom line in the black is convincing evidence that an organization is creating value for society.[45]

Five Critical Differences in Context
In the public sector, however, this concept of the bottom line loses its moorings, and with them not only its conceptual and practical simplicity but also its philosophical and social significance. That is what the confusion in Bratton's metaphor reveals.

It may seem unfair (not to mention pedantic) to put Bratton's use of a familiar metaphor under this microscope, but it seems worth doing for two reasons. The first is precisely because Bratton's remarks are so familiar. Countless public officials and pundits have made similar remarks about what and how the public sector and its managers should learn from the private sector and its managers. The more these comments get repeated, the more social legitimacy they acquire and the greater their influence on choices made by managers, and evaluations made by citizens. It matters that the metaphors that gain this kind of social legitimacy be accurate and useful rather than confusing and distorting.[46]

The more important reason to look closely at the metaphor, however, is that the frictions and incongruities that stand out will reveal the key differences in context that have to be accommodated if we are to construct some approximation of a bottom line for the management of public agencies. The goal is to find out which parts of the private-sector metaphor can do useful work in the public sector despite some fundamental differences in the context in which public managers operate. Five interlocking features seem particularly important.

Private Value versus Public Value. In pursuit of economic value, free societies allow their citizens to create myriad commercial enterprises. But free societies also tax and regulate themselves to create and sustain public agencies that they hope will improve the quality of individual and collective life.

Society values commercial enterprises partly because they provide wealth to shareholders and jobs to employees. But their most important social justification is that they offer value to their customers.[47] When individuals pony up their hard-earned money for a product or service, they give strong, objective evidence that they value it. If society values an economic system that delivers value to individual consumers, then customer satisfaction counts as a kind of social value creation. When customers cover the costs of production and then some (i.e., when the company earns a profit), shareholders are happy and (arguably) some net value has been produced for society.

Society—and the individuals who comprise it—expects the public agencies it creates to produce a different kind of value. Citizens, acting through the complex processes of representative democratic government, decide which public purposes are important enough to tax and regulate themselves to produce, and those purposes define public value and the mission of the public agency. Thus the "bottom line" for public agencies is not whether they produce revenues in excess of costs but whether they satisfy the aspirations of citizens at the lowest possible cost in terms of money and authority.

The success of private-sector firms in producing financial returns can be measured relatively simply and objectively. The creation of public value for citizens is much harder (but no less important and urgent) to define and measure.

Private Financing versus Public Resourcing. Private-sector enterprises mobilize financial resources to create and sustain their activities in two different ways. They mobilize investment capital from investors by promising long-term gains, and they secure revenue streams through sales to willing customers. Public agencies, in contrast, mobilize financial resources by promising to achieve social outcomes that citizens and their elected representatives consider valuable and taxing their income, purchases, and property.

Both the mobilization of private capital and the sale of products and services to individual customers depend on voluntary individual transactions. The mobilization of tax revenues to support public agencies, in contrast, depends on a collective decision to use the authority of the state to require individuals to contribute to common goals.[48]

Individual versus Collective Arbiters of Value. In the private sector, the social actors that determine the value of goods and services and confer legitimacy on the activities of a company are individuals making decisions about how to spend their own money. While one might have some doubt about the ultimate social value of producing Ouija boards or Chia Pets, when a company successfully sells such things, no one condemns it. The fact that individuals choose to purchase these goods demonstrates the value of the enterprise.[49]

In the public sector, where citizens collectively define the social purposes of public agencies, the collective's willingness to continue to tax and regulate itself to achieve social outcomes establishes public value and confers legitimacy on the agencies that help produce it. In the public sector, we the people, acting through the imperfect processes of representative government, are the final arbiters of public value (whether you or I personally like it or not).

Voluntary versus Obligatory Transactions. Private-sector organizations seek to achieve their goals primarily through a large number of voluntary transactions. They invite investors to buy a stake, employees to work in exchange for a salary, and customers to purchase goods and services.

Public agencies also depend on voluntary transactions to achieve social outcomes. They expect that citizens will voluntarily pay the taxes they owe, consider employment in government agencies, visit the national parks, and take advantage of various social service programs when their need qualifies them. But public agencies also rely on the power of the state to compel individuals (as well as private companies) to contribute to public purposes when voluntary compliance is not enough. They garnish the wages of tax evaders, draft individuals into military service, require children to enroll in school, regulate the disposal of industrial waste, and restrict access to public services to those whom the public has decided are entitled to them.

Efficiency and Effectiveness versus Justice and Fairness. The fact that public agencies routinely use state authority to raise money and achieve their objectives has implications for how citizens evaluate the performance of government. In the private sector, shareholders usually focus on whether companies have used their material assets efficiently and effectively.

In the public sector, individuals and the broad public also evaluate public agencies in terms of their efficiency and effectiveness. But because state authority is often engaged in the operations of public agencies, another evaluative frame becomes relevant. We ask not only whether the organization has acted efficiently and effectively but also whether it has acted justly and fairly. We also judge public agencies by assessing the degree to which the ends they seek are consistent with the creation of a good and just society, the degree to which the means used accord with ideals about right relationships between citizens and the state, and the degree to which the burdens of achieving the collectively desired goals have been fairly distributed across society.

A More Limited Metaphor: Value-Oriented Management
in the Public Sector

If the differences in private- and public-sector contexts throw up obstacles that prevent the general private-sector metaphor from easily passing into the public sector, perhaps there is a somewhat narrower or more particular idea that can usefully go through. Maybe the lesson of Compstat is not to borrow everything (profits, customers, competition) from the private sector but simply one thing. Maybe all public managers need do to improve the performance of their agencies is borrow the private sector's disciplined commitment to "bottom-line" value.

The following four simple steps should suffice for public managers to achieve this discipline:

1. Articulate a clear, complete, and compelling idea of the public value that their agency exists to produce.
2. Develop a set of measures to record the agency's performance in producing that public value.
3. Invite and embrace external accountability for defining and creating that value.
4. Create management systems that distribute internal accountability for public value creation across the managers and the employees of the agency so that they will feel motivated to perform in the short run and to innovate and learn over the longer run.

From a private-sector perspective, there is nothing complicated, novel, or controversial about this idea. It is Management 101. Indeed, to many in the private sector, the failure of public-sector managers to use these techniques seems like nothing but managerial incompetence or, worse, a determined effort to resist the demands for accountability and performance that characterize life in the private sector.

One key to making this more limited metaphor work is to develop a conceptually sound and practically useful basis for reckoning the (net) public value produced by a given public agency. There has to be a simple accounting concept that compares the good things that happen as a result of investing in and operating a public agency with the costs of doing so.[50] That much, at least, has to carry over into the public from the private sector.

A "Public Value Account" for Public Agency Managers

Public managers could imagine starting with something analogous to the "income statement" for private-sector firms.[51] An income statement in the private sector records revenues earned on the right side of the account and costs incurred on the left. The difference between the revenues earned and the costs incurred is the "bottom line."

PUBLIC VALUE ACCOUNT	
Financial Costs	Gross Public Value

Figure 1.1. Public value account I.

To create the equivalent in the public sector, we need an accounting scheme that can name the particular dimensions of value that an organization is supposed to pursue, and the various kinds of costs incurred in the pursuit of those values. The accounting scheme needs not only specific categories of valued effects and costs but also real quantitative and empirical data to fill out those categories and capture some sense of the net value produced. In this section we will develop a kind of "income statement" for public managers that holds onto the idea of a bottom-line value while taking account of the unique features of their situation. We will call this concept the "public value account" for a given organization in a particular setting. The public value account will cover the major conceptual categories of public value accounting that could create a rough equivalent of a bottom line for government organizations. Because many of these dimensions of value do not pass through markets in which money changes hands, they are neither captured in existing financial measurements nor easily monetized. Instead, the public that authorizes and pays for the activities of the organization determines the value of these categories of effect—often by reacting politically to movements in the particular categories that concern them.[52]

We begin with the simplest idea of a public value account, based on a financial income statement. One side of the account names and measures the *positively valued* effects of an agency's activities and recognizes those effects as (gross) public value creation. The other side names and measures the economic and financial costs that must be charged against the gross public value produced, as shown in Figure 1.1.

*Financial Costs versus Public Value: The Lack of Revenue Data
and Its Consequences*

The cost side of the account begins with the sum of the public dollars used to create the goods, services, and outcomes that the agency produces—the cost of raw materials, salaries paid, buildings and facilities, and so on. This looks very much like cost accounting in the private sector. Indeed, in principle, the public sector can and should have as great a capacity to recognize financial costs as the private sector, and even to allocate these costs to particular governmental activities and results.[53] The problems begin when the public sector turns to the right side of this ledger and tries to account for the *value* public agencies produce. For the most part, public agencies do not generate revenues through the sale of products and services to willing customers.[54] As a result, no financial data on the right-hand side of the ledger correlate to the value created. Instead, public managers have to measure material accomplishments with regard to the particular purposes—or dimensions of public value—that constitute their agencies' mission.

The fact that the gross value of what public agencies produce is not captured in revenue data creates a huge problem for "bottom-line accounting" in the public sector. Consider briefly just how useful a revenue earned from the sale of goods and services is in accounting for the value produced by a commercial company, and how much is lost when that measure is not available.

Revenues earned have the following five features that make them extremely useful in reckoning the value produced by a commercial enterprise:

1. Revenues earned by the sale of products and services to willing customers provide a relatively clear, objective, and precise estimate of the value that individuals attach to consuming those products and services.
2. Data about revenues earned are captured inexpensively right at the boundary of the organization at the time a purchase is made.
3. Because revenues earned are denominated in the same terms as costs (money), it is easy to compare the value of the goods and services produced with the costs expended and to calculate a net value for the effort as a whole.

4. Because revenues for all products and services are denominated in money, it is easy to compare the net value of producing one product or service compared to others.

5. The information systems needed to capture revenues earned have been developed over hundreds of years and are so widely used and accepted that no company could think of operating without them.

In contrast, consider what would happen if automobile manufacturers were forced to operate in a world where they could have all the *cost* information they wanted but could not know how much *revenue* they earned by selling the cars they made. Presumably, both managers and investors would be at a total loss. They could not know whether they were succeeding or failing as a business or which car model was most profitable. To get some guidance about whether they are producing anything of value, they would have to turn to a variety of other means. They would have to survey their customers, asking if they liked the cars they produced. Or, they might ask some expert engineers about the physical characteristics of the cars they produced. Were they good cars, in the sense that they performed their function well and were efficiently designed and manufactured? Some might try to figure out whether their cars had increased mobility for those who purchased them and enlarged the capacity of the nation's transportation system. But none of these methods would produce as precise and reliable information about value as revenues do.

It comes as no surprise that these are the very methods on which the public sector relies to determine gross public value. Public managers use surveys and other consultative mechanisms to provide feedback on the character and ultimate value of the services provided to clients.[55] They seek out the expert judgment of engineers and policy analysts to learn whether their activities and the results being produced are valuable, and how they could become more efficient and effective. And they often try to determine whether the enterprises they lead have produced the social outcomes that were intended.[56] It is good that government has found ways to try to capture and recognize the value of what it produces. But the lack of revenue data is a perpetual thorn in the side of those who yearn for a quick, inexpensive, objective expression of public value.

The fact that public agencies do not have revenue data leads to a painful conclusion: simple arithmetic will not help us calculate a bottom line for performance. We have to set a bundle of financial costs against a complex set of material effects that are hard to measure in their own right, and difficult to compare with the costs of production or with one another.[57] Finding better ways to measure the *positive* effects of agency operations on the right-hand side of the account is essential to constructing a conceptually sound and practically useful approximation of the "bottom line." But it will always be difficult to compare these effects with costs. To move forward, public managers need to find a way to cope with the philosophical complexities of their particular circumstances rather than simply ignoring them or relying on ill-fitting metaphors. Instead of losing their minds in the quixotic pursuit of a single numeric value that will allow them to get the benefits of "bottom-line management," public managers have to engage in "value-oriented" management that puts the production of public value front and center but acknowledges the complexities of defining and recognizing value in the public sector.

The Mission of Public Agencies as the Starting Point for a Public Value Account

The first place to look for a rough definition of the public value we expect a given public agency to produce is the agency's "mission."[58] The mission statement offers a more or less concrete description of the particular values that the political community behind the public agency seeks to achieve through the agency's work.[59] The mission of a public agency, whether established by tradition, statute, professional aspiration, or informal agreement, embodies a collective conception of the purposes for which the agency exists and how it ought to behave in trying to achieve those purposes.[60] For instance, the current mission of the NYPD is "to enhance the quality of life in our City by working in partnership with the community and in accordance with constitutional rights to enforce the laws, preserve the peace, reduce fear, and provide for a safe environment."[61] One police chief may look at that statement and conclude that the single metric of "crime reduction" serves as a good enough indicator for all of those outcomes (law enforcement, fear reduction, a peaceful and safe environment). Another, spending a bit more time musing over the mission, might search for some ways to measure the NYPD's community involvement, its policing of "quality-of-life offenses," the general level of fear among New Yorkers, and the degree to which it is satisfying individual citizens who call the police for service.

Whatever the approach, the mission is a solid basis for beginning the philosophical inquiry that will help a public agency draft the public value account that will ultimately allow its managers to reveal value creation and develop a strategy to produce more public value for citizens. Figure 1.2 is a more precise iteration of the previous figure.

Before leaving the simplest of public value accounts, it is worth noting that the achievement of a given mission is not the only dimension of public value recognized in this account. It also recognizes costs and counts the reduction of costs as an important value-creating move. Public managers often develop a very strong and commendable commitment to advancing the mission of their organization, but sometimes they focus so much attention on mission achievement that they pay less attention to managing costs.[62] They may think their mission is so important that all necessary costs to achieve it should be paid, or simply view their goal as maximizing mission performance subject to the (unreasonable) constraint of current budgets.[63] Few government managers think that their goal is to find significant cost reductions by abandoning outmoded procedures or eliminating parts of their operations that have become obsolete. They want to hold onto what they have and, ideally, get more to pursue their important public goals.[64]

In this respect, public managers' values are probably not fully aligned with those of citizens and taxpayers. Citizens and taxpayers would certainly like costs per unit of performance to go down over time in the public sector as they usually do in the private sector. And sometimes they simply want the total costs of government to go down even

PUBLIC VALUE ACCOUNT	
Financial Costs	Mission Achievement

Figure 1.2. Public value account II.

if that means reducing government services.[65] Public managers have to respect and embrace the public's interest in controlling costs as well as achieving mission results. Just as private-sector managers have to try to increase revenues and reduce costs simultaneously, public-sector managers have to try to increase mission performance even as they reduce their financial costs.[66] That is the reason there is a left side of this account as well as a right side.

Thinking beyond the Current Mission: Unintended Consequences, Unexploited Opportunities

An organization's mission statement provides an invaluable guide to the most important dimensions of public value to be recognized on the right-hand side of the account. But the particular dimensions of value that the existing mission statement nominates may not capture *all* the important effects of an agency's current operations, nor all those dimensions of value that the organization could pursue or reflect in its activities.

Many have observed that government enterprises produce unintended as well as intended consequences.[67] This happens in part because we lack the foresight or imagination to see that an effort to advance one or two dimensions of value would end up affecting other values as well, and also because governmental actions often have many rippling consequences that make it difficult to keep track of all effects and to guess which will be large and important enough to track in evaluating an agency's performance. We ought to focus on what we intended to do. But if what we do in pursuit of those goals has a side effect that dwarfs the value of what we intended to accomplish, it would be foolish not to notice (and measure) that effect.[68]

The idea that an effect was unintended does not necessarily imply that the effect was negative, however. Sometimes we produce an unexpected valuable result. For example, a public library established as a place to store and deliver media could have value as a kind of indoor park where individuals could gather to socialize and enjoy cultural events. But, certainly, there are some unintended effects—such as the threats to individual liberty, fairness in law enforcement, and the legitimacy of the police associated with aggressive "crime reduction" efforts—that should be evaluated negatively rather than positively.

Whether positive or negative, the unintended consequences of governmental initiatives have to find their way onto the public value

PUBLIC VALUE ACCOUNT	
Financial Costs	Mission Achievement
Unintended Negative Consequences	Unintended Positive Consequences

Figure 1.3. Public value account III.

account. The positively valued effects go on the right-hand side of the account. The negatively valued side effects go on the cost side of the equation, as shown in Figure 1.3.

By definition, we will not know these effects for sure at the outset, and there may be many of them. Consequently, there is a real risk that adding this complexity to the account will undermine an agency's focus on the core mission. But the benefit of adding this concept is to increase the overall diagnostic capacity of public managers and their overseers as they deploy government assets and produce complex results in the world. The category is a kind of invitation for managers and overseers to stop every now and then to imagine all the potential consequences of their actions. The category could also be a place to park external claims made about values that a given agency could advance or unintentionally harm.

Having a category that is a placeholder for "everything we didn't think of that did/could happen" encourages managers and overseers to look for effects (both negative and positive) that they had not originally considered and can prevent some significant errors and encourage some important successes. For example, concerns about the fair and moderate use of authority and force eventually did find their way into the Compstat system but were not there at the outset. Having an unanticipated side effects category in the accounting scheme might have sped up that process.

To hammer this point home, consider the example of the U.S. Department of Energy's (DOE) nuclear weapons program.[69] Initially the DOE was charged with responsibility for building nuclear weapons. It faced intense pressure from its overseers to produce the maximum number of weapons at the lowest economic cost. Consequentially, the department generated huge environmental problems in pursuit of this core mission. Then the cold war ended and with that the urgent need to keep manufacturing nuclear weapons. Simultaneously, the growing environmental movement was gradually succeeding in stripping the DOE's weapons program of the special protections it had enjoyed as it pursued its security mission. The result was that the mission of the organization turned 180 degrees. Instead of maximizing weapons production while ignoring environmental costs, the agency was charged with cleaning up the mess it had created while pursuing its original mission.

Of course we may have needed the bombs quickly, and we may have judged the environmental price small enough to pay for that result at the time. But we might have saved some time and money and spared ourselves a great deal of worry if the original mission of the DOE had accounted for environmental costs, or at least kept open some accounting category to determine how those costs were accumulating.

Just as a lack of awareness can allow negative effects to accumulate, it can also cause managers to miss valuable effects that are well within its capacities. A police department focused exclusively on crime reduction may fail to see the important value it contributes to dealing with medical and social emergencies such as traffic accidents, suicides, or marital disputes. A library can not only lend books but also accommodate latchkey children who have no safe place to go after school.[70]

The fact that public agencies produce both negatively and positively valued effects beyond those named in their missions poses a challenge for effective value-oriented management. Should the accounting scheme recognize these effects or leave them aside, unmeasured? Should public managers try to produce and enhance the positive effects or simply treat them as by-products of the core mission?

This question becomes even more important and difficult if the world is changing around a public agency in ways that make its old mission seem less relevant for the future than some of the side effects. If, for example, the former uses of a public library are becoming outmoded because the Internet allows people to do research from home, and the current uses of a library as a safe haven for latchkey kids are becoming more important, it might be time to change the mission of the library not only to recognize and accommodate these new uses but to make them central to its purposes. Effects that were once viewed as side effects might become the basis for a reformulated mission statement.[71]

Because there are liabilities associated with defining public value either too narrowly (tunnel vision, neglected costs, missed opportunities, etc.) or too broadly (lost focus, insufficient discipline, etc.), those who construct systems for accounting for public value production might find it useful to make a distinction between the core mission and effects that lie outside the core mission but that citizens and their elected representatives still value positively or negatively. This category can then become the basis for continued exploration of the value a given agency can and should produce.

This idea is not all that different from the increasingly popular private-sector idea that companies should add double and triple bottom lines to their income statements to show the (unpriced) effects that they are producing on environmental and social conditions.[72]

Client Satisfaction as a Dimension of Public Value
In recent years, as private-sector concepts have made their way into the world of public management, the concept of mission accomplishment as a representation of public value has been joined by the concept of "customer satisfaction."[73] But as we have seen, in trying to be faithful to the idea that public value includes satisfying customers as well as achieving publicly mandated missions, public managers can easily get confused about who their customers are, and what they want.

As noted earlier, those who receive benefits at the service end of government agencies often do not pay for them directly, and those who receive obligations often would prefer not to have them. Given that those on the other side of the counter lack some vital characteristics of customers in the private sector, we should probably not describe them as such. For lack of a better choice, I use the word "client" to describe such individuals, and recognize that clients come in two different forms: direct beneficiaries of government services, on one hand, and those on whom obligations are imposed, on the other. I call these clients "service recipients" and "obligatees," respectively, bearing in mind that many clients of government simultaneously receive services and obligations.

To some it might seem like hairsplitting to distinguish between mission achievement and client satisfaction. But the particular case of policing reveals exactly how important the difference can be. If we think of those stopped, cited, or arrested by police as clients, it seems pretty clear that their satisfaction is not the point of the exercise. Indeed, they have become the means to the end of achieving the publicly sanctioned mission of the police, and to some degree their interests are subordinated to the greater good.

While it is obvious that the police do not exist to satisfy those they stop, cite, or arrest, it is plausible that they exist largely to satisfy those who call for assistance. But even in this case, a certain tension shows up between achieving the mission of the police and satisfying service recipients. The tension is revealed in a culturally significant bit of police procedure and language.[74] When officers on patrol arrive at the scene to respond to a service call, they radio the dispatcher and announce that they are "going out of service." They say this at precisely the moment they step out of the car to meet the citizen caller! Then, when the officers get back into their cars, they radio the dispatcher to say they are "back in service." Given today's focus on customer service, serving the individual citizens who call seems more important than serving the dispatcher. Yet the dispatcher embodies another kind of public value—the capacity of the police department to respond quickly to a serious crime or a major emergency. The dispatcher is the agent not only of individual clients requesting service but also of the wider society that established the department's mission.

This reminds us that the various dimensions of value that public agencies produce in the form of social outcomes (whether intentional or unintentional, positive or negative) are ultimately enjoyed or endured by the collective public. As noted earlier, given that virtually all the assets that pay for public agency operations come from the broader public, it is only natural that the collective public is the proper arbiter of the value of these outcomes. Of course, none of this means that public managers should be indifferent to the impact their work has on service recipients and obligatees. Public managers are legally bound to protect the rights of all their clients. And, as a practical matter, treating clients respectfully often makes it easier to achieve the ultimate results defined in the mission. The public is free to direct public managers to give lots of attention to client satisfaction, as shown in Figure 1.4.

PUBLIC VALUE ACCOUNT	
Use of Collectively Owned Assets and Associated Costs	Achievement of Collectively Valued Social Outcomes
Financial Costs	Mission Achievement
Unintended Negative Consequences	Unintended Positive Consequences
	Client Satisfaction
	Service Recipients
	Obligatees

Figure 1.4. Public value account IV.

The Costs of Using Public Authority

The fact that public agencies impose duties on clients as well as deliver services reminds us that they often use more than money in the pursuit of their mission; they also at least sometimes—maybe often, maybe always—use the coercive power of the state.[75] Sometimes they use that authority directly to require individuals to contribute to public purposes (pay your taxes, go to school). Other times they use it to prohibit individuals and organizations from acting against the public's interests (do not steal, do not pollute, do not neglect and abuse your children). Public agencies also use authority to ration access to public goods and services and to ensure that public benefits and services go only to those the public intended to help.[76]

If these uses of authority produce the desired results—if they cause individuals to do good things for themselves and society and to resist doing bad things, and if they ensure that public benefits go only to those who are entitled to them—then the use of authority creates some public value. But the use of public authority should not be considered free of charge. A free society should be reluctant to use the authority of the state casually, for every time the state uses its authority, some of the freedom or privacy available to individuals in charting their own course

PUBLIC VALUE ACCOUNT	
Use of Collectively Owned Assets and Associated Costs	Achievement of Collectively Valued Social Outcomes
Financial Costs	Mission Achievement
Unintended Negative Consequences	Unintended Positive Consequences
	Client Satisfaction
	Service Recipients
	Obligatees
Social Costs of Using State Authority	

Figure 1.5. Public value account V.

in life is lost. If it is possible to produce the same gross public value using less state authority, doing so guarantees an increase in net public value. For these reasons, agency uses of public authority have to be reckoned as a cost in the public value accounting scheme.

What is more, financial costs are associated with every use of state authority. Rules require enforcement agents and courts of appeal. Regulations require paperwork and people to file that paperwork. If cutting the social cost of using state authority also means saving taxpayers some money, there is an opportunity to eke out that much more net public value, as shown in Figure 1.5.

Valuing Fairness and Justice in Agency Operations
The use of state authority does not register only on the left-hand side of the ledger; it also changes things on the right-hand side. The revenues side can and should pay attention to mission achievement, positive side effects, and client satisfaction. But once a public agency engages state authority, justice and fairness in both operations and outcomes become just as important as efficiency and effectiveness in achieving outcomes

PUBLIC VALUE ACCOUNT	
Use of Collectively Owned Assets and Associated Costs	Achievement of Collectively Valued Social Outcomes
Financial Costs	Mission Achievement
Unintended Negative Consequences	Unintended Positive Consequences
	Client Satisfaction
	Service Recipients
	Obligatees
Social Costs of Using State Authority	Justice and Fairness
	At Individual Level in Operations
	At Aggregate Level in Results

Figure 1.6. Public value account VI.

and satisfying clients. Public managers have to worry about whether the burdens they place on individual clients are just and sufficiently protective of their rights, and whether they are treating differently situated clients fairly. They also have to look at the aggregate results of their agencies' performance and ask whether they have advanced an appropriate idea of justice, as shown in Figure 1.6.

Blending Utilitarian and Deontological Conceptions of Value
In Western philosophy it is conventional to distinguish between utilitarian normative systems (which are primarily concerned with the practical relationship between ends and means and take individuals' well-being as the most important social goal) and deontological normative systems (which are primarily concerned with acting in accordance with some theory of right relations that defines the rights and obligations of social actors to one another and evaluates social conditions in terms of the degree to which existing social relationships do or do not approximate

an ideal of justice).[77] Often these different ethical worlds are held apart and seen to be in conflict with one another, in part because these different ethical systems are rooted in distinct academic disciplines that guide public managers: economics, which mostly relies on utilitarian thinking, and law, which relies more on deontological ideas. Whatever the reasons for holding these worlds apart, in the ordinary practice of public management, they cannot be allowed to stand apart. Public management as a philosophy and a practice demands that they be integrated.

Public management presents itself principally as a utilitarian effort. Managers are supposed to deploy the assets granted to them in intelligent ways that create value. Value creation is most often calculated in utilitarian terms such as satisfying individual clients, or bringing about desired aggregate conditions in the world. But public management cannot be a purely utilitarian enterprise. Managers occupy a particular fiduciary role in a democratic system that requires them to behave in certain ways regardless of the consequences for themselves and others. They are entrusted with both public authority and with money raised through public authority. This obliges them to use the assets entrusted to them fairly and equitably, as well as efficiently and effectively. Consequently, utilitarian values alone cannot guide the value they seek to produce and to reflect in the operations of their organizations. They also need to rely on deontological ideas about their own proper role, right relationships between government and citizens, and what makes a society not only good but just.

Apart from any philosophical reasons for combining these philosophical traditions in this inquiry, the fact of the matter is that public managers, like police chiefs, are routinely called to account for their performance in both terms: police chiefs sometimes get in trouble for spending too much money and failing to control crime, but they are far more likely to be fired for allowing their organizations to become brutal, racist, and corrupt.

Table 1.1 outlines how a public value account could be constructed to capture the value of an agency's activity in both utilitarian and deontological terms. The most familiar quadrant in this matrix is the top left, which conceives of public value as a relationship between money and practical results. Public value accounts I–IV are closely associated with this box.

Table 1.1.   Blending philosophical frameworks in recognizing public value.

	Public purposes	
	---	---
Public assets	Public welfare (utilitarian)	Social justice (deontological)
Public money	Efficient and effective use of public money	Fair use of public money
Public authority	Efficient and effective use of public authority	Fair use of public authority

Only slightly less familiar is the bottom-right quadrant, which finds public value in using public authority justly and fairly to enforce justice in social relationships. These deontological values appear in public value accounts V–VI.

The remaining quadrants combine utilitarian and deontological values in public value accounting. The bottom-left quadrant reminds us that we have some utilitarian interest in using as little authority as possible to achieve desired social results. The top right reminds us that we have some deontological interest in how we spend public money.

The Collective Arbitration of Value

A lot of the aforementioned discussion used the word "we" when discussing the valuation of police departments and other public agencies. So it is reasonable to ask, who is this collective "we"? Remember this apocryphal exchange?

> *Lone Ranger:* Tonto, we're surrounded by hostile Indians.
> *Tonto:* What do you mean "we," white man?

It is a very important question—one at the core of Bratton's confusion about "customers," on one hand, and "the public," on the other. If there is a "we" (a public) that values public agencies, then figuring out who "we" are and what "we" want is crucial. In principle, "we" could refer to two quite different ideas.[78]

"We" could refer simply to the sum of individual members of the public.[79] Each individual has some idea of what he or she wants or expects from a public agency and weighs those expectations against personal experiences. The value that this "we" attaches to a public agency is the sum of those individual valuations.[80]

In a second definition, however, "we" could refer to the result of a political process that produced some agreement about what "we" collectively wanted from a public agency.[81] In this formulation, each of us has to subordinate some of our individual ideas of what we want from government to what the collective public wants from it.[82] The value of a police department, then, would lie not in the satisfaction of clients nor in the satisfaction of the desires of individual citizens and taxpayers but in the extent to which the police force lived up to a collective understanding of what it ought to produce and through what means. To return to Bratton's metaphor, it is at this point that the public becomes something other than a collection of individual customers.[83]

Given that public agencies are in the business of using the collectively owned assets of the state—its authority, and tax dollars raised by state authority—the proper arbiter of the value those agencies produce is not necessarily their clients but, rather, the collective body politic that has mandated their purposes. In the public sector the proper arbiter of value is "we the people." It is we who are willing to tax and regulate ourselves to produce collectively valued and just ends through efficient, fair, and just means. Of course, the collective "we" is never perfectly constructed or perfectly articulate about its preferences. And it seems to keep changing its mind about what is valuable. Nonetheless, it is that "we"—constructed through the institutions and processes of democratic government—that is the only appropriate arbiter of the public value that "our" government produces.

What Is the Public Part of Public Value?

To be as clear as possible about what we mean by public value and how it might be distinguished from the concept of private value, Figure 1.7 sets out some distinctions that might be useful in marking boundaries of public versus individual value.

The *rows* in the table distinguish between *individuals* as arbiters of value, on one hand, and *collective* arbiters of value, on the other. Of course, free societies are defined by the special standing they give to individuals to evaluate both individual and collective conditions in society, and the opportunities that their economic, civic, and political institutions offer individuals to pursue their own ideas about their well-being

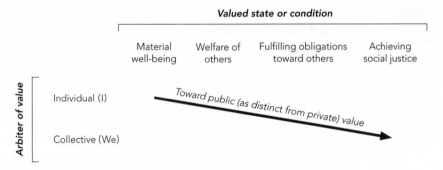

Figure 1.7. Degrees of "publicness" in the concept of public value.

and that of others.[84] They encourage the development of free markets that allow individual purchases to guide much of the economy. They give individuals significant rights not only to elect individuals to represent their interests and values in government but also to petition the government through many different channels.

But while individuals are privileged, free societies also understand that sometimes a collective must be formed and become articulate about its collective interests.[85] Each time the government decides to use its collectively owned assets (authority and tax dollars), a collectively defined purpose has to justify that act. That is true even, or perhaps especially, when we use public assets to promote what seems to be the narrow economic interest of a corporation, for example, or a single mother. To have a democratic government is to accept not only the idea that individuals are the core elements of society but also that some collective decisions have to be made, even if the decision is to reduce government's size and power. So while it might seem unfashionable to suggest that there is such a thing as a public that determines the value of government action, that idea is crucial to the idea of a liberal democratic state.

The *columns* in the table focus on the values held by the individual or collective arbiter. We know that individuals care about their own material well-being, or their own status in the society. But many individuals also value—that is, are willing to absorb some personal costs to achieve—other purposes.[86] They empathize with others and have some sense of duty to them. And they are willing to spend blood and treasure to pursue ideas of a good and just society. What is true of individuals is also true of the collective public.[87] The collective can be interested in protecting and advancing its material interests as well as concerned about the plight of the least fortunate. The collective may feel compelled by an idea of duty to those less fortunate. And within the collective body public are many smaller collectives formed explicitly around ideas of the good and just society that they would like to see realized.[88]

The concept of *public* value could refer to the interests and values pursued—the well-being of others, the common good, and the just. But it could also refer to whether the arbiter of value is an individual or a collective body public. The most purely private value in this scheme would be individuals valuing their own material well-being. The most purely public value would be the collective public's valuing of aggregate social conditions against some standard of the common good or the just.[89] In between are individual views of the good and the just that the public has not yet ratified,[90] as well as collective decisions to advance the material interests of some particular individual or class of individuals.

Given that the private and the public, the individual and the collective, and material interests and commitments to the welfare of others are spread across Figure 1.7 in some unexpected ways, a sharp line is not drawn between private and public values. Instead, values are identified as more or less public, with collective arbitrations of value having more legitimacy as a definition of public value than idiosyncratic individual ideas of public value.

Citizens versus Clients
The distinctions made in Figure 1.7 between individuals and collectives and between material interests and relational interests (associated with altruism, duty, and justice) suggest another key distinction for public value accounting: the distinction between *citizens*, on one hand, and individual *clients*, on the other. It is not a difference in groups of individuals; most individuals in a democratic society are both citizens and clients.

The difference is in the point of view an individual takes when thinking about what she or he would like and value in a public enterprise. A client is rooted in his or her particular position in society. Clients know whether they are rich or poor, black or white, or living in a dangerous or safe area. Because clients have particular known positions in society, they have particular interests to advance.[91]

The word "citizen," on the other hand, has, for our purposes, a special meaning. In *A Theory of Justice*, philosopher John Rawls argued that just social institutions would be those that individuals would choose *without knowing what particular position they would occupy in society.*[92] Rawls described this as thinking behind a "veil of ignorance." The intuition was that if one did not know what social position one occupied, one would have to imagine oneself in any or all positions before choosing a particular institution or set of institutions. That act of imagination and empathy, in turn, would reveal the institutional arrangement that was fair in the sense that it responded to the interests and needs of each and all individuals in the society. Thus, for example, a citizen could envision a police department that would be satisfactory whether he or she turned out to be a victim of crime, a criminal offender, someone falsely accused of a crime, or a taxpayer who has no pressing need for the police department.

In the real world, of course, we do not confront the question of what values we would like to see created and reflected through public policing as individuals considering an abstract issue. Our individual interests and social position shape our views. But so do some wider social values.[93] The values attached to public services like policing do not simply hang in the air as ideals; they are deeply rooted in our collective ideas about what makes a just and a fair society. To the extent that citizens hold such values as aspirations for police departments and other public agencies, public agencies need to monitor the degree to which they operate faithfully in accordance with these principles.

Summary: A Public Value Account for Public Agencies in General and Police Departments in Particular

Thus far we have seen that a proper accounting for the public value produced by an agency like the NYPD entails the following steps:

1. accounting for the financial costs of agency operations;
2. enumerating the dimensions of value named or implied in the agency's mission and finding measures that can capture their accomplishment;
3. imagining or learning about unanticipated consequences of the agency's performance and beginning to collect data on these;
4. finding the means to record client satisfaction (whether service recipients or obligatees);

5. accounting for the use of public authority as a cost; and
6. noting justice and fairness in organizational ends and means.

The goal is not to generate financial returns nor to satisfy individual clients but to satisfy the demands of citizens and their representatives as they articulate a particular conception of public value for a given public agency at a particular time.

The Technical Challenge of Developing a Public Value Account. Looking over this list of steps, one cannot help but notice how far we have moved away from the private sector's simple financial bottom line. Only one component of the public value account is denominated in dollars. All the rest have to be physical measures of events that occur in the world. Only some of the effects are valued by individuals in terms of their own satisfaction and well-being. Others are valued against the desires of individual citizens as they have been aggregated and expressed through the political processes of democratic government.

Measuring these effects is difficult, but far from impossible. We have well-established measures for many things that once seemed hard to measure. In policing, performing surveys of criminal victimization to get an accurate measure of crime, determine levels of fear in the community, measure a community's satisfaction with the fairness and effectiveness of police operations, or determine the degree of client satisfaction once seemed impossible. Yet over the last decade or so, these measures became familiar and widely used and, as we have learned how such measures behave, have improved in their technical quality. In order to measure public value, public managers have to give the matter serious thought and attention, make investments in new instruments for performance measurement, and accumulate experience in how the measures work.

Given these requirements, developing and using the metrics that can create a rough public-sector equivalent of a "bottom line" seems like a costly proposition—one that will test the patience of citizens, elected representatives, and managers who want a quick, cheap, and objective way to assess government performance. And these facts make successfully developing a public value accounting system a tough assignment. Often, individual managers make an enthusiastic start, only to find that it is much more difficult, expensive, and time consuming than they thought. In fact one can find relics of these past efforts in the information systems in any public agency, in dusty files, or in a small office producing a small report that no one reads. The challenge in this work is neither to surrender to simplicity and convenience nor to be overwhelmed by complexity. It is to forge ahead in a cumulative effort to develop a reasonably coherent, complete, and useful measurement system.

One Conception of a Public Value Account for Policing. Challenged by the example of Compstat, and curious about the practicality of creating a public value account for police departments, some colleagues and I spent several years developing such a tool for police departments in New York City and in Milwaukee, Wisconsin.[94] The effort was partly a philosophical inquiry into what dimensions of public value citizens should expect their police departments to produce. Beyond crime reduction, what other values did we want them to produce, or to reflect in the way they operated? How should we organize and name these dimensions of performance? But the inquiry also focused on the practical question of how to measure performance on these different dimensions of value. To what extent did current reporting systems contain information about the effects that we thought were valuable? What could we find in the files of departments that would reveal something important about the agency's performance? To what extent would we have to invest in new data collection efforts?

Presented in Figure 1.8 is a list of seven dimensions of public value in policing that we nominated as the beginning of a public value account for public police agencies, our first-round answer to the aforementioned philosophical question.

Once these dimensions were nominated as philosophically important, we had to figure out how they might best be measured—how to turn the abstract ideas into operational definitions, and how to develop metrics consistent with the operational definitions. Some dimensions of performance were relatively easy to measure using existing information systems. Established measures of reported crime could reveal crime reduction reasonably well. Clearance rates could measure success in calling offenders to account for their crimes. Response times to calls for service revealed one important dimension of service quality.

Figure 1.8. Seven dimensions of public value in policing.

We realized, however, that the only reason these things were easy to measure was that years of investment had gone into making them measurable. It was not that they were intrinsically easy to measure. Indeed, we eventually learned that reported crime numbers were not particularly accurate measures of total criminal victimization—there was a dark figure of unreported crime that victimization surveys could help us gauge more accurately. We learned that the process of clearing

PUBLIC VALUE ACCOUNT	
Use of Collectively Owned Assets and Associated Costs	Achievement of Collectively Valued Social Outcomes
Financial Costs	Mission Achievement
Internal	Reduce crime
External (private security costs	Reduce fear
to citizens)	Promote civility
Unintended Negative Consequences	Unintended Positive Consequences
Police corruption	Provide emergency medical and
Vigilante justice	social services
	Client Satisfaction
	Respond to citizen callers (service
	recipients) with speed and courtesy
	Respect the rights of criminal
	suspects (obligatees)
Social Costs of Using State Authority	Justice and Fairness
Citizen/Client dissatisfaction	At individual level in operations
Illegal search complaints	• Protect individual rights
Excessive force complaints	• Ensure fair and equal protection
Use of force	of citizens
Firearm use	• Call offenders to account
Civilian casualties	At aggregate level in results
	• Help ensure the quality of justice
	in society at large
	• Call offenders to account

Figure 1.9. A proposed public value account for policing.

crimes was relatively haphazard, and that we could not be sure we had good measures of the degree to which individuals were called to account for their crimes. We also learned that there were many attributes of police service beyond speed of response that mattered to those who called.

These findings reminded us of two key facts about performance measurement in the public sector. First, whether something is easy or hard to measure depends a great deal on how much effort has gone into trying to measure the effect. There are many values that start off as abstractions that seem hard or impossible to measure that eventually yield to efforts to create metrics. For example, the police thought it would be impossible to measure something as subjective (and potentially irrational) as fear of crime. But we learned how to construct these measures, and what sorts of police activity help reduce fear.

Second, in developing public value accounting schemes, we can take either a short-term or long-term view. If we take a short-term view in order to develop and use a public value account quickly, we will be mostly limited to the values for which we have established concepts, metrics, and data collection systems. More often than not, this short-run account will give a limited and biased picture of the full set of values at stake. If we take a longer view, we can give ourselves the space to develop a fuller accounting system that could better represent the real public value produced, but we have to spend more on development and be more patient in waiting for the results. Figure 1.9 sets out a more complete public value account that a police department could use as the basis for its information systems.

Figure 1.10, developed at the same time as Figure 1.8, presents a proposal about the sequence of investments that a given police department could make to develop information systems around the proposed public value account. The columns of the figure represent dimensions of public value. The rows represent where overseers and managers of the police could gather information about each of the values. The target symbols represent our best judgment about where investments should be made to develop and use information.

As expected, in the short run, only some items nominated to be part of the general ledger can be easily captured. Over the longer run, after some conceptual work, some experimenting with instruments for measurement, and some initializing of data systems, many more of these dimensions could be filled in.

	1	2	3	4	5	6	7
Administrative Records (*existing*)							
Reported Crime Data	◉	—	—	◉	—	—	—
Arrests and Clearance Rates	—	◉	—	—	—	—	—
Response Times	—	—	—	—	—	—	◉
Repeat Calls	—	—	◉	◉	—	—	—
Expenditures Per Capita	—	—	—	—	◉	—	—
Sworn Personnel	—	—	—	—	◉	—	—
Civilian Complaints	—	—	—	—	—	◉	◉
Firearm Use/Civilian Casualties	—	—	—	—	—	◉	◉
Surveys of Citizens (*new*)							
People Cited or Arrested	—	—	—	—	—	◉	◉
Callers	—	—	—	—	—	—	◉
General Population	◉	—	◉	—	—	◉	◉
Evaluations of Programmatic Initiatives (*new*)	◉	—	◉	◉	—	—	—

◉ = *High-priority targets for investment*

Figure 1.10. Priority investments for police information systems.

All of the aforementioned categories for measurement may or may not be useful for every police department. Subsequent real-world experiments with this accounting scheme have shown that these measures can at least be implemented and gain some political traction.[95] But these figures sketch a relatively serious and thoughtful approach to developing a public accounting scheme for a complex public agency like a police department.

Summary

With all this in mind, let's return to the case of Bratton in New York City and consider his success in formulating a "bottom line" (or a public value account) for New York's finest and driving them toward increased public value creation.

Seeking to align himself with a "businesslike" approach to running the NYPD, Bratton promised to reduce crime by 10 percent in the first year and 30 percent more in the years following. Like a chief executive officer speaking to a group of potential investors and analysts, he defined his purposes, committed himself to a certain level of performance that could be measured objectively, and exposed himself and his organization to the risk of failure, hoping that it would generate a sense of urgency throughout the NYPD.

There is much in what Bratton did that is worthy of unmitigated admiration. He embraced rather than resisted accountability. He focused that accountability on what he judged to be the NYPD's most valuable core purpose. He developed the administrative means to generate a strong sense of internal accountability that translated into focused efforts to improve performance across the organization. And he created conditions inside his organization that made it possible for police of every rank to learn how to improve their performance. By embracing external accountability, attaching it to an important and a measurable goal, and redistributing the accountability across the midlevel managers of his organization, Bratton generated a behaviorally powerful demand for performance. And the NYPD responded as though its life depended on improved performance, just as Bratton had hoped.

But the behavioral power that Bratton's leadership generated made it all the more important for Bratton to get the public value account right—including accurately identifying the true and the full value that the NYPD could and should produce and embody. It is here that we might begin to have some doubts.

Comparing the original iteration of Compstat with the public value account proposed earlier in Figure 1.8 would reveal that Bratton was focused on the first two or perhaps four dimensions of public value creation. He assumed that the existing financial control systems were taking care of the sixth. But he was not paying much attention to dimensions five and seven.

We could give Bratton a great deal of credit for getting most of the important dimensions right. But, as noted previously, omitting certain dimensions of value can set a public agency up to pay a terrific price in reduced performance on the other dimensions of value. Indeed, over time, the NYPD learned to acknowledge the importance of the sixth and seventh dimensions of performance and to include these in Compstat.

If the case of William Bratton and Compstat has helped public managers take seriously the idea of value-oriented management, then that is a valuable and commendable thing. Despite all the challenges of defining and recognizing public value, described earlier, Bratton forged ahead and developed a simple conception of the public value that the NYPD produced, sustained a political consensus behind that goal, and used it to animate and guide the operations of the NYPD. The most valuable lesson here for public managers is that all the apparent obstacles to developing and using a public value account as an approximate bottom line to manage public agencies are not insurmountable.

The case inspires, but it also cautions. The increase in citizen complaints and the discussion in this chapter point to some of the costs of failing to develop a more comprehensive and accurate account of the public values at stake in police operations, and the risks of moving too quickly and decisively to a fixed idea of what constitutes an agency's public value. The case suggests that instead of imagining that one can leap quickly to a clear, comprehensive scheme for recognizing public value, it might be better to think of the drive to create a strong bottom line for public agencies as a cumulative process of collective learning and adaptation. This learning approach is necessary at least in part because "we the people" may not be quite sure what we want, or what our public agencies can actually produce. To find out, we have to keep developing and using some kind of public value accounting system.

The price of being hasty and incomplete in a public value accounting system can be steep. When performance measures guide a public agency, the dimensions of value that do not get measured get short shrift. Bratton's failure to measure the costs associated with producing crime reduction meant that the NYPD could ignore the fact that it was spending citizens' liberty at a higher rate, and perhaps in a more unfair manner than before. The inevitable consequence was that complaints increased. The legitimacy of the police—something that is intrinsically valuable as well as instrumentally valuable in encouraging the cooperation of citizens—also declined.

Whether instances of discrimination and brutality were truly on the rise is hard to say, since the NYPD was not making special efforts to track these numbers, but those who complained energized a political discussion about fairness and restraint in police action. As discussions like these gather steam, police have to respond with measures designed to capture information on how fairly and extensively they are using force. The communities and the citizens get to decide what they want out of their police departments, and they are the ones who nominate one dimension of value or another as a candidate for measurement.

We have spent a lot of time and analytic effort on the particular case of policing because the case of policing focuses a bright light on some important dimensions of public value that would be easy to overlook, such as:

1. the important role that public authority plays in the operations of public agencies;
2. the fact that the important arbiter of public value is the collective of citizens forged through the processes of democratic governance (i.e., the public) rather than individual clients;
3. the public typically wants socially defined outcomes rather than the satisfaction of individual clients; and
4. the collective values fairness in government operations and wants government to create justice as well as material well-being.

But one might worry that the case of policing is odd and unique in this respect, and that these lessons are less important when considering how to create a useful bottom line for other public agencies. We will consider that question as we go through the remaining cases in this volume.

2

━━━⊰♦⊱━━━

Mayor Anthony Williams and the D.C. Government

Strategic Uses of a Public Value Scorecard

Mayor Anthony Williams and the Politics of Performance

When Anthony Williams was elected mayor of Washington, D.C., in November 1998, he inherited a city that was just getting back on its feet after a harrowing brush with insolvency.[1] Although the "District" (as locals called it) had balanced its budget for the last two years—thanks in good part to the efforts of Williams himself, who had been its chief financial officer since 1995—the effects of its fiscal distress were still evident. After years of little or no capital investment, the city lacked the equipment to consistently deliver basic services to its citizens. Its employees were saddled with antiquated information systems and poor facilities. The city workforce had been slashed, and citizens found many of those remaining on city payroll ill trained and unresponsive. Williams had campaigned on a platform stressing improved services and accountability, and voters seemed to endorse these aims by handing him a convincing victory.

Independence, Bankruptcy, and Independence Restored

Prior to 1973 a committee of the Congress of the United States governed the District. All of its funding came from the federal government. Special congressional committees controlled local government activities. But the passage of a home rule amendment gave the citizens of the District the right to establish their own government and elect those who would govern them. The legislative committees in Congress retained some oversight responsibilities and powers, since they continued

to appropriate the funds that provided the bulk of the District's revenues (essentially payments made in lieu of taxes for the federal government's use of its land and services).

For nearly twenty years, the choice of the people in this largely African American city had been Marion Barry, a charismatic politician
and civil rights leader. Over the years Barry had allowed the city to fall
into grave financial difficulties. By 1997 the District was running a huge
deficit. Congress stepped in with a massive bailout package that relieved
the city of its most onerous burdens, but the price of the federal bailout
was a loss of autonomy. The same legislation that provided the money
stripped the mayor of important powers and transferred authority over
the city's nine largest departments to a new entity: the "Control Board."

Barry complained that the federal government was trying to "re-
colonize the citizens of the District," but federal lawmakers laid the
blame for the District's financial problems squarely on Barry. Lauch
Faircloth, chairman of the United States Senate's Appropriations Committee for the District, noted that the mayor had failed to comply with
the terms of annual "performance accountability plans" that had been
mandated for three years in a row and suggested that "accountability is
apparently beyond the reach of the mayor's office." He added that this
failure to be accountable "confirms what I've said all along: the District's problem is management, management, management."[2]

Within a year of the Control Board assuming operational responsibility for the management of the city, the District's fiscal conditions had
dramatically improved. One of the heroes of this turnaround was Anthony Williams, a young African American technocrat. Williams first
came to D.C. in 1993 to take the job of chief financial officer (CFO) at
the U.S. Department of Agriculture. In 1995 he was appointed to the
post of CFO for the District of Columbia, where he made his mark not
just for his financial skills but for his overhaul of the city's troubled tax
department—a feat that made him the stuff of "bureaucratic legend,"
according to the *Washington Post*.[3] However, his corporate-style management of the department—in particular his firing of some 165 employees—
led some to view him as a heartless hatchet man. His opponents
portrayed him as a "cold-blooded, calculating manager more interested
in spreadsheets than people."[4]

Prior to the 1998 election, Williams had held only one elected
office—serving as an alderman in the city of New Haven while he was

a student at Yale. Since then, he had operated mostly as a self-described "Ivy League bean counter," and "managerial geek." In these respects he could not have been more different from Marion Barry. One commentator described Williams as "a stranger to street rhetoric, community activism, and small talk."[5] Another wrote, "If Marion Barry was a black power guy and a street dude, Tony Williams was happy to be a nerd."[6]

Despite his technocratic commitments, however, in the summer of 1998, at the urging of a citizen coalition, Tony Williams threw his hat into the ring and ran for mayor.[7] In a light voter turnout, Williams won the Democratic primary on September 15 with 50 percent of the vote in a field of seven candidates. He then trounced his Republican opponent on November 3 by a margin of better than two to one. On the eve of his inauguration on January 2, 1999, some District residents expressed reservations about Williams's commitment to the city's less prosperous citizens, but others were more hopeful. "We're looking forward," said one, "to having a well-run, well-organized city government that will do what city governments are supposed to do."[8]

Once inaugurated, the mayor moved quickly to improve some of the basic services that affected the quality of life of all citizens in the District. In his inaugural address, Williams ran down a laundry list of "basics" that city government needed to provide. "We need to fill the potholes," he declared. "We need to sweep the streets. We need to exterminate the rats, wash away the graffiti, repair the road signs, and collect the garbage. We need to beautify the parks, inspect run-down buildings, organize our records. We need sewers that drain. We need 911 that responds."

There was plenty of room for improvement in these basic services. The fiscal crisis of the mid-1990s had dealt a devastating blow to an already shaky service delivery system. According to Williams, the rigorous efforts to control costs had forced "a severe level of capital disinvestment." Significant layoffs (recommended by Williams himself as the District's CFO) had demoralized the city's workers. The combination left city services "in another world, in terms of not [being] exposed to modern trends and practices. [There was] a kind of besieged mentality," Williams said. "Service delivery was basically abysmal in agency after agency."

Knowing he had some political capital to spend with his overseers, Williams convinced Congress to restore to the mayor's office the authority to hire and fire midlevel managers. The administration then identified some "quick wins" that Norman Dong, Williams's deputy chief of staff, hoped would produce "visible, concrete, tangible benefits" within six months.[9] The list of twenty-eight improvements included increasing the pace of pothole repairs, expanding rat control and graffiti removal efforts, and setting up a centralized phone number for inquiries concerning city services. "I thought up the short-term action plans," Williams recalled, "as a way to get everybody focused on deliverables, to show the government could do something. . . . [O]nce they were under way, and people felt something was happening, then we started working on a longer term plan."[10]

Williams's long-term plan focused on two key objectives: "I came into the city to do two things: to rebuild the fundamental operations of the government, while at the same time building greater respect, affinity for, [and] identification with the government by citizens." He conceived of the plan as a way to foster "an identity of interests" between the city and its residents and an organizational culture in city government that "was fueled by an appetite for performance."

Williams and his staff spent several years developing a citywide strategic plan. Williams's original objectives grew into five strategic priorities: building and sustaining neighborhoods; strengthening children, youth, and families; making government work; promoting economic development; and enhancing unity of purpose and democracy. The mayor took these objectives to a "citizen summit," where the three thousand-plus people in attendance cast votes ranking their priorities and then submitted comments and suggestions using electronic keypads and laptops.[11] Their comments and suggestions were analyzed and sorted into "citizen priorities" under the headings of each of the five strategic priorities. Those who managed city agencies were asked to devise their own strategic plans based on these priorities and to develop performance measures that could show progress toward concrete goals. The Williams administration integrated the goals into the contracts of agency directors and used them as the basis for a yearly review.

In a more controversial move, in the fall of 1999, Williams offered a choice to nine hundred midlevel municipal managers: forfeit their civil service protections and join the "management supervisory service" (MSS), making them, like their bureaucratic overseers, subject to performance-based reviews and accompanying pay raises or dismissals;

or, stay in the civil service and be demoted from their managerial positions.[12] Over 90 percent elected to join the MSS.

Famously, Williams also created "scorecards" for city managers modeled after baseball cards, with the image of a city manager on one side and on the other "a few critical measures" of his or her agency's effectiveness, Norman Dong explained. The first series of scorecards merely listed the performance goals. The following series would include progress toward those goals and a new set of goals for the next series.

Inside the Department of Motor Vehicles

When Williams asked Sheryl Hobbs Newman, a customer service manager in his administration, to become director of the Department of Motor Vehicles (DMV), she initially hesitated. "Oh no, I don't think that's a good idea," Newman recalled saying. "That place is a mess." The DMV was making do with an outdated and unreliable computer system, makeshift procedures, and shortages of basic resources like staff and office supplies. Wait times in the DMV line ran three to four hours, and waiting customers were rewarded with surly attitudes from DMV staff.

Since lines were the biggest complaint, the performance measures that Newman selected for the DMV's scorecard goals all concerned wait times—for licenses and registrations, inspections, and hearings on parking fines. Newman met with Williams and Norman Dong, now deputy mayor, to finalize target wait times and to request funds to hire new staff and update the computer system. The central goal was to reduce wait times for licensing and registration to thirty minutes for 80 percent of transactions (the mayor's office initially pushed for 100 percent, but Newman felt that even 80 percent might be a long shot).

Mitchel Dennis, head of the DMV's customer services administration, was enormously relieved to see the mayor's office finally setting standards and funneling resources into the DMV. "There were times when I would dig in my pocket and buy pens, and the staff would dig in their pockets and buy pens and staples and staplers," said Dennis of the pre-Williams era.[13]

Dennis was one of a few in the District who had faith in the DMV staff. "If they have the wherewithal to do a good job, they want to do a good job," he said. Still, the DMV's veteran staff was circumspect about the targets. "One of the biggest battles that I've found in government in general, but particularly here," said Newman, "is the notion of getting the word down to the front line. . . . It was very difficult to convince people that things were going to change, and things were going to get better."

Investment in a technological innovation, however, made the task of reducing wait times much easier. An automated line management system called "Q-matic" provided the issuance of tickets from a reception desk to each DMV customer, who received a number indicating the type of transaction and place in line. Customers could then sit down and wait for their number to flash on an electronic board. Q-matic also gave the DMV immediate and precise information on wait times for each transaction and the number of customers waiting in line. Each time employees completed a transaction, they hit the "next" button, and, after a brief pause, the next number flashed on the board. Because of the lag between pressing the button and the number appearing, Dennis "exhorted" employees to hit "next" as they were concluding business with each customer rather than waiting for the transaction to be completed. The staff began referring to their boss as Mitchel "Next" Dennis.

Employees who may have been hazy on the details (or even the existence) of the DMV's scorecard goals had a concrete relationship with Q-matic. "After I do a customer," said Dewan Sales, a fourteen-year DMV veteran, "I always check and see—I spent three minutes, I spent five minutes. . . . We bet like a football pool who can work faster." The feedback from Q-matic, providing real-time evidence of slowdowns and backups, empowered the floor staff to get help from administrative staff when volume was heavy. Customers were less agitated, and DMV staff no longer had to worry about keeping the seething customer lines orderly.

Inside the Department of Consumer and Regulatory Affairs

The Department of Consumer and Regulatory Affairs (DCRA) for Washington, D.C., is responsible for a host of regulatory matters under three main headings: building and land regulation; business and professional licensing; and housing regulation.[14] Like the DMV, the DCRA had a reputation for slow and spotty service. "There was a perception that you call in and no one answers the phone," said David Clark, whom Williams appointed director of the DCRA in 2001—the eleventh person to take the reins in twelve years. At the time of Clark's arrival, the agency had recently relocated from a run-down building to more spacious, modern offices and had upgraded its computer and information systems. Its budget had swelled by almost $3 million to support new staff and to help the agency reach its performance goals. But the complaints continued unabated.

Clark found that most of the grumbling came from two kinds of clients. "One is a neighborhood person [who doesn't] like the blight . . . across the street," said Clark. "The other high-leverage customers are the developers. When they don't get their permit quickly, when they run into zoning problems, [when] they run into whatever, then DCRA is seen as the [source of the problem]."

Clark's predecessor at the DCRA had responded to these two groups of customers by setting scorecard goals for demolishing and boarding up "nuisance" properties and speeding up the process of granting building permits for residential and commercial projects. But Clark, like Newman, discovered that the DCRA's frontline workers had little knowledge of the scorecard goals. Worse, the agency's midlevel managers did not have effective processes in place for reaching or measuring progress toward the goals. Clark initiated a series of retreats with management staff members to help them focus on the scorecard goals, the strategic plan, and their individual roles in achieving the agency's objectives. "[W]e laid out the process at the lowest level, literally, in the organization, and said, 'These are the steps; every place there's a handoff, we'll build in a process measure and . . . a results measure,'" said Clark. Clark also took care to remind staff that the scorecard goals had been ratified by District residents at the citizen summit and were being publicized by the mayor's office.

James Aldridge, the head of the DCRA's Housing Regulation Administration (HRA), had been helpless to address the District's many "nuisance properties" for many years. The mayor's office bumped up the building repair account, "severely underfunded" at $100,000, to $1 million. The scorecard goals were so ambitious, however, that Aldridge had to find a way to turn a tenfold budget increase into a hundredfold increase in performance.

Aldridge hired a few new staff members, but mostly he focused on "streamlining processes." First, rather than having private contractors compete for each job (a process that often took months), the HRA established a roster of contractors who would take jobs on a rotating basis. Second, to shorten the period of time before properties could be razed, the HRA asked "code officials" from the Building and Land Regulation Administration, a partner agency in the DCRA, to declare the properties life-threatening hazards. "[W]e actually had a code official riding around with us one day a week," said Aldridge. "We would identify thirty or forty properties, buy him lunch, put him in a vehicle and say, 'Let's go.' " To further expedite the demolition and cleanup process, Aldridge sought help from other public agencies. The National Guard barricaded buildings under the auspices of its drug and addiction program, which provided job training and placement assistance for recovering drug users. Aldridge contracted with the Department of Corrections to have inmates clean vacant properties for thirty-three cents an hour.

Ronald Duke, a senior rehab specialist in the Enforcement Division, was grateful for the expeditious new process for hiring contractors but had some concerns that the focus on numbers could interfere with the thoughtful handling of individual cases. "We're in a position where we can really do some damage to people," he said. He cited a case where there was a demolition order on the home of a ninety-year-old man. "He's trying to negotiate a sale," said Duke, "and it's the last asset he has that he's going to live on. . . . I have to listen to these folks, and I have to temper what I do because, hey, you could destroy a life, you know."

Reflections at Midpoint

The first round of scorecard results was reported in January 2001. Overall, the city had met or exceeded 67 out of 98 published goals, or 68 percent. Later, a more complete tally of the goals for 2000 showed that the city had done better than first reported: agencies had met or exceeded targets for 78 out of the 98 goals, or 79.6 percent. Total figures for the second round indicated a slight dip—79 out of 105 goals, or 75.2 percent, were met or exceeded.[15]

Looking back, Williams said, it had taken "an enormous amount of time and effort to do this in a city environment"—not just to design and institutionalize it, but to structure it to inform and coincide with the District's budget process. "It does take a lot of front-end load," remarked the city administrator John Koskinen. As overseer of the performance management system, Koskinen worked to overcome resistance to the system and to keep agency managers focused on the citywide strategic plan and the scorecard goals. "It takes a lot of my time and a reasonable amount of prodding and pushing and making sure it happens," he said. "If you're going into a city that's never done it before, you're going to have a lot of people grumbling about the meetings."

The mayor's involvement in the scorecards and the performance management system was decisive in motivating city employees to take both seriously. "It's clear to me," Koskinen maintained, "that if the mayor were not asking about this, if he were not sitting down with the agencies and cross-examining them about how they're doing on their scorecard goals, we wouldn't have made anything like the progress we've made."

"Clearly we've put ourselves on the spot," Williams said when he unveiled the scorecards in April 2000. "Citizens need to make a judgment [about our progress], and I'm willing to be held to that judgment."[16] Privately, however, he acknowledged that success as well as failure in this venture might have its costs. While falling short of a target could undermine public confidence in his still-young administration, meeting a scorecard goal could mean that "people will automatically raise the bar."

Nonetheless, Williams encouraged the District's public managers to set challenging goals for themselves and their agencies. "I think it's better to have an aggressive goal and fail to meet it," he said, "than have an easy goal." Agency officials, however, expressed some concern about public reaction to subpar results, Koskinen recalled. "I think there's a hesitancy on the part . . . of public managers about having goals and then posting them. You figure with performance, people will only notice when you don't make it, and not care so much when you do make it."

But Koskinen believed the public would be forgiving. He pointed to the experience of officials in the British subway system who had worried about the response when their performance goals and results were made public. "What they discovered was that everybody loved it because, first, it demonstrated that somebody cared about performance, and people were going to give you information. And that's been my experience—what people worry about most [about] government service is that nobody cares, and nobody notices, and it's never going to get better." He added, "You have a lot more credibility with the public when you have goals you missed, since they understand that not everything ever goes according to plan."

There were other risks involved in giving scorecard goals a prominent role. "The downside," Williams observed, "is that you'll be criticized for being a micro-manager and not really a leader. . . . In this city—in any city, [but] certainly in Washington, D.C.—the media are very, very cynical. They look at it just as a political ploy."

"These were very broad brush goals," said one critic, "that were achievable with a minimal investment and very little measurement of real results in people's lives." But others labeled the goals as a "brilliant public relations move." It was "great PR," one resident told the *Washington Post*, because Williams "gets to hold his managers accountable if they don't deliver, which is really popular with residents."[17]

Williams saw the positive and negative comments alike as indicators of the public engagement he sought to encourage. "People pooh-pooh [the goals], and they're cynical about them, but at the end of the year, everybody talks about them. The paper writes about them," he said.

Though press coverage of the scorecards waned, Williams believed that interest in—and approval of—the goals, and the larger citywide planning process out of which they grew, remained high among District residents. "The public," he said, "keep[s] telling us that we're moving in the right direction with our emphasis on performance management." As evidence, he pointed to the turnout for the second "citizen summit" on October 6, 2001, to begin work on a new strategic plan: over thirty-five hundred people showed up for the event, several hundred more than had participated in the original summit. "So," Williams concluded, "there's still a strong interest in the process, in the transparency, in the objectivity, the concreteness of this."

Regardless of how vocal they were about the goals, Koskinen believed that people were paying attention to performance. "At the local level particularly," he maintained, "you're judged on whether the place works or not. . . . [E]ven if the public went sound asleep on it, you'd have to do it because you want the place to run better." The scorecard goals gave city officials something to "manage against" and the public a say in what was managed. "Ultimately," said Koskinen, "you share all this with the public not so much for the goals themselves, but for the prioritization. You want the public to be telling you . . . what [it] thinks is most important."

Similarly, Congress kept a close and critical eye on the city's performance, though not necessarily on the scorecard goals themselves. Members of Congress continued to be "very supportive" of the administration, Koskinen noted, "but primarily because they recognize and appreciate the actual improvement in performance." Only the "experienced managers among them," he added, had "looked behind the figures to see and appreciate how we're doing on the performance system."

As for the scorecard results themselves, Williams contended that, while far from perfect, they showed that the system was working. "Basically," he reflected, "the government has to do a zillion things. If I tried to do a zillion things without setting up an organization and delivery system to do it, it's hopeless."

Still, it was a challenge to keep the public eye on the improvements made and not on the many still on the to-do list. In an ambiguously worded editorial, printed in late December 2001, shortly after Williams announced his intention to seek reelection, the *Washington Post* mildly chided Williams for touting the achievements of his administration in his first term. "Where is the District now?" the *Post* asked. "The mayor said the other day that his administration has racked up a long list of successes. While to some extent that's true, we think the answer is more complex." Pointing to persistent social problems—unsafe streets, a still-high homicide rate, and underperforming schools—the *Post* warned that voters would "scrutinize the mayor's claims and carefully judge the extent to which he has achieved the goals he outlined nearly three years ago." Williams, however, appeared confident that his administration could withstand the scrutiny. "It's a hard record to knock down," he declared.[18]

Strategic Uses of Performance Measurement: From Public Value Accounts to Public Value Scorecards

In many ways Anthony Williams's story closely resembles William Bratton's. In each case, a high-level public manager made a personal commitment to improving government performance.[19] In each case the manager announced his commitment publicly, transforming the personal commitment into a highly visible public pledge with real consequences for his personal standing and reputation if he failed to deliver. And in each case the manager's drive to improve performance—given standing by the authority of his office and energy and force by his personal and public commitments—gained a sharp focus through the development and use of specific, quantitative performance measures that could reveal real progress made in pursuit of the announced goals.

Having made themselves accountable for achieving specific, measurable goals, Bratton and Williams each found the administrative means to push accountability down and out through the organizations they led. They tied strong performance management systems to the performance measurement systems that recognized progress made toward their goals.[20] Compstat meetings—a forum in which the efforts of precinct captains to reduce crime could be assessed and discussed—were the centerpiece of Bratton's performance management system. Williams relied on the power of "scorecards" to identify individual agency directors to citizens and to publicize the performance goals their agencies pledged to meet. In response, Bratton's precinct captains and Williams's agency directors found ways to improve their performance along the dimensions of value that their bosses had nominated for their attention. Presumably, these gains came from some combination of new resources, new pressure on employees all the way down the line to stay focused and work harder, and experimentation with new methods.

From the perspective of the private sector, there is little that is novel in these stories. Using objective measurements of performance to enhance accountability and improve performance is about as old an idea as there is in management. The only thing that makes Bratton and Williams unusual is that they apply these principles thoughtfully and energetically in government.

This raises an important question: Why is such managerial action uncommon in the public sector? Perhaps, one might hypothesize, there is little public demand for the kind of accountability that could be generated through the development and use of even a rudimentary kind of public value account. Perhaps the managerial work required of public managers to create suitable conditions for value-oriented management is too great and too complex. Perhaps it is unclear whose job it is to build an effective performance management system anchored in a public value account. Perhaps there are few incentives for public managers to do this work. Any of these hypotheses could explain why developing some kind of public value account, and using it in a tough, value-oriented management system, takes unusual managerial commitments and actions.

But there is an even deeper problem. Hard as it is to make a public agency accountable for producing all the values named in a comprehensive public value account, developing a performance management system that can do this and position the organization for increased value creation in the future may be even harder. It is one thing to develop a public-sector approximation of a financial bottom line to reveal past public value production and press for productivity gains, another to develop a public value account that can capture the future value-creating potential of a public agency, and still another to develop and use additional information systems that can focus managerial and organizational attention on the actions necessary to execute the forward-looking strategy. This move, from a public value account that records a public agency's past value-creating performance to a broader performance measurement system that helps position the organization for improved performance in the future, follows a path staked out by Robert S. Kaplan and David P. Norton in the 1996 book *The Balanced Scorecard: Translating Strategy into Action.* In that book and in subsequent work, the authors argued that to ensure a strong financial performance in the future, private-sector managers had to look beyond financial measures to the conditions in their environment that would enable the firm to sustain or increase profitability in the future. They proposed the "balanced scorecard" as a measurement and management system that would allow managers to put a forward-looking strategy for value creation into action.[21]

In the rest of this chapter I will consider why effective performance measurement and management are relatively rare in the public sector. I will also take a close look at what kind of work is necessary to create the conditions for value-oriented management guided by a public value account in the public sector. But I will spend most of my time focusing on why it is important to go beyond the development of a public value account, and to put that work in the wider context of a "public value scorecard" that can fully exploit the strategic potential of performance measurement in the public sector.

Why Effective Performance Measurement and Management Are Rare in the Public Sector

We could think about why effective performance measurement and management are rare in the public sector in terms of both the strength of the demand for such a thing and the capacity of the system to supply it. If there is no demand for effective performance measurement and management, there is no reason to expect such things to arise. If responding to the demand is exceedingly difficult, or if it is not clear whose job it is to respond, then even with the demand, there might be little response.

The External Demand for Accountability

Some critics of government performance view a lack of accountability in the public sector as the root of government performance problems. But to anyone who has managed in the public sector—including, in particular, those accustomed to managing in the private sector—the claim that there is no accountability in the public sector seems patently false. To public managers the demands for accountability seem ubiquitous and incessant. If anything, it seems like there is too much accountability: individuals complain when they feel mistreated as government clients and join forces to create interest groups that add the power of numbers to their individual grievances and desires; the media amplify the complaints of both individual citizens and interest groups; and the elected representatives of the people, acting through various legislative oversight committees, also routinely demand accountability from public agencies.[22]

The real problem seems to be the form that these demands for accountability take. Ideally, public agencies, like private corporations, would be held accountable for their ability to improve their (net) value-creating performance over time. This kind of accountability would require not only a public value account that could reliably identify the important values at stake in an agency's operations but also enough political agreement among those who call the agency to account to ensure that the public value account would be at least the primary, and perhaps the only, terms in which the agency would be held accountable. While the agency could respond to other concerns raised by citizens and their representatives, the commitment to producing results that registered in the public value account would trump many smaller nitpicks about organizational performance. That kind of demand for accountability would provide an operational focus for managers and create a context in which they could mobilize increased effort from the organizations they led.

But instead, as noted, demands for accountability arise from many different places and focus on many different aspects of government performance. From the point of view of a public manager, these demands accumulate in four broad systems—some more disciplined, consistent, and durable than others.

The Auditing System. Perhaps the firmest and most consistent pressure for accountability comes from government agencies specifically constructed to ensure that the money entrusted to public agencies not be stolen, wasted, or misused (the General Accounting Office, or the Offices of Inspectors-General, or the Office of Management and Budget at the federal level, and their counterparts at the state and local levels).[23] Bad audit reports from any of these agencies can tar the reputations of government managers, and can sometimes land them in jail.

The presence of these agencies and the threat of audits create a powerful, continuous current of accountability that runs through public agencies. But it is a kind of accountability that is focused primarily on money and expenditures, and on compliance with existing policies and procedures rather than the satisfaction of clients or the achievement of social outcomes. These forms of accountability do not allow much room or provide much incentive for innovation and organizational learning; rather, they create a kind of accountability that tends to keep agencies rooted in existing policies and procedures for better or for worse.

Accountability to Elected Officials in the Legislative and Executive Branches. The second system of accountability seeks to ensure that government agencies respond to the expectations and demands of the people's elected representatives. A constitutional system that allows citizens to elect those who sit at the pinnacle of government's executive branch and allows those elected executives to appoint the next level of executive managers to carry out their program establishes this system of accountability. That same constitutional system also allows citizens to elect legislators who have the collective power to create and oversee public agencies and to provide them with government money and the authority to produce valued results. In the American political system, because there is no guarantee that those elected to executive or legislative branch positions will agree about the important values to be pursued by government agencies, there is always the risk that the definition of the values to be pursued and the appropriate ways to measure those values will continue to be contested.

When political accountability is attached to a clear, consistent, and durable statement of the public value to be produced by public agencies, democratic accountability functions as intended. The purposes of government action are ratified by elected representatives of the people and encoded in measurement systems that managers can use to set targets, monitor results, and look for improvements. But, of course, this kind of political accountability does not always work well. Democratic elections often produce divided governments in which politicians in legislative and executive branches fight over values and purposes. Furthermore, elected politicians often seem to lack the time, energy, skill, or incentives to exercise thoughtful oversight and management of public agencies.[24] As a result, the political oversight that could provide the strongest and most fundamental form of democratic accountability is weaker, less committed to performance, or less able to make its claims felt throughout an organization than we would like. Even worse, sometimes the energy that could create strong political oversight is wasted on very limited, parochial, or self-interested concerns.

The Pluralist Demand for Accountability. The third system of accountability is the least disciplined and focused. Indeed, one can hardly call it a system. It consists of the uncoordinated demands of anyone with an interest in some aspect of an organization's performance, and some kind of platform and/or megaphone to make their particular concern heard. In a democratic society this includes nearly everyone. As noted earlier, individual citizens and interest groups can become highly independent and demanding agents of accountability by using their rights to speak out and petition their government. They do not have to wait for special authorization from elected officials to press their claims. Nor do they have to wait for their concerns to come up in elections. They can move on their own, whenever they want, and force both public managers and elected representatives to pay attention.[25]

The media play important roles in broadcasting and amplifying the diverse demands of stakeholders and self-appointed accountability agents. Indeed, democracies have established the free press specifically to create an informed public that could call the government to account.[26]

While the media have no direct, legal authority to demand account-ability from government agencies, in practice they play a critical role in focusing the attention of elected representatives on the issues they cover.[27]

From the point of view of government managers, this kind of ac-countability that emerges from the daily swirl of democratic politics is both powerful and problematic. In informal polls of public managers attending executive sessions at the Kennedy School, students who were asked to weigh the relative importance of the three nonjudicial systems of accountability consistently reported that it was this last system that commanded most of their attention. While this is consistent with the goal of making government agencies accountable to the people, it is inconsistent with the goal of producing an exacting, consistent, broad demand for improvement on a limited number of dimensions of perfor-mance. This kind of accountability too often focuses on individual inci-dents over aggregate performance, on process over outcomes, and on only one dimension of value creation rather than on the full spectrum of values at stake in most government operations. And it often comes straight out of the blue. While an ideal accountability system runs a steady current of electricity through an organization to keep everyone focused on creating public value as defined in a public value account, this kind of accountability often strikes like lightning; all of a sudden a bolt of accountability can burn an unsuspecting public manager to a crisp.

Complaint Systems and Legal Recourse. The fourth system of accountabil-ity includes the institutions that hear and respond to citizen complaints about the conduct of government agencies. Some of these institutions are narrow and specialized, such as civilian complaint review boards set up to hear complaints from citizens about their treatment at the hands of the police. Others, such as offices of ombudsmen, are more generalized. Increasingly, public executives—particularly mayors like Williams—establish call centers where citizens can get information about government services and obligations, register complaints, and have their problems forwarded to agencies for resolution and/or aggre-gated for review. Governments also increasingly create formal consulta-tive mechanisms with client groups to try to make government services more responsive to the interests of those they seek to help.[28] And, in some rare circumstances, individual citizens or classes of citizens can go to court to complain that their rights have been violated by a government agency, and to ask for relief from that injustice.[29]

Ideally, these four systems of accountability would meld into a coherent, compelling demand for performance. Ideally, their demands for accountability would be focused on an explicit public value account that could simultaneously clarify expectations for public managers and create a context in which they could produce a record of increased value creation. In the real world, however, these four accountability systems rarely cohere into anything like a stable and usable public value account. Indeed, many of them do not focus on overall performance at all! The audit system tends to focus on cost controls and procedural compliance. The political system tends to focus on the issue of the day. The pluralist system focuses on whatever piques the interest of any organizational stakeholder. And the complaint system focuses on the bad experiences of individual clients.

Despite the heavy demands for accountability, then, the demands do not accumulate into a coherent system that focuses managerial attention on sustained improvement in the overall performance of government agencies.[30] Moreover, the unruly nature of the demands for accountability tends to discourage managerial efforts to create a coherent demand for accountability, since there is no guarantee that managers' hard work to negotiate a public value account with their political overseers would protect them in the future from capricious demands for accountability.

More and Different Kinds of Managerial Work

A second, closely related explanation for why effective performance measurement and management are rare in government is that both more and different kinds of work are required to create the conditions necessary for such systems to work. Private-sector managers typically inherit a broad agreement on the goal to be pursued, an established set of measures and information systems that can reveal progress toward the goal, and an organization accustomed to being held accountable for performance against those measures. In contrast, public managers have to work to create those conditions. The work is of the following four different types:

1. philosophical work associated with naming and justifying the important public values to be achieved by a public agency (or reflected in its operations)
2. political work associated with building a broad, stable agreement about the important dimensions of value that those who can call the organization to account will use to evaluate agency performance
3. technical work associated with finding or developing empirical measures that can reliably capture the degree to which the nominated values are being realized (or reflected) in agency operations
4. managerial work associated with linking a performance measurement system to a performance management system that can drive public efforts toward improved performance

To see exactly what this work entails, let's look a bit more closely at each kind of work.

Philosophical Work: Creating a Normatively Strong Public Value Account. The first challenge of constructing a public value account is to explore the philosophical basis for the values encoded in a policy mandate or an organizational mission. Though the ultimate arbiter of public value in a democracy is the public as a whole (acting through the messy processes of democratic politics), public managers do not have to remain silent on this question. Indeed, we depend on our elected public executives and the political executives they appoint to take a major role in identifying and pursuing publicly valuable purposes. And we depend on the knowledge and experience of career civil servants to help political executives estimate what is possible to achieve, what unintended outcomes might occur, and what opportunities for value creation lie before them.

Many public managers would prefer to treat the question of public value as though the answer were self-evident, or settled long ago, or a technical issue rather than deal with the philosophical aspects of constructing a public value account. But as revealed in Chapter 1, managing a public agency raises complex issues about the good and the just, and the appropriate roles of the individual and the collective. If Bratton had taken the philosophical questions about policing more seriously as he thought about the public value to be produced by the NYPD, and considered the fair and economical use of force as an important value question, the NYPD might have performed better with respect to the full set of values embodied and produced by police action. It does the polity no harm and some potential good for public managers at all levels to think philosophically about the values that are at stake as they deploy the assets of the state to achieve a publicly valued purpose. Simply writing down those values in a clear and comprehensible way might help managers and their enterprises stay focused on their ultimate goals. The public, in turn, could enjoy the improved performance that came from that focus.

Political Work: Negotiating Terms of Accountability. In democratic societies, getting clarity about the values to be produced by and embodied in a public agency is always a political as well as a philosophical task. To seek political consensus for the values that they think they ought to be accountable for producing, public managers need to make some kind of public value proposition—a list of the values that would show up on the right-hand side of the public value account. In forging a sustainable political consensus around a public value proposition, there are many ways to fail. Arguably, even though Bratton had a strong political mandate from Mayor Giuliani for focusing the police on "quality-of-life" offenses, the political consensus they formed together was flawed insofar as it seemed to ignore the costs of that strategy with respect to an important political constituency: the city's minority community, which rightly suspected that the burdens of the new crime control approach would fall particularly heavily on them. A public value proposition might equally fail if it did not connect or resonate with all, or most, or the most important of those in a position to call the agency to account, exposing a public manager to indifference, or angry criticism for neglecting cherished values. Even a public value account conscientiously and meticulously constructed through intensive negotiations with elected overseers and "market testing" with the wider public can unravel when those who seemed to agree change their mind and begin to find fault with what they had previously considered appropriate (as we shall see in Chapter 3). Thus the work of sustaining a political agreement about the values to be pursued is relentless and ongoing. It is partly for this reason that Mayor Williams initiated a broad public discussion about the overall goals for Washington, D.C., to ensure that the public value account for the D.C. government made a connection with the aspirations of citizens above and beyond their desire for better city services.

Technical Work: Developing Operational Measures for the Public Value Account. While the philosophical and political work is important, it only gains real leverage in the world when the concepts of public value can be operationally defined and empirical measures developed to show the degree to which the philosophical values are being realized in the real world. That is the technical work required to create the conditions for performance management in the public sector. The challenge is to develop, test, and adapt methods or instruments for measuring progress toward both abstract values and concrete operational goals. It is a long and expensive process, but without the technical means to measure performance, it is impossible to manage performance with regard to the dimensions of value in the public value account.[31]

Both Bratton and Williams found some existing measures in their organizations that could be used to monitor value-creating performance. But they both eventually saw that they would need new performance measures to capture a broader set of the values at stake in the performance of their organizations. When Bratton moved to Los Angeles, he widened the focus of Compstat to include a managerial focus and some data collection on the legitimacy and support that the police had in minority communities.[32] Likewise, Williams eventually had to find some way to measure progress toward meeting the aspirations that the D.C. community had articulated in his "citizen summit"—aspirations that went beyond improved quality of service and customer satisfaction.

Managerial Work: Turning Performance Measurement Systems into Performance Management Systems. At the risk of stating the obvious, value-oriented management also requires a great deal of managerial work.[33] For a public value account to succeed in animating and guiding the day-to-day operations of government agencies, public managers have to engage in two different kinds of managerial work. On one hand, they have to invest in developing measurement systems that can capture whether the agency is creating value. On the other, they have to find ways to make the public value account a powerful behavioral lever for motivating greater effort and enabling organizational learning. Indeed, it is precisely this second type of managerial work that transforms a performance measurement system into a performance management system. To realize the full potential of performance measurement, managers must link performance data to the evaluation and compensation of midlevel managers and workers, and do so in a way that builds the organization's commitment to performance measurement and accountability. They also have to find ways to use performance data to facilitate conversations and collaborations that allow the organization to learn and innovate.[34] As noted earlier, Williams accomplished this with respect to service delivery, but he still had work to do in finding a management system that could drive the D.C. government to help the D.C. community achieve the broad goals defined in his five "strategic priorities."[35]

Whose Work Is This?
Government fails to engage in performance management not only because the structure of accountability is divided and chaotic, and not only because there is so much complex work involved, but also because it is unclear who bears responsibility for doing all the work described earlier. In the private sector, it seems clear that the chief executive officer (CEO) is ultimately responsible for building and deploying performance management systems. In the public sector, however, this responsibility seems to be distributed across different kinds of officials who have different claims to legitimacy and stand in somewhat uneasy relationships to one another.

Who Is the General Manager of Government Agencies? The officials who most resemble CEOs, and are therefore perhaps best positioned to assume responsibility for performance management, are those in senior management positions in the executive branch—appointed officials like Bratton, elected chief executives like Williams, and, in some cases, senior civil servants (who may be in the best position to sustain performance management efforts over the long periods of time it often takes to develop and use management systems).

Unfortunately, because the work of developing these systems is simultaneously political, philosophical, technical, and managerial, it challenges some basic boundaries between different types of public officials. In public administration theory, elected executives have the right and responsibility to develop philosophical ideas about public value and build public support for those ideas. Appointed executives do some of the same work with regard to the particular organizations they lead but must align their ideas about value with those of the elected executives who appointed them. Appointed executives also have the right and the responsibility to do the managerial and technical work of building public value accounts and performance management systems if such work is necessary to achieve the goals of their organizations. Senior civil servants have the right and the responsibility to do the technical and managerial work of developing performance measurement and management systems, but they might also help with the philosophical work—particularly the work of linking abstract values to more concrete and measurable values.

So each of these public managers owns some part of the problem of constructing public value accounts and the management systems that give the accounts behavioral and operational power. While they all feel qualified in their own domain, they feel a bit awkward entering into one another's.[36] As a result, often no one steps forward to create the systems that could increase value production. And when one steps forward without the other, the result is often a system that is only partially developed, and only partially effective. To create a functional system, either they must act together as a team or one brave soul must cross the boundary and do the work of others. The elected executive has to engage with the managerial and technical work or the appointees and career civil servants must venture into the realm of politics.

How Elected Public Executives Think about Performance Management. Williams, as mayor, had to think of himself principally as a leader of a political community.[37] He was ultimately accountable to an electorate that consisted of citizens, taxpayers, and clients. Because politicians know that their personal success lies in future reelection, most of them are skilled in the particular practices that help them produce that result (or, more idealistically, that help call a political community and a public will into existence).[38] Although they know that there is some relationship between the performance of the piece of government they lead and their public support and future electability, elected chief executives like Williams are not sure how strong that relationship is. They tend to think that good performance is helpful in winning elections (and something for which they should take responsibility in any case), but they are not sure that better performance across the board is either necessary or sufficient as grounds for reelection. If government performance matters in an election, it is more likely to be the kind of performance attached to "making good" on campaign promises, or to one's ability to improve performance significantly in an area that touches many citizens, or in the capacity of the agencies in their domain to avoid serious errors. For these reasons, elected chief executives are generally less inclined than the average private-sector CEO to invest in the development and use of performance measurement and management systems.

How Appointed and Career Public Executives Think about Performance Management. Appointed public executives like Bratton tend to be more familiar with the common tools of administration and the day-to-day work of the organizations they lead. This experience makes them better equipped to develop and use performance measurement to animate and guide the performance of their organization. Yet in the face of all the different kinds of work described earlier—the philosophical challenge of defining public value, the political challenge of focusing their overseers on a viable public value account, the technical challenge of measuring public value, and the managerial challenge of creating internal accountability for creating public value—many appointed and career public executives fail to fully exploit this opportunity.

Furthermore, any efforts these managers make to negotiate the terms of their agencies' accountability may well be treated as an inappropriate incursion into the proper domain of elected officials. The politicians won the election, and with that the right to define the terms of accountability for public agencies. Appointed managers or senior civil servants who put forth their own ideas about how to represent public value risk their reputation for discretion and responsiveness to their elected superiors.

Taking the Initiative and Creating a Team. All this makes the question of who will take the responsibility for creating public value accounts and developing the capacity to use them for performance management in public agencies surprisingly difficult. There is a good chance that no one will. Ideally, one intrepid manager would take the initiative in creating a team that includes all three kinds of managers and collaborates in developing and implementing these systems. For example, an elected executive might commission or authorize such a team and delegate all the work to political appointees in charge of different agencies. They, in turn, would work with the senior civil servants in their organizations to develop appropriate performance measurement and management systems. In the end, whether any public manager takes this kind of initiative depends at least in part on the incentives that these different kinds of managers face.

Why Do the Work? The Absence of Personal Incentives
This question brings us to the fourth reason that developing a public value account to enable value-oriented management is less common in the public sector: the public managers who are in a position to do the work may lack the incentive to do so. Indeed, their incentive may push them in exactly the opposite direction. As a public manager might reasonably ask: "Why should I manufacture a gun and put it in the hands of others who can and probably will use it to shoot me?"[39]

Faced with that question, public managers (of all types) have often used their wide discretion in how to respond to public demands for accountability to resist those demands. The tactics are all too familiar, and might include any of the following:

- setting goals so vague that it is impossible to say how much progress is being made in achieving them
- setting concrete and measurable goals and objectives but setting targets at levels that are easy to achieve
- setting goals that are reasonably concrete but for which no measurement system exists

It seems there are at least three reasons that public managers should embrace accountability and develop the performance measurement and performance management systems that can render that accountability effective. Unfortunately, however, these incentives for public managers to go beyond lip service in developing the potential of performance measurement and management systems are not very strong. The first possible incentive we have already considered is that public managers are vulnerable to demands for accountability from citizens and their (official and unofficial) representatives. Because these demands are so often narrow and transient, however, they generally fail to create the kind of pressure that causes public agencies to invest in systems that will allow them to make steady, significant improvements in performance.[40]

A second reason for public managers to embrace accountability and measure performance is that it is morally and ethically the right thing to do. Public managers have long accepted their fiduciary responsibility to the public and gotten used to meeting the financial part of that responsibility through financial audits. As the focus of public and auditing attention has shifted from financial management and bureaucratic compliance to issues of value-creating performance, public managers have begun to talk about being accountable for the quality of services and the efficient and effective achievement of desired social outcomes.

But observers of the actual conduct of public managers often find them more interested in the general idea of this kind of accountability than in any concrete efforts to enable it. It is the rare public manager who nominates particular targets on which to stake his or her career. It is rarer still for managers to nominate performance targets that challenge their organization's capabilities, especially if their pay and promotion depend on achieving those results. However strong the commitment to accountability and performance may be in the abstract, when it comes to making a concrete deal for accountability and agreeing on how performance will be measured, many public managers demur.[41]

In the end there is really only one reason to run the risk of embracing external accountability and to invest heavily, over a long period of time, in developing public value accounts and using them in a broader performance measurement and management system, and it is this: it is only by embracing (external) and imposing (internal) accountability that managers can really improve the performance of the organizations they lead.[42] This may seem surprising. Those who lead public agencies seem to have a great deal of formal authority over their organizations. They have powerful administrative levers to use in directing and animating the performance of their organizations. Why single out performance measurement and accountability as the most powerful levers for managing performance? Why insist that it is the combination of external and internal accountability (and the congruencies between them) that makes all the difference? The answer requires a look into the basic deal made between those who lead and manage public agencies, on the one hand, and those who work and make their careers within those agencies, on the other.

All organizational executives hold their executive positions in trust to those who have invested in the organization. In the private sector, executives are the fiduciaries of shareholders. In the public sector, executives are the fiduciaries of citizens. The essence of their job is to manage the resources committed to them to create value for those who have made contributions: shareholders want long-term equity returns for their investment, and citizens want the long-term production of public value.[43] This means that those in positions of authority have to commit to strong performance and continuous improvement in the organizations they lead.

In basic economic theory, an organization's performance can be improved through the following three possible avenues:

1. securing and deploying additional resources
2. working a bit harder to squeeze some slack out of operations
3. working smarter by finding value-creating innovations

Most organizations, when called upon by their bosses to improve performance, would prefer the first method: receiving additional resources to accomplish their goals. The flow of additional resources signals success and allows workers to achieve more without having to make too many painful changes. Indeed, with enough resources, workers might be able to actually improve their working conditions even as they increase their output.[44] Unfortunately, the path of improvement through increased spending is not always available to public agencies. Moreover, this path may not even represent a performance gain when a public value account includes the cost of producing desired results.

This leaves the second and third options—working harder and working smarter—and it is here that trouble starts. Those in positions of authority may well want their organizations to work harder and smarter. Much experience tells us, however, that both "speedups" and "organizational change" initiatives are likely to meet significant resistance from employees accustomed to doing their work in a particular way.[45] While elected representatives of the people lodged in oversight positions might expect the leaders of organizations to challenge and improve overall performance, most workers have different hopes and expectations for their bosses. Most of them would rather be reassured that they are doing a good job than challenged to improve their performance. If what workers really want from their bosses is reassurance that the status quo is just fine and the future is bright, then it is hard to know how a boss could say anything else—say, that there is a lot of slack in the existing system, that there are probably much better ways of doing the work, and that if they do not get on the stick, the organization will fail.[46]

On the other hand, many workers might like a chance to develop themselves in their jobs and find better ways of achieving results.[47] With the right kind of managerial encouragement and incentives, they might enjoy challenging themselves, experimenting with new methods, and learning new things. Despite the fact that the cards are stacked in favor of the status quo, there is always some latent energy in an organization that can be mobilized for innovation and improvement.[48]

But even if the employees are willing to give change a chance, a public manager has to find some kind of ace in the hole to get leverage over the natural resistance that arises in response to pressure for changes. That extra leverage cannot come from his or her office alone. Nor can it come only from personal charisma—though both the office and the charisma help. The extra leverage has to come instead from powerful forces outside the organization that make the demand for change look serious, objective, and unavoidable rather than personal and arbitrary.[49] It is one thing for an incoming manager to say that the organization has to make changes when the only thing that has changed is the management; it is quite another when there is suddenly a clamoring mob of citizens, taxpayers, and politicians hammering at the doors. In the latter case, the manager is transformed into an agent of reality, expressed as the public will. If the manager represents real outside pressures on the organization, the staff might stop debating whether change is necessary and instead look for some guidance and leadership about how best to meet these demands.

Bratton and Williams in Perspective

Considering the chaotic demands for accountability that public managers face, the various and challenging kinds of work that managers who decide to develop and use performance management systems must take on, the confusion about whose work this is, and the lack of incentives to motivate the work, it is easy to see why Bratton's and Williams's willingness to embrace accountability, to name the values they were trying to produce, and to create performance measurement and management systems to make the organizations they ran perform with respect to those values was relatively rare in the public sector. What is surprising and hopeful about these cases is that Bratton and Williams seemed to overcome so many of the obstacles identified earlier. They were bold enough to reimagine and fully exploit the potential of their particular positions as elected and appointed government managers. Each decided to operate at the edges rather than well within the usual practices of those in their positions, exploring and revising the frontiers of effective public management.

On the question of what motivated their efforts, it is hard to know for sure, but they seemed to think that embracing accountability by developing performance measurement and management systems was both an important part of their professional responsibilities and a worthwhile investment in powerful tools that would help them improve government performance.

On the question of whose work it was, they each decided that it was theirs—despite their different positions. The elected mayor followed his technocratic instincts into the technical and managerial world of performance measurement. The appointed police commissioner tied his performance measurement system to the political aspirations of a city and the commitments of an elected mayor. The barrier between politics and administration was successfully breached—at least for a time.

But Bratton and Williams differed in their approach to the work. Both began with a straightforward operational approach in which they defined important values to be pursued by their organization and built management systems to drive their organizations toward improved performance through more exacting accountability. Bratton developed the Compstat system to focus the attention of precinct commanders and line officers on controlling crime. Williams developed scorecards that reminded public managers of their agreed-upon performance goals.

But Williams went farther than Bratton to position his organization for value creation in the future. Three moves mark this change.

First, even though he had run for election in a campaign that emphasized service improvements in city government, Williams decided he needed a more sustained and detailed discussion with the District's citizens about their aspirations for their community life, and the role that government was to play in that vision.[50]

Second, Williams used that discussion with citizens to inform a shift from the idea that the value to be created by D.C. government lay only in the quality of services he could deliver to clients of the District's agencies to the idea that the value lay in the D.C. government's performance with respect to broad social outcomes. Like Bratton, he shifted the focus of accountability from particular processes and procedures to social outcomes that would register in the collective lives of citizens. But Williams's public value account covered both social outcomes and client satisfaction. These outcomes became the focus of a broad strategic vision for the District's government.

Third, Williams recognized that producing broad social outcomes required a broader and more flexible idea about how the work of city agencies could be combined to produce those outcomes. To engage the managers of the District's agencies in this collaborative work, he required them to adapt their agencies' missions and the terms of their accountability to the strategic vision of D.C. government.

These three acts—engaging in political mobilization, focusing accountability on the achievement of broad social outcomes, and adapting existing organizational missions to enable successful contributions to the larger goals—carried Williams from the purely operational realm into the strategic realm.

Strategic Management in Government and the Public Value Account

Williams's efforts to build a performance measurement and management system that reached out politically to create an "identity of interests between citizens and their government," that recognized value not only in client satisfaction but also in the achievement of social outcomes, and that incorporated many different organizations in his conception of the productive capacity he needed to achieve the desired results provide a glimpse of a purpose for performance measurement and management systems that goes beyond the effort to construct a public value account for a government organization that can be linked to internal management control systems and enable it to improve its performance in its current mission. It suggests that there might be more strategic, less operational uses of performance measurement and management systems.

The rest of this book will focus on the ways in which public managers can use performance measurement, accountability, and performance management systems not merely to understand and learn from past performance but to execute sound strategies for improved government performance in the future.

My previous book, *Creating Public Value: Strategic Management in Government,* set out a framework that public managers could use to manage strategically in the complex conditions they confronted.[51] The core idea was that public managers were responsible for using the assets entrusted to them to achieve the maximum public value possible in the particular context in which they found themselves. The framework assumed that context was both complex (in the sense that the public and its representatives held public managers responsible for producing and protecting many different kinds of value) and dynamic (in the sense that the values the public was interested in changed over time). To develop a strategy that could identify and guide the pursuit of the maximum public value attainable in a particular context, public managers had to imagine their particular context transformed by a vision that successfully aligned:

1. a new conception of public value they could produce using the assets entrusted to them;
2. sources of legitimacy and support for that vision of public value; and
3. the operational capacity they would need to materially produce the envisioned public value.

While public managers could hope that these three elements would naturally align, there were no processes that guaranteed that result. If they were to be aligned, it would be the result of a public manager's efforts to diagnose both their political authorizing environment and their task environment, imagine and test different strategic concepts of

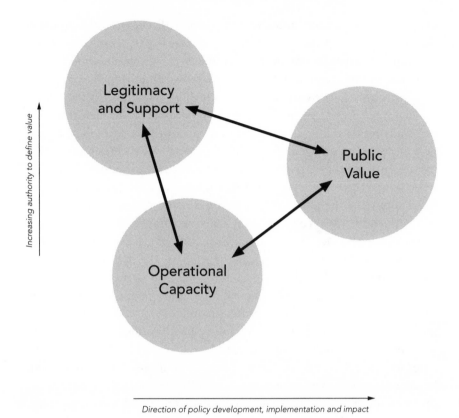

Figure 2.1. The strategic triangle.

public value creation, and determine which managerial actions could maximize public value in a particular situation. The analytic framework developed to guide that effort is known as the strategic triangle (see Figure 2.1).

The triangle is drawn here with the points positioned with respect to two axes. The horizontal axis represents the direction and flow of policy from development to implementation and to impact, while the vertical axis represents the degree of authority to define public value inherent in the different points on the triangle. This particular concept of strategic management in government has gained some traction as a useful guide for public managers in police departments, public defenders' offices, and even in state arts agencies and public broadcasting systems.[52] But as these managers worked with the strategic triangle, they discovered repeatedly that the key to making the framework work both analytically and practically was to develop a solid method for recognizing value creation when it occurred—something like a public value account. To see why this is true, consider how the effort to build a public value account would work at each point of the strategic triangle.

Starting with the obvious, it should be clear that developing a public value account answers the question of what constitutes public value for the purposes of managing a particular organization in a given context. That is the whole point of the exercise. Yet it is important to realize that putting the public value account in the context of the strategic triangle implicitly recognizes that constructing the public value account cannot be merely a philosophical and technical calculation. The strategic triangle reminds public managers that the definition of public value is conditional on the support of the political authorizing environment that has the right and responsibility to define public value and on the existence of some organizational and operational capacity that must be animated and guided to produce public value.

This also means that the concept of public value used to manage the enterprise could change as environmental conditions change. If new political aspirations arise, or new problems show up to challenge the organization's performance or present the organization with new opportunities to create public value, then a strategic public manager might have to adjust or adapt the old public value account and suggest a new public value proposition to accommodate the new realities and possibilities that have appeared.

At the next point of the strategic triangle, the managerial effort to create and adapt a public value account can play an important role in building legitimacy and support. It does so in the first instance by giving clear evidence of a public manager's willingness to be held accountable for the performance of the enterprise he or she leads, and in the second instance by allowing citizens and their representatives to be sure that their conceptions of the public value to be produced by an agency align with the purposes the organization has committed itself to pursuing.

Turning to the third point of the strategic triangle, creating the public value account can also help generate and direct the operational capacity necessary to achieve the results by giving the organization

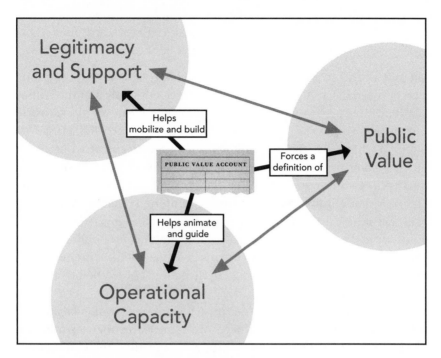

Figure 2.2. The public value account helps build, integrate, and test a strategy for public value creation.

clear targets to shoot for and steady feedback about how well the organization is performing. A well-constructed public value account can also help guide and manage efforts that cross organizational boundaries through these same mechanisms.

It is in this sense that a public value account that is at once philosophically sound, politically supportable, technically measurable, and operationally exacting helps align and integrate a concept of public value, a source of legitimacy and support, and the operational capacity needed to produce the desired effect. Figure 2.2 illustrates how a public value account helps managers build, integrate, and test a strategy for public value creation. The public value account connects a conception of public value with a source of legitimacy and support and the operational capacity necessary to deliver the results, thereby moving the strategic triangle from the realm of abstraction to the concrete reality in which a particular manager finds himself or herself.

The Public Value Scorecard: A "Balanced Scorecard" for
Strategic Management in the Public Sector

There is a third strategic challenge that a public value account standing alone cannot meet. A public value account includes only a limited number of possible performance measures—those that capture the ultimate (net) value of what the organization is trying to produce. Sometimes, as noted in Chapter 1, the ultimate value that an organization produces includes some procedural aspects because those procedural aspects are intrinsically valued, for example, the fair use of state authority. But the criterion that admits some measures to a properly constructed public value account is not that they are ultimate results of government action but that they are intrinsically valued. It is precisely because the public value account covers only these intrinsically valued dimensions of performance that it operates as an analytic equivalent to the private sector's financial bottom line.

To guide a governmental enterprise toward public value creation in the future, however, one may need other measures that describe the conditions that must be created to produce that value, and that monitor the work that is being done to produce those enabling conditions. For example, managers may want to track the speed with which staff members implement a new operating method that could improve the organization's performance as it is revealed in the public value account. Or, they may want to monitor their standing with some important overseers, such as a legislative committee, and use that measure to monitor the success of efforts launched by the organization to strengthen that relationship.

To many, the focus on such "process measures" that track the success of a manager and a public organization in the activities that build the capacity of the organization to perform in the future represents a retreat from the goal of value-oriented management. The whole point of trying to develop performance measurement systems was to shift the focus from processes that are not valued in themselves to social outcomes that are intrinsically valued.

Yet once one is in the dynamic world of a manager guiding an organization's activities and development over time, the usefulness of knowing how much value the organization created in the past cedes some of its importance to the pressing question of how the organization is positioning itself for the future. A public value account is best at revealing what has been produced in the past. A strategic public value proposition is an idea about how more public value can be created in the future. This suggests that a truly valuable performance measurement and management system would not stop at measuring an organization's past value-creating accomplishments but would go on to identify the work necessary to sustain or improve that past performance and track the performance of the organization with respect to these actions.

This transition from the public value account to a public value scorecard derives from Kaplan and Norton's simple—but powerful—observation in *The Balanced Scorecard*: while financial statements produced vital information about the past performance of firms, they alone could not help private-sector managers figure out how to sustain their firm's profitability in the future.[53] To do that, they needed to gather and use additional information about the internal performance of their organizations and the external state of their relationships with customers.[54] To organize the need for information to support the development and execution of a future oriented strategy, they constructed a "balanced scorecard" that included all the usual information about financial performance but added information about the conditions necessary to improve that financial performance. To the financial account they created additional measurement systems that could support a "customer perspective," an "internal business processes perspective," and a "learning and growth perspective." See Figure 2.3 for a graphic illustration of these ideas.

The book has helped many private-sector managers organize their information to better reveal how they were positioned to sustain or improve their future financial performance. But the book also resonated strongly with managers in the nonprofit and governmental world.[55] To them, Kaplan and Norton, private management gurus, had finally articulated the very issue that dogged them daily: the financial bottom line is not enough! Some defenders of public interest in the public and nonprofit sector saw in this logic an opening for businesses to add multiple bottom lines—to become concretely accountable for their social and environmental impact.[56] But Kaplan and Norton did not go this far. In *The Balanced Scorecard*, financial performance remains the ultimate aim and measure of a firm's success. Kaplan and Norton recommended monitoring nonfinancial information, but only for purposes of sustaining or increasing profitability.

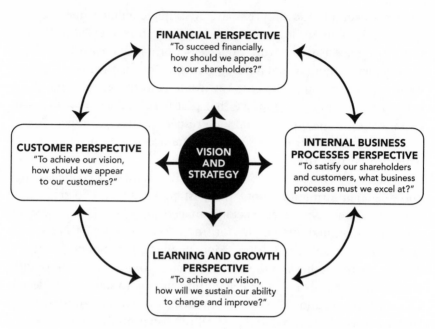

Figure 2.3. The balanced scorecard (adapted from Kaplan and Norton, *The Balanced Scorecard*).

In subsequent work, Kaplan and Norton argued for linking performance measurement systems even more closely to a "strategy" for increased value creation, and they showed that private-sector organizations that did this performed better than others.[57] The difference between tracking routine performance and tracking progress in implementing a forward-looking strategy is one between imagining that a firm can continue in a steady state and imagining that a firm has to change continuously to hold onto its competitive (value-creating) position. If a firm's strategy called on it to innovate, or to alter, its internal processes or its position in the market, information systems would have to be created to support performance measurement and management systems that track efforts to implement the change strategy as well as maintain current operations. As such, performance measurement systems stopped being devices for monitoring financial performance in the rearview mirror and became vehicles for managing future performance. Developing performance measurement systems thus became an occasion for the public sector to get specific about an organization's theory of change and check the assumptions and logic of a proposed strategy as well as its performance.[58]

Given the shortcomings of "the bottom line" as a guide for strategic action even in the private sector, it seems all the more evident that developing a conceptually sound and actionable public value account only gets one part of the way to a performance management system capable of driving forward a strategy for future value creation. Public managers also need a "balanced scorecard" to complement the public value account and to enable them to manage for results in the future.

Combining Kaplan and Norton's insights with the strategic triangle, a public manager's "balanced scorecard" could include three different "perspectives" closely aligned with the three points of the triangle. The "public value perspective" would depend on information gathered to fill out the values represented in the public value account. The "legitimacy and support perspective" would monitor performance in maintaining relationships and mobilizing support from citizens, taxpayers, their elected representatives, and others in the political authorizing environment. The "operational capacity perspective" would focus attention on the public-sector production processes that turn inputs of public money and authority into changes in the world that the public values. Figure 2.4 sets out the general form that a public value scorecard might take. Each of the particular categories would have to be examined for relevance in a particular circumstance, and concrete measures would have to be developed. But like the balanced scorecard, the public value scorecard helps distribute managerial attention not only to the valuable results that were produced in the past but also to the conditions that must be constructed to improve performance in the future. This means that it pays attention not only to current operational capacities and current conditions in the political authorizing environment but also to the investments needed to maintain or create favorable political conditions and to improve operational capacity.

Developing this scorecard as a general conception, and as something that is useful in individual cases, is the main purpose of the rest of this book. Just as Kaplan and Norton urged private-sector managers to create performance measurement systems that went beyond the

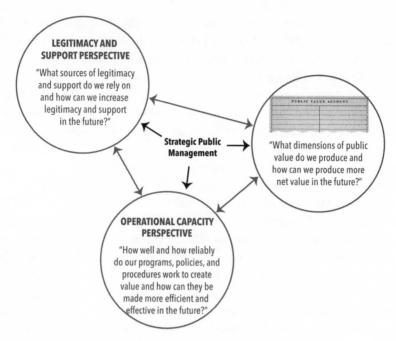

Figure 2.4. A public value scorecard for public managers.

bottom line to define and pursue a value-creating strategy, this book urges public managers to embrace a wide set of measures to articulate and execute a forward-looking strategy for value creation. This framework, which I will call the "public value scorecard," translates an abstract idea of public value creation into a concrete set of performance measures that can both monitor value creation in the past and guide managerial action necessary to sustain or create greater value in the future. On the political side this work typically focuses on monitoring the political environment, imagining how developments there might transform the public value account, and taking actions to keep the enterprise highly responsive to public aspirations. On the operational capacity side this work typically focuses on searching for productivity gains that can be made through experiments, innovations, and investments in operational procedures, on the one hand, or reallocations of resources among units producing different outputs, products, and services.

How a Public Value Scorecard Can Support
Strategic Public Management

To see how all this might work, let's look a bit more closely at the strategic triangle, the questions it puts before public managers, and how developing a public value scorecard might help a manager not only see and define public value but also find the means for engaging the political support and operational focus needed to produce it.

Developing a Public Value Scorecard Forces a (Contingent)
Definition of Public Value

The "public value" point on the strategic triangle challenges public managers to lay out for themselves, their organization, and their overseers the ultimate values their enterprises seek to produce and embody in their operations. That requirement is met by the development of a public value account that can identify the value the enterprise intended to produce, what it actually produced, and the costs incurred along the way.[59] Just as a "balanced scorecard" requires a financial perspective that focuses on a firm's (past) financial performance, a public value scorecard requires a public value account to capture the net public value that a public agency has produced.

The sharp focus on value creation emphasized by the development and use of a public value account is essential to overcome the tendency of all organizations to become more concerned about their survival and comfort than their value-creating performance.[60] The need to overcome this tendency is particularly strong in public organizations where many of the established accountability systems focus on processes rather than on results, or on small incidents rather than on steady improvement in overall performance. In this respect, at least, it helps a great deal to have something like a bottom line that can focus the attention of the organization on real public value creation.

To do its work well, however, the public value account has to do work at several different levels, and in several different parts of the strategic triangle. It has to work at the philosophical level in the sense that it recognizes the important values the enterprise should create and embody. It has to work at the political level in the sense that it responds to the authorizing environment's concerns and engages its commitment. It has to work at the technical level in the sense that suitable measures have been developed to populate the categories set out in the public value account. And it has to work at the managerial level in the sense that it inspires staff, focuses staff on creating valuable results, and helps staff learn how to best maximize public value creation.[61]

Moreover, the public value account has to be forward looking. As noted in Chapter 1, while the public value account can usefully begin with the existing mission of the organization and record accomplishments with respect to that mission, it has to have some room to adapt. In public value accounting, the basic frame can be challenged by unintended effects, by a renewed political focus on particular dimensions of value, or by the emergence of new challenges that the enterprise is well positioned to face, or new opportunities the enterprise can exploit. Seeing such changes in their environment, public managers could propose a modification of the existing conception of public value and the measures used to track it. With political support, that public value proposition could serve as the basis for a new public value account to help animate, guide, and evaluate organizational performance.

In this crucial respect the public value account requires a measurement system quite different from the fixed bottom line of the financial perspective in Kaplan and Norton's balanced scorecard. It has to meet philosophical and political tests as well as technical and managerial tests. It cannot be fixed in time but has to adapt in varying degrees to changing circumstances. To do so the public value account has to have some unusual properties. It has to speak to concerns for large, abstract, public values such as the public good and the pursuit of justice but also has to be sufficiently specific, concrete, and measurable to recognize the value that the agency produces and the costs it incurs. It has to speak to the diverse concerns of a dynamic political system and be alert to possible future concerns as well as those already expressed. And it has to distinguish between the value associated with satisfying clients, on the one hand, and achieving desired social outcomes, on the other. For reference, the general form of the public value account is reproduced here as Figure 2.5.

The two cases we have already considered reveal the tensions between a focus on satisfying clients and a focus on achieving social outcomes and the strategic choices that public managers have to make between them. Bratton and Williams initially took different positions on this crucial philosophical question. Bratton's efforts to improve the

PUBLIC VALUE ACCOUNT	
Use of Collectively Owned Assets and Associated Costs	Achievement of Collectively Valued Social Outcomes
Financial Costs	Mission Achievement
Unintended Negative Consequences	Unintended Positive Consequences
	Client Satisfaction
	Service Recipients
	Obligatees
Social Costs of Using State Authority	Justice and Fairness
	At Individual Level in Operations
	At Aggregate Level in Results

Figure 2.5. The public value account: general form.

performance of the NYPD focused initially on achieving a desired social outcome at the core of his organization's purposes: reducing crime. Williams's efforts to improve the performance of the District's public agencies focused on what he understood to be the core mission of municipal government: improving the quality of service provided to individual citizens (whether that service involved educating students, delivering a driver's license promptly, or responding to a crime victim's call).

Over time, however, each moved toward the other's position. Williams moved to an effort to build a political and organizational system that could focus on achieving broad social outcomes as well as producing client satisfaction. Similarly, Bratton was eventually forced to pay attention to the individual experiences of those who had encounters with the police—both those who called for service and those who were stopped, investigated, cited, or arrested by the police even as he pursued the desired social outcome—though only after he had left the NYPD.

The discussion of public value in Chapter 1 outlined the important difference between public value as client satisfaction and public value as the achievement of collectively desired social outcomes. The moves Bratton and Williams made as they initiated and adapted their public value accounts testify to the importance of both ideas of public value and the likely necessity of including both in any plausibly effective public value account.

Developing a Public Value Scorecard Helps Build Legitimacy and Support
The second point of the triangle focuses managers' attention on how they plan to build legitimacy and support for a particular nominated conception of public value, written down and measured through the public value account. By far the most straightforward way for public managers to build legitimacy and support for themselves, the agencies they lead, and the cause they champion is to embrace accountability for advancing the values, purposes, and goals "the public" has specified as valuable. That is why the public value account begins with the established mission, or the desired outcome of a particular public policy. In making themselves faithful agents of those articulated purposes, public managers gain credit not only for acting properly in their role as a fiduciary for the public but also for producing what the public wants.

Unfortunately, as we have seen, "the public" usually does not articulate a clear and coherent view of what it wants in prospect, or how it will evaluate performance after the fact. When looking at Washington, D.C.'s DCRA, for example, some of those demanding accountability for performance may focus on reducing costs and trimming the budget. Others may be most interested in adding eco-friendly regulations to the building codes, the speed with which building permits are processed, the quality or accessibility of the DCRA's consumer education programs, or simply budgetary compliance.

My earlier work, *Creating Public Value*, identified the complex set of social actors who were in positions to hold accountable public managers and their organizations as the "political authorizing environment." That concept includes all those actors who were identified as part of different accountability systems: the financial oversight agencies, the elected representatives of the people in executive and legislative branches, the interest groups that could press their particular concerns, the media who appoint themselves to defend the public interest, and the individu-

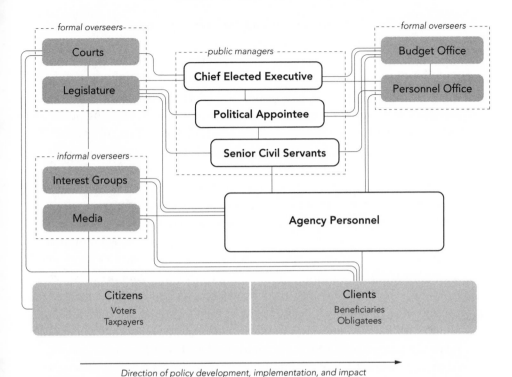

Figure 2.6. The authorizing environment.

als in whose name government acts (citizens, voters, and taxpayers), and the individuals with whom government organizations interact as clients (both service recipients and obligatees). Figure 2.6 offers a rough sketch of the different components of a public manager's authorizing environment.

This picture includes all the actors and agencies that make external demands for public agency accountability, mentioned earlier in the chapter. The reason that those demanding accountability are the same as those who can authorize public action is that authorization and accountability are two sides of the same coin. Authorization is what gives legitimacy and support to a new public value proposition. Demanding accountability is what happens after an initiative has been launched and has begun to produce its effects. The same actors show up for both acts of the drama. It follows that the main way a public manager can maintain her or his legitimacy and support is to meet demands for accountability.

Public managers could react to the chaotic nature of this "authorizing environment" by throwing their hands up and refusing to act until the political world gets its act together and gives them a clear, coherent mandate. But it might be a better strategic move to keep making public value propositions to these authorizers, and asking them to propose changes in the existing public value account. Choices made to add or subtract dimensions of value could be seen not only as a process of learning about which values the public and their representatives deem important but also as a way of responding to new concerns and engaging the public in ways that add legitimacy and support to the enterprise.

The previous discussion explains how a public value account and its adaptation might be helpful in building legitimacy and support in the authorizing environment. But the legitimacy and support perspective might include measures that are not directly related to the form or content of the public value account. A strategic view of the individuals and groups populating one's political authorizing environment could reveal some potential sources of legitimacy and support that might be tapped, or strengthened. There might be a core of support that is tied to a particular set of values and limits the organization to the pursuit of those values. But outside that core base of support (and constraint) there might be other constituencies representing other values that could be mobilized to enlarge the set of values included in the current public value account. There might be other authorizers demanding an account whose support could be enhanced by paying a bit more attention to the values they would like to see expressed in the organization's operations.

Efforts to connect with these authorizers could be an important part of strategic management, and a strategic manager might want to have measurement systems that captured the state of her or his agency's relationship with the many active and passive authorizers in its environment and recorded the success of efforts made to strengthen those relationships. Just as the balanced scorecard's customer perspective encourages private-sector executives to track their customers' desires and satisfaction with the firm's products and services constantly, the legitimacy and support perspective of the public value scorecard encourages public executives to track the desires and satisfaction of those who support and authorize their enterprises—elected representatives in legislatures, but also interest groups or opinion leaders and random samples of citizens, taxpayers, and clients (of both types).

In the case studies we have considered so far, both Williams and Bratton were fortunate that social and political conditions had built a broad constituency for improved performance by government agencies. New Yorkers were tired of the serious crime and widespread minor offenses that had rendered life in the city threatening and disheartening. Residents of Washington, D.C., had been frustrated and humiliated by the near bankruptcy of their city and the shoddiness of the public services they received. This meant that Bratton did not have to overcome the political limitations of his position to swing public opinion his way, and Williams did not have to use much of his broad political privilege to build a constituency for reform. The constituency for improved performance along particular substantive dimensions of public value was already there. It just had to be consolidated and focused on a limited number of concrete objectives.

Although Bratton and Williams were broadly similar in their use of public demands for accountability to build and focus pressure on their organizations, there was one key difference in their political approach. In the early days of Williams's tenure as mayor, he was content to focus on urgent, short-run demands for accountability. In his previous position as the District's CFO, he had already demonstrated that he understood the need to bring costs under control, and that he could make cuts where necessary. He also understood that he needed to improve the quality of service to the citizens of Washington, D.C. Circumstances in the District and Williams's electoral strategy created a mandate for cutting costs and improving services. To align with that mandate, Williams focused on controlling costs and providing basic public services to citizens (objectives he called "quick wins"; see Table 2.1).

But soon into his tenure, Williams began working to build a different constituency for a different public value proposition, and a different mandate for action. He launched a citywide planning process to develop a broader and more deeply involved constituency for improving the overall performance of city government. As Williams said, "I came into the city to do two things: to rebuild the fundamental operations of the government, while at the same time building greater respect, affinity for, [and] identification with the government by citizens." He intended to build an "identity of interests" between the city and its residents, as well as an organizational culture "fueled by an appetite for performance." These strategic objectives are included in Table 2.2.

Williams's statements capture the tensions that public managers face when they take a strategic approach to performance measurement and management. On one side is the public-spirited goal of trying to build "an identity of interests" between citizens and their government—an effort tied to the legitimacy and support perspective of the public value scorecard. On the other side is the more straightforward drive to

Table 2.1.   Williams's strategic goals I.

	"Quick wins" in operations
Get costs under control	Improve quality of government services to D.C. citizens
	• Pothole repairs
	• Rat control
	• Graffiti removal
	• Public sanitation and garbage collection
	• New centralized phone line for inquiries about city services

Table 2.2.   Williams's strategic goals II.

Build an "identity of interests" between citizens and government

Five strategic priorities (link to legitimacy and support perspective):

- Building and sustaining neighborhoods
- Strengthening children, youth, and families
- Promoting economic development
- Enhancing unit of purpose and democracy
- Making government work (see below)

Rebuild the fundamental operations of government

Making government work (link to operational capacity perspective):

- Increase productivity in D.C. public agencies
- Improve quality of public services to citizens across D.C. public agencies

THE LEGITIMACY AND SUPPORT PERSPECTIVE: General Form

Mission Alignment with Values Articulated by Citizens
  (Link to Public Value Account)

Inclusion of Neglected Values with Latent Constituencies
  (Link to Public Value Account)

Standing with Formal Authorizers:
  Elected Executives
  Statutory Overseers in Executive Branch (Budget, Finance, Personnel)
  Elected Legislators
  Statutory Overseers in Legislative Branch (Audit, Inspectors-General)
  Other Levels of Government
  Courts

Standing with Key Interest Groups:
  Economically Motivated Suppliers
  Self-Interested Client Groups
  Policy Advocacy Groups
  Latent Interest Groups

Media Coverage:
  Print
  Electronic
  Social

Standing with Individuals in Polity:
  General Citizenry
  Taxpayers
  Clients
    • Service recipients
    • Obligatees

Position of Enterprise in Democratic Political Discourse:
  Standing in Political Campaigns
  Standing in Political Agendas of Current Elected Regime
  Standing in Relevant "Policy Community"

Status of Key Legislative and Public Policy Proposals to Support
  Enterprise *(Link to Operational Capacity Perspective)***:**
  Authorizations
  Appropriations

Engagement of Citizens as Co-Producers *(Link to Operational Capacity Perspective)*

Figure 2.7. The legitimacy and support perspective: general form.

use increased accountability to improve the operating performance of government—a managerial approach focusing on the operational capacity perspective of the public value scorecard. A general form of the legitimacy and support perspective is presented here as Figure 2.7.

Some categories for information gathering and performance measurement coincide with categories in other perspectives of the scorecard. Categories associated with citizen sources of legitimacy and support appear at the top of the form because the values that the public articulates are the primary and fundamental sources of legitimacy and support. Categories associated with the flow of resources to the organization and the supportive role of citizens as coproducers appear at the bottom of the form as legitimacy and support begins to transform into operational capacity.

Developing a Public Value Scorecard Helps Animate and
Guide Operational Capacity
This brings us to the third point of the strategic triangle, which focuses managers' attention on developing and directing operational capacity to achieve desired social outcomes. It is useful to think about operational capacity in terms of a "value chain" that links inputs of public resources (money and authority) into a production system consisting of public policies, programs, procedures, and activities that produce transactions with clients and, ultimately, create some socially desired outcome, as shown in Figure 2.8.

The diagram is meant to focus managers' attention on the reality that at any given moment the operational capacity of a public production system generates costs and produces results that register as social outcomes and/or transactions with clients. Viewed in terms of a public

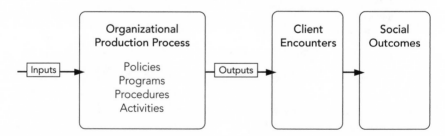

Figure 2.8. The public value chain.

value account, client satisfaction and social outcomes are on the right-hand side of the ledger, while the resources flowing into the production process are on the left-hand side. Viewed in terms of the strategic triangle, the public value chain can be superimposed on the arrows connecting legitimacy and support to operational capacity, and operational capacity to public value. Public value recognition, in turn, helps generate legitimacy and support. Figure 2.9 shows how the value chain fits into the picture of the strategic triangle.

There is nothing novel about a flow diagram that shows a material, causal process through which resources are deployed in a production process to achieve results. It is the drive to improve performance along the value chain that motivates good operational managers to use performance measurement and management systems. Examining the existing value chain allows public managers to learn whether and how

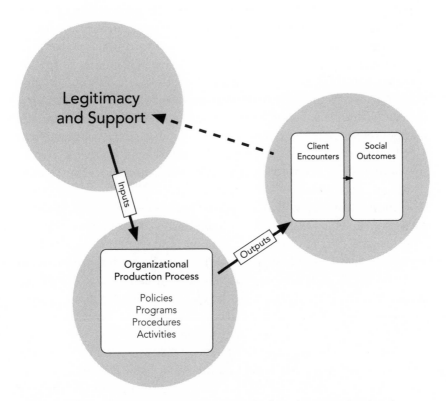

Figure 2.9. The public value chain superimposed on the strategic triangle.

operational capacity and current operations could be reengineered to increase valued output per unit of cost, or reduce costs per unit of valued results. It is in the value chain that opportunities for increasing productivity lie. In order for the value chain to reveal those opportunities, however, there has to be a performance measurement system that tracks not only the ultimate results produced but also the activities undertaken by many different actors to produce those results. Just as the balanced scorecard includes the organizational process perspective and the learning and growth perspective to focus private managers' attention on the production processes that generate the costs and revenues that show up in the financial perspective, the public value scorecard calls for the development of an operational capacity perspective that can direct public managers' attention to the processes on which they are relying to produce valuable results at a low cost.

To complicate matters, however, because the activities and outputs of public enterprises often have intrinsic as well as instrumental value, information about those processes belongs not only in the operational capacity perspective but also in the public value account. As noted earlier, the measures included in the public value account are limited to those with intrinsic rather than instrumental value. I also noted, however, that one of the important features of public value accounting is that the public places value on the character of activities and processes, without reference to their impact on producing customer satisfaction or social outcomes. Thus many parts of the production process are designed to achieve client satisfaction and social outcomes that have intrinsic rather than merely instrumental value.

Another complication arises when we consider that operational capacity functions to create public value in terms of both publicly desired outcomes and individual client satisfaction. And both concepts also have a place on the public value account. This is what Williams discovered when he started with the first concept and eventually moved to embrace the second. The costs of producing the results that register as client satisfaction or the achievement of social outcomes also enter directly into the public value account, since the polity values them directly.

Thus the value chain covers territory that is relevant to both the operational capacity perspective and the public value account. The connection between the public value account and the operational capacity perspective is the focus of Chapter 4 in this volume.

In addition, the value chain reminds us that the public agency at the center of the production process does not operate alone. The operational capacity to produce public value includes "partners" and "coproducers," emphasizing the fact that most public agencies have to achieve results in contexts where they represent only a part (often a small part) of the overall system that produces desired results. While Bratton could energize the police, he depended on the willingness of citizens to support them, and even to defend themselves from victimization. While Williams might have been able to use municipal agencies to improve conditions for economic development in Washington, D.C., economic development also depends on the actions of private banks and companies. The implication is that public managers have to see their efforts in the context of the productive efforts of others and think about how they might leverage that external coproduction for maximum advantage. We will consider this idea from the legitimacy and support perspective in Chapter 5.

While features of the value chain can show up in all three parts of the public value scorecard, the operational capacity perspective reminds public managers to maintain a lively interest in the instrumental aspects of organizational processes, policies, and procedures. Assets are deployed through these mechanical processes that determine exactly how much gross public value one can get out of the use of a particular quantity of public money or authority. Knowledge of these processes can reveal where opportunities for increasing productivity lie. In manufacturing operations this is the work of production engineers and efficiency experts. And for a long time it seemed that this work was limited to manufacturing operations. But the private sector soon discovered that it could use the same principles in the design of service organizations. The public sector has since followed, imagining that there is some public value to be claimed through the rigorous engineering of the procedures on which public-sector organizations were relying to produce their valued results. The existing procedures of an organization for investigating a homicide, handling a domestic dispute, handing out building permits, or assembling a jury, like the operating technology of a manufacturing operation, can be reengineered to produce more value at less cost.

To take advantage of this opportunity, managers need information about the processes they are using and the results they are achieving.

THE OPERATIONAL CAPACITY PERSPECTIVE: General Form

Flow of Resources to Enterprise *(Link to Legitimacy and Support Perspective)*:

Financial Revenues Flowing to Public Agencies:
- Appropriations
- Intergovernmental grants
- Fees

Legal and Statutory Authorizations/Mandates

Public Support/Popular Opinion

Human Resources:

Current Status of Workforce
- Size
- Quality
- Morale

Recruitment and Selection Processes

Training/Professional Development of Staff

Compensation Levels

Advancement Opportunities

Performance Measurement Systems for Individual Accountability

Public Volunteer Efforts

Operational Policies, Programs and Procedures:

Quality of Operational Performance
- Documentation of current procedures
- Compliance with tested procedures
- Auditability of performance recording methods

Organizational Learning
- Evaluation of current untested policies
- Stimulation and testing of innovations
- Institutionalization of successful innovations

Internal Resource Allocation

Performance Measurement and Management Systems
- Investment in systems
- Use of systems

Organizational Outputs *(Link to Public Value Account)*:

Quantity of Outputs

Quality of Outputs
- Attributes that produce desired results
- Attributes that increase client satisfaction
- Attributes that reflect justice and fairness in operations

Figure 2.10. The operational capacity perspective: general form.

When they have processes they think work very well, the problem is to use the information about processes to ensure compliance with those validated processes. But many processes in government have never really been tested. Consequently, public managers also need data on processes to test them against desired results. They also need a certain number of innovative ideas and experiments to explore what was actually possible to produce. And when they find a valuable new process, they need some way to monitor investments made to roll out the improved process across the enterprise.

All this becomes a bit more complex once we realize that the relevant production system often includes actors outside the organization. Once partners and coproducers are involved in a network of capacity, information about processes becomes an important tool for keeping the network together and focused on achieving valued results. For all these reasons, the public value scorecard insists on developing an operational capacity perspective filled with information that describes the activities and outputs of the organization, as well as its costs and results. After all, these processes are actually generating the costs and the results, and if we want to find ways to improve them, we have to first know what we are doing, and what results are being achieved. A general form of the operational capacity perspective is presented here as Figure 2.10.

Categories related to the legitimacy and support perspective appear at the top of the form, as they concern the flow of resources into the organization. Categories related to the public value account appear at the bottom of the form, as these are the organizational outputs that lead to the ultimate creation of public value. In this way, the form follows the flow of the public value chain (see Figure 2.8).

Summary

To improve government performance it is vital for public managers to develop a public value account that captures a philosophically and politically sound conception of public value, and to use that set of measures in the development of a management system that can increase accountability and drive the performance of public agencies to new heights. That is the promise of a public-sector version of "bottom-line" performance management that I explored in Chapter 1.

But to exploit all opportunities to create public value, public managers must learn to *manage strategically* and build broader performance measurement systems that can help them implement the value-creating strategies they imagine. Strategic managers have to develop a strong capacity to notice and respond to important changes in their environment: changes in both the political aspirations that flow through their organizations and the material challenges they face in trying to meet those aspirations. To realize the value-creating potential that exists in their organizations, managers need a concrete plan for articulating and measuring the public value that their organizations create, galvanizing legitimacy and support for that concept, and investing in the operational capacity they need. That is their strategic challenge, and meeting that challenge requires them to have concrete ideas about how they will both engage their political environments and transform their operational capacities. To execute their strategy for creating value in the future, managers need a performance measurement and management system that goes beyond a public value account; they need a public value scorecard. Indeed, one could say that it is only the creation and use of a public value scorecard that will allow a strategic manager to see how an abstract vision of public value creation could be realized in a particular circumstance, and to keep the organization honest in its pursuit of that vision.

Applying the abstract concepts of the strategic triangle to a particular set of circumstances helps managers test in their own minds an idea about how they could increase the public value of the enterprise they lead. But the abstractions of the strategic triangle do not really provide much detailed operational guidance. Bringing the strategic triangle into contact with the concrete reality that managers face begins with becoming much more concrete and specific about the particular dimensions of public value they intend to pursue in a public value account.

Beyond the public value account, however, the managers need the guidance that comes from a public value scorecard that includes both a legitimacy and support perspective and an operational capacity perspective. The legitimacy and support perspective will guide a diagnosis of the particular political authorizing environment that managers face. The operational capacity perspective will guide managers along a value chain in which they deploy the public resources available to them in activities and processes to produce organizational outputs that ultimately lead to the achievement of desired social outcomes. Some of that operational capacity lies within the organization, under the formal control of the managers, but much of it probably lies outside the organization's boundaries in the capacities of both organized partners and individual coproducers. The operational capacity perspective will enable managers to focus on how to animate and guide these external actors as well as their own organizations.

When these perspectives are brought to bear on the particular circumstances facing public managers, they produce many particular observations and can be used in many different ways. First, the perspectives can be used to describe the existing state of the environment within which (and on which) managers are trying to operate. They can show managers the world as it is, and as it affects their strategic ambitions.

Second, the perspectives can be used to diagnose potential problem areas and focus managerial attention on them. The legitimacy and support perspective can point to a crumbling coalition of support, to a key policy that is about to sunset, or to a latent constituency that might be mobilized to support an important strategic innovation. The operational capacity perspective can distribute managerial attention across the complex network of actors and activities to influence the social conditions that managers seek to change. That, in turn, will help managers envision the programmatic and operational innovations necessary to deliver desired results and focus on developing the working relationships necessary to animate and coordinate a complex network of capacity to take effective action to produce the desired results.

Third, and most important, the perspectives can help managers keep track of whether and how their efforts are changing the conditions that they have determined are essential for producing desired results. They can set goals for engaging authorizers to provide legitimacy and support for their effort. They can set goals for building and deploying the operational capacity they need to achieve the desired results. In this respect the perspectives become useful not only as diagnostic aids but also as vehicles for setting targets and managing change in their particular context. They become tools for seeing not only what public value has been produced in the past (the main work of the public value account) but also what managerial work needs to be done to build legitimacy and support and operational capacity to produce greater public value in the future.

What distinguishes the public value scorecard from the public value account is that the scorecard includes measures that keep track of efforts to build legitimacy and support for one's enterprise and to develop and

PUBLIC VALUE ACCOUNT for Anthony Williams and Washington DC

PUBLIC VALUE ACCOUNT	
Use of Collectively Owned Assets and Associated Costs	Achievement of Collectively Valued Social Outcomes
Financial Costs	Mission Achievement
	Build and sustain neighborhoods
	Strengthen children, youth, and families
	Promote economic development
	Enhance democracy and unity of purpose (create "an identity of interests")
	Make government work
	Client Satisfaction
	Improve client services
	Licenses and permits
	Mail delivery
	Emergency response
	Garbage collection and sanitation
	Etc.
	Create centralized call center
Social Costs of Using State Authority	Justice and Fairness

Figure 2.11. Public value scorecard for Anthony Williams.

THE LEGITIMACY AND SUPPORT PERSPECTIVE
Progress and Planning for Anthony Williams and Washington DC

Mission Alignment with Values Articulated by Citizens:

Held citizen summits to allow citizens to nominate dimensions of public value to pursue

Inclusion of Neglected Values with Latent Constituencies:

Gave attention to broad economic and social development

Standing with Formal Authorizers:

Elected Legislators
- Secured increased autonomy from Control Board

Statutory Overseers
- Received good reports from federal and local financial oversight agencies

City Council
- *Develop strategy for re-engaging Council in city governance*

Media Coverage:

Received favorable coverage of service improvements and "scorecards"

Standing with Individuals in Polity:

General Citizenry
- Built "identity of interests" through citizen summits
- Increased transparency in government operations through widely publicized "scorecards" for agency managers

Clients
- Reduced wait times and improved client services in city departments

Status of Key Legislative and Public Policy Proposals to Support Enterprise:

Authorizations
- Recovered authority to hire and fire managers

Appropriations
- Secured increased funding for service improvement

OPERATIONAL CAPACITY PERSPECTIVE
Progress and Planning for Anthony Williams and Washington DC

Flow of Resources to Enterprise:

Financial Revenues
- Increased appropriations from federal government

Legal and Statutory Authorizations/Mandates
- Increased autonomy for Mayor's office
- Reclaimed authority to hire and fire public managers

Public Support/Popular Opinion
- Engaged public in defining and pursuing public value
- Increased transparency of government operations through scorecards

Human Resources:

Professional Development
- Increased discretion and accountability for midlevel managers

Performance Measurement Systems for Individual Accountability
- Integrated "scorecard" goals into agency directors' contracts, as basis for annual reviews
- Removed civil service protections to make rewards and sanctions for midlevel managers subject to reviews based on performance data

Public Volunteer Efforts
- "Scorecards" invited public interest and assistance in pursuing governmental goals

Operational Policies, Programs, and Procedures:

Performance Measurement and Management Systems
- Required agencies to adapt mission statements to Mayor's "strategic priorities"
- "Scorecard" goals forced innovations in operations and service delivery

Organizational Outputs:

Performance scorecards created for each city agency

Process and results measures developed for each step of DCRA work

Q-matic installed to provide detailed information on customer volume, wait times, and transaction speeds at DMV deploy the operational capacity that can deliver the desired results. When a vision of public value creation is combined with a set of measures that can recognize not only whether an organization is producing public value but also whether it is taking the political and operational steps necessary to achieve that vision, a real chance for enhanced value creation opens up.

Developing a fully operational public value scorecard linked to a strategy for creating public value seems like a great deal of work. But managers should be encouraged by the fact that getting even part of the way to the finish line produces valuable results. Indeed, a recent international study of performance management in the public sector found that using performance measurement in a performance management system "connects what an organization does—setting outcomes and objectives, planning, budgeting, allocating resources, managing people, and reporting—to its mission and its intended results." The same study revealed that public agencies that committed themselves to performance management "share an adaptive ability to work within the constraints of their political systems, a determination to overcome barriers, and a willingness to grapple with the thorny management dilemmas involved with implementing and using performance management. As a result, they are transforming their organizations from reactive, inward-focused entities into proactive agencies focused on creating greater public value."[62]

In the remainder of this book I press forward with developing the idea of a public value scorecard as an essential aid to value-creating public management. I will do so in the way I started—by looking at public managers who face up to strategic challenges and find ways to use performance measurement and performance management systems to help them get on with the job. The cases will include managers who have focused a lot of attention on the legitimacy and support side of the strategic triangle, those who have grappled with the philosophical questions underlying the definition of public value, those who have focused much attention on managing a complex production process across many different organizations, those who have faced the problem of how to mobilize tolerance and assistance from the broader public, and so on. At the end, readers should have a greater appreciation for why a public value scorecard is important, what it consists of, and how it can be created and effectively used in strategic management in government.

At the end of this and each subsequent chapter (with the exception of Chapter 6, which presents the case of an agency focused soley on performance measurement without having any operational capacity to create social outcomes in the usual sense) I present a public value scorecard for the manager in the case at hand. The general form of the public value scorecard, introduced in this chapter, is reproduced for convenience at the end of the book as the appendix (see there Figures A.1, A.2, and A.3). Each manager's scorecard will include only the categories I see as points of leverage worthy of the manager's attention. Categories that are not particularly applicable to the manager's position and categories in which the manager can leave well enough alone without significant strategic hazard are omitted. Readers are nonetheless invited to consider what the managers in question could do to gather information and measure performance in omitted categories. Under the general headings for each manager's public value account, legitimacy and support perspective, and operational capacity perspective, readers will find actions taken and goals accomplished in the case, as well as suggestions and challenges for improving performance through performance measurement in the managers' particular enterprise. Suggestions and challenges will be set in italics. Figure 2.11 is the public value scorecard for Anthony Williams.

3

John James and the Minnesota Department of Revenue

Embracing Accountability to Enhance Legitimacy and Improve Performance

John James and the Legislative Oversight Committee

In late 1987 John James was appointed commissioner of the Minnesota Department of Revenue (DOR), an organization with an annual budget of $65 million and a staff of over twelve hundred employees.[1] Like all revenue departments, the Minnesota DOR was responsible for two critical government functions: collecting revenues owed to the state and offering technical advice to policy makers about tax policy. By far the most money and staff were devoted to the first task. Most DOR employees thought the DOR performed this admittedly unpopular function in a highly professional, effective, and fair manner. They also believed that the department got no respect from the legislative committees that authorized its existence, appropriated funds for it, and reviewed its operations.

Legislative Oversight

The principal legislative oversight committee to which the DOR reported was the State Departments Division of the House Appropriations Committee, which was responsible for the budgetary review and oversight of forty-three different "accounts"—including the Department of Natural Resources, the Supreme Court, and the state zoo. It carried out its budgetary and oversight responsibilities primarily through hearings authorizing two-year budgets for the accounts it oversaw.

Phyllis Kahn, the chair of the State Departments Division, judged her committee to be the most conscientious and hardworking in the entire state legislature. On average, its members held more advanced degrees and put in longer hours than their fellow legislators. The Division also exhibited an unusual sense of community. Part of what joined them was a shared resentment of their fellow legislators' apparent contempt for their cause. During periodic budget crunches, the State Departments Division felt that agencies within its jurisdiction routinely took disproportionate cuts because the agencies were part of the "overhead" of government and did not directly provide goods and services to Minnesota clients.

Members of the Division typically refused to vote along partisan lines, which helped bolster their outsider status in the legislature. They loved to tell the story of Rep. Tom Osthoff, a Democrat from Saint Paul, who was assigned to the Division by House Speaker Robert Vanasek to bring more partisanship to the proceedings. Instead, Osthoff adopted the ethos of the group he had been sent to reform, and the Division continued its nonpartisan approach to budgeting and oversight.

Perhaps because of its independent spirit, the State Departments Division had acquired a reputation for tough (some would say nasty) hearings. For many Division members, this was a point of pride. (Osthoff, when summoning an agency representative to the table as a witness, once exclaimed, "Fresh meat! Get 'em up here!") Kahn contrasted the Division's ethos with that of other legislative committees that tended to "just kind of consider themselves to be the advocate for their agency."

The Division's contentious hearings often involved conflicts at two different levels. On one hand, there were conflicts among members. On the other, members thought that tough oversight required them to adopt a skeptical attitude toward the agency representatives who came before the Division. They believed that the citizens and taxpayers of Minnesota expected them to scour out waste in government and ensure high-quality services. To do so, they had to be tough, and to avoid being co-opted by the agencies they reviewed. The legislators viewed themselves as being subjected to a kind of bureaucratic blackmail in which the DOR showed up to ask for budget increases and threatened dramatic reductions in revenue collections if its requests were not met.

This dynamic had been in place for so long that the hearings had come to feel like a stylized game. Substantive discussions about how much money the DOR needed to sustain or improve its performance were sacrificed to a public ritual in which the legislators pilloried the

DOR's representatives who, in response, tried to reveal as little as possible about their operations. The frustrated legislators would then attack even more aggressively. Eventually, the collision would end—not because shared understandings of the problem they faced had emerged and a plan for dealing with the issue had been agreed upon but simply because time ran out. Both sides went back to their corners to await the next encounter two years later.

The legislators thought that this process was beneficial, but James and his staff did not. They decided that this dynamic was long overdue for a change. As Deputy Commissioner Babak Armajani put it, "At the Revenue Department, we decided to change the paradigm of the dialogue—unilaterally." To implement this new approach, James made three important moves.

First, he hired Connie Rae Nelson, a former fiscal analyst with the State Departments Division, to work with the DOR as the assistant commissioner for administration. Nelson had an insider's knowledge of how the legislative committees thought and worked, and she had maintained excellent working relationships with her former bosses in the legislature.

Second, James, Armajani, and Nelson set in motion a (locally) novel strategy they called "invest/divest" as a key element of their own internal budgeting process.[2] That process called on midlevel managers to submit proposals cutting 5 percent from their annual budgets despite the fact that the DOR was under no explicit instructions to reduce its costs. "Invest/divest" also asked managers to develop proposals to improve DOR operations that could be submitted to the governor and the legislature for approval. Though the DOR could have kept this process internal and concealed potential cost reductions, James was willing to gamble that transparency on "invest/divest" would benefit the agency.

Third, and perhaps most important, the agency crystallized its conception of how it thought the rules of the budget game should be changed. The DOR developed two slides to explain its new approach to staff and overseers. The content of the slides is shown in Table 3.1.

The legislature's budget oversight hearings began in mid-March 1989, with Commissioner James appearing before Rep. Phyllis Kahn and the State Departments Division. James began with a frank statement: "We heard that we are considered something of a black hole—that you throw a lot of money down it, and you don't really know where

Table 3.1. The old and the new budget games.

The old budget game	The new budget game
Provide as little information as possible to upper management, the governor, and the legislature.	Winners will be: managers who get the most out of resources they are given;
Winning means getting as much money for your unit as possible.	managers who innovate even without extra resources;
Spend all that you get; if you don't, it will be taken away.	managers who make themselves accountable for measurable results;
Never, under any circumstances, give up what you've got.	managers who voluntarily offer savings to fund higher priorities in other areas; and
New initiatives require new funding.	managers who are constantly reviewing their activities and giving up what has the least benefit to our customers in order to fund that which has the greatest benefit.

it goes. And we heard that we are not accountable for outputs [and] that some folks viewed us as engaging in what amounted to extortion in terms of saying 'Give us this money or you are going to lose a lot more.' We are concerned about that. What we want to do now, frankly, is to move out of this past that I have described into a future that is rather different."

He then elaborated on the DOR's self-conceived mission of making the tax system "fair, efficient, stable, competitive, and understandable." Then, to the surprise and interest of the legislators, he projected the overhead slides about the old and new budget games. He also explained the invest/divest process but emphasized that the job was by no means complete.

Despite this bold opening, the hearing soon relapsed into the "old budget game." The legislators found 130 "ghost" positions in the DOR's budget—jobs for which funds were allocated but which were never filled. The money was used instead to provide a cushion against unexpected increases in operating costs in other parts of the budget. The Division was also "outraged" to learn that the DOR estimated that fifty thousand incoming telephone calls had gone unanswered. Legislators also criticized proposals to spend additional funds on two large computer systems on the grounds that the DOR was taking on too much too fast. After reviewing the DOR's budget request for a 17.4 percent increase, the State Departments Division voted to hold the increase to 11 percent, cutting specific planned activities such as the second computer system. The Division made no change to the DOR's base and allowed $7.5 million in new spending.

The response from the DOR's other legislative oversight committee, the State Departments Senate Finance Subcommittee, was quite different. The Senate committee, seized with a sense of urgency about reducing a potential overall budget deficit, recommended almost $15 million less than the House had recommended.

A conference committee of the House and Senate appropriations subcommittees met and recommended a (two-year) budget of $131 million, an 8.3 percent increase. The budget bill included a base cut of $1.2 million for the two years. Unexpectedly, the governor chose to veto the base cuts.

The DOR was pleased by the governor's veto but generally confused by the results of this new approach to the budget process. The DOR officials thought they had made a good-faith effort to change. They had cut costs and fired workers. But they seemed to still be in the old budget game. Nelson noted one key feature of the old budget game that continued to plague the process: it was by no means clear what sorts of incentives the legislative committee could offer the DOR to improve performance. It was not clear whether good performance in controlling costs and achieving results could or should be rewarded with more money, either for the agency or for individual managers who performed especially well.

Getting Back on Track: A Joint Focus on Performance

Thinking about how to move forward, Armajani and Nelson thought one thing was apparent: the legislators did not really seem to understand what the DOR was trying to achieve. It seemed to be more focused on the DOR's ability to account for its inputs and control costs than its ability to deliver results. Further, the legislators did not seem to understand much about the relationship between the DOR's costs and the results it was able to achieve, nor did they trust the agency to tell them about these relationships.

Armajani and Nelson thought that it might be valuable to hold a performance-focused "oversight hearing" before their next budget hearing in order to better inform the committees about DOR operations, and the value they could produce for the state if they were allowed to increase investments and expenditures. The House's State Departments Division agreed to schedule a hearing for the next winter or spring.

Armajani wanted this process to be "a model, a first step towards opening a dialogue about accountability between the legislative and executive branch outside the context of budget hearing." He went on: "My broader objective is to introduce a whole new pattern of interacting in government. We all work for the same people—the citizens of Minnesota; and we really have a very common purpose there in serving the people. So I think one objective is to get away from the notion that we are on different sides. I don't mean to overcome the Constitution, which sets up deliberately some tension between the executive and legislative branches. But I think we could round the corners a little bit and serve the citizens better."

For the first meeting, however, Armajani kept his expectations more modest and practical. He wanted to change the terms in which the Division called the DOR to account:

> [They have to understand that] they don't know anything about running an organization. . . . Our opinion is that they should stick to strategy and policy and hold us accountable for managing. But don't tell us how to manage, because they don't know a thing about it. . . . They think that if they control inputs, that they're doing a good job. . . . What we're trying to do is to get them to control outputs. We're telling them, "Don't talk to us about how many computers we buy or even how many people we've got or what we spend on travel or how we use our consulting dollars, or whether people are going to training or not. . . . What we think you should do is to make us tell you what it is we produce. You know, how many people are paying their taxes, how many people are getting answers to their questions, how many people are getting refunds, how many of the people that owe us money are we tracking down and collecting from. Results, that's what citizens want! And that's what you should control!" If you look through the budget process, there's nothing about results in there.

Armajani also wanted to talk about the legislators' behavior in oversight proceedings: "I think most of them on that committee are just sincere, honest people who are trying to be good legislators, who care about Minnesota government. [But] they're incredibly rude in the deliberations process . . . and disrespectful and hostile, and we can't figure out why because we consider them our bosses, and we are trying to be accountable to them. We think of them as our board of directors."

Armajani's goals for the hearing were quite simple. "[I want] a really good discussion about what they want. I also want the legislators to hear what each other wants because, of course, they have conflicting interests. One of them wants us to be efficient, another wants us to be fair, and the two are not always compatible." He also had a clear picture of how the performance evaluation hearing and the next budget hearing should unfold: "We'll listen to them, and then we'll come back, and next year we'll say, 'Okay, last year here's what you said, and so now we've thought about it, and we've planned and budgeted, and here's our proposal.' And I think they'll really appreciate that. And I think that's the way that government ought to work."

In preparation for the hearing, the DOR developed the following set of "critical outcomes" as criteria for judging its performance:

- Transactions are processed with speed and accuracy.
- Citizens and their elected representatives are confident in the integrity of the tax system and the Department of Revenue.
- There is compliance with the tax laws.
- Customers of individual work units are satisfied with the services of that unit.
- State and local revenue policies are congruent with [the] DOR's mission.
- The DOR is effective and efficient in using its resources to achieve these outcomes.
- The Revenue organization is prepared to carry out its mission and strategies, and its employees are fulfilled through their work.
- Taxpayers and employees have the information they need when they need it.

In the last few weeks leading up the critical oversight meeting, the State Departments Division and the DOR carried on fraught discussions about the agenda, content, and style of the meeting. Finally, Phyllis Kahn circulated an agenda for the meeting with a cover letter explaining the following:

[The DOR] has undergone its own self-evaluation and has implemented a strategy of re-ordering priorities. The invest/divest strategy is an attempt to critically examine the Department and its mission, while directing internal resources to the highest priorities before requesting additional funding. This evaluation is to identify strengths and weaknesses of the Department, identify outcomes which the Department and Division would like to see accomplished and provide the means for measuring these outcomes for the purposes of evaluating the Department during the next budget season and beyond. In short, it is an attempt to change the oversight process from one of just looking at inputs to one of emphasizing outcomes.

Kevin Kajer, a Division staff member, opened the meeting by describing the central purpose of the exercise: to focus for the next two hours on what committee members "want the Department of Revenue to do, and how we're going to judge them." Kahn added, "We're not sure that we handle Revenue appropriations in the best way." She then introduced the DOR representatives with the observation that "we actually appreciate" its management redirection, even though the DOR might not think so after the 1989 hearings. The meeting, she said, recognized that "despite the fact that we're sometimes set up as an adversarial system, the management of the Department is one of the critical issues in the management of state finances because you're such an important part of the state financial picture. And whatever happens in the future, we'd like our relationship to be one that ends up with the best solution for the state." Ron Nickerson, a second Division staff member assigned to facilitate the discussion, set the agenda for the evening:

- Develop a process for agency evaluations
- Develop a process transferable to other agencies
- Develop meaningful performance measures
- Start an ongoing dialogue

The Division and the DOR then met separately to discuss what each side would like to see emerge from the meeting. The next half hour set the tone for the evening: DOR representatives tried to do as the moderators requested, while Division members began with the point under debate, then flipped quickly onto other topics, often laughing and whispering among themselves. Nonetheless, each side's concerns became clear over the course of the evening.

Nelson presented the DOR's hopes to her former colleagues in the State Departments Division:

> We'd like to have a healthier, more open and honest working relationship between the executive and legislative branches. We think that you would like to improve agency performance without necessarily giving us more money. We would like to improve our dialogue with you and be more accountable to you as overseers separate from the money cycle as well. We would like to talk about ways to improve rewards and incentives to improve performance without it necessarily being dollars and cents. And rewarding for you as well as rewarding for us. We would like to have a dialogue that puts us to a point where we have some shared public purpose about why we exist and some shared expectations about what outcomes we're going to be held accountable to you for.

Commissioner James added, "We have some ideas about how we might be able to interrelate better with you." He then presented some slides describing the agency's operations. He concluded, somewhat plaintively, "We don't have anyone else out there as constituents who really love us. If you people don't love us, who will?"

As the evening wore on, despite Division staff moderators' efforts to bring the discussion back to the agenda, the Division's internal concerns began to dominate the proceedings. Members seemed glad of the opportunity to tell outsiders about the burdens under which they functioned: the chronic shortage of time inherent in being a part-time legislator; the lack of appreciation for the Division's work from state agencies and the legislature; and the frustrations of minority members.

On occasion, the committee's griping gave the DOR an opportunity to explore issues it considered central. For example, as Nelson had foreseen, the Division considered her presence at the DOR crucial to building trust. Nelson testified, "These people are as competent, credible, honest, sincere public people as you have said you believe I am. And I should be irrelevant. It should be a discussion about what do you want from this department, how do you know whether you're getting honest information, and having ongoing dialogue." The DOR representatives were pleased and surprised to learn that the Division considered the DOR the most honest and best-run of the agencies it dealt with. That did not mean, however, that the DOR was in the clear. Rep. David Battaglia commented: "Once someone gives you a reason to believe that something has been done less than in an honest manner, it's almost impossible to correct that. And the big point is, what can we do to never have that happen? . . . Let me say this, and it's not disrespectful: After having gained a certain amount of confidence in the Revenue Department, how much of that do you think I retained when I found out that you had 100 paid positions with 100 less people? Do you think that really instilled a great amount of enthusiasm in me?"

The Division's chief message to the DOR was: How can we trust the information you give us and, even if we trust it, how does it help us make responsible budgeting decisions? Kahn raised the related matter of identifying the point of diminishing returns on investment, and Commissioner James promised that with better data—to be available soon—such calculations could be made. Representatives spoke to the issue of fifty thousand unanswered telephone calls from taxpayers, which the DOR agreed was inexcusable.

Later in the evening, Rep. Rick Krueger raised a different question: How should he interpret an honest report from the DOR on a program that was doing poorly?

> *Krueger:* Let's say I'm concerned [and] you tell me you're doing
> a poor job in a certain area. What does that tell me? Does
> that tell me we've got to spend more money . . . because
> we've got to beef up our efforts in that area? . . . Does it mean
> that if you're doing a good job in an area, conversely, that we
> should reduce the funding in that area?
> *Armajani:* I guess I don't think it necessarily should tell you that
> wherever we're screwing up, that means you have to spend
> more money. . . . You should focus on what it is you want
> from us. And if you're not getting what you want from us,
> then you should say, either "Are these the right people to be
> delivering this service?" or "Do we really want to invest?"
> *Krueger:* You're telling me that's what I want from you. I'm not
> sure that's what I want from you. I don't even know the
> questions to ask what I want from you.

The moderators did achieve their central goal for the evening: to compile two lists of desired DOR outcomes—one from the Division and one from the DOR. The DOR list was the one the executive team had compiled over months of internal discussion, presented earlier. The

Division's list of concerns was somewhat different. As the legislators voiced their concerns about the DOR, Nickerson recorded them as the Division's list of desired outcomes. It read:

- At what point do increased resources = diminishing returns?
- Lower the percent of uncollected taxes.
- Identify what types of income are not being reported.
- Follow not just the letter but the intent of legislative directives.
- No complaints from taxpayers.
- Organize the department as efficiently as possible.
- Be sensitive to the political process.
- Answer telephones with accurate information.
- Develop a sound tax policy based on consistency, honesty, and fairness.
- Provide equal access to information for all legislators.
- Seek input from local governments and tax experts.
- Relate program evaluation to the budget process.

As they dispersed, the mood was somber among the DOR officials. Many of them felt that the Division had been listening principally to its own concerns and less to what the DOR had to say. Hope was fading that the legislators could function in the way a corporate board of directors functions vis-à-vis a private company.

The next morning, members of the Division and the leadership team from the DOR resumed their meeting. This time, instead of dividing into two groups, everyone sat together. The goal for the day was to see whether there were areas of common concern between the two groups and, if so, what could be done about them.

To get the discussion going, Division moderators Nickerson and Kajer "matched" the DOR's "critical outcomes" list with the legislators' list. The exercise went very well. For those items on the lists that the staffers had been unable to match, the participants jumped in and found correlations. For example, the first item on the Division's list ("At what point do increased resources = diminishing returns?") seemed to align with the sixth item on the Revenue Department's list ("The DOR is effective and efficient in using its resources to achieve these outcomes").

The moderators also asked the DOR to go through the Division's list of outcomes and give a brief report on where it stood on each item.

The ensuing discussion found the Division members mostly complimenting the agency. On the thorny subject of the "ghost" positions, Rep. Ron Abrams leaped to the DOR's defense, saying, "The Department of Finance basically produces a budget that makes no sense. . . . You're beating up on John James and the DOR for what is essentially a Finance Department problem. I think John would love to come up with an honest budget." Rep. Dave Bishop was the most forthright in his praise: "I think I speak for the other members of the Division in saying that of all the agencies that we deal with, we probably have more trust in and are getting more honesty from the Department of Revenue than any of the other agencies."

For its part, the DOR voiced empathy for the Division members. On the contentious subject of the relationship between DOR spending and its capacity to deliver additional revenues to the state, Commissioner James stated: "We can tell you with a straight face—because it is true—that if you give us more people, we will bring in more money. We are just operating at such a low level compared to what all is out there that I think that is true. But yet, I don't blame you for not believing us because one, we screwed up once before, and two, we never really relate it to the whole universe [of the Department's activities]."

On the instructions of the moderators, the group unanimously selected the outcomes from the Division's list that could be applied to the Department of Revenue and to other agencies. These "outcomes" included the following:[3]

- At what point do increased resources yield diminishing returns?
- Follow not just the letter but the intent of legislative directives.
- Organize the department as efficiently as possible.
- Answer telephone calls with accurate information.

The group also discussed which remaining outcomes were within the power of the DOR to fix. Commissioner James said he intended first to address measurement issues. The question of performance incentives also incited much debate. Although Division members such as Osthoff argued sympathetically that "it is kind of hard for an agency to offer incentives when they don't have anything in their budget to do it with," James demurred, "We would endeavor to produce results even if we didn't get more money." Armajani agreed, adding, "You guys greatly underestimate the impact [of a word of praise]."

As the meeting concluded, the moderators quickly reviewed five items that, judging from the discussion, the Division wanted the DOR to pursue as both worked to improve their relations:

- Continue the dialogue for shared purposes.
- Improve communication and information flow by circulating regular updates from [the] DOR.
- Try harder to consider what is on legislators' minds.
- Provide reliable information.
- Maintain a healthy, open relationship between the two branches of government.

Facing the Problem of Democratic Accountability

John James, like most public managers, faced insistent, urgent demands for accountability. For the most part, democratic citizens think it is a good thing for public agencies to be called to account. This is how they can ensure that the government is "for the people" and reflects their aspirations for an efficient, fair, and responsive public administration. But, as noted in Chapter 2, there can be too much of a good thing. When the demands for accountability come from many voices in an unpredictable and uncoordinated stream, and when those voices cannot be engaged in a constructive dialogue about how performance could be improved, they tend to distract managers from, and undermine their commitment to, the value-creating tasks they have taken on. Public managers can (and to some degree should) seek to build their legitimacy and support by making themselves accountable to those who can call them to account. But in order for the accountability to work, the demands for accountability have to be somehow sustained and rendered coherent to focus attention on the most important dimensions of value creation: ideally, named and measured in a skillfully negotiated public value account. The accountability process should keep consistent pressure on a public agency to increase its productivity in current activities and to become more responsive to new political aspirations and new operational risks. But to organize the demand for accountability in this way, public managers have to engage in the political work of developing both a suitable forum for negotiating accountability and a suitable form of accountability. If the forum consists of individuals taking potshots from any number of political or institutional positions, and the form forces managers to answer for minor incidents rather than overall value-creating performance, then the accountability process cannot function in this way.

James's Accountability to His Authorizers

James's accountability began with a responsibility to pursue the mission that the elected officials of the Minnesota state government had faithfully set out for him and his agency—that is, collecting taxes owed to the state efficiently, fairly, and effectively and providing expert advice on tax policy. While there were many who could call him and his agency to account, the dominant official player in James's authorizing environment was the House Committee that was responsible for overseeing his operations and authorizing his budget. Unfortunately, that particular forum for accountability was severely flawed. There was little apparent respect or trust and, therefore, no real opportunity for the two parties to reach an agreement about what precisely the legislature wanted the DOR to accomplish. It also meant that when disputes emerged, it was hard to engage in constructive problem solving. The DOR leadership also found the form of accountability inappropriate. From their point of view, the legislative overseers should have been concentrating their attention on the ultimate ends of the organization, not on process or compliance measures that tended to reduce the DOR's flexibility and innovativeness in pursuing its objectives.

Hoping for a stronger, more strategically useful relationship with their most important overseers, the DOR leadership took it upon themselves to build trust with the legislative overseers by increasing their transparency, on one hand, and focusing on ways to reduce costs, on the other. That was the force behind "invest/divest"—a serious effort to look for cost savings and efficiency gains in the agency's operations. In exchange for their move to accept and emphasize the legislature's right to demand information and performance, the DOR leadership wanted two things. First, they wanted a more respectful dialogue with their legislative overseers. Second, they wanted the focus of the conversation to shift from the control of inputs and costs to the definition and pursuit of performance. In short, they wanted to work together to develop a public value account to which both they and their legislative overseers could commit themselves.

Dimensions of Value: The Rudiments of James's Public Value Account
Revenue collection is one of the few government activities that can be easily denominated in financial terms. We can calculate the costs of the agency in financial terms, and we can calculate the financial return of the agency's operations in terms of the amount of money it brought into state government. That calculation would reveal a hugely profitable enterprise! As in the case of policing, however, this calculation conceals the degree to which the authority of the state is the real asset that is producing the financial returns. The use of public authority obligates the DOR to ensure fairness in the tax-collecting process and to make the burden of paying taxes as easy to bear as possible.

Because the DOR imposes obligations on Minnesota citizens, it is hardly a popular agency. In fact, it tends to generate a great deal of citizen dissatisfaction and complaints. Whenever taxpayers can connect their general reluctance to pay taxes with a reason to be offended, they are free to lodge complaints with the DOR or with their state legislators. It is at least partly for this reason that support from the House Appropriations Committee seemed particularly important to James. He knew he could not win a popularity contest among his taxpaying clients; the best he could have hoped for was that his legislative overseers would represent the interests of Minnesota citizens as well as taxpayers and support his agency's efforts to impose the (unwelcome) burden of taxation as efficiently, fairly, and effectively as possible.

James also knew that if the elected representatives of the citizens did not support the DOR, then taxpayers might be less motivated to pay their taxes, hence his plea "If you people don't love us, who will?" The more Minnesota's taxpayers resisted, the less efficient and effective the DOR would be in collecting taxes. Because the DOR depends on the "voluntary" contribution of taxpayers to achieve its desired results, the cost to them per dollar of revenue collected could be very different depending on the degree to which the legislature and ordinary citizens judged the DOR to be efficient and fair.

James also knew that whenever the government is under pressure to reduce its size and scope, the DOR comes under pressure to collect taxes at a lower total cost. Since James and his team believed that they would become more efficient and effective if granted the resources and motivation to refine their methods, however, it seemed clear to them that their budget should increase, when in fact the Minnesota legislature may have been interested in reducing James's budget—even if the price was reduced revenue collections for the state!

Focusing on costs often highlights a real difference in the values of public managers versus elected representatives. Public managers often say that they are interested in controlling costs, and they invariably say that they are interested in finding innovative methods for accomplishing their work more efficiently and effectively. The trouble usually starts, however, when they succeed in developing innovations that create productivity gains. With expenditures more highly leveraged, it might make sense to spend more on the agency, but it might also make sense to cut the budget. The agency managers tend to think that they, like their private-sector counterparts, ought to be rewarded financially and otherwise when they develop productivity-enhancing innovations. Elected representatives, on the other hand, are inclined to think that the productivity gains should be more widely distributed—that money saved in one agency could be diverted to urgent needs in another, or even returned to the citizens and taxpayers in the form of a tax dividend. This blind spot on the part of many public managers is a chronic problem in public value accounting.

Figure 3.1 sets out a rough approximation of a public value account that could be constructed for the Minnesota DOR.

The fact that James would be called to account for performance with respect to each of these dimensions of value—collecting taxes fully and fairly, providing excellent customer service, and minimizing costs—created a significant managerial problem. It was not clear whether he could improve his performance on all these dimensions of public value at the same time. In fact, at the outset, it looked as though there should have been significant trade-offs among the values he was pursuing. (Later in this chapter I will discuss the question of value trade-offs in more detail.) In an aggressive effort to collect more taxes, the DOR risks angering citizens, and the increased expense of chasing down delinquent taxpayers. If the DOR focuses on satisfying clients, it risks effectiveness in collecting revenues or increased operating costs, and so on. Indeed, it is precisely this set of questions that seems to concern the

PUBLIC VALUE ACCOUNT for John James and the Minnesota DOR

PUBLIC VALUE ACCOUNT	
Use of Collectively Owned Assets and Associated Costs	Achievement of Collectively Valued Social Outcomes
Financial Costs	Mission Achievement
Internal (administrative costs)	Collect taxes owed to state
External (tax preparation costs to citizens)	Provide advice to policy makers
Unpaid revenues owed to the state	
Unintended Negative Consequences	Unintended Positive Consequences
Distortion of efficient production and consumption (deadweight loss)	Encouragement of socially constructive activity
	Client Satisfaction
	Provide accurate information
	Facilitate compliance
	Reconcile taxpayers to tax burdens
Social Costs of Using State Authority	Justice and Fairness
Intrusiveness of government	Protect individual rights
Perceived abuses, injustices in tax collection	Impose aggregate burdens fairly

Figure 3.1. Public value account for John James and the Minnesota DOR.

legislators. They want to know the relationship between increased DOR expenditures and increased revenue collection. They want to collect more revenues even while reducing costs and complaints.

The Constitutional Structure and Common Process of Public Accountability
Ideally the people's elected legislators and executives would have guided James in prioritizing these basic performance goals and given him some room to explore ways to improve performance on all dimensions of value through innovation and experimentation. For these purposes, he had hoped that his legislative overseers would share the burden of managing the DOR's performance, like an experienced board of directors that could (1) represent the interests of the DOR's "owners" (the citizens of Minnesota), (2) define the dimensions of public value that should guide operations, (3) provide steady pressure for improved performance, and (4) share in some of the strategic decision making and risks involved in seeking to improve performance in uncertain, changing environments.[4]

The kind of accountability he actually faced was much different. Constitutionally, James was legally accountable to at least three separate institutions: the governor's office, the Senate, and the House of Representatives. All three had to sign off on the legislation giving him the authority and money to operate. And all three had the right and responsibility to direct and oversee the DOR's use of public money and authority. Beyond these official overseers were a large number of self-appointed agents of accountability who felt authorized to advise James and to demand accountability from him.

The diversity of actors making claims, and the different dimensions of value that are the focus of their concerns, would not necessarily be a problem if there were some mechanism to prioritize or integrate them into a coherent whole. And while legislative processes do integrate and prioritize the claims to some degree, the capacity of the legislation that emerges from these processes to construct a useful structure of accountability typically has four crucial weaknesses.

First, legislators and political executives often deal with conflicting goals by papering over the conflicts—raising the level of abstraction in the agency's goals to obscure contradictory objectives, or naming important dimensions of value without any indication of which should be regarded as more important.

Second, because legislation is passed at a particular political moment, it generally reifies the political agreement that was possible at that moment. But the world does not stand still. Unanticipated effects occur, new technologies emerge, political aspirations and values change, and new constituencies press their views on the agency. The deal encoded in the legislation is constantly under pressure, and constantly shifting under the surface.

Third, precisely because unresolved conflicts were pushed into the implementation stage, and because the world continues to change, statutes cannot fully protect public managers and agencies from emergent demands for accountability. A particular resolution of a conflict creates a political backlash that unsettles the apparent agreement, unanticipated effects attract new constituencies, and so on. For these reasons, the integration of competing demands for accountability that should occur at the time of legislative enactment does not occur in a way that creates a durable, coherent form of accountability.

This much is well known. But there is a fourth problem that is less widely acknowledged: while legislatures can set out the formal and legal terms of accountability, they cannot necessarily protect the agency from demands for accountability that come from other interested stakeholders. As noted in Chapter 2, almost any actor in a democratic society can find a platform from which to demand accountability from a public agency for some particular aspect of its performance, and none of these actors feel morally or practically obligated to integrate their claims with those of the others, leaving public managers to sort them all out.[5]

In the research my colleagues and I carried out to determine whether the particular public value account we developed for policing would work in the political authorizing environment for public police departments, we examined the degree to which the dimensions of value were, in fact, the focus of concern of important authorizers. To answer that question, we had to gather empirical data on (1) who the important authorizers of the public police were and (2) what particular dimensions of police performance seemed to concern them.

The results are presented in Figure 3.2. The rows of this figure describe the formal and informal overseers of the New York City Police Department (NYPD). The columns define the valued dimensions of police performance. The cells of this matrix use an eye symbol to represent empirical observations about whether a particular agent of

Formal Oversight: Continuous							
Federal Government	—	—	—	—	—	—	—
Governor	—	—	◉	—	◉	◉	◉
State Legislature	—	—	◉	—	◉	◉	◉
Mayor	◉	—	◉	—	◉	⟨◉⟩	◉
Office of Operations	—	—	◉	—	◉	—	—
Office of Management and Budget	—	—	—	—	◎	—	—
Criminal Justice Coordinator	—	—	◎	—	—	—	—
Law Department/Carpenter Council	—	—	—	—	—	◉	◉
Office of Investigation	—	—	—	—	—	◎	◎
City Council	◉	—	—	—	◉	—	◉
Community Boards	◎	—	◎	—	—	—	—
Civilian Complaint Review Board	—	—	—	—	—	◉	—
Police Commission	—	◉	◉	—	◉	◉	◉
Formal Oversight: Specially Commissioned							
Mollen Commission	—	—	—	—	—	⟨◉⟩	—
Gighenti Crown Heights Commission	⟨◉⟩	⟨◉⟩	—	—	—	⟨◉⟩	⟨◉⟩
Informal Oversight: Citizens and Nonelected Representatives							
Electronic Media	—	⟨◉⟩	⟨◉⟩	—	—	—	—
Print Media	—	⟨◉⟩	⟨◉⟩	—	—	—	—
Citizens Budget Commission	—	—	—	—	◉	—	—
ACLU	—	—	—	—	—	◉	—
Police Unions	—	—	—	—	—	—	—
Alliance for Professional Policy	—	—	—	—	—	◎	—
Community Groups	◎	—	—	—	—	—	—
Informal Oversight: Partners in Criminal Justice							
Courts	—	◉	—	—	—	—	—
District Attorneys	—	◉	—	—	—	—	—

◉ = Continual Intense Oversight ◎ = Continual Less Intense Oversight
⟨◉⟩ = Intermittent Intense Oversight ⟨◎⟩ = Intermittent Less Intense Oversight

Figure 3.2. Oversight of the New York City Police Department.

accountability is paying attention to the particular dimension of value. Through this device, one can see that overseers tend to be somewhat specialized in their oversight. Most pay attention primarily to one or two dimensions of performance.

The eye symbols also reflect the intensity and steadiness of the overseer's scrutiny. The darker the eye, the more intense the focus and the pressure. The presence of eyelashes indicates intermittent and flickering attention, while the absence indicates a steady gaze.

The figure gives a relatively clear picture of an authorizing environment, or a system of oversight and accountability, that is fractured and inconsistent. One way to solve this problem is to decide which among the overseers has the greatest legal, moral, or practical capacity to demand accountability and to focus attention on the dimensions of value that are the concerns of the most compelling overseers. A second, quite different way is to try to integrate the diversity of the authorizing environment by including many dimensions of value that are of concern to the varied overseers.

Thus James could have tried to solve his accountability problem by focusing on the terms of accountability that he set with the legislative committee, which, among his large and varied set of other stakeholders and overseers, seemed to have the most legal, moral, and practical power to make a claim on him. But that approach may not have helped all that much because divisions and unresolved conflicts about the important dimensions of value were present even within the legislative committee. In the end James's best bet was to construct a public value account that included many dimensions of value—enough dimensions that he could be reasonably sure at the philosophical level that he had covered most of the bases and would not have too many unintended consequences, and at the political level that he was being responsive to the concerns of most of the key political actors.

Drawing the Line between Policy and Operations in the Public Sector
As suggested in Chapter 2, one issue that frequently arises as legislators and agency managers seek to negotiate terms of accountability is that public managers will often spend a great deal of time trying to draw and enforce a sharp line dividing policy issues (the proper objects of legislative oversight) and operational matters (the responsibility of public managers) in order to resist legislative micromanagement.[6] Despite

the best efforts of public managers, however, this line remains stubbornly fuzzy. This is true in part because the public often assigns intrinsic value to features of the process as well as to the desired result. The public wants to know how fairly the DOR used its legal powers as well as how successfully it collected tax revenues. But even if this were not true, it seems that legislators would still feel free to scrutinize every aspect of agency performance, from the broad and strategic to the anecdotal and mundane. And, in less public settings, legislators often focus on particular, idiosyncratic issues that are important to their key political constituents rather than on improving performance.

Faced with overseers who seem undisciplined in their oversight and uninterested in improving the overall performance of their organizations, public managers often react with less than full cooperation and trust. To protect some degree of professional autonomy and operational control (and professional self-respect), many public managers choose to remain standoffish in their relationship to legislative overseers and tight-lipped in their explanations of operations and results. Indeed, at a basic, human level, James's motivation to transform the terms of accountability and accommodate legislative demands for more accountability seemed to grow out of professional frustration and humiliation at the DOR. As a professional committed to performing well, he hoped to work with professionals on the other side who shared his commitment.

James would quickly recognize the scenario described previously as the "old" system of budgeting and accountability. What was inspiring about this case, however, was that James and his staff did not feel that this system was immutable. It may have been the most likely result of the particular constitutional system that was created, but it was not the inevitable result. James thought he could work with legislators to develop both a new forum and a new form of accountability that would make better use of performance measurement and be more effective in helping the DOR and other public agencies improve their performance and responsiveness to citizens' aspirations. He was convinced that he could influence the procedural and substantive terms of public agency accountability, giving him and other public agencies a chance to manage their organizations more effectively and build the legitimacy and support their organizations needed to create public value.

An Analytic Framework for Diagnosing and Evaluating
Accountability Relationships

To help public managers negotiate appropriate terms of their accountability with legislators and the wider public, it is useful for managers to
have a basic framework in mind for understanding and guiding efforts
to improve the accountability systems under which they labor. That
analytic framework might also serve as a guide to the construction of
the legitimacy and support perspective on their public value scorecard.
This perspective of the scorecard, as explained in Chapter 2, takes managers systematically through the question of their standing with regard
to the many different actors who hold them accountable.

Accountability as a Legal, Moral, and Practical Relationship
Analytically, the concept of accountability describes a relationship between two or more actors.[7] In that relationship, one actor (A) can make
some kind of claim on the conduct of another actor (B). At a minimum,
A can demand that B provide information about B's conduct and performance with respect to A's interests (e.g., the State Departments Division of the House Appropriations Committee can demand from the
Minnesota Department of Revenue an accurate, detailed account of its
activities and performance). But this is usually just a prelude to a more
substantive claim: A asks B to act more responsively with regard to A's
interests (the Division can recommend actions to the DOR that it thinks
will improve the DOR's performance along dimensions that it considers
important).

The accountability relationship is partly rooted in legal structures.
The Minnesota legislative committee could have, as a legal matter, compelled James to appear at public hearings to give an account of what he
did with the public's money and authority. But the relationship was
also rooted in moral ideas about what each actor owed the other. The
Minnesota legislators and James would probably agree that the legislators had a moral right to command James's appearance and testimony.
Both the legislators and the DOR work for the citizens of Minnesota.
James knew that it was a matter of honor and duty for him to act as a
faithful fiduciary of the public's will and long-term interests. He also
thought, however, that the legislators had moral duties attached to
their office—that they should represent the interests of the people and

resist corruption, and that they should have helped him and his agency do the best job they could by clarifying what constituted a good job. Finally, the relationship was rooted in practical concerns. James could have made legislators' lives difficult by frustrating their legitimate inquiries and threatening dramatic decreases in revenue collections when legislators sought to cut his budget—concerns that the legislature had freely expressed. The legislature could have made James's life difficult by increasing oversight burdens, cutting his budget, or reducing his authority to pursue noncompliant taxpayers.

At the outset it might have seemed that the accountability relationship between the legislative committee and James ran only one way, with the legislators making claims on the manager. That was certainly the legal structure of the relationship. But the moral and practical aspects of the relationship suggested that some degree of mutuality also existed. Indeed, the central question in the case concerned the degree to which legislators and agency heads could recognize their interdependence and common goals and act with mutual accountability, as peers sharing responsibility for advancing the public interest through the work of the DOR. They had a formal reason to do so; neither could ignore its fiduciary responsibilities to play its respective roles in carrying out the public's will. But it was also a question of behavioral impact. A respectful forum in which to enact their mutual accountability provided more opportunities to improve the performance of government in general and the DOR in particular. The public, for whom they both worked, wanted public overseers and managers to find ways to outperform adversarial accountability structures and to operate jointly to improve government performance.

Initially, the main terms of the accountability relationship between the DOR and the Division were contained in the budget document—a contract that specified how much money the legislature would supply to the agency and the purposes for which that money could be used. It had a lot of information about inputs and costs, but it said nothing about the public value the agency was supposed to produce. At best, the budget incorporated some workload numbers that measured organizational outputs. But it did not reach out to specify the kind of values that the Minnesota citizens might want to see reflected in client encounters with the DOR—for example, whether the DOR made it relatively easy and convenient for taxpayers to understand and pay their taxes. Nor did the budget document mention the goal of collecting all taxes owed in the interest of both getting money into the state coffers and ensuring that each Minnesota citizen contributed her or his fair share.

This form of accountability did nothing to direct or gain from the skills and talents of DOR employees. Its focus on inputs emphasized the goal of avoiding theft and malfeasance over finding optimal ways to use available assets to accomplish the DOR's goals. It is as though the DOR existed not to achieve results but to spend exactly the amount of money the legislature provided in precisely the categories it agreed to support. Budgetary compliance is a good goal for public agencies insofar as it rewards good planning and offers assurance that no money has been stolen or diverted to unauthorized purposes. But it offers an agency like the DOR no chance to innovate or respond to unanticipated changes in its operating environment, and it gives its workers no real sense that they are creating value for citizens.

The Principal-Agent Model of Accountability

Scholars studying accountability relationships in both economics and political science have explained these relationships in terms of the principal-agent theory.[8] According to this theory, the principal is the actor in the accountability relationship whose purposes are understood to be legally, morally, and practically compelling. The principal, who puts up the capital, has the dominant interests; the agent exists as a means to the principal's ends.

The problem in this accountability relationship is motivating the agent to act in the principal's interest. There are two difficulties.[9] First, the interests of the principal and the agent may not be fully aligned. The principal would like the agent to eat, sleep, and breathe the principal's goals; the agent might have additional interests and priorities. Second, the agent may well have more information than the principal about the technical means available for accomplishing the principal's goal. In fact, this is almost always the case, since the principal likely sought out the agent for his or her superior know-how in the first instance. If the agent has somewhat different goals, and more knowledge about what can be produced, then the agent can act to advance her or his interests at the expense of the principal's, and that represents both a practical and a moral problem from the point of view of the principal.

One solution to this problem is to write a performance contract that brings the incentives into alignment.[10] Principals define their purposes, propose a way of monitoring the degree to which they are being achieved, and offer agents rewards contingent on their performance. Ideally, this kind of contract will motivate agents to find and exploit the best opportunities for advancing their principals' goals, and to deliver most of the value created to principals, taking only the portion established as their fair share in the contract. But if agents create some surplus value and use their discretion to take a bit of the surplus, principals could view that as an acceptable price to pay.

Public policy and management professor Herman "Dutch" Leonard has suggested that all principal-agent relationships consist of at least the following four components:[11]

1. a description of the principal to whom an agent is accountable;
2. a description of the substantive terms of the agent's accountability—the dimensions of value that will count in monitoring and evaluating the agent's performance;
3. the development of specific, objective measures linked to the terms of the agent's accountability that the principal can use to monitor and evaluate the agent's performance; and
4. a set of contingent sanctions that the principal can use to motivate the agent to attend to the principal's interests, and to divide up the benefits and losses that come from good or poor agent performance.

The last three features of Leonard's "accountability regime" can also be seen as the terms of the contract binding the principal with the agent.

This form of accountability recognizes and insists on a significant asymmetry in the relationship between principals and agents. Because principals create the relationship and put up the capital, they have the legal, moral, and practical power to define the purposes of the working relationship and to judge the value of what it produces. Agents have no standing to define the purposes or values of the enterprise. And principals are free to change purposes without seeking their agents' approval or to make unilateral decisions to terminate the relationship with their agents.

For agents—particularly those who entered into relationships with principals not simply for personal gain but because they share their principals' desires to achieve particular social results—this relationship may be unsatisfactory. Principals, for their part, might want a bit of room to take advantage of such an agent's sincere desire to help. If the principal can rely on the agent's loyalty (to either the principal or the principal's purposes), getting good performance from the agent is relatively easy. The burdens of monitoring, creating incentives, and so on fall more lightly on the principal, and the working relationship can become a source of satisfaction and pleasure in achieving a joint task rather than a struggle marked by suspicion and distrust. If, on the other hand, a principal cannot fully trust the agent, then the principal may have to treat the agent as an actor to be subordinated and controlled rather than as a partner in a shared enterprise.[12]

Democratic theory makes particular use of principal-agent theory in the context of government accountability. In the public sector "the public" is the principal to government agencies. The public has the right to say what is worth doing, to review the agency's operations, to decide whether to carry on, and to suggest and encourage improvements.[13] Those who run public agencies are accountable for performance with respect to the public's goals. They are expected to use their talents and energy to find the most efficient and effective means of achieving the results the public has mandated.

The traditional theory of public administration has embraced principal-agent theory.[14] However, the practical difficulty has always been finding some concrete way for the public to become articulate and insistent about what it wants from public agencies.[15] The traditional solution has been to give the task of defining public value to the elected representatives of the people in both the legislative and executive branches of government.[16] The people's representatives are expected to develop coherent policy mandates that define the purposes of public agencies. Agency managers, in turn, are accountable for realizing those purposes efficiently and effectively.

The problem with this clean and simple notion of public-sector accountability is (again) that a single, coherent principal can never be sustained. In fact, using Leonard's conditions for constructing a suitable principal-agent relationship in the public sector, trouble emerges at every point:

- Public agencies are accountable—legally, morally, and practically—to many different actors, not just one, and (again) there is no mechanism that integrates their demands in a coherent whole, and no simple principle for ordering the conflicting demands.
- The substantive terms of their accountability are also numerous, and varied in kind. And there may be necessary trade-offs among competing values.
- For many important dimensions of value, there may be little or no useful information on performance available. Using the few well-developed measures available risks distorting the agency's overall performance because they show only a small number of the potentially valuable dimensions of performance.
- It is not at all clear what sanctions principals can use to motivate public agents when civil service laws designed to protect public managers from inappropriate political influence have made it difficult to hire or fire or even to adjust levels of compensation based on performance. The overseers of public agencies are more likely to increase or decrease overall budgets than adjust managerial salaries in response to performance, but the problem remains that when public agencies fail, budget cuts will likely only make things worse. Thus to experienced public managers the threat of budget cuts often seems idle.[17]

Incomplete Contracts and the Need for Strong Working Relationships

The fact that the conditions for a principal-agent kind of accountability break down relatively quickly in the public sector means that however desirable it might seem in theory, we might not be able to rely on this theory in practice.[18] But there are important reasons we might prefer a different, more mutual form of accountability even if there were no empirical difficulties with the principal-agent form of accountability.

The principal-agent relationship is problematic because it is rooted in a powerful asymmetry between the principal and the agent. The principal is not only the sole arbiter of value but also is the one who is in a position to define the performance-based contract to be written with the agent. It is true that the agent can refuse the contract. But there is a great deal of power that comes from being the principal who can propose the contract on a take-it-or-leave-it basis. The principal-agent theory also assumes divergent rather than convergent interests and is based on distrust and suspicion rather than on trust and mutual confidence. Citizens seeking effective control over unreliable bureaucracies may have to be content with that kind of relationship. But if they are, then the only way the relationship can be managed is through a tight contract.

If contracts could be complete between principals and agents (in the sense that they fully and accurately specified the principal's goals and values, and the conduct of the agent that would best serve them), and if human beings were the rational maximizers these models assume (in the sense that principals understood their goals and values, and agents responded in their own self-interest to the terms of the contract), these arrangements would be fine. The problem is that contracts are never quite complete, and human beings are a bit more complicated psychologically. Principals can never quite control what agents do, and agents have information that principals need—not only about the best means for achieving established goals but perhaps also about opportunities to pursue new or better goals. Agents react to the way in which they are treated and the degree to which they are trusted—sometimes in good faith, and sometimes not. And principals may have limited capacities to reward and punish their agents, and the process of rewarding and punishing may unleash all kinds of unexpected consequences. Finally, if working relationships remain locked in contractual language, some significant opportunities for additional value creation might be lost.

The implication of these observations is that while principal-agent forms of accountability can work to guarantee one level of production through the working relationship, there might be another form of accountability that could, under certain circumstances, outperform this kind of accountability. We could call that form of accountability "mutual accountability for achieving a common goal." This kind of accountability would make a less sharp distinction between the principal (the people and their elected representatives) and the agents (the public agency). In this conception legislative overseers and public agencies would be jointly and severally responsible for accomplishing important public purposes. The public would recognize the capacity of those in both the legislative and executive branches to nominate ideas about what the public purposes might be, and what priority they might be given, and to search for a more efficient and effective means for accomplishing the desired result. To many, this might represent an elevation of the status of the public agency and a degradation of the status of the public and its representatives, and this might sound both inappropriate and dangerous. But it seems as though this is the kind of relationship that the DOR is trying to create, and what it is offering in exchange for this change in its standing is increased transparency, increased focus on cost control, and improved performance over the long run. As Armajani insists: "We all work for the same people—the citizens of Minnesota."

Groping toward Improvement

The abstract ideal of a regime of mutual accountability that structures relationships among citizens, their elected representatives, and public executives through a shared commitment to a public value account that focuses public agencies on goals and purposes (that managers and overseers alike acknowledge are important) gives us a picture of the target we would like to hit. But it also reveals just how far the reality is from the ideal. Instead of a coherent principal, we have a divided principal. Instead of a consistent set of well-developed, commensurable performance measures, we have bits and pieces of partially developed ideas that are hard to compare. Instead of contingent sanctions reliably connected to performance, we have weak sanctions disconnected from performance. Instead of respectful forums in which principals and agents can meet in good faith to deal with the incompleteness of the contracts that structure their relationships, we have encounters in which the principals seem more interested in shaming the agents than in helping them perform well.

Progress probably does not lie in trying to overhaul the structure of accountability. The problem of multiple principals, each with its own ideas of public value, is constitutionally cemented in the formal structures of democratic government. But in order to bridge the gap between the real and the ideal, overseers and managers could begin rethinking and experimenting with the practices that they use to manage their encounters with one another.

Diagnosing the Authorizing Environment

Public managers can begin this work by performing an "inventory" of their political authorizing environment. As the research that my colleagues and I carried out on the overseers of public policing showed, delving into organizational files and media archives can reveal those who have called the agency to account for its actions and results in the past, the nature of their claims, and the particular dimensions of value on which they focused. With that information, managers can draw a picture similar to the one we developed for the police for their own agencies (see Figure 3.2). While it might seem unnecessary to go through this simple historical analysis, there are three compelling reasons to do so as part of the legitimacy and support perspective of the public value scorecard.

The Authorizing Environment Explains Current Performance. First, a historical understanding of the pressures that have operated on a public agency will help managers understand current performance. Organizations, like most things, adapt to their external environments. Over time, their performance tends to reflect the demands made on them. Thus the observed performance of a given agency probably reflects the balance of external actors making value claims on it.

When a new force shows up in the authorizing environment— when a constituency capable of making a legally, practically, or morally compelling claim on a public agency nominates a new value for consideration in operations, or emphasizes an old value that has fallen off the radar screen—it upsets the existing balance of pressures. If that new force has sufficient intensity and staying power, it alters the performance of the agency. If the new force is weak, or short-lived, it falls under the implacable force of the usual demands for performance and accountability.

A Normative Evaluation of the Current Authorizing Environment. Second, a close look at the structure of accountability affords public managers and other interested parties an opportunity to reflect on the quality of the accountability structure—whether it has the power to confer legitimacy on the agency's operations and to keep it focused on creating public value. The quality of the existing accountability structure can be evaluated against at least two different standards.

First, there is a procedural question about the degree to which those with legitimate interests in the agency's operations have been consulted in the process of establishing the accountability structure.[19]

If some constituencies are neglected and/or others seem to have a disproportionate role, it stands to reason that a more balanced representation of those with interests in the agency's performance could improve the responsiveness and legitimacy of the agency's operations.[20]

There is also a substantive question about the degree to which the accountability system acknowledges and defends particular dimensions of value, and whether that is adequate.[21] In James's case, if there is no one in the authorizing environment concerned about controlling costs, pursuing tax delinquents, the fairness of DOR operations, or the respect that the DOR shows for individual rights, then one might conclude that the DOR's accountability structure is substantively unbalanced and therefore diminishes its responsiveness and legitimacy.[22]

Imagining a Different and More Legitimate Authorizing Environment. This observation leads to the third and most important reason to undertake a detailed analysis of the demand for accountability—namely, that public managers can use their detailed knowledge of the authorizing environment to manage their agencies better. If managers want to pursue a neglected or underemphasized dimension of value, they can improve production along that dimension of value by developing (1) a performance measure for it and (2) a constituency interested in monitoring performance with regard to this dimension of value. We have observed that managers cannot run their organizations very well if they do not embrace external accountability for improved performance, but managers can also help shape the external demands for performance—not just by nominating a particular dimension of value to measure but also by recognizing and mobilizing a latent political constituency interested in advancing it. In effect, they can create a force for innovation and improvement on a particular dimension of value by advertising their agency's performance in that area to an interested outside party.

A similar opportunity exists in noticing an underrepresented voice in the authorizing environment (rather than a neglected dimension of value). Mayor Williams's effort to orchestrate a discussion about strategic objectives for Washington, D.C., with citizens of the District was essentially a bid to reconstitute the accountability structure he faced. Including new voices in a discussion about public purposes may make a public manager aware of new dimensions of value worth producing, or may bring a new emphasis to a neglected dimension of value. But even if no new values emerge, the consultation has the potential to increase the overall legitimacy and support that a public manager enjoys. To the extent that a wave of public support lifts morale, stimulates imagination, and helps mobilize citizens to assist a public agency in reaching its goals, a move to include new voices can dramatically improve performance.

Diagnosing the Complexity and Dynamism of the Authorizing Environment
A detailed empirical analysis of one's authorizing environment also helps managers gauge how complex and dynamic that environment actually is. Getting some clarity about how the accountability structure has been arrayed in the past helps managers make predictions about the future. Additionally, it helps them figure out ways to accommodate and manage the system that is demanding accountability from them.

The Complexity of the Authorizing Environment. Two key findings reveal the complexity of the authorizing environment. The first is the total number of different dimensions of value that interest the authorizers. The more dimensions of value involved, the more complex the authorizing environment. James's authorizing environment would have been much simpler and more coherent if the only thing anybody had wanted him to do was to collect taxes. As soon as he had to account for client satisfaction and reducing costs as well, his authorizing environment became more complex (as did the public value account that he needed to create to respond to the concerns of his environment).

The second key finding is the degree to which the interests of the existing authorizers are highly specialized and differentiated. Imagine two different worlds. In world one are three authorizers, each paying attention to one dimension of James's performance as though that were the only dimension that mattered. In world two are three authorizers, each paying attention to all three dimensions of agency performance. The problem with world one is that those calling James to account might not realize that the value they hold dear might have to be traded against competing values. World two is preferable, since it makes it easier for James to encourage a conversation among his overseers, and to accept a common responsibility for achieving all three dimensions of value.

Whether overseers are willing to stop insisting on their one-dimensional concerns as a full representation of agency performance is a critical matter for James. If they can, James has a chance to construct a coherent mandate for his organization. If they cannot, James and his agency will remain vulnerable to partial attacks masquerading as general attacks on the agency's performance.

The Dynamism of the Authorizing Environment. The authorizing environment's complexity reflects the number and variety of actors and interests at play; its dynamism is about the frequency and speed with which the demands for accountability change.

Sometimes, as social and political conditions change, dimensions of public value have to be added to or subtracted from the total dimensions of value that matter to actors in the authorizing environment, and that managers might hope to capture in a public account. For example, for many years police agencies neglected concerns about reducing fear and providing quality services to crime victims. Eventually, as police came to the shocking realization that more money was being spent on private security than on public police, and that there were more private security guards than there were police officers, these concerns got put on the agenda for evaluation.[23] Similarly, concerns about police corruption tend to appear and disappear from the accounting for police performance in twenty-year intervals.[24]

Other times the emphasis or priority that the authorizing environment gives to established dimensions of value shifts, and public managers have to be prepared to adjust the accounting scheme accordingly. For example, as the elected officials of Minnesota became preoccupied with controlling the overall costs of state government, the DOR had to find ways to reduce its costs—even if that reduced its performance in collecting taxes.

The institutions of government establish a stable of overseers in official oversight offices, but the incumbents of these offices change. And there is even more dynamism in the many self-appointed accountability agents who appear and disappear in the authorizing environment. Any citizen or group can make an issue of some aspect of an agency's performance at any time.

A "Deep Structure" of Accountability? While the ideal of a simple and stable structure of accountability contrasts starkly with the reality of public-sector accountability, the appearance of constant change may also be a bit deceptive. Stepping back and taking a slightly longer view, a public manager might uncover a hidden and stable core. Perhaps there is a deep, unchanging structure of public value governing the performance of a given public agency.[25] In the case of police performance, for example, a review of the accountability structures in several cities over time revealed that the dimensions of police performance that become the focus of public evaluations remain relatively limited and constant. Only occasionally were new values introduced into the evaluation of police operations.[26]

Much more common were changes in the relative emphasis given to the various dimensions of police performance. When the NYPD was intensely focused on controlling corruption, it did not stop feeling accountable for reducing crime and holding offenders accountable. It was just that, at the margin, the relative importance of reducing corruption went up.[27] When the NYPD was focused on reducing crime and disorder, it did not stop being accountable for minimizing the use of force and acting lawfully and fairly when intruding into the private lives of citizens, but again, the relative importance of these goals shifted.[28]

These changes may correspond to shifts in political sentiment and aspiration, or to changes in the objective conditions in which citizens live. They may be progressive (the authorizing environment's focus moves in a predictable direction from less important dimensions of value to more important dimensions of value) or cyclical (an emphasis on one value is replaced by an emphasis on a second value, only to be replaced once again by an emphasis on the first value). But however often the emphasis on the different values changes, the full set of values used to evaluate an agency's performance may not change much over time. A responsible public manager could ignore the occasional flaps and focus instead on continuously improving performance on those core values that an empirical analysis of the demands for accountability reveals.

If there is a deep structure of accountability that defines the enduring values at stake in a given agency's operations, that is good news for those who want to build public value accounts and focusing public agencies on the value they produce. They could simply build those accounts around the enduring values. At any given moment, one value or another might be highlighted on the public value account but rarely would a wholly new value appear. A strategy-oriented manager might even be able to use the account to guard against swings in public attention that treat a single dimension of value as though it were the only thing that mattered. In effect, a public value account could provide a more consistent, comprehensive anchor to everyone's understanding of the mix of values to be produced.[29]

If the diagnosis of the authorizing environment does reveal a highly complex and volatile authorizing environment, that diagnosis can help managers think strategically about how to harmonize conflicting demands and respond appropriately to volatility.

Responding to Complexity in the Authorizing Environment

If multiple authorizers call public managers to account for multiple dimensions of value, managers face a serious problem in trying to harmonize performance expectations in a single public value account, and an even bigger problem in keeping a lid on the total number of dimensions of public value that they would have to recognize. A basic premise in the development and use of performance measures is that too many measures will diminish their ability to focus organizational effort and work. The ideal, of course, is to have a single "bottom-line" measure, but we have long ago left that particular dream aside. So the important question is, what should managers do when they cannot rely on a single measure of financial performance and have to rely instead on empirical, quantitative measures that capture levels of performance with respect to many different and incommensurate dimensions of value?

A Social Utility Function. There is a simple technical answer to this problem. If a manager is trying to improve performance on multiple dimensions of value, then, in principle, the manager (in consultation with overseers) could construct a "social welfare function" specifying the particular weight to be given to each value relative to all the other values.[30] This makes incommensurate, hard-to-quantify values commensurable by specifying the rate at which we would be willing to trade gains on one value for losses on another value, for example, the Minnesota legislature telling James at what rate they would be willing to spend more money and accept more citizen complaints in exchange for increased revenue collections.

In the book *Unlocking Public Value*, the Accenture Institute for Public Service Value suggests weighting outcome-related performance measures in order to clarify strategic priorities.[31] As priorities shift over time, the weights shift also, and the idea is that this process makes it possible "to aggregate the metrics data into a type of 'total outcome score'"—an approximation of the ever-elusive "bottom line" for a public agency's performance.[32]

In practice, of course, it is virtually impossible for a political system to produce a clear social utility function. Even the architects of the detailed weighting and filtering processes described in *Unlocking Public Value* acknowledge that "the thinking and deliberation that the weighting process provokes" is more important than arriving at the "total outcome score."[33] So citizens and public managers alike are left with no satisfactory way to sum up the overall performance of a given public agency or unit of government, and no way to resolve questions about trade-offs among the tangle of incommensurable values. This might seem to preclude any consistent, reliable method for managing the production of public value. But if we could get used to managing public agencies with multiple dimensions of value—if we could agree to name all the important values and take them seriously—maybe our ability to recognize and manage the creation of public value would improve.

Working with Multiple Values. A second possible answer, which might seem bizarre at the outset, would be for public managers to take the stance that they would allow any dimension of value nominated for attention by any democratic overseer into their public value account. This sounds crazy to public managers who do not want to be overwhelmed by diverse measures of performance.[34] It sounds crazy even to most overseers, since a large number of measures could become a screen for public managers to hide behind. But the idea that public managers should simply say yes to any particular dimension of value nominated by actors in their authorizing environment has some merit.

First, at a minimum, the willingness to embrace any demand for accountability sends a strong message that the manager wants to be accountable and responsive. In agreeing to track a particular value, a manager can attract the support of those who value it, and whatever legitimacy they happen to possess then attaches to the manager's commitments. Saying yes to legislative oversight committees that have the legal, moral, and practical power to make claims on public managers may be not only valuable but necessary. Choosing to say yes to the demands of others in the authorizing environment depends on the relative legal, moral, and practical power of those actors and the claims they make. Sometimes the effort required to meet a demand for accountability is less than the effort that would otherwise be spent on defending oneself against it or resisting it.

Second, committing to measuring any dimension of value nominated by the authorizing environment forces public managers to be creative in searching for useful and convenient metrics. In the course of searching they learn what information their agencies currently collect and begin to consider how that information might be arranged in reports that could meet the demand for accountability.[35]

Third, by accepting accountability for all nominated dimensions of value, managers could help shift the discussion away from whether they were "accountable" in a sweeping sense and toward the more interesting question of which dimensions of value they should be accountable for. Legislative overseers often score easy political points by complaining about the general "lack of accountability" in public agencies. While this makes hay for the politicians, it does not help public managers improve their agencies' performance. If public managers responded to these criticisms by asking what new dimension of value they should be producing and measuring, the public dialogue might shift from procedural concerns about levels of accountability to substantive concerns about the values at stake.

Fourth, public managers can use this kind of radical accountability to both contain and reveal the political conflicts that prevent a useful structure of accountability. For a political faction seeking to increase revenue collections and willing to spend additional funds on the DOR to get them, revenue collections are the right measure of public value production. For another political faction, seeking to minimize government expenditures and reduce both the costs of tax collection and the revenues claimed, minimizing costs at the DOR is the key value. These factions are free to insist that the process of evaluation be simple, and that it focus primarily on overall revenue collected, on one hand, or overall costs and budgetary compliance, on the other. But if the DOR and its overseers listed all the values of interest to all the different political factions, both authorizers and managers could see more accurately what could be produced, and what is at stake in the DOR's operations. The political conflict can be revealed in the public value account that enumerates the values held dear by each faction and forces the different factions to either acknowledge or reject the importance of the values.[36]

Finally, a necessary condition for normatively compelling and practically useful public accountability is that the dimensions of value for which public managers are held accountable be those that the public deems important. If there are multiple dimensions of value, the accounting system has to accommodate that fact. We cannot shrink the number of values deemed important without losing the connection to the public that would give a public value account legitimacy and behavioral power in guiding public agencies.

There is an understandable preference for a simple bottom line over multiple indicators. But, again, well-run businesses do not rely exclusively on a single bottom line.[37] Business executives live in a "data-rich" environment consisting of information about costs, processes, outputs (quantity and quality), customers, and many other features of their operating environment.[38] This data bank supports diagnosis and learning. While having an array of outcome measures in place of a financial bottom line makes public management a more complex challenge than corporate management, the fact that the best-managed corporations rely on myriad measures of both internal operations and their external operating environment to guide the execution of a value-creating strategy leaves no particular reason to believe that creating an equally data-rich environment for public managers would undermine their focus and efficacy.

Searching for the Production Possibility Frontier. Critics may also object that there are always trade-offs between values—that in order for a police department to succeed in controlling crime it must use its authority more aggressively, or that a revenue department can only increase revenue collections by spending more money on enforcement. Such trade-offs may exist, and a public manager can look to the authorizing environment for some guidance about which value should be emphasized over the other at a particular time. But public managers cannot really be sure they face such trade-offs until they have explored all the possibilities in trying to produce all of the valued results.

In economic theory the "production possibility frontier" is the set of points representing the best anyone can do with existing resources when trying to produce two or more values (e.g., reducing crime and protecting liberty, or assisting taxpayers and chasing tax evaders).[39] Presumably, these values can be produced in many different combinations, but the points along the production possibility frontier represent the maximum value that can be produced with the given resources. At the frontier there is a choice: Which value is worth pursuing at the other's expense? But public agencies do not have to answer that question if their performance lies somewhere inside the production possibility frontier. Inside the frontier it is technically possible to produce more of both values. Of course, public agencies generally do not know where they stand with respect to the production possibility frontier. The only way to find out is to try different methods and observe the results.[40]

Political discourse often implies, even insists, that we citizens face painful trade-offs, but there is no particular reason to believe that our public agencies are close to the production possibility frontier.[41] Indeed, it seems extremely unlikely that most public agencies operate anywhere near their production possibility frontier.

In the private sector relentless competition and active shareholders and boards scouring organizations for any small increment of value creation may push productivity out to the frontier.[42] But even under these conditions, private-sector organizations often operate well inside the production possibility frontier. Public agencies, which do not face much competition and have far fewer motivations to make value-creating innovations, are even less likely to be on the production possibility frontier. Public managers can probably assume that it is possible to improve organizational performance simultaneously on many different dimensions until hard, documented experience tells them that they are wrong. They should not assume that they face "tough choices" before exploring their options. The real challenge of managing performance in the public sector may not be making value judgments but finding the energy and authorization to search for, experiment with, and exploit innovations that can improve overall performance.[43]

In the unlikely case that a public agency is on the production possibility frontier with respect to all the values it seeks to produce and needs some guidance about which values currently deserve more or less emphasis, a full set of measures showing value creation with respect to the values at stake in its operations could help facilitate that tough political conversation. But when a public agency looks to the authorizing environment for a value judgment, the political process often devolves into a shouting match. Politicians grab hold of their favored value and insist on its primacy without discussing the degree to which losses will register elsewhere. Keeping all the relevant values in the public discussion can help those in the authorizing environment understand that they are making an incremental adjustment in the relative importance of competing values.[44] Political sound bites may demand fidelity to one value, but the pursuit of (net) public value requires cognizance of all.

The problem with orchestrating this deliberation about the various dimensions of performance that matter to a given agency's conception of public value is that it takes a lot of time and political skill. And even with time and skill, one still may have to hope against hope that the political environment is willing to be disciplined and focused in its deliberations. It is not at all clear that even the best public managers can summon the requisite time, skill, and political wherewithal at any one moment, let alone all the time. But if demands for accountability persist, it is probably worth the effort. To achieve what is doable, one may have to act unilaterally and contrary to conventional wisdom and practices. James and his deputies at the DOR have shown what these efforts might look like, warts and all.

Responding to the Dynamics of the Authorizing Environment
Responding to the complexity of the authorizing environment is only part of the challenge facing public managers. The dynamism of the authorizing environment—the fact that both the actors demanding accountability and the dimensions of performance they value change over time—creates an even greater challenge: How can public managers negotiate the terms of their accountability with a diverse authorizing environment that will not hold still?

Accommodating or Resisting Changes in the Authorizing Environment. Public managers can and should make conscious strategic decisions to resist or integrate new demands for accountability. The natural reaction is to resist. At a minimum, new demands mean more reports. But the new demands could also entail new data-collecting and reporting systems, or (worse) reviewing operations in light of the new demands for accountability.[45] Given the yawning scope of this work, the temptation is to treat demands for accountability on new and unaccustomed dimensions of performance as inappropriate claims that come too late and out of left field. Thus the NYPD found it difficult to adapt to the demand that it use force and authority more economically and fairly while reducing crime successfully. And thus even though James anticipated the demand for cost reduction, he still made the case that increasing spending on the DOR would increase revenues for the state.

However, to repeat a point made earlier, rather than resist new demands reflexively, managers could consider the legal, moral, and practical basis of the new demand and make a strategic judgment about how, and how much, to respond. If the newly nominated dimension of value threatens to carry the agency away from its established strategy, managers and overseers might choose to stiff-arm the new demand as an unwanted distraction. If, however, the new demand is consistent with the strategic direction that the agency is pursuing, managers and overseers might welcome it as an aid to their efforts, using the leverage that comes from this new demand for accountability to amplify their efforts to improve agency operations. Both Bratton and James made this strategic response to particular performance demands—Bratton by treating police corruption as a crime on par with murder, rape, and robbery and James by creating the invest/divest process.

Developing a Constituency for a Neglected Dimension of Value. Public managers can also exploit the complexity and dynamism of their authorizing environment to mobilize constituencies that can help them pursue particular values. With a comprehensive list of the values at stake in their agencies' operations, managers might well discover that there are values on the list that concern no one in their current authorizing environment. If their organization is not doing particularly well with respect to producing these neglected values, the observed vacuum of attention might explain why. But this vacuum could also identify a strategically useful piece of political work for managers to undertake. If, from a philosophical point of view, there is an important dimension of public value going unnoticed among political authorizers, then a strategic public manager could nominate that dimension of value for attention and develop the means for measuring its attainment in hopes of creating a constituency focused on the pursuit of that value. This might fill the political vacuum and round out the perception of public value.

These ideas about how to deal with the complexity and dynamism of the authorizing environment suggest that public managers need not be hostage to the bewildering twists and turns of that world. In fact, both the complexity and the changeability of their political oversight provide important opportunities for strategic leadership. Public managers might be able to help the public (and its many official and unofficial representatives) articulate its aspirations and desires, as James tried to do, through seeking to negotiate terms of accountability. If managers were to enter their authorizing environments with an open mind, listen closely to the conversation, note the ideas about the dimensions of public value that seem to be at stake in the public mind, and simply feed that information back to the authorizing environment in a proposed public value account, perhaps that would help overseers converge on a particular set of dimensions to be included in a complete public value account. And, to the degree that public managers see gaps in the authorizing environment that surrounds them—important dimensions of value going unrecognized, stakeholder voices lost in the din—they can make an effort to correct the problem by nominating neglected values for attention, or amplifying underrepresented voices. Such actions are not inconsistent with democratic governance. On the contrary, they strengthen the quality of the democratic process that is guiding the agency toward public value production.

Using Public Value Propositions to Engage and Manage the Authorizing Environment

Whether public managers respond to the authorizing environment as it develops autonomously or try to influence its shape, a public value proposition that names the set of values to be advanced through the work of the agency can be a powerful tool in organizing its political oversight and accountability. As noted in Chapter 2, making the effort to name and measure progress toward a particular set of values helps force a discussion within the authorizing environment about how to define value-creating performance. If public managers engage elements of the authorizing environment with a concrete proposal specifying the terms in which they would like to be held accountable, they get two valuable results.

First, they demonstrate a commitment to accountability consistent with their fiduciary responsibilities. They are aligning themselves with the following principles:

- embracing rather than avoiding accountability;
- fully accepting a fiduciary responsibility to the public;
- making accountability as easy and as effective as possible through thoughtful performance measurement; and
- doing everything possible to produce desired results for the public with the public assets dedicated to producing those results.

Taking such a stance automatically increases the legitimacy and support that public managers can enjoy from their authorizing environment.

Second, the public value proposition forces a substantive conversation among overseers about what the public really wants from a given agency. They have to decide whether to accept or reject the public value proposition. If they do not like it, the public value account compels them to say in what particulars they disagree and allows them to suggest changes. They might also have to recognize their different perspectives on the relative importance of those values and be encouraged to face one another and begin resolving the conflicts among themselves rather than pushing them onto the public manager. All of this might help forge a more coherent understanding and agreement among overseers and between overseers and managers.

Finally, a well-crafted public value account might succeed in getting the authorizing environment to stick with its thorough conception of public value—at least for a time. If overseers (in both executive and legislative positions) commit to a particular public value proposition, managers might have a rare opportunity to work on advancing those values (and to chart their successes and failures in a public value account) without worrying that a sudden shift in the demands for accountability coming from their political authorizers will undermine their efforts.

Incentives for Performance and Cost Control
One serious problem identified early in the Minnesota case remained both unresolved and largely unaddressed at the end of the case—namely, how the legislature could create incentives for improving managerial performance through the budget process. As noted, public agencies and those who manage them often face perverse incentives: if they are failing to produce desired results, managers and their organizations often get more money so that they can meet the need left by their (apparently)

poor performance. When they hit their objectives, resources are often diverted elsewhere to areas of greater need despite their (apparently) good performance. This troublesome pattern follows from the idea that public dollars should flow to need (measured in terms of some gap between desired and actual social conditions) rather than to accomplishment of desired objectives. If a school fails, it is hard to reduce its budget without injuring already disadvantaged students still further. Conversely, when a school succeeds, it is hard to increase its budget without increasing inequality in outcomes. Thus (apparently) poor performance gets rewarded with more funding, and (apparently) good performance gets punished with less.

This certainly seems like a serious problem if the legislature is trying to motivate managers to improve their performance through resource allocations. But the legislature can solve this problem by separating rewards and sanctions for individual managers from budgeting processes and being more specific about what it wants from the managers—even when all it wants is cost reduction (while maintaining as much valuable output as possible).

In most public personnel systems, managerial salaries are tied to the size of the agency the managers lead. This, along with the fact that it is always easier to maintain staff morale and ensure cooperation with a rising budget than a falling one, causes many public managers to believe that their goal is to increase the resources granted to their agencies.[46] If the legislature changed these common practices and rewarded public managers not by increasing budgets but by raising salaries based on success in achieving valued results while improving cost-effectiveness, and/or reducing total costs, managers would likely respond with productivity gains.[47]

Rewarding managers for increasing productivity in current activities and/or reducing costs by shedding unproductive activities is, of course, a common practice in the private sector. In Jack Welch's General Electric, for example, managers were handsomely rewarded not only for building a high-performing division but also for liquidating or selling their poorly performing divisions.[48] Rather than suffer the same fate as their employees, they got promotions for saving company money and freeing up resources for more profitable investments.

In the public sector, however, managers tend to rise or fall with the fate of their organizations. This causes them to identify too closely with the "success" (i.e., growth) of the agencies they lead.[49] To deal with this dilemma, legislatures could instead reward public managers for improving performance even as they reduce funding to the agencies they lead, and punish managers for bad performance even as they provide additional resources to a failing agency to keep it afloat while they look for a better manager.

Because cost control is one of the most important areas of managerial performance, the reward system must take costs into account. Often the public thinks about public agencies' performance in terms of whether they do or do not produce the desired results. We look at the right-hand side of the public value account (where valued results register) rather than the left-hand side (where costs are incurred.) We often assume that budgeting processes that limit spending on public agencies will keep costs under control and compel public managers to maximize publicly valued output subject to constraints on public spending (and the use of public authority).

But sometimes the public focuses intense attention on the left side of the public value account and demands real cost reductions, not just cost restraint. Sometimes it does so as a matter of ideology—a belief that a smaller government will produce a better and more just society. These concerns can become particularly compelling in times of growing government deficits. In such times the public and its elected representatives often demand that officials minimize cost while meeting a certain (perhaps lowered) standard of performance. They may even demand reductions in cost without worrying too much about what happens to performance—judging the cost reduction objective to be more important than the level of government output. In these times cost reduction can seem to be a publicly valuable result in itself.

In principle, of course, we should consistently call public managers to account for both cost reduction and the achievement of desired results. Indeed, what we should want public managers to do is constantly explore the possibility of increasing valuable results even as they reduce costs—in effect, to be searching for the production possibility frontier in order to allow us to make better judgments about both what is worth doing and how to allocate resources among different government activities. In reality, however, we often fail to make public managers feel accountable for cost control and the need to reassert the public's interest in controlling costs—in individual activities to achieve productivity gains as well as across the board to keep costs in some prudent relationship to revenues.

This is almost impossible to do when the government managers identify very closely with their organizations and are committed to producing given levels of output regardless of cost. It is easier, but still hard, when the managers' fates have been separated from those of their organizations, and when the authorizing environment has emphasized cost reduction as an important form of public value creation. In constructing incentives for managers, then, it is crucial that we remain attentive to costs as well as the relevant dimensions of public value. It is important that rewards and sanctions be tied to managers' success in improving the performance of their agencies or divisions (given the conditions they face), and it is important to recognize cost reduction as a valuable goal—whether for purposes of achieving productivity gains or keeping the government within responsible fiscal limits and preserving as much freedom for individual choice and liberty as possible.

Summary

James, like all public managers, faced the usual demands for accountability that emerge from the swirling politics of the authorizing environment. Unlike most public managers, however, he joined Bratton and Williams in embracing rather than resisting the general demand for accountability. In doing so he hoped to find not only increased legitimacy and support for his agency but also a vital source of energy he could use to drive his organization toward improved performance—even if that improved performance included overall cost reduction as an important dimension of public value creation.

But James's efforts went beyond Bratton's. He sought to engage his key political authorizers in a serious discussion about the important values to be produced by his organization, how they would be measured, and how he could otherwise meet executive, legislative, and wider public demands for performance and accountability. Two years of effort in wooing the legislative committee did seem to increase the respect and trust between the agency and its legislative overseers. And it brought them tantalizingly close to reaching an agreement about the terms in which the agency could be called to account.

To see how close they were, Table 3.2 presents the dimensions of value that each side nominated as terms they considered appropriate to use in calling the DOR to account and evaluating its performance, and

Table 3.2. A comparison of the dimensions of public value nominated by the DOR and the legislative committee.

Legislators' dimensions of value	The DOR's dimensions of value
Legitimacy and Support	
Be sensitive to the political process.	Citizens and their elected representatives are confident in the integrity of the tax system and the DOR.
Provide equal access to information for all legislators.	
Follow not just the letter, but the intent of legislative directives.	State and local revenue policies are congruent with the DOR's mission.
Develop a sound tax policy based on consistency, honesty, and fairness.	
Seek input from local governments and tax experts.	
Public Value	
Lower the percent of uncollected taxes.	There is compliance with the tax laws.
Identify which types of income are not being reported.	
There are no complaints from taxpayers.	
Operational Capacity	
At what point do increased resources = diminishing returns?	The Revenue organization is prepared to carry out its mission and strategies, and its employees are fulfilled through their work.
Organize the department as efficiently as possible.	
Relate program evaluation to the budget process.	The DOR is effective and efficient in using its resources to achieve these outcomes.
Answer telephones with accurate information.	Internal DOR "customers" of departmental overhead units (e.g., human resources, information technology) are satisfied with the services of those internal units.
	Transactions are processed with speed and accuracy.
	Taxpayers and employees have the information they need when they need it.

PUBLIC VALUE ACCOUNT for John James and the Minnesota DOR

PUBLIC VALUE ACCOUNT	
Use of Collectively Owned Assets and Associated Costs	Achievement of Collectively Valued Social Outcomes
Financial Costs	Mission Achievement
Internal (administrative costs)	Collect taxes owed to state
External (tax preparation costs to citizens)	Provide advice to policy makers
Unpaid revenues owed to the state	
Unintended Negative Consequences	Unintended Positive Consequences
Distortion of efficient production and consumption (deadweight loss)	Encouragement of socially constructive activity
	Client Satisfaction
	Provide accurate information
	Facilitate compliance
	Reconcile taxpayers to tax burdens
Social Costs of Using State Authority	Justice and Fairness
Intrusiveness of government	Protect individual rights
Perceived abuses, injustices in tax collection	Impose aggregate burdens fairly

Figure 3.3. Public value scorecard for John James and the Minnesota DOR.

THE LEGITIMACY AND SUPPORT PERSPECTIVE
Progress and Planning for John James and the Minnesota DOR

Mission Alignment with Values Articulated by Citizens:

Build citizens' trust in fairness of taxpaying system

Standing with Formal Authorizers:

Elected Executives
- Maintained governor's support

Elected Legislators
- Strengthened relationship with House subcommittee
- *Provide more reliable, accurate, and continuous reports on performance and problems*
- *Secure support from subcommittee in Senate*

Other Levels of Government
- *Seek input from local governments*
- *Ensure that state and local revenue policies are congruent with mission*

Standing with Key Interest Groups:

Develop relationships with tax accountants and preparers

Media Coverage:

Review media coverage to identify values and challenges

Standing with Individuals in Polity:

General Citizenry
- *Survey citizen attitudes towards taxes and taxpaying*
- *Initiate public information campaign about taxpaying*

Taxpayers/Clients
- *Survey clients about experience and satisfaction*

Position of Enterprise in Democratic Political Discourse:

Distinguish efficient, fair, responsive tax collection from tax burden

Engagement of Citizens as Co-Producers:

Help citizens meet obligations

THE OPERATIONAL CAPACITY PERSPECTIVE
Progress and Planning for John James and the Minnesota DOR

Flow of Resources to Enterprise:

Financial Revenues
- Secured budget increase recommendation from House subcommittee
- *Secure support from Senate subcommittee*

Public Support/Popular Opinion
- *Build capacity for surveys and marketing efforts*

Human Resources:

Workforce
- *Survey employees to gauge satisfaction/fulfillment*
- *Strengthen working relationships between departmental overhead units and operations units*

Performance Measurement Systems for Individual Accountability
- Initiated "invest/divest" to focus midlevel managers on efficiency and cost-effectiveness

Operational Policies, Programs, and Procedures:

Organizational Learning
- *Develop methods for estimating unpaid taxes*
- *Devise and test methods of improving tax collections*
- *Develop methods of calculating likely returns of operational innovations*
- *Relate program evaluation to the budget process*

Internal Resource Allocation
- Initiated "invest/divest" to improve resource allocation
- *Increase spending on support to reliable taxpayers?*

Performance Measurement and Management Systems
- *Develop Compstat-like system for tax collections relative to owed*
- *Develop systems for surveying general citizenry*
- *Develop systems for surveying client experiences*

Organizational Outputs:

Quality of Outputs
- Ensure accessibility and accuracy of information provided to taxpayers
- Ensure courtesy, speed, and accuracy in client transactions
- Maintain consistency in client treatment

organizes them in terms of the three points of the strategic triangle, introduced in Chapter 2. There are differences between the legislators' views and the agency's views. Predictably enough, the legislators place a lot of emphasis on being responsive to politics and politicians and their concerns; the agency focuses more attention on its mission and operations. Interestingly, the politicians offer more specifics in describing the public value they want the agency to produce than the agency does. And neither side emphasizes cost reduction as an important goal, even though concerns about cost reduction were a critical part of the general political context at the time, and a central concern on both sides of the relationship.

Table 3.2 reveals another interesting aspect of the accountability relationship. Even though the conversation was ostensibly about the value that the DOR could produce, only some of the nominated concerns would naturally fit into a public value account. Many of the concerns of both legislators and the agency fit more neatly into the other parts of a public value scorecard. There are concerns about processes that would be measured in the operational capacity perspective. (For example, the DOR's focus on the idea that "The Revenue Organization is prepared to carry out its mission and strategies, and its employees are fulfilled in their work," and the committee's focus on "relating program evaluation to the budget process.") And there are concerns about issues that seem to belong in the legitimacy and support perspective. (For example, the DOR's focus on ensuring that "citizens and their elected representatives are confident in the integrity of the tax system and the DOR," and the committee's desire to ensure that the DOR would be "sensitive to the political process" and "follow not just the letter but the intent of legislative directives.")

These values come into the DOR's terms of accountability to the legislature partly because they are understood by the legislature and the agency to be instrumentally valuable in producing ultimately valued results; but it also seems that at least some of the concerns that would appear in the legitimacy and support and operational capacity perspectives are on the list because both the agency and the legislators thought they had intrinsic value. This means that some of those values might be measured in the public value account as well. (See Figure 3.3 for an idea of how a public value scorecard might encompass the parties' concerns.)

Unfortunately it seems that on the verge of making a serious agreement on what was, in effect, the outline of both a public value account and a public value scorecard for the DOR, they backed away. The terms that they agreed to in the last moments of the meeting were less complete, comprehensive, and compelling than the sum of each party's nominated terms of accountability that were previously on the table. It is as though, after having done all the work and seen the possibility of a binding agreement, they could not quite bring themselves to make the commitment. The legislators did not, in the end, want to be disciplined by this agreement and give up their right to raise whatever issues they wanted to raise. The DOR managers were again left with their worries about whether they would be able to make the improvements they wanted to make, and how they would be treated if they failed to produce. Right there at the brink, the deal collapsed. The structural conditions anchored in constitutional provisions, the ordinary practices that had sprung up over time to deal with those structural conditions, and the incentives facing elected politicians and agency managers conspired to undermine the deal.

Still, the effort is worthy of both study and emulation. James and his team represented the kind of bold managerial action that is needed to improve the quality of our democratic accountability systems. In this case the managers embraced rather than retreated from their democratic overseers' demands for accountability and sought to facilitate it. They did so in part to reclaim their self-respect as skilled and professional public managers, but also because they believed that they could actually improve the overall quality of the oversight process by helping their overseers become more articulate and precise about what they wanted and expected. And in doing so they hoped to help themselves by creating a clearer and more durable mandate that they could use to animate and guide their organization's efforts. Without such action, much of the useful democratic energy that is expressed through citizens and their elected and self-appointed representatives calling government organizations to account is wasted. It never coheres or crystallizes in a public voice that is articulate and exacting about what should be produced, and it fails to engage public managers and their staffs in a shared effort to create public value.

Figure 3.3 shows what a complete public value scorecard might have looked like if the DOR and the legislators had worked together to create one.

—➤•◆•◄—

4

Jeannette Tamayo, Toby Herr, and Project Chance

Measuring Performance along the Value Chain

Jeannette Tamayo, Toby Herr, and Performance Contracting in Illinois

In 1990 Jeannette Tamayo was appointed director of the Division of Employment and Training in the Illinois Department of Public Aid.[1] The division was responsible for developing, managing, and improving the government's efforts to help welfare clients make the transition from welfare to work. The program was called "Project Chance" to emphasize its mission to give welfare clients a chance to end their welfare dependency.[2] Most of the casework associated with Project Chance—providing advice, support, training, and encouragement for welfare clients—was contracted out to independent social service agencies. Tamayo felt she had a mandate to clean up, rationalize, and guarantee the performance of the social service providers that received funding from Project Chance. Her boss, Robert Wright, the deputy director of Public Aid, observed: "Project Chance . . . had gotten to the point where there was no really rational scheme for what was happening with the money. Employment and training contracts were often given out because someone had convinced the department or the director that theirs was a good program. . . . Once the contract had been awarded, they expected to have it renewed again and again."

Tamayo's strategy to clean up the system was to shift nearly all Project Chance contractors to performance-based contracts, specifying exactly how much would be paid for predetermined program accomplishments.[3] She sent out a standard request for proposal (RFP) specifying the purposes that Project Chance was trying to achieve and the basis on which it would pay the contractors for their work.

Project Match

Among the many contractors receiving the RFP was Toby Herr, director of an organization called "Project Match." Project Match opened its doors in 1985. Herr believed that welfare recipients—particularly long-term recipients—needed both assistance and prodding to change their lives.[4] In her view the standard job training and placement programs had skewed priorities, at least where the hard-core poor were concerned. These programs saw getting a job as the *end* of the welfare-to-work process, while Herr suspected it was just the beginning. Formal evaluations and anecdotal evidence showed that training and placement programs did not rapidly move large numbers of people directly to self-sufficiency.[5] For many, staying on the job was at least as big a challenge as getting a job in the first place. Herr explained: "All the attention and all the help comes before the job. The job is the end of it. Programs do these very complicated assessments, they track people into education or training, they do job development and placement, and teach résumé writing and interviewing skills—they get people jobs, and that's it. . . . We have no idea why people who lost their jobs lost them, or when, or what we could do to improve that; we have no idea why people kept jobs and what we could learn from that."

To Herr, this seemed particularly nonsensical for the long-term welfare clients she served. For them, she suspected that social supports and individual behavioral factors would be at least as important as their reading level or technical skills, and that help in dealing with post-placement crises or stagnation would be as important as help in getting a job in the first place. But since programs did not stay with their clients after placing them, there was no way to know if that was true, or what to do about it if it was. Herr decided to find out. She envisioned Project Match as a combined social services program and research center. It would try to help people get off welfare, with an emphasis on the realistic and the long term.

The initial state funding for Project Match's work with clients (the program's research component was largely foundation funded) had come through a demonstration grant from Project Chance, which was also looking for some fresh ideas at the time—particularly about how to deal with the hard-core population. Randy Valenti, Tamayo's predecessor, explained, "Project Match appealed to us as a locally-based program that could help show us whether we could serve this very difficult population while they were on aid, and even afterward."

Project Match based its operations in a community health center near the notorious Cabrini-Green Housing Project. Cabrini-Green was the very image of a failed American housing project: a cluster of isolated high-rises on Chicago's North Side—dilapidated, dangerous, and drug- and gang-ridden. Most of Project Match's clients came from the project: 99 percent were African American; 77 percent were female; 95 percent were single; 72 percent were parents; 60 percent were age twenty-five or younger; just over a third had never finished high school; 60 percent grew up on welfare; two-thirds had been on aid, steadily, for at least the last four years; 80 percent were on aid when they enrolled in Project Match; and nearly half had never had any job to speak of.[6]

Herr directed a staff consisting of a "job developer" who recruited employers to take Project Match placements, three caseworkers, and an office worker. Herr also employed Research Director Lynn Olson, who managed a staff of two researchers at Northwestern's Center for Urban Affairs and Policy Research.

The first and most ironclad Project Match rule was that clients *always* came first. Herr said:

> From the very beginning, I always said, if a client comes in, drop everything. I wanted Project Match to be a place where people felt important and welcome. I wanted it to provide family-like support. We'll visit you in the hospital, we'll send you a card when your father dies, we'll come to your graduation, we'll come to your wedding. We'll be there for you. If you come in and get a job and everything's going fine and you're getting promoted, great: we'll call once a month to check in. If you just flunked the GED exam for the third time and you want to come in every afternoon for a week and grumble, that's fine too. If it takes you two years to get your first job and you need a lot of help keeping it, you can count on us. We are here for the duration.

All this casework was recorded and sometimes driven by an elaborate computerized tracking system that Project Match personnel considered the backbone of the operation. Herr said, "Every client had a file that followed her or his [progress] at one-month intervals: course enrollment, participation, and dropout, failure, or graduation dates; getting, starting, keeping, and losing jobs; whether Project Match or the client had gotten the placement; salaries and raises; contact people and their telephone numbers; and more." Project Match also maintained a paper file, recording the nature and content of office and field visits. It was an unusual system. Olson explained:

> Most programs' information systems have been set up to capture units of services. You're supposed to report on the number of clients you served this month, the number of clients in employment this month. That is not helpful information at all when what you are trying to do is trace the history of a person. Ours is focused on history and outcomes.[7] You will rarely go into any other program and open up a book and see the history of somebody you're working with. A lot of programs talk about doing case management, but they couldn't show you just where that person was and where they are today. Our tracking system tells us that. It lets us do our research, but it's had a very strong influence in shaping the day-to-day operations of the program.

All of Project Match's clients were volunteers. Initially, most were referred through the local health clinic and other social service agencies; some—more and more over time—came in through word of mouth from other participants. By 1990 the program had some four hundred individuals on its rolls. All clients had to attend a three-day orientation workshop, which included goal-setting exercises and group conversation about employment histories and aspirations, and it was immediately apparent that many were far from even contemplating full-time work and self-sufficiency. Project Match staff members were prepared for this but surprised to find themselves unsure about what to do for people who *did* seem ready. Many clients did not want training; they wanted work. "I could see right away that 'basic skills first' wasn't working," Herr said. "Many of them have had some sort of training that didn't lead to anything," added caseworker Warrine Pace. "It had to sink in that you're dealing with adults who have ideas of their own about the way they want their lives to go," said Pace. "I finally started to say, all right, you know, maybe you do need a job first."

What happened next came as a rude shock to Herr and her staff. Project Match could get clients jobs, but most clients subsequently lost them—early and often. Some of the job loss seemed due, as expected, to a lack of skills, but there were other problems as well. Some employees were chronically late. Some did not understand that they should call in if they were sick. Some did not understand what it meant to have a boss. "I had one of my clients, the first job she ever had she was fired—I think it was that, or she quit—in three days," said caseworker Meg Santschi. "[I asked] 'Michelle, what happened?' She said, 'The lady, she was telling me what to do. *Nobody* tells me what to do.'"

To Herr, the implications of these early findings were clear. Project Match needed a robust, flexible strategy to help people who were not ready for work or self-sufficiency. It had to be prepared for people to fail and had to have ways to catch them and keep them on track. It had to be able to attend to social and psychological issues, as well as skills. Some of the most important and hardest work was going to come *after* the first placement. "This is a very long, very difficult transition for a lot of our clients," Herr said. "A program has to face that and respond to it, or it's just going to spin its wheels." The idea she was evolving seemed so different from traditional train-and-place notions that she wanted a new image, a new metaphor, to go with it. What she came to, eventually, was the "ladder and the scale."

The Ladder and the Scale

The ladder and the scale offered an illustration of the pathway that welfare clients typically followed from dependency to self-sufficiency (see Figure 4.1). The "scale" recognized that there were different kinds of independence being sought. The "ladder" recognized different stages of progress in each particular realm. At the top might be full-time, stable employment. In the middle might be a training program or part-time work. At the bottom, for people who were not ready for jobs but had to get used to getting out of the house and keeping commitments, might be community volunteer work or even attending a prenatal course. Self-sufficiency might be too much to ask of many, but being *on* the ladder—and having a plan to ascend it—was not. Herr believed that many Cabrini-Green residents were going to start close to the bottom, and that they might stay there a while. But the ladder provided a picture of valuable progress as clients reached new rungs—and avoided backslides.

In 1991 Herr wrote "Changing What Counts" with Robert Halpern and Aimee Conrad, an article arguing that for many long-term poor,

Steps to Social Involvement and Economic Self-Sufficiency

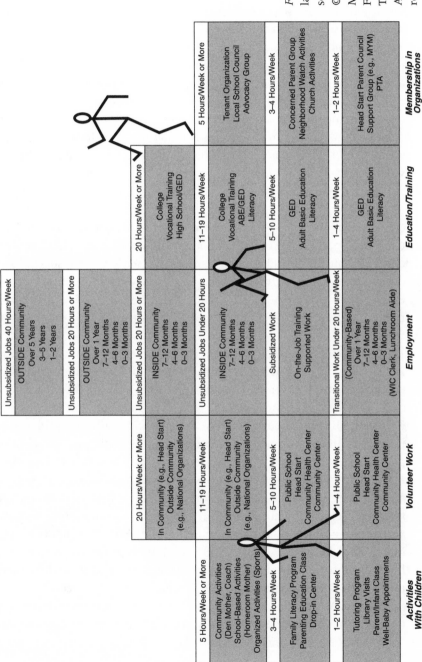

Activities With Children	Volunteer Work	Employment	Education/Training	Membership in Organizations
		Unsubsidized Jobs 40 Hours/Week OUTSIDE Community Over 5 Years 3–5 Years 1–2 Years		
		Unsubsidized Jobs 20 Hours or More OUTSIDE Community Over 1 Year 7–12 Months 4–6 Months 0–3 Months		
		Unsubsidized Jobs 20 Hours or More	20 Hours/Week or More	
5 Hours/Week or More	In Community (e.g., Head Start) Outside Community (e.g., National Organizations)	Unsubsidized Jobs INSIDE Community 7–12 Months 4–6 Months 0–3 Months	College Vocational Training High School/GED	5 Hours/Week or More Tenant Organization Local School Council Advocacy Group
11–19 Hours/Week	11–19 Hours/Week In Community (e.g., Head Start) Outside Community (e.g., National Organizations)	Unsubsidized Jobs Under 20 Hours INSIDE Community 7–12 Months 4–6 Months 0–3 Months	11–19 Hours/Week College Vocational Training ABE/GED Literacy	
3–4 Hours/Week	5–10 Hours/Week Public School Head Start Community Health Center Community Center	Subsidized Work On-the-Job Training Supported Work	5–10 Hours/Week GED Adult Basic Education Literacy	3–4 Hours/Week Concerned Parent Group Neighborhood Watch Activities Church Activities
Family Literacy Program Parenting Education Class Drop-in Center				
1–2 Hours/Week Tutoring Program Library Visits Parent/Infant Class Well-Baby Appointments	1–4 Hours/Week Public School Head Start Community Health Center Community Center	Transitional Work Under 20 Hours/Week (Community-Based) Over 1 Year 7–12 Months 4–6 Months 0–3 Months (WIC Clerk, Lunchroom Aide)	1–4 Hours/Week GED Adult Basic Education Literacy	1–2 Hours/Week Head Start Parent Council Support Group (e.g., MYM) PTA

--SOCIAL ISOLATION--

Figure 4.1. The ladder and the scale. Copyright © 1991 Project Match—Families in Transition Association; reprinted with permission.

seemingly minor steps were notable achievements and should be recognized and rewarded.[8] The idea, Herr said, using language familiar
around Project Match, was to "construct a future" for recipients, starting wherever they happened to be and sticking with them until they
were ready to stand on their own.

Casework was the heart of Project Match's efforts to move clients
up the ladder. Herr explained, "[I]nstead of doing a one-shot assessment
as an intake procedure, like most programs do, we're doing assessment
constantly. . . . Moving out of dependency is a process of *change.* People
change as they do it." The idea that there was any basic path to follow
or any standard way to help clients make the transition disappeared
completely. Project Match was to be a job shop, custom fitting the services that each client required at any particular moment.[9]

Clients had a hard road to travel. Caseworkers discovered that many
of them were under heavy pressure from family and friends not to
change their lives. The reasons were sometimes material: one individual bringing in money or going off aid could hurt a household's welfare
check or housing subsidy. Often, though, the reasons were social. Children, friends, and boyfriends resented the outside obligations. One client's mother was a drug abuser whose parties kept the daughter up all
night. Another client was expected to babysit all day after returning
from a night shift.

Work itself was often not what clients expected. Some had unreal-
istically high hopes. "There are many times," said Santschi, "when they
go into a training program, say, and come out thinking they have these
skills and life is going to be wonderful. They have an idealized view of
what life is like for people who have money, and they don't think about
the actual process of earning the money." Some could not roll with the
punches. And, as Santschi pointed out, there was always a known alternative to fall back on. "When they're not working, when they're getting
an aid check, they're masters of their fates. They have some level of autonomy." Some did well, some quit, and some were fired, but the overall pattern was clear. Olson examined a sample of 180 clients Project
Match had placed by February 1987 and found "a startlingly rapid and
high" rate of job loss.[10] Forty percent lost their jobs within three
months, 57 percent within six, and 70 percent within a year.[11]

Project Match did think, however, that it was finding ways to help
its clients handle employment more successfully. One way was simply

staying with them through their first cycle of failure. Losing their first job was often a clarifying experience for clients. Project Match worked hard to help clients focus on the positive in their painful experiences, sort out what they needed to improve, and move on. Pace started to run reemployment workshops. "She really pushes people," said Linnea Berg, a member of Olson's research team. "Okay, so the boss is racist. What are you going to do next time? What did you contribute to that? You're going to face lousy customers, you're going to have low pay. Here's what you have to do to get away from that."

Project Match also tried to prepare clients for the roadblocks to success that they would inevitably encounter. "I learned to anticipate what the problems were going to be, having been through them with so many people," said Santschi. "It was a question of working with them on issues they didn't even see as issues yet."

As much as anything else, Project Match was there to provide moral support. Noted in the Project Match office, as well as in its newsletter, *The Independence,* was each class enrollment or graduation; each volunteer position; each new job; each job retained; and each bit of progress. The aim was both to celebrate success and create an atmosphere in which hanging in was a powerful norm.

And when none of it worked, caseworkers could still offer clients a bit of rough wisdom. "There was always an acknowledgment that life is hard," Santschi said. "It was critical to give them a sense that no matter what the situation was, they could bounce back."

Project Match's casework was complex, subtle, and sometimes overwhelming. Each caseworker carried approximately one hundred clients, some twenty of whom seemed to need a lot of attention at any given time. Caseworkers were expected to talk to each client (and, where appropriate, her or his employer) once a month, usually by phone, assessing the client's status, charting progress, and updating the tracking system. If clients were not doing well, caseworkers followed up with more frequent conversations, face-to-face sessions with clients and supervisors, and intervention with public aid, health, and housing authorities. Caseworkers seized every opportunity to emphasize the need to cope and act responsibly.

There was constant tension between caseworkers' efforts to teach clients to be reliable and responsible and their desire to keep them connected to the program. Many clients, if not most, were terrible about returning phone calls and keeping appointments. "Very rarely did they come on time," Santschi said. Project Match tolerated such behavior. "I would let them know that I had been expecting them at the time they were supposed to be in," Santschi said. "And then I would go on."

Not everybody was comfortable with this. "In some cases, we didn't ask enough of clients," said Greg Goldman, another caseworker. "Nobody ever said, 'You have done this, or not done this, [and] these are the consequences.' . . . That's something that I'm still somewhat uncomfortable with, in the Project Match model. At the same time, I really feel that—and this is now from more and different experience—it's not about the program, it's about the clients. . . . If you're going to stay with certain clients, that's just how you have to do it. But it cuts a little bit both ways."

Performance and Accountability

By 1990 the Department of Public Aid's Division of Employment and Training, now led by Tamayo, wanted to see Project Match put on a performance basis with all the other welfare-to-work programs it funded. Tamayo appreciated Project Match's commitment to its clients and could see that other contractors within the Project Chance network had picked up some important ideas from Herr's program, but Tamayo believed it was time to get serious about accountability. She and her staff wanted to ensure that Project Match received no special treatment. Liz Hersh, manager of Project Chance's field staff, explained:

> The dilemma is how to set outcomes that allow you to work with those people who may take five years to make real progress. I basically like Project Match. I think it's a good program. I like the fact that it's in the community. I like the long-term approach. I think the fact that Toby is trying to document what people actually go through is a really important contribution. . . . My problem with the program is that I feel they don't set high enough expectations for people. . . . I have never really been able to overcome my gut feeling that they're very good at getting people to buy in but maybe not so good at helping people become independent. I think it's reasonable to fund the demonstration end of Project Match, but it's also fair to insist that we see some results of what she's doing.

Herr did not think it was fair. The "Life Skills Request for Proposal," issued by the Department of Public Aid for all contractors seeking funding under Project Chance, seemed fundamentally at odds with

Herr's ideas about what constituted the valuable work of her program. First, the RFP counted only educational and vocational programs and full-time jobs as valid placements; achievements on the lower rungs of the ladder would not register at all. Second, the RFP required an "Action Plan/Employment Plan," laying out the steps the program and client would take from enrollment to placement; there was no provision for the flexibility and learning-while-doing that Project Match believed was so important. Third, the RFP indicated that the state would only pay to track clients through the first two months of a full-time job. There were no provisions to keep people in the program or to reenroll them if they lost their jobs. Finally, there was no category that recognized (and would pay for) the manifold, often idiosyncratic client services that Project Match provided. Herr thought that she would have to break Project Match to fit it into the new mold. She also worried that her methods and her particular segment of the welfare population would make her look like a very high-cost contractor.

Some Project Chance officials recalled thinking of Herr less as being principled in her objections than intransigent. "Project Match's expectation, because of past experience, was that they would be awarded a contract under any circumstances," said Jan Valukas, head of contract operations. Herr got news of Tamayo's new requirements on May 7, 1990, and the formal RFP on May 18. On June 1 she wrote Tamayo a letter explaining why "it is not possible for us to change our contractual relationship with the Department of Public Aid and operate under a performance-based contract." Tamayo, however, was equally immovable. Herr found her calls unreturned and her pleas for discussion unanswered. The Public Aid contracting staff would only restate Tamayo's position: performance-based or nothing.

In an attempt to combine Tamayo's interest in strict accountability with Project Match's commitment to custom fitting the service to the client, Herr and Pace sat down and started to work out a plan for all of their participants, based on their history to date and setting key milestones for the upcoming six months or year. This approach, though forced on Project Match by outside events, "made us focus on exactly where everybody was and what they should do next," Herr said. "I think we're working more effectively right now because of that." It was also very time-consuming and unwieldy, however, and, contravening the basic Project Match philosophy, plans were not developed in consultation with participants. "There would have been no time to do that," Olson said.

It was unclear what status the plans had, or could have, as tools of accountability for either the program or the clients. If clients deviated too far from a plan—even a negotiated, agreed-upon plan—Project Match's instinct was still to believe that somehow the assessment and the plan had been wrong, and to start over, perhaps at a lower rung of the ladder. The program's commitment to long-term, flexible services remained complete, making it hard to imagine any specific short-term performance measures that would be compatible.

No one at Project Chance really wanted Project Match terminated; there was hope that Herr would find a way to meet both her own and Public Aid's objectives. "Project Match could figure something out," Valukas said. "I think that we could have come up with something that would have been not only acceptable but maybe a unique model that might have been able to be transferred somewhere else. I would love to be able to incorporate some of these long-term concepts into my performance-based contracts. I think it's possible, if I can find some people with good ideas who are willing to work with me."

But Tamayo exhibited little interest in Project Match's compromise, and—further complicating the situation—Northwestern University (for whom Herr worked and under whose auspices Project Match operated) flatly refused to sign a performance-based contract. Herr continued to search for some common ground. "I know we have to be accountable, and in a way a state bureaucracy can deal with on a routine basis," she said. "I think we're really onto something here, something that could reshape how we think about and deliver welfare-to-work services. I'd like to see a lot of programs taking up the long-term approach, using the idea of the ladder, using our tracking system so they really know what's happening to people. But if funders don't think this kind of program can be held accountable, it's never going to happen."

Frustrated and fearful for the future of her organization, Herr finally contacted Beth Langen, associate deputy director of Public Aid. Seeing Herr's operation, Langen noted, "It was so clear that if we are ever really going to make a difference, we are going to have to look at the long term. . . . I was really impressed with Toby and with the program. And she did have this alternative proposal for maintaining accountability. I just went back to Garry [Veicht, deputy director of Public Aid] and said, 'This one makes sense.'" Neither she, nor Herr, nor the local Project Chance bureaucracy ever learned just what happened next, but Project Match's contract was renewed in essentially its original form. The program was safe, at least for the upcoming year.[12]

Deciding What to Measure and Where along the Value Chain

Tamayo, as director of the Division of Employment and Training in the Illinois Department of Public Aid, sought to use the same value-oriented management principles that William Bratton, Anthony Williams, and John James used to improve the performance of their enterprises. Specifically, her job was to:

- give a clear operational definition of the public value that Illinois citizens wanted to produce through Project Chance;
- develop measures that could record whether and to what extent that value was being produced; and
- use that measurement system to guarantee that those who received public money to do the work would be accountable.

Two features of Tamayo's position distinguish her work from that of any of the managers we have seen so far. First, Tamayo was a civil servant in a midlevel management position. She was neither an elected chief executive, like Williams, nor a politically appointed public manager, like Bratton or James. Partly because of this, she may have been more inclined to view the job of developing performance measures for her enterprise as a technical rather than a philosophical or political challenge, even when (as we will see) important philosophical and political questions were at stake.

Second, Tamayo had no direct authority over those whose performance she sought to manage. While Bratton, Williams, and James directly supervised many public employees, Tamayo oversaw a network of contractors bound to the state through service contracts. This reflected a broad national trend toward privatizing public services, spurred by a belief that government agencies could be more effective in demanding performance from private contractors competing for government contractors than from government employees.

Traditionally, when the public mandated the government to use tax dollars in pursuit of some public purpose, government would create a public agency that was to be accountable for achieving that purpose. The managerial tools designed call agencies to account focused primarily on controlling internal processes: financial controls to prevent fraud, waste, and abuse in public spending; compliance reviews to ensure that the agency was operating fairly and using professionally established best practices; and so on. Workload measures also focused some attention on direct organizational outputs. But the traditional systems generally did not measure the important dimensions of public value that these agencies were established to produce: desired social outcomes and (to the extent the public deemed appropriate) client satisfaction.

To many critics the government's reliance on process measures had failed to make public enterprises accountable for creating value. Instead, citizens got monolithic government organizations with one-size-fits-all solutions that could not accommodate the diversity of clients the organizations sought to serve. Worse, the systems seemed to stagnate, with productivity either flatlining or falling over time. Compared to the efficiency, responsiveness, and steady productivity gains that private-sector firms could demonstrate, government enterprises seemed costly, inefficient, and resistant to change.[13]

To get improved performance, critics of government suggested government become a buyer rather than a producer.[14] As a buyer, the government could fulfill its responsibility for pursuing public purposes by spelling out the outcomes it wanted the private-sector providers to deliver in concrete detail. Private sector-firms could go after those outcomes unencumbered by the policies and rules that had hamstrung government. And, over the long run, government could benefit from competitive pressures to stimulate productivity-enhancing innovations among private contractors, as experimentation and innovation began to reveal the production possibility frontier.[15]

To make all of this work for Project Chance, Tamayo had to shift to a system of performance contracts that specified the public value the state wanted the contractors to produce rather than the state-approved means for pursuing that value. The contracts she wrote would fundamentally change the way in which contractors like Toby Herr and Project Match would be evaluated and paid.

Observed in this chapter is the limited capacity of the process-oriented performance measures traditionally used for public agency accountability to reckon the value of a public agency's work or to create opportunities for experimentation, innovation, and increased productivity. It was these concerns that led Tamayo to contract for desired social outcomes rather than rely on traditional methods. But her story also reveals that defining the ultimate public value of welfare-to-work programs is a bit harder than it might appear. Further, we will see that even when managers focus on achieving outcomes, there are many reasons to measure processes all along the value chain. Some processes, like outcomes, have intrinsic value; other processes are worth measuring because they help reveal opportunities for increased productivity and guide innovations that can bring us closer to the production possibility frontier. These latter process measures are central to an operational capacity perspective on a public value scorecard that could guide a manager like Tamayo more reliably toward public value creation.

Measuring along the Value Chain

In Chapter 2, I introduced the concept of a value chain that sketched the process through which public assets (tax dollars and authority) were transformed into publicly valued results through a particular set of policies, programs, or activities (see Figure 2.8). Figure 4.2 reproduces that image with *costs and activities* on the left side of the value chain and *valued results* (represented here as some combination of client satisfaction and the achievement of social outcomes) on the right. The figure also indicates key points for measuring along the value chain: control over inputs, compliance with policies, production of outputs (measured in terms of quantity and quality), levels of client satisfaction in encounters with the organization, and success in achieving socially desired outcomes.

The push for performance-based contracting in government has grown up alongside the trend toward focusing on outcome measures over process measures. This trend corrects the problem of public-sector reliance on accountability systems focusing on the left-hand side of the value chain (inputs, processes, and outputs) rather than on the right-hand side of the chain (client satisfaction and social outcomes). The

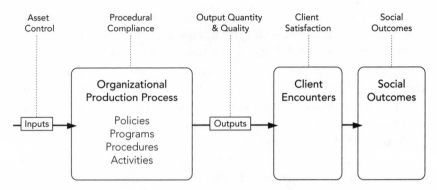

Figure 4.2. Measuring along the public value chain.

pressure to develop outcome measures, welcome as it was, led many public managers to ignore or downplay the importance of the process measures on the left side. This may have amounted to throwing the baby out with the bathwater. Without information about activities and outputs, some important values that attach to processes would go unrecognized. Further, without process measures, public agencies could not explore production methods to learn what works and achieve productivity gains through innovation. Indeed, performance measures that run *all along the value chain*—from costs, through processes, through outputs, to client satisfaction and, finally, to social outcomes—are critical to developing the operational capacity perspective of the public value scorecard. So before we consign those bad old systems that focused on processes to the dustbin of history, it might be useful to remind ourselves of what they are and how they might continue to be important even in the brave new world of outcome measures and performance contracts.[16]

Measuring and Controlling Costs
In the public value account, costs are the public dollars and uses of public authority that must be set against desired results to indicate whether a public agency is increasing or decreasing its net public value. As we have seen, in moments of fiscal crisis, sometimes reducing costs becomes the most important dimension of public value to be pursued—even at the price of reduced performance on the right-hand side of the public value account. Reducing costs can also become an important

route to public value creation when changes in the operating or political environment render programs or activities obsolete. In the effort to increase the net value of any public enterprise, minimizing costs is always essential. If public agencies can reduce costs without sacrificing the quantity and quality of output, degree of client satisfaction, or the social outcomes that can be achieved, then they can increase net public value merely by saving money. But from the operational capacity perspective, the old tried-and-true input measures—tallies of the tax dollars and units of labor that go into operations—provide public managers with data that help them understand the relative costs of distinct activities and programs (or, in Tamayo's case, distinct contractors). Such activity-based cost accounting is crucial to efforts to improve organizational performance, for several reasons.[17]

Cost Accounting to Improve Efficiency and Performance. First, breaking down costs into particular organizational units with accountable managers (e.g., precincts in the New York City Police Department [NYPD], departments within the D.C. government, or district revenue collection offices in Minnesota) and comparing the unit costs against the results these units achieve can create a powerful mechanism of internal accountability. If midlevel managers each have to account for their own unit's costs and outputs, they will respond to the pressure to reduce costs, increase output, or both.

Linking cost and performance data to organizational units with similar responsibilities (such as police precincts and revenue collections offices) strengthens this incentive effect. Making comparisons across producers of relatively homogenous products and services is quite simple; if everyone is producing apples, we do not have to worry about the relative value of apples and oranges. Those producing fewer "apples" than their peers will feel strong pressures to improve. This, in turn, motivates the low-producing units to learn from the more productive units, boosting efficiency not only through competition but also through learning.

When public managers have to look across organizational units that produce quite different kinds of value, however, things get more complicated. They have to weigh the relative value of precinct patrol operations versus homicide investigative units, tax advising services versus a fair and effective audit system, or, for a mayor like Anthony

Williams, a responsive and helpful Department of Motor Vehicles (DMV) versus clean and safe parks. But by treating similar organizational units as essentially competing with one another for performance, managers like Bratton and James could generate some of the same kind of leverage over operations that Tamayo could generate by setting up competition among suppliers.

Measuring Costs to Improve Allocative Efficiency. The ability to break down costs and outputs for even dissimilar organizational units allows public managers to understand the degree to which their organization has efficiently allocated its resources across different kinds of activities and/or distinct product lines. An organization engaged in multiple activities can make productivity gains in two distinct ways. First, it can find and exploit productivity gains in one or more of its activities without changing the allocation of resources across different activities (an operational productivity gain). Second, it can notice that one of its activities is worth more than the others and reallocate resources from other activities to the more valuable activity (an allocative productivity gain).

The Minnesota Department of Revenue (DOR), for example, allocates resources to district offices that seek to collect taxes from those who paid less than they owe, either by design or neglect. It also allocates resources to a much smaller unit that provides taxpayers with filing information. James could have called on district offices to cut costs and hoped that they would find the means to become more efficient and effective in their task (an operational productivity gain), or he could have invested in information services in hopes of reducing the number of taxpayers who failed to pay what they owed because of honest error (an allocative productivity gain).[18]

These kinds of allocative choices can be made not only among various activities within individual public agencies but also among various public agencies within larger units of government. Indeed, ordinary government budgeting processes depend on some ability to reckon the public value of various activities within and across public agencies.[19] Whether within an organization or a larger unit of government, performance measurement and management systems that connect the costs of particular activities to the public value they produce are the key to realizing both kinds of productivity gains.

Making operational productivity gains is particularly important when an organization is basically doing the same thing across many operational units. Making allocative productivity gains is particularly important when an organization is engaged in various different activities of greater or lesser value. But allocative productivity gains are often difficult to ferret out because the value of the activities cannot be easily compared. If the different activities are complementary approaches to the same goal, it might be empirically possible to determine the degree to which, say, the DOR's information office can reduce the burden on its tax-collecting units. But if an organization has different units designed to produce quite different results—the D.C. government, for example, which runs a school system, on one hand, and an economic development office, on the other—it is much harder to know whether allocative gains are possible.

Documenting and Monitoring Operations: Compliance Audits

As with cost accounting, the public sector has well-established systems for "compliance audits."[20] As the name suggests, these performance measures gather information about the degree to which a public agency's activities comply with official policies and procedures. Indeed, the main purpose of the dreaded bureaucratic "red tape" is to ensure that a public agency's activities comply with its policies and procedures.[21] Compliance is generally cheaper and easier to measure than values like client satisfaction or the achievement of social outcomes. These measures can also provide a useful description of organizational processes and activities. They do not reach the end of the value chain where ultimate value is realized, but they can and do, under certain conditions, help public managers increase the public value that their agencies produce, and they should therefore be tracked in the operational capacity perspective of a public value scorecard.

Compliance Audits Guard against Fraud, Waste, and Abuse. Like cost controls, compliance audits help prevent theft and the diversion of resources. While cost controls prevent the appropriation of public resources for private purposes, compliance audits prevent the failure to focus public spending on tried-and-true (or at least democratically mandated) methods for achieving desired results. In the Minnesota case, for example, the legislators did not object to the existence of "ghost positions" in the DOR budget because they thought that someone in the DOR was stealing money; they objected because there were more transparent and efficient ways of dealing with budgetary uncertainties.

Compliance Audits Promote Efficiency and Effectiveness? In guaranteeing consistent application of policies and procedures, compliance audits can theoretically help ensure that public agencies are performing with optimal efficiency and effectiveness, but only if the existing policies and procedures capture the most efficient and effective means to produce desired results. With foolproof policies and procedures, there is no need to monitor values farther down the value chain; managers would only need to ensure that everyone follow the rules. Reliable execution guarantees the desired results. If, however, existing policies and procedures are not the most efficient and effective, insisting on compliance dooms the organization to mediocre performance and locks it into "permanently failing" working methods.[22]

In reality, few public policies and procedures have been fully tested for efficiency and effectiveness. As noted in Chapter 3, in most cases government has experimented with only a small range of imaginable policies and procedures to achieve the desired results. It may even be uncertain whether existing policies or procedures actually produce the desired results, much less whether they represent the most efficient methods!

Compliance Audits Ensure Consistency and Fairness. Even when it is uncertain that existing policies and procedures represent the best possible methods, compliance audits can help ensure a certain kind of fairness. Fairness is a slippery concept, but one common understanding focuses on consistency: like cases should be treated alike.[23] If public agencies have standard operations to deal with cases that are alike in all important respects, then compliance audits can help guarantee consistency.[24] It might not be the best possible performance, but it will at least be consistent and, in that sense, fair rather than arbitrary and capricious.

Compliance Audits as Blueprints for Reengineering Processes. The last argument for using compliance audits is that precisely because they describe operational technologies in some detail, and because they encourage both public managers and their overseers to examine operations, they provide a baseline for considering how operations could be improved. In effect, they are the first step toward process reengineering.[25] In commercial manufacturing there is often a gap between the "designed capacity" of a technical system (whether a single machine or a whole production line) and its real capacity. Only those observing, working, and reflecting on the system can make it meet (or surpass) the design standard. The blueprints that explain how things were supposed to work make possible the process of reflection and reengineering. Compliance audits can function the same way in public agencies. Organizational policies and procedures are "blueprints" of production processes that managers and overseers can use to investigate whether the agency operates as intended and whether and how performance could be improved. If public managers and their overseers treated compliance audits as serious investigations into the value of the operating methods, these performance measures could become vital aids to learning and innovation. Only when they become a straitjacket preventing thought about improving operations do compliance audits become a problem.

Measuring the Quantity and Quality of Outputs

The next link in the value chain focuses attention on outputs—the actions that bring the public agency into contact with clients and the conditions in the world that it seeks to change.[26] Here the actual production of public value begins to come into sight. Delivering services and obligations to clients affects their current and future condition and, by extension, the overall public good. Public agencies also carry out tasks—building dams, cleaning up polluted rivers, protecting wilderness areas, and so on—that alter material conditions in society.

Measuring the Quantity of Outputs. Measuring the quantity of work carried out by public agencies has long been a staple of government management. Most agencies have "workload" measures to show how much work they have done in the past and how much money they will need to meet anticipated changes in their workload. The police track the number of calls they answer, the DMV counts licenses issued, the DOR counts its audits, and so on. Such numbers also help auditors and budget analysts make empirical estimates of productivity gains: if the police answered an increased number of calls with the same workforce, then that constitutes a productivity gain in one dimension of police performance. Demonstrations of both increased demand and increased productivity can sometimes be used to justify budget increases.[27]

Measuring the Quality of Outputs. Whatever the quantity of outputs, recognizing public value creation requires public agencies to focus on the *quality* of outputs as well. For purposes of strategic performance measurement and management, there are several reasons to measure the quality of organizational outputs.

First, as noted previously, the public often values particular features of organizational outputs intrinsically. In a welfare-to-work program, for example, the public might want to know that client encounters did not violate clients' rights to privacy, or that they did put pressure on the client to move toward independence. If the public attaches intrinsic value to certain outputs, these values should register in the part of the public value account that records concerns about justice and fairness in client encounters.

Second, certain features of organizational outputs turn out to be critical to an agency's capacity to produce public value. If the agency's public value account includes making beneficiaries happy or easing burdens on obligatees, then those features of client encounters that affect client satisfaction are instrumental in creating public value and important to track in the operational capacity perspective of a public value scorecard.[28]

Looking farther down the value chain, however, we also have to record those features of organizational outputs that are instrumental in achieving desired social outcomes. For example, Herr believes that in order for Project Match to succeed in moving clients from welfare to independence, caseworkers have to establish personal relationships with their clients—not only because this encourages clients to provide caseworkers with all the relevant information but also because the established relationship provides some instrumental power to urge the client forward. Without ensuring this quality in its primary output (client encounters), Project Match will not succeed in moving individuals to independence.

Using Output Measures to Create Accountability and Learning. Meeting the challenge of developing good output measures that capture both quantity and quality can yield enormous dividends for the managers and overseers of public agencies. Only when satisfactory output measures are in place does it become possible to compare costs with outputs of specific activities in order to learn whether productivity is going up or down. Recognizing productivity gains and losses is important in itself, but it is also what allows managers to analyze differences in performance among various organizational units producing similar outputs. Observed variations in the quality and quantity of outputs can point the way toward improved performance.[29]

Because outputs are more directly under managerial control than values farther down the value chain, a performance management system that holds midlevel managers accountable for the quantity and quality of outputs often seems more fair to those managers than a system that holds them accountable for ultimate outcomes, which are often beyond direct managerial control.

Output data are also easier and cheaper to collect than information about client satisfaction and social outcomes. One does not have to spend time and money surveying clients or tracking down past clients to determine what became of them. Output data usually come right from the operating records of the organization at no additional cost. And they come in real time, while outcome data often can only be observed in the future—far away in time and space from the outputs that (we hope) produced the desired results. Consequently, managers can get relatively precise feedback on outputs early and often.

For all the reasons previously set out, public managers need to develop and use output measures—in both the public value account and the operational capacity perspective of their public value scorecard. Such measures are often crucial for the development of a performance management system that can drive performance and promote learning in public agencies. While they might not be sufficient to guide organizations toward public value creation, they are necessary.

Measuring Client Satisfaction and Social Outcomes

As useful and important as input, process, and output measures can be in the effort to manage and improve the performance of public agencies, those who criticize the government's overreliance on these measures are absolutely right. The ultimate value that public agencies produce cannot be found at or within the boundaries of the organizations. The public value account requires public managers to have performance measures that capture the satisfaction of individual clients, and the agencies' success in producing the social outcomes that the public desires.

Public Value as Individual Client Satisfaction versus Socially Desired Outcomes. The commitment to measuring effects beyond the boundaries of public organizations has led in two distinct directions. On one hand, as discussed in Chapter 1, oversight and managerial attention have focused on increasing the *satisfaction of individual "customers"*—a trend that has drawn considerable strength from the private-sector analogy it invokes.[30] On the other hand, oversight and managerial attention have focused on achieving *publicly desired social outcomes.* The collective public may or may not consider the satisfaction of individual clients a desirable outcome.[31]

Strangely, the current discourse about how to improve public management often treats these two distinct ideas about how to understand and measure public value as though they were interchangeable. In fact, as demonstrated in Chapter 1, the concepts of "customer" satisfaction and the achievement of socially desired outcomes represent two fundamentally different answers to the question of *who is the arbiter of public value,* and therefore what constitutes public value and how it might best be measured. In the former case the arbiter of public value is *each individual* who is plausibly affected by a given public operation. Value lies in individual, subjective judgments; the overall valuation is equal to the sum total of individual satisfaction and dissatisfaction. In the latter the arbiter of public value is a *collective* that becomes articulate about its public policy purposes through the (flawed) processes of representative democracy.[32]

When we think of individuals as the arbiters of public value, we tend to see public value in terms that apply to them in their particular positions. As clients of government agencies, they would like easy access to the services to which they are entitled, and to be treated with respect and fairness. As taxpayers, they assess the organization in terms of the costs imposed on them. When we think of the collective as an arbiter of public value, however, we see value in terms of a complex set of public value dimensions that includes improving individual welfare, advancing the public good, and enacting and achieving a vision of a just society.

Gauging Individual Citizen and Client Satisfaction. As a philosophical matter, treating individual "customer satisfaction" as an important element of public value creation has brought the treatment of individual clients—an oft-neglected value—into sharp focus. While emphasizing client satisfaction risks distorting perceptions of public value by diverting attention from the achievement of desired outcomes, it has been practically useful in encouraging public managers to reconsider operational methods in light of their effects on individual satisfaction and to develop tools for measuring client satisfaction as well as citizen satisfaction.

Indeed, a booming survey industry has arisen to create myriad questionnaires asking individual clients about the encounters they have had with public agencies. In response, public agencies have reengineered their processes and outputs to make them more "customer friendly." Making these encounters as convenient, respectful, and easy as possible is a value-creating move whether government is delivering a benefit or service or an obligation. Public agencies have also learned to survey individual *citizens* about their satisfaction with government activities, directing questions at a general sample of the population to seek advice or participation in deciding matters of public policy or in overseeing and commenting on government performance.

Measuring the Achievement of Desired Social Outcomes. The principal alternative to evaluating the performance of public agencies against values held by individuals is to evaluate performance against collectively defined public aspirations, often expressed in mission statements or in the statutes establishing public agencies. But sometimes public aspirations are expressed in terms other than established organizational missions.

On some occasions, public aspirations can be expressed above the level of a single organization. Anthony Williams, for example, sought to develop a set of goals for Washington, D.C., as a whole, and he held individual agency managers accountable for contributing to goals that went above and beyond their agencies' particular missions.

On other occasions, public purposes can be expressed in terms of the desired outcomes of particular policies and programs. In fact, public agencies are often built on the accretion of policies and programs that were independently passed and then handed off to the organization that seemed to have the most relevant capacities for implementation. In the case of Project Chance, for example, the social aspiration that justifies the use of public assets to help welfare clients make the transition to economic and social independence is attached not to the mission of a particular public organization but to a particular program lodged in the Illinois Department of Social Services.

Since the 1960s a large professional community has arisen to meet a demand for the evaluation of particular government policies and programs. Government oversight agencies as well as private and nonprofit organizations offer myriad program evaluation services, and many public agencies have their own offices of policy evaluation.

The core practice of the program evaluation community is to try to determine the degree to which a particular policy or program worked to achieve the desired social outcomes. This means program evaluators must identify the desired outcomes that justified a particular policy or program, develop empirical measures to determine the extent to which the objectives were achieved, and use established social science methods to determine whether the changes observed were, in fact, caused by the policy or program. This allows them to make a reliable estimate of the likely effects of a given policy if it were reproduced.

Such efforts have contributed a great deal to our knowledge about what we can expect from the adoption and successful implementation of particular government programs. They have not, however, done much to help public managers manage their organizations strategically. Part of the reason is that policy and program evaluations are so expensive that only a small fraction of organizational policies and programs will be subject to program evaluations at any given moment. This reduces their utility for helping managers allocate resources across organizational activities. Program evaluations are also not particularly helpful to managers because they focus on ultimate outcomes, which take time to produce. By the time the evaluation has been completed, a whole new set of managers has shown up to take the credit or the blame. A third problem is that in order to maintain the conditions necessary for sound social science research, managers are discouraged from adapting programs even in the face of obvious problems.

Measuring Overall Organizational Performance

This book seeks to provide public managers with a wide set of performance measures to be used in performance management systems that will allow them to improve the performance of their organization over time. Like program evaluation, it encourages managers to measure social outcomes empirically, but the focus is on developing measures that enable managers to manage whole organizations strategically rather than determining to scientific standards the effects of particular activities. Strategic management does not mean having perfect, comprehensive knowledge of the consequences of planned actions; it means developing and executing a plausible theory in the face of great uncertainty until there is good evidence that one is headed in the wrong direction. For that, one needs measures that cover *all* organizational efforts, and that can be used to motivate, guide, and enable the rapid learning of managers entrusted with the task of producing public value. There is a place for rigorous policy and program evaluation, but there also is a place for less ambitious forms of policy and program evaluation that emerge as important research and development (R&D) efforts as managers adapt and undertake new policies and activities to meet political and economic realities.

Given the public's constant demands for government accountability, it seems surprising that an industry focused on evaluating overall organizational performance in government has not appeared. But the experience of the General Accounting Office (GAO) under Charles Bowsher revealed something unexpected: not only were methods for such evaluations difficult to develop but the demand for the work was unexpectedly tepid.

As comptroller general of the United States, Bowsher was responsible for calling public organizations to account. The GAO had the primary responsibility for carrying out financial audits of federal programs to ensure that public money went only to activities authorized by Congress, and for ensuring that public managers used approved methods for functions such as strategic planning, human resource management, and procurement. The GAO also carried out policy and program evaluations. But Bowsher, a former private-sector manager, noticed that no one carried out what he described as a general management review of public organizations over time. He resolved to fix this situation.

He asked his staff to carry out a review of the five-to-ten-year performance of the Department of Health and Human Services and the Department of Justice. Predictably, the teams carrying out these general management reviews found it difficult to establish the proper criteria for measuring the overall performance of organizations with diffuse missions and multiple programs. They were also unsure how to obtain data about value creation. Once his staff had completed this difficult work, however, to Bowsher's great surprise, no one was interested in reading the reports! The president and his staff were not interested, because they did not really see the president's work as managing the government departments for superior performance. They were much more interested in developing and implementing the policies that would be the hallmarks of the president's administration. Congress was not very interested either. There was no equivalent of a stock market focused on the equity value of individual government organizations. There were only individual constituents focused on particular policies and programs.

This is a sobering lesson for those who wish to develop and use performance measurement and management systems that can measure and drive the performance of whole organizations rather than individual policies and programs. To keep their efforts relevant and useful, they have to focus instead on measuring and managing performance with respect to the dimensions of value that resonate with public systems of accountability. This certainly includes the dimensions of value contained in organizational missions. But it may include other dimensions as well. Thus the Bratton case raises the question of whether reduced crime was the only social outcome that citizens expected or wanted from the NYPD; the Williams case raises questions about how improved service delivery would affect broader social conditions in Washington, D.C., and how the District's agencies could contribute to the strategic priorities set by the mayor's office (in consultation with citizens); the James case raises the question of how legislators' ideas about which measures define the public value created by the Minnesota DOR could be reconciled with the ideas of James and his team; and Tamayo's case raises the question of what ultimate public value she should ask her contractors to produce.

Creating a Public Value Account for Welfare-to-Work Programs

Any public contracting system focused on producing socially desired outcomes depends on there being a measurable concept of the public value that the contractor is to produce. The system simply cannot work without a technically sound, objective measure of valued results. But, importantly, the measure has to meet philosophical and political standards as well. And this is where trouble can arise. Managers nearly always face some difficulty in resolving political and philosophical conflicts about the values to be advanced. In the rush to develop a serviceable measure, efforts to clarify the values to be advanced through a public program are often shoved aside. When managers treat the development of measures as a purely technical problem, an opportunity for social and political learning about what the public wants to accomplish is lost, and, with that, some capacity to find out what is really possible to do is sacrificed.

What Should Count as Public Value Creation in a Welfare-to-Work Program?

Central to this case is a dispute that begins as an apparently technical discussion about the right way to measure the results of a welfare-to-work program between Tamayo (the official responsible for creating value through Project Chance contracts) and Herr (one contractor in this larger network). Tamayo is eager to develop a simple and universally applicable set of measures to focus and galvanize the network of contractors. If this can be done, it will solve many of her problems. She will look like a tough-minded, performance-oriented manager who demands and gets value-creating performance from the contractors. She can also be seen as acting fairly among contractors, since every contractor is held to the same standards. And she can maximize her leverage over the contractors not only by paying them just for performance but also by being able to make simple, objective comparisons among providers.

Herr, on the other hand, is concerned about Tamayo's proposed measures. Part of her concern may be that the measures that Tamayo has chosen could put Project Match at a disadvantage—making it look like a high-cost, low-performing program in the larger field. But she is also concerned because she thinks the proposed measures of value are unreliable measures of the public value that Project Chance claims to want to produce.

Two Conceptions of Valuable Outcomes in Welfare to Work. In her RFP, Tamayo committed to a particular way of measuring the value her contractors produced: the number of placements made in educational institutions or jobs that would last two months or more. Herr had a different, and somewhat more complex, but still measurable concept of public value creation: movements of individual clients toward economic and social independence sustained over variable periods of time.

Herr's vision of public value creation was informed by her knowledge of how welfare clients experienced and navigated the transition from welfare to work, in general, and when they had great obstacles to overcome, in particular. Her image of the ladder and the scale embodied her vision of what the process was like and the value she was trying to create. Rather than setting an arbitrary level of achievement to be maintained for an arbitrary period of time, her measurement system continuously monitored the status of clients to capture any movements up or down the ladder and how long clients sustained improvements or losses.

For her part, Tamayo thought Herr's stance too soft and forgiving to both welfare clients and welfare-to-work providers. She wanted to set the bar high for both and, therefore, restricted the operational definition of value creation to reaching a particular rung on the ladder and the scale and staying there for a specific period of time. Table 4.1 illustrates these two different conceptions and shows the relationship between them. One can see that Herr's scheme includes, but is not limited to, Tamayo's concept.

The Political Appeal of Tamayo's Measure. The usual political discourse would treat Herr's and Tamayo's differences on the appropriate opera-

Table 4.1. Two measurable conceptions of public value creation in welfare-to-work programs.

Tamayo		Herr	
Successful placements supporting economic independence		Improvements in social independence and economic self-sufficiency	
Employment (two-month duration)	Yes/No	Positions measuring level of social development	Time spent in each
Education and training (two-month duration)	Yes/No	Activities with children	Low–High
		Volunteer work	Low–High
		Employment	Low–High
		Education and training	Low–High
		Membership in organizations	Low–High

tional definition of public value at least partly as a question of whose definition was "tougher" and more demanding, on one hand, and which was more practical and "commonsense," on the other—as though these should be the principal issues in constructing a useful public value account. But upon close inspection, it is by no means clear which of these ideas is "tougher" or more "commonsense" than the other.

On the question of "toughness," Tamayo could argue that her value proposition is more exacting than Herr's because it refuses to recognize any public value creation until the participants ascend quite high on the ladder—to an educational or a job placement. But Herr might respond that her value proposition is tougher because it focuses on the long-run status of clients. She knows from her research that welfare dependency is a chronic, relapsing state, which gives her good reason to doubt the long-term value of a three-month placement. Herr's system continued to hold clients accountable for working toward independence *after* a three-month term of employment or education.

On the question of practicality, Tamayo's concept of value would undoubtedly be easier to implement using existing data systems throughout the state. Determining whether a client was enrolled in an educational program or had held a job for two months is a relatively simple matter. Herr's investments in developing the concept of the ladder and the scale and the corresponding information system, however, reveal that what seemed impractical was in fact quite doable. Thus both value propositions could survive the transition from the political and philosophical realm to the practical (technical and managerial) realm.

In the end, of course, the question should not be which system is tougher but which concept works better as a political and philosophical statement of what constitutes the value that the Illinois public would like to achieve through Project Chance. At the technical level, Herr's method can do everything that Tamayo's system does, and then some. Beyond three-month placements in schools and jobs, Herr can note improvements in client status that fall short of job placements but might still have value for the client and the public (depending on how the public perceives the value of the program). Her system tracks how long clients maintain progress toward independence, leaving no questions about the value of a program that produces three-month placements that may fall apart shortly thereafter. The question that remains is, if Herr's system can do everything that Tamayo's can, and then some, why would Tamayo not embrace it?

The answer could be simply that Tamayo's concept works better politically. It is a more familiar and straightforward idea that aligns with the public goal of getting clients off the welfare rolls (or at least with becoming better equipped to join the workforce) and holds providers accountable for producing that result. But that answer may not be entirely satisfactory if Tamayo's understanding of the process of transitioning to economic and social independence and her definition of success in that transition conceal an important truth about welfare-to-work programs.

Different Assumptions about the Transition from Welfare to Work. Beneath the argument about how best to measure the public value produced by welfare-to-work programs is a pretty deep difference in assumptions about the nature of the problem that both Tamayo and Herr were trying to fix. Tamayo's implicit model for helping move people from welfare to independence seemed to treat welfare dependency as a kind of acute illness. There is a problem: a client is on welfare. The state makes a relatively short-term, one-shot intervention to solve the problem. The client either does or does not get better. Everything is nice and discrete.

Herr's model, in contrast, treated welfare dependence like a chronic disease. There is a problem: a client is on welfare. The state intervenes (through Project Match) with a continuous program of assistance and encouragement, while the client struggles to make the adjustment. The problem improves but does not go away. Indeed, the problem may even worsen from one period to the next, especially if some of the support is withdrawn. With some continuing support (and nudging), the client makes some modest advances up the ladder of economic and social independence.

These very different ideas about the process through which individual clients can become economically self-sufficient, and the ways in which public funds and authority can be used to help them along this path, have implications for the imagined costs and benefits of these programs. On the surface, it seems that the first model would be less expensive and more effective than the second. The taxpayers pay for only one intervention and receive a permanent effect. It may be that it is precisely for this reason that Tamayo wants to think in terms of an acute curable rather than a chronic relapsing condition. If she had to report to the citizens of Illinois and their elected representatives that the real process of supporting transitions from welfare to work would be closer to the second model, she might well worry that they would stop supporting the project altogether. Perhaps the program would look too expensive, too unreliable, and too long term for the citizens and taxpayers of Illinois to support.[33]

Yet if Herr were right about the transition process, then Tamayo's model of the process and her system for recognizing value creation when it occurs might well fail. If there are many lapses and pitfalls on the road to economic independence, then many of those clients Tamayo thought cured would show up in the future for another dose of treatment. The relapse would not be recorded as a loss. Nor would the cost of additional treatment for that client be recorded as an additional cost in the treatment of that same client. To guard against the error of wrongly attributing a low-cost success to clients who relapse, Tamayo would have to maintain records of individuals continually treated so that she could check for repeat visitors and charge both the failure implied by the repeat visit and the extra costs of the repeat visit to the program that had previously claimed success in treating the individual. Otherwise, what looks like the successful treatment of a thousand people with acute illnesses might turn out to be the continuous management of a chronic disease among a hundred people.

Thus Tamayo's method for recognizing public value creation may overestimate the value of placing a person in a job for two months. Two months of employment does not represent the end of welfare dependence. It is far more likely that the client will return shortly for another shot of help and encouragement or simply give up. Herr suggested that the value of Project Match is really contained not in large, permanent changes in a person's status (which rarely occur) but instead in smaller, more herky-jerky movements toward independence—a way of more accurately recognizing public value creation that takes a more pessimistic view of the net public value that can be produced with welfare-to-work programs focusing solely on job placements.

Beyond Utilitarian Social Outcomes: Deontological Issues in
Welfare-to-Work Programs
The aforementioned considerations about how best to measure the value of welfare-to-work programs focused on the progress individual clients

make toward independence. To the degree that the individual clients value these changes in status, their increased happiness and material well-being would count as value creation by any utilitarian standards. But, again, the arbiter of value for public programs is not simply the clients but also the wider body politic (the public). The public may value the satisfaction of individual welfare clients who succeed in the program, but it has interests in other dimensions of value as well.

Reducing Future Welfare Costs. First, the public has a clear material interest in reducing welfare costs in order to reduce future tax burdens. Taxpayers invest in welfare-to-work programs not only to increase the happiness, dignity, and autonomy of their fellow citizens but also in hopes of avoiding the expense of supporting those fellow citizens on welfare in the future. By this accounting, the value of welfare-to-work programs lies in reducing future welfare payments. Compared with many other dimensions of public value, this is relatively straightforward to express and measure by estimating the degree to which the program enabled clients to move off the welfare rolls and calculating an estimate of future welfare payments avoided. This fits easily within a utilitarian calculus of the social benefits of welfare-to-work programs and seems closely aligned with Tamayo's approach. In her view the goal is to get folks off the welfare rolls and into permanent jobs so that the state can save money for citizens and taxpayers.

Of course, if Tamayo were solely focused on saving the taxpayers money, paying contractors to make educational placements would not seem to make sense. In the short run, welfare clients in educational programs are more rather than less expensive to the state because the clients continue to receive welfare payments and use public dollars for education. To this extent Tamayo seems to acknowledge Herr's view that the public might have to pay for intermediate steps toward independent employment. But the core utilitarian idea that society is paying money now so that it will not have to pay money in the future remains.

Welfare to Work as an Instrument of Social Justice. Herr, in contrast, seems to view the welfare-to-work system in much less utilitarian terms. This does not mean that she is indifferent to the costs or the practical results of her program. If she can reduce costs without sacrificing valuable results, or find more solid methods for advancing Project Match clients toward economic and social independence, she will do so. She is, after all, a manager. But, to Herr, welfare-to-work programs like Project Match provide value beyond their ability to reduce public spending on welfare; Herr sees the use of public assets to help individuals become socially and economically independent as a way of creating a more just as well as a more prosperous society. Her conception of justice includes the idea that individuals who have fallen into a state of dependency should be given a chance to work their way toward economic, social, and political independence. She thinks the public values such opportunities as a matter of justice as well as practical benefit. This deontological stance creates a competing framework for understanding the public aspirations that motivate and legitimate expenditures on welfare-to-work programs.

Thinking about welfare-to-work programs from a combined utilitarian and deontological perspective raises two other crucial issues in how the public value of welfare-to-work programs should be evaluated in general, and how Herr's particular program should be evaluated as one element of the larger system.

Special Credit for Dealing with the Poorest of the Poor? As Herr sees it, her clients represent the most hard-core segment of the welfare-dependent population. Her practical experience has shown her that there are differences among clients in both the quality and quantity of the help they require to achieve independence. As a matter of justice, Herr believes that the services should be available to all who meet eligibility requirements, that the level of help should be adjusted to individual needs, and perhaps that it is particularly virtuous to help those who seem to require the most help, as she has chosen to do. This strategic decision shows up in the public value account for her program as higher average costs per client, and fewer placements in educational programs and jobs, than Project Chance contractors who work with less severely disadvantaged clients. This raises the question, is there any extra or special public value associated with helping those who are the worst-off?

There are several reasons the public might attach a special value to moving a long-term welfare client to independence—some practical and utilitarian, and some regarding matters of justice and fairness. The first (decidedly utilitarian) reason has to do with ensuring that the state gets its money's worth out of its contractors. The performance contract guarantees that the state will pay contractors what it estimates is the average cost of achieving the program goals. If contractors can find a way of attracting a segment of the welfare population that they know to be easier to place than the average welfare client, then they can earn revenues beyond their costs. Their ability to cherry-pick their clients comes at the expense of the state's interest in providing an equal chance to welfare clients to make the transition from welfare to work.[34]

A second reason to pay more for working with more intractable welfare clients has to do with treating contractors fairly. If hard-core clients need more assistance, the contractors who work with them should be paid more when they achieve the desired results.

A third reason to pay extra for moving hard-core clients focuses less on the total costs for different clients and more on the differential social benefits of succeeding with different kinds of clients. Tamayo could have decided to pay more for hard-core clients not simply because it cost more to help them but also because the public value of making these placements is higher. The benefits of succeeding with hard-core clients can be reckoned in familiar utilitarian terms such as the greater happiness to the individual that comes from moving from the very bottom (client satisfaction), or the achievement of broader social outcomes such as reduced welfare expenditures in the future, or reduced crime and drug abuse.

But there are ideas about social justice and fairness that would also guide citizens and their representatives to see greater public value in the progress of those who are the worst-off than similar progress made by those who are relatively better-off.

At the core of all of these arguments is the idea that the public value of Project Chance is something more than maximizing the number of individuals who leave the welfare rolls. There are concerns about the rights of individual clients and about the justice and fairness with which the program operates, and the degree to which it helps create a more just Illinois society. In paying more for working with hard-core clients, Tamayo would have been saying that the public values she is pledged to protect and advance include not only the utilitarian idea that vendors should be paid only for the net value they add to the lives of their clients along particular dimensions but also the following deontological ideas: (1) Project Chance should give differently situated clients an equal chance to succeed, and (2) a certain vision of justice makes it a virtue to give special attention to advancing the economic and social independence of the least well-off. Figure 4.3 presents a public value account for Project Chance that adds these concerns to the public value conceptions first presented in Table 4.1.

A Service or Obligation Encounter? Whether the welfare-to-work program should be evaluated in utilitarian or deontological terms depends a great deal on how citizens view the ends of the program—as a way of reducing their individual tax payments, or as a way to create a more just society. But it also depends on the nature of the program itself. If the program makes extensive use of public authority, then the public value account should include deontological as well as utilitarian values. Thus one has to consider whether the encounter between welfare clients and Project Chance's contracted caseworkers is a service or an obligation encounter.

Initially the encounter appears to be primarily a service encounter. The clients are voluntarily seeking a service that will benefit them as individuals. The only way in which they do not seem to be typical "customers" is that the service provided to them is free. Upon closer inspection, however, one can see how state authority creeps into this transaction, and how obligations begin to attach to the service provided. Caseworkers must ask clients about economic status, work history, family background, and so on. These questions help determine what the agency might best do to help the client, but they are also designed to determine whether the client is eligible to receive services at the public's expense.

The idea of eligibility includes a concept of justice as well as efficacy. The public wants to be sure that the services go not only to those who can use them but to those who need and are officially *entitled* to them. The notion that some are entitled to the services and others are not is not simply a question of how to efficiently target those with the need and capacity to use the service; it is also a question of who can make a *legitimate* claim for the service. Once eligibility rules are established, it becomes the state contractors' duty to obtain all relevant personal information and to admit those who are eligible and reject those who are not.

Once clients are admitted to the program, they benefit from services, but they are also pressured to go as far as they can in meeting the goals of the program, and the more specific expectations of their case-

PUBLIC VALUE ACCOUNT for Jeannette Tamayo and Project Chance

PUBLIC VALUE ACCOUNT	
Use of Collectively Owned Assets and Associated Costs	Achievement of Collectively Valued Social Outcomes
Financial Costs	Mission Achievement:
Internal (administrative)	Move welfare clients to
External (costs to clients)	independence
	• Economically
	• Psychologically
	• Socially
	Reduce future welfare costs to
	taxpayers
Unintended Negative Consequences	Unintended Positive Consequences
Alienating clients from programs	Shift cultural norms toward
designed to help	independence
Extending welfare dependency	
	Client Satisfaction
	Treat clients with respect
	Meet client needs
	Engage client aspirations
Social Costs of Using State Authority	Justice and Fairness
Rationing of services	Protect individual rights
	Impose obligations fairly
	Provide access for all welfare clients
	Offer extra help to neediest clients (?)

Figure 4.3. Public value account for Jeannette Tamayo and Project Chance

workers. The caseworkers not only provide services but also keep nudging their client toward economic independence (or at least toward a state-approved "placement"). The fact that the clients choose to submit themselves to interference and intrusions in their lives from caseworkers makes their encounters less onerous to the clients and less obviously a use of state authority. But when the public as a whole becomes impatient with the progress of the clients enrolled in the program, the pressure on clients can be increased, and the whole enterprise can tilt more decisively in the direction of an obligation rather than a service encounter. The state can refuse to let clients continue participating in the program if they do not make sufficient progress, or it can cut their welfare benefits entirely if they fail to cooperate with welfare-to-work services.

These observations suggest that caseworker-client encounters are simultaneously service and obligation encounters. Public dollars pay for the service and public authority rations access to it and creates obligations consistent with some public idea about an efficient, effective, and just way to deliver welfare-to-work services. As Figure 1.7 in Chapter 1 illustrated, this means that the value of Project Chance will be reckoned *by individual clients* in terms of both their material interests (as service recipients) and their notions of their rights and duties (as obligatees), as well as *by the collective public* in terms of both social welfare (utilitarian concerns) and social justice (deontological concerns). A complete public value account has to recognize all these dimensions of performance.

The Price of Political Expediency in Defining and Measuring Public Value

Tamayo's public value proposition for Project Chance (and the understanding of the welfare-to-work process it seemed to embody) may have been the most politically expedient. And political support for a particular value proposition is hardly irrelevant to the task of building a strong public value account. But taking advantage of this expediency comes at a cost to the public. First, it precludes recognition that creating the value that Project Chance is supposed to create is more difficult than it might appear. Second, it prevents the public, its representatives, and its managers from debating what it really wants and considering many deontological questions about what a just society should be willing to do for those who have become welfare dependent. Third, by treating welfare dependency as an acute disease that can be treated with a single intervention, Tamayo's value proposition does not encourage Project Chance contractors to learn how the transition actually occurs, and what they can do to facilitate it. In this way, embracing an established (but a faulty) understanding of the ends and means of a public program can prevent the public from learning what is desirable and doable.

If the public embraced Tamayo's measurements, and the implied conception of welfare dependency as an acute problem that can be solved with a one-time intervention, it would hardly be the first time that a performance measurement system had obscured rather than revealed what was both desirable and possible to do in government operations. But that does not let Tamayo off the hook. A more strategic, value-oriented approach in this case might have helped her create a public value account that better reflected what the Illinois public really wanted to accomplish with Project Chance. Tamayo could have then used that account not only to drive performance but also to lay down a record of real operational performance that could help everyone learn what is possible to do in this domain.

An Operational Capacity Perspective on Project Chance

In Chapter 2 I introduced the public value scorecard as a device that would enable public managers to manage their enterprises strategically—that is, with an eye to changing environmental conditions and the managerial actions necessary to sustain or improve past and current value-creating efforts (as recorded in some kind of public value account). I also introduced the value chain as an analytic concept that could focus managerial attention on the core operational processes that were producing (or not producing) the desired social results. I made use of the value chain earlier in this chapter to distinguish among different kinds of performance measures in terms of the part of the value chain that was the focus of their attention. I noted that contemporary pressures had moved public managers to develop measurement systems that could recognize value creation in terms of client satisfaction and desired social outcomes, and that while that move represented an improvement in the ability to manage for public value creation, creating outcome measures did not eliminate the need for process measures in effective performance and management systems. To understand not just the outcomes that Tamayo wanted to achieve but also the processes on which she relied (the operational capacity perspective), I next consider the value chain from Tamayo's point of view.

The Value Chain for Project Chance

The original concept of the value chain described the process by which managers deployed assets in specific policies, programs, and procedures to produce particular outputs and (ideally) socially valued outcomes in a single organization. Project Chance, however, is not a single organization; it consists of a network of contractors. Compared to the size and reach of that network, the organization that Tamayo led (in effect, a contracting office and an audit team) is very small. Figure 4.4 draws the value chain with Tamayo's organization at the head of the line, receiving public dollars and authority from the authorizing environment and deploying those collectively owned assets through contracts with suppliers like Herr's Project Match.

Contractors then use the state's money and authority to hire and pay staff and to provide services to (and impose obligations on) clients. Exactly how contractors use their staff is based on the set of policies, programs, and procedures they design to produce client encounters in hopes of producing the desired results. These particular policies and procedures represent the operating methods or "technology" of a particular welfare-to-work program.[35] These may be either proprietary and held closely by the provider, or part of the public domain and the focus of professional dialogue among different providers. Clients react to their encounters with providers and caseworkers, and then either do or do not make significant changes in their lives. The degree to which the clients move toward self-sufficiency represents an important part of

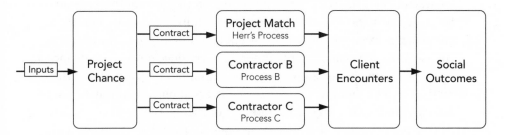

Figure 4.4. Tamayo's public value chain.

the public value that justifies the public's choice to support Project Chance's mission.

Performance Contracting to Control Production in a Network. In the early days of Project Chance, before Tamayo's performance contracts, contracts specified activities or functions that the contractor would carry out rather than outputs or outcomes. The terms might have been as broad as "provide welfare-to-work services to eligible clients," with little mention of the means to be employed, the character of the results to be delivered, or even the number of clients to be served. Or, the contracts might have described some operational requirements that had to be met—the qualifications of those working in the programs, or the frequency of contact with clients, for example.

Tamayo's shift from contracting for *activities* to contracting for *outcomes* was designed to change the form of the contract between the state of Illinois (the principal with the right to define value) and the contractors (the agents pursuing the principal's purposes). As noted earlier, this shift matters for two reasons. First, because outcomes constitute the end value to be produced, the state gets to contract for the direct production of what it wants. Second, in relaxing constraints on methods, the state gives contractors room to innovate and experiment with production processes that might work better in general, or for particular populations. In both cases the state hopes that the move to performance contracts will improve the overall performance of the system, whether by motivating greater effort, encouraging the spread of innovation, or customizing programs to particular client populations.

Designing Production Systems at the Contractor Level. While Tamayo can afford to be indifferent to the particular operational methods that her contractors use, the contractors live or die on the basis of their methods for achieving the contractually mandated results. Each contractor has to engineer processes that transform public money into a workforce of counselors, job developers, and others who produce outputs in the form of contact with clients, employers, and educational institutions. If their method allows them to achieve the contracted objectives reliably, at a low cost, and with many different kinds of clients, they will continue to receive public assets. Those with methods that work only occasionally, only with some clients, or only at a high cost will be weeded out of the system. Even with better-than-average results, a relatively high-cost provider like Herr could fall to Tamayo's efforts to improve the overall performance of the system.

Two Different Kinds of Innovations. Changes in production processes are called "innovations." Innovations can be large or small. They can be new in either a global or local sense. They can be changes in the processes used to produce outputs or changes in the actual outputs produced to create the desired outcomes. Each innovation, by definition untested in a particular context, carries risks and uncertainties. Arguments and data indicating that the innovation can improve performance have to justify the costs of both development and uncertainty.

At least two different kinds of innovations can be used to improve performance. The first kind is associated with changes in administrative systems (e.g., organizational structures, human resource management, budgeting, or performance measurement). The second kind changes basic operating programs—the particular ways in which an organization deploys labor and materials to produce specific outputs.

In shifting to a performance contracting system, Tamayo introduced a significant administrative innovation to Project Chance. In order to make that shift, she had to develop performance measures and new methods of paying contractors for demonstrated performance. She made these changes in hopes that contractors would improve performance through reduced costs and/or increased quantity and quality of outputs. And, insofar as these changes created opportunities and incentives for experimentation and revealed what organizations and processes seemed to work best, there was a good chance that her administrative innovations would produce programmatic innovations. But the administrative innovation will not produce the desired programmatic changes desired if contractors do not respond to the opportunities and incentives with improved designs. And, if administrative systems cannot recognize improved performance and help increase the use of improved methods (by spreading innovation, or increasing support for organizations with superior methods), then the administrative change will not necessarily move the value chain in a desirable direction.

For example, William Bratton relied on an administrative innovation (Compstat) to create both opportunities and incentives for midlevel managers to find a more effective means to reduce crime.[36] If precinct commanders respond with operational and programmatic innovations, the NYPD can learn how to improve performance. But the Bratton case can also be seen as an effort to introduce a programmatic innovation in policing—one that seeks to control crime and reduce fear through enforcement against minor disorder offenses. If Bratton's principal intervention is a top-down programmatic innovation, and Compstat is just the means for ensuring that the NYPD pursues this strategy, then we get a very different interpretation of how Compstat worked to improve performance; instead of using outcome objectives to stimulate precinct commanders to imagine better crime-control methods, Compstat was an administrative control system for ensuring compliance with mandated policies and procedures.[37]

Similarly, in the case of Project Chance, Tamayo's RFP caused Herr not only to imagine new ways to produce the outcomes requested but also to comply with Tamayo's preferred methods. The RFP from Tamayo called for "action plans" for moving each client to the desired goal. While this seemed consistent with Herr's individualized focus on clients, the necessity of writing a plan for each and every client seemed unnecessary, costly, and potentially damaging to Herr. Project Match caseworkers were continuously creating and updating plans with clients; writing down plans meant more busywork and less flexibility to adapt to changes in clients' environments or motivations. Moreover, Project Match caseworkers were supporting clients to make progress— not to achieve an arbitrary goal that may have been beyond their current capacities. Even though Tamayo's requirements seemed relatively neutral with respect to specifying the means to accomplish a given goal, they still imposed procedural burdens on contractors that could increase costs and reduce performance and the freedom to innovate.

The Essential Role of Partners and Coproducers. It is a relatively easy matter to take stock of the production processes *within* the boundaries of a given organization, but there are also myriad activities and actors that lie *beyond* organizational boundaries that affect an organization's success. For Project Chance this includes not only contractors but also potential educators and employers of clients. And, as Project Match's caseworkers noted, the families of clients can greatly help or hurt their ability to become independent. The "process" of producing public value extends well beyond organizational outputs—both over time and across social actors.

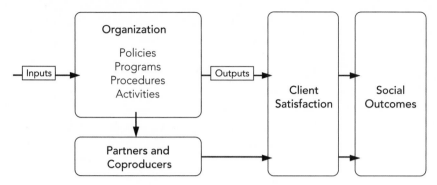

Figure 4.5. The public value chain, with partners.

Figure 4.4 showed the difference between a value chain that was fully contained within a single organization (also see Figure 2.8) and one that was entirely contracted out. Figure 4.5 presents a more generalized diagram, showing public agencies alongside other actors (partners and coproducers) that contribute to the achievement of social outcomes.

The figure gives explicit recognition to the fact that for many public agencies, the necessary operational capacity for value production lies outside organizational boundaries. Sometimes this help lies in the individual willingness of citizens to lend operational support for achieving agency goals. Thus, for example, without citizens willing to provide information, police cannot solve crimes and arrest offenders. Other times the external capacity that is needed lies in independently governed organizations with whom the public organization contracts for services, as in Tamayo's reliance on private welfare-to-work agencies.

Figure 4.6 shows in a bit more detail how public agencies work with other organizations as partners to produce desired results through the effective engagement of their clients. Those encounters can be service encounters (in which clients receive information, benefits, or services that they can use), obligation encounters (in which clients have more or less compelling obligations imposed on them through the direct authority of the state, or informal pressure to conform to a social norm), or, most commonly, some combination of the two.

In Project Chance, organized partners like Project Match provide clients with ongoing advice, encouragement, and prodding from caseworkers, as well as referrals to others who can help (organizational

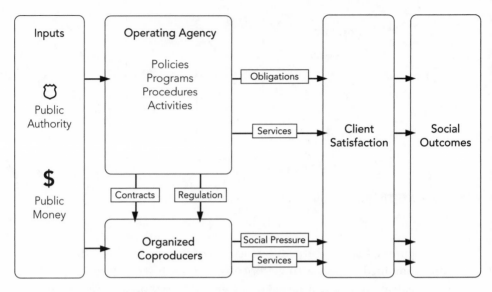

Figure 4.6. The public value chain, with organized coproducers.

outputs). They may hate or enjoy this experience (client satisfaction). But Project Chance's ability to achieve its ultimate goals depends on both the capacity and willingness of the clients to turn the advice and referrals from Project Chance contractors into independence (desired social outcomes). Only when clients find the motivation and support they need to become financially independent is public value created. It is in this sense that clients are "coproducers" of social outcomes (public value). This principle applies especially to public agencies that impose obligations as well as provide services. James could not collect taxes from Minnesota's citizens unless they cooperated—either voluntarily, or through coercion.

When public agencies have to rely on their clients to produce valued results, their managers have to understand what is happening beyond organizational boundaries. Finding the means to engage clients in producing the desired outcomes is an essential part of process and program design.

Heterogeneous Client Populations and Cherry-Picking. If clients play a central role in achieving desired results, the process that public agencies (or their contractors) use to recruit and select clients also becomes a critical part of policy or program design. As noted earlier, if a welfare-to-work program can screen out unmotivated and/or unskilled participants, it can probably make more placements with less effort than if it took any eligible candidate or focused on assisting those clients who were most disadvantaged.

Again, this means that Tamayo (1) has to account for differences in clients when considering the likely costs for the contractor and (2) has to face the philosophical question of what the overall goal of the system is. If the goal is the utilitarian goal of maximizing the number of individuals who can be removed from the welfare rolls at the lowest possible cost to the state, then it would make sense to grant contracts to programs skilled in finding the clients best able to use their services. In essence, the successful programs would be selling two valuable things to the state: (1) a capacity to help clients make the transition from welfare to work and (2) a kind of triage capacity for finding the candidates who can most easily make the change. If, however, the goal is the deontological goal of providing equal access to all eligible individuals, or providing extra help to the most disadvantaged so that each individual gets an equal chance at making a similar degree of progress, then allowing contractors to screen for the most resourceful clients would be a mistake.

For their part, contractors would have to decide how to position themselves in a heterogeneous market of need. Whether they choose to focus on the hard-core or the relatively better-off segments of the population depends to some degree on their own ideas of what constitutes public value and the mission of their organizations and how they understand and evaluate their own capacities. But the choice will also be influenced by what Tamayo decides to purchase and the price she is willing to pay.

As long as Tamayo assumes that one welfare-to-work client is pretty much like another and ignores the client's role in coproducing the results that Project Chance is trying to achieve, she does not have to confront the philosophical question of whether advancing one kind of client is worth more than advancing another, nor the operational question of how to recognize differences in client populations in her performance measurement system. As soon as she recognizes that populations differ in terms of how much help they need to achieve similar levels of independence, she has to confront both questions.

At Project Match, Herr made a commitment to developing a method and a program for dealing with the hard-core client population—those with little work experience and with years (sometimes generations) of welfare dependence behind them. In essence, Herr did the opposite of cherry-picking: she went for the hardest-core population. To assist that population, she provided highly individualized, sustained, and responsive casework on an as-needed basis. These methods were difficult to manage, but Herr made it easier over the long run by developing an information system, a personnel system, and an organizational culture that allowed her to manage this complex process. Such individualized and complex systems may be generally necessary to make progress with the hard-core population. But it is also possible that these methods would work better with all welfare clients, and that they could compete on the basis of cost as well as effectiveness for a broad segment of the client population.

Assuming, however, that Herr's methods are tailored to the hard-core population, and that her average costs are higher than those of providers working with other client populations, the burden is on Tamayo to decide whether to recognize differences in the client population, and whether to pay more to aid the hard-core population.[38] In the case discussed, Tamayo offered one price for particular outcomes regardless of the characteristics of the population served. This implied that the particular outcomes she named were a relatively complete description of the public value citizens wanted Project Chance to produce, making the question of how inexpensively welfare-to-work programs could find and move individuals off the welfare rolls the only really important issue.

Tamayo could have decided instead to pay more for success with hard-core clients, acknowledging not only that there were different costs associated with treating different kinds of welfare clients but also perhaps that there was added value in helping the most disadvantaged individuals, and that helping those who were the worst-off would produce a valuable kind of social justice. Had she done so, she would have not only increased the fairness of the compensation system for providers but also removed incentives for providers to cherry-pick. The contracting system would work to stimulate innovations that could reduce the costs of helping all kinds of welfare clients make the transition rather than innovations that could help contractors find the easiest to treat.

Recognizing the Value of Research, Experimentation, and Innovation

Tamayo, as the manager of Project Chance, was responsible for improving the long-run efficiency, effectiveness, and fairness of the welfare-to-work system. To some degree she could count on the incentives created by her performance contracts to encourage her contractors to search for and exploit productivity-enhancing innovations. But there was no guarantee that these innovations would spread throughout the industry or allow the government to benefit from the gains. Contractors could treat their innovations as proprietary, refuse to share them with others or the government, and, instead of trying to expand in the market, stay in a particular market niche using the productivity gains for their own benefit.

The alternative was for Tamayo to take a more activist approach in encouraging particular kinds of R&D activities, using both philanthropic and governmental funds to support experiments and innovations designed to improve performance in the welfare-to-work field, and spreading these research findings across the entire field. Rather than wait for individual contractors to make innovations and then try to structure the market to give those firms a larger share, she could use her agency to sponsor an exploration of the field's position relative to the production possibility frontier and learn how to improve its performance.[39]

A public value scorecard that focused Tamayo's attention on the operational capacity perspective and particularly the role of experimentation and learning in building operational capacity might have encouraged Tamayo to view Herr's activities in a different light. Project Match was unlike other contractors not just because it had developed a special method for dealing with the hard-core welfare population but because it was engaged in research and in producing findings that could boost the performance of the system as a whole in the future. In this respect Herr's program could have been part of an R&D program designed to support long-term productivity gains in Project Chance.

Including investments and activities designed to support innovation, experimentation, and learning in the operational capacity perspective of the public value scorecard raises some important questions for Tamayo, and for the broader public: first, whether there is, in fact, public value associated with the kind of research that Herr is conducting; second, whether the government should pay for the research; and third, whether Herr's program represents the best method of carrying it out.

While Herr's original funding from the newly created Project Chance had come through a "demonstration grant," the research end of the program was primarily funded through grants from foundations and in-kind contributions from Northwestern University rather than through public funds. Presumably, Tamayo could have recognized Project Match's research role by continuing to fund it through a demonstration grant, but this would have created three problems. First, it would have compromised Tamayo's ambition to commit all the contractors in the system to performance contracts and reap the benefits of a standardized and competitive bidding process. Second, it would have created the impression that there was political favoritism and a lack of discipline in the system, undermining both the effectiveness and the fairness of the procurement system she managed. Third, continuing to support demonstration grants would have suggested that Project Chance still did not know what it was doing after six years of operation. Would her overseers not think that the time for experimentation was over, and that the time for squeezing out of the program cost reductions and improved results had begun?

Gauging the Need for Research, Innovation, and Experimentation. Tamayo doubted whether her overseers would see public value in supporting research because the public and its representatives lacked well-developed views about the value of R&D in public-sector operations—despite the fact that government routinely supports basic research designed to create value in many different fields.[40] Indeed, government supports research even in areas where commercial enterprises will likely be among the first to use research findings, turning them into life-saving drugs, high-yield crops, and faster computers and reaping huge profits.[41] In light of this, it seems only natural for government to support research into public enterprises as well. Still, most public managers remain reluctant to do so.[42]

As noted earlier, Tamayo's competitive procurement system was, in many ways, designed to support a high level of research, experimentation, and innovation. Under the competitive procurement system, all contractors had an incentive to create innovations that would allow them to produce more of what Tamayo wanted at a lower cost than their competitors. Suppliers presumably had access to some private capital to help develop their ideas. Ideally, the combination of competitive procurement and private financing would produce many important product and process innovations. As previously noted, however, it was unclear how these proprietary ideas would spread in a market dominated by public spending.

If Tamayo (perhaps in partnership with private foundations) were to take on some responsibility for developing value-creating innovations in the welfare-to-work field, she would, in effect, recognize that some portion of her spending should be used to create a "risk portfolio" of R&D ideas. Of course, in a world that expects government agencies to already know the best methods for achieving desired results, it does not make much sense to invest in a risk portfolio to explore the production possibility frontier. But what if government officials do not really know the best way to accomplish a particular goal? Suppose their practices have never been subjected to empirical testing? Suppose they could be easily improved upon if only they tried to develop alternatives?

Most public agencies would be hard-pressed to answer the question of how large their risk portfolios should be, even though many could point to various pilot projects, demonstration grants, and so on that might constitute a rudimentary effort to construct one. Advanced industrial economies spend about 3 percent of their total resources on R&D, on average. Some sectors of the economy focusing on technological innovation spend as much as 30 percent on R&D.[43] In deciding how much to invest in innovations, four slightly different standards could guide public managers.

First, if citizens are not satisfied with the performance of a public agency, a public manager would be wise to shift more resources toward innovative activity. Failure cannot be met with more of the same; something new has to be tried.

Second, if the agency faces a new task, more resources should be dedicated to innovation. When confronting a new problem, it usually takes several attempts to find a workable and efficient solution, even under the best of circumstances.

Third, if the population of a public agency is trying to serve or if the problems it is trying to solve are either highly varied (heterogeneous) or rapidly changing (dynamic), then it might have to invest in developing distinctive approaches to those different populations and circumstances. The more heterogeneous and dynamic the world that public managers face, the more they might want to invest in R&D.

The fourth consideration concerns changes in technologies and practices. Technological changes can sometimes suggest or enable important changes in practices. An improved diagnostic capacity for identifying learning disabilities or emotional problems might allow kindergarten teachers to respond to differences among their pupils more effectively than in the past. Devices to keep automated teller machines (ATMs) and those using them more secure might produce a technical answer to the question of how to stop a rash of ATM robberies. Not all important innovations in a given field come from that particular field. Many are borrowed and adapted from other fields, or they emerge as new applications of technologies developed elsewhere for different purposes.

Many—perhaps even most—public agencies have underinvested in R&D. They have long operated as though they were standard production-line organizations confronting steady, homogeneous conditions. They may have adopted this style to meet demands for accountability and consistency as virtues in themselves, but whatever the reason, public agencies tend to resist any tinkering with operating methods. They do so despite the fact that they are often perceived to be failing, taking on new problems, facing highly diverse and rapidly changing operational tasks, and living in a world in which knowledge and technology are rapidly changing.

Jeannette Tamayo faced all these conditions to one degree or another, suggesting that she would indeed benefit from experimentation. Herr may not be the only or even the best supplier of the R&D required to improve the long-term performance of Project Chance, but Tamayo would have been wise to include some R&D in her strategy to ensure the long-run, continuous improvement of her enterprise as well as its short-term operational efficiency.

Different Kinds of R&D. If Tamayo wanted to build learning and innovation into the system, she would have to consider what kind of R&D efforts would be most valuable. For her part, Herr was already engaged in at least four kinds of research that Tamayo might find valuable: (1) problem/market research; (2) materials and process research and production engineering; (3) program design and evaluation research; and (4) management research.

First, through long hours of close observation and individual attention, Herr and her staff were gathering a great deal of information about the problem they were taking on, and about the individual clients who constituted the problem but also held the solution. They studied the condition and character of their clients. They analyzed the transition from welfare to work in anthropological detail and learned that the process often *began* rather than ended with a job placement. They discovered that relationships outside the program—families, friends, and role models—played a critical role in supporting or sabotaging the transition. Because Project Match was a fairly large program that maintained continuous contact with the clients, it was possible to identify and anticipate the full range of issues that individual clients would confront and how often particular issues came up.

To many sociologists, anthropologists, and behavioral economists, such work looks a lot like social science research into the problem of welfare dependency. But these efforts are also analogous to "market research" in the private sector. In hopes of making Project Match services more useful, relevant, and accessible, Herr looked outside her organization to find out how her clients saw and made use of its services and built a client-oriented staff culture.[44] The "market" being investigated was not a consumer market consisting of individuals with money to spend on services but a market of individuals with needs to which the broader public, acting through the government, was trying to respond. And, as in private-sector marketing, the ideas of the individuals with needs became an important part of the methods that the organization used to engage them.

The detailed knowledge of the problem Herr intended to solve, and the individuals she meant to recruit in the solution of the problem led to a second kind of applied research—described here as materials and process research, for lack of a better term. The goal of materials and process research is to develop an understanding of the materials with which one is working to produce a particular result, and the ways in which that material can be engaged and worked to achieve the desired result.

Obviously it is not only in bad taste to talk about individual clients of welfare-to-work programs as "raw material" in a production process but also empirically inaccurate, since these individuals are independent human beings with purposes of their own. Yet from an instrumental perspective, when Herr was looking closely at her clients' struggles to achieve independence, she was not simply learning about her clients as human beings—she was also looking at their individual motivations and capacities that constituted the material she had to work with in trying to help them make the transition that she, they, and the collective public desired.

Like the "market research" component of Herr's enterprise, this "materials" aspect of her research initially looked like basic social science research about the characteristics of her clients and the problems they faced as they tried to enter the mainstream economy. She tried to find out what would happen if she did not intervene at all, and looked for some of the important causal factors that made the process uncertain, slow, and costly to both clients and her program.

There is a crucial difference, however, between Herr's aims and those of social scientists. Herr's research agenda was set by a desire to solve a practical problem rather than an intellectual question. She was not looking to investigate the nature of human society, the laws that shape the operations of the economy, or the nature of government's response to individuals who are shoved aside by socioeconomic forces. She was interested in finding, among all the factors shaping her clients' prospects, some point of leverage she could use to help some of the individuals who had been marginalized find their way into the economy.[45] The causal variables that interested her were not just those that could explain the most variance in the outcomes (the usual focus of social science investigation) but those that *she could change to improve the results.* Because she was interested in particular prescriptions rather than in general causal explanations, she acted more like an engineer trying to produce a particular result under particular circumstances than a social scientist trying to understand general laws of social behavior.[46]

The third kind of research in which Herr was engaged could be described as program design and evaluation research. Typically, this kind of research follows on the heels of materials and process research. Program design research seeks to develop an intervention that could plausibly be successful in exploiting the points of leverage identified through materials and process research, and evaluation research seeks to learn whether the carefully imagined intervention actually works.

With respect to program design, Herr seemed to have engaged in a kind of intellectual brainstorming that was disciplined by her understanding of the problem to be solved. Her problem, market, and materials research produced many valuable insights that helped her imagine a plausibly effective intervention. She recognized that caseworkers had to start with a detailed diagnosis of clients' current situations in order to create a baseline for measuring individual progress and engage clients in the joint process of diagnosing their situation and making plans for the future. Herr's hard-won understanding of the transition process led her to imagine a kind of intervention that looked very different from the standard methods or any kind of standard production process: an intensive, long-term, and highly flexible engagement with clients.

Once Herr had a particular idea about what kind of intervention might work with her clients, she had to test the efficacy of that intervention more rigorously through the formal processes of program evaluation. Viewed through the lens of program evaluation, the apparent strength of Herr's research efforts breaks down a bit. For one thing, they fail to identify precisely what results the citizens of Illinois want produced (though she might be forgiven for this fact if the people of Illinois have not given this question the consideration it deserves).[47] But Herr's methods also break down because she failed to run the program as an experiment. The failure to use an experimental approach is a serious problem not only to social scientists but also to those who would like to replicate Herr's methods with confidence in getting the same results. But Herr's looser standards may not be too damning, since this kind of confidence comes at a high price, and the confidence is not always merited.

If a public agency needs to be very confident in its methods, has a lot of money to spend on research, and is prepared to wait a long time to find improved methods, then it can afford a systematic experimental approach. If, however, it does not need to be so certain, or has little money for R&D, or needs to move more quickly to improve performance, it might be prepared to adopt a faster, more pragmatic, but possibly less certain, means for developing improved performance.

Finally, Herr engaged in research into the development of a performance measurement and management system that could be used to guide agency operations and observe valued results. I argued in Chapter 2 that an important part of a strategic approach to performance measurement and management in public enterprises is the assumption that developing these systems will take time. There should be no expectation that the performance measures that managers need already exist in the organization. They might all have to be developed—sometimes from scratch.

Arguably, Herr's most important invention was "the ladder and the scale," which embodied her public value proposition and the corresponding computerized tracking system that guided and controlled her program's complex operation. This system allowed a small staff to keep in relatively constant contact with a large number of clients. It gave caseworkers a way to think about and record the progress of their clients and to figure out when interventions were needed, and what kind. It also allowed Project Match to see what it actually produced in the form of activities and client contacts. This helped Herr maintain some degree of administrative control and meet the demands for external accountability focused on activities and outputs. It also provided the data necessary to trace the connection between the operations of the program and the results it achieved.

The ladder and the scale allowed Herr to suggest a different way of evaluating Project Match—a different conception of the public value the program produced. Until Herr developed the ladder, the citizens of Illinois were stuck with an acute disease model of the problem they were trying to solve through Project Chance. Arguably, that model failed to identify the real value that the public wanted to produce through a welfare-to-work program. Whether Tamayo embraced it or not, the ladder provided citizens with a different public value proposition for welfare-to-work programs. Herr was thus an innovator with respect to the development of concepts and instruments for recognizing public value, as well as the methods for dealing with one of the public's most intractable and frustrating problems.

Summary

This chapter opened with the story of Jeannette Tamayo, who was charged with managing Project Chance—an innovative program designed to help Illinois welfare clients make the transition from welfare to work. The story of Project Chance reveals some fundamental differences between public agencies that create and monitor their own production systems and those that rely on a network of private service providers mobilized and supported by a public contracting system that pays for particular outcomes. But Project Chance has one important thing in common with the other cases examined so far. If Tamayo wants to run the program in a strategic way, she will have to develop a public value account that can recognize and measure all the important values the public has implicitly and explicitly mandated the program to achieve, a legitimacy and support perspective that tracks the political conditions under which it is operating, and an operational capacity perspective to help develop the program's capacity to improve productivity over time.

Tamayo has to develop a concept of public value that works not only technically and managerially but also philosophically and politically. A conflict between Tamayo and one of her contractors about the terms of the contract that seems to be technical and managerial actually goes straight to the heart of philosophical and political ideas about the ultimate ends and appropriate means of welfare-to-work services. Tamayo sees the question primarily in collective, utilitarian terms: her job is to move as many clients as possible off the welfare rolls for as little money as possible. She hopes contracting for the results she takes to be indicators of success in moving individuals off the welfare rolls will encourage contractors to design processes that deliver those results robustly, quickly, and effectively. Herr, for her part, thinks of the work largely in deontological terms. She thinks the goal should be to give all welfare clients the best possible chance to overcome their welfare dependence. She also thinks the process is inherently slow and only intermittently successful.

Tamayo and Herr do not find a suitable forum in which to air and resolve their differences with the help of elected officials. They get stuck at the contractor/contractee level. As a consequence, they are left with a measurement system that recognizes only part of the public value that Project Chance could produce and creates incentives for welfare-to-work programs to cherry-pick clients rather than assist every client requesting services—including seemingly hopeless cases. In sticking with a flawed but politically supportable measurement system, Tamayo denied the citizens of Illinois an opportunity to discuss and define the public value they wanted Project Chance to produce and denied herself an opportunity to develop a management system for Project Chance

PUBLIC VALUE ACCOUNT for Jeannette Tamayo and Project Chance

PUBLIC VALUE ACCOUNT	
Use of Collectively Owned Assets and Associated Costs	Achievement of Collectively Valued Social Outcomes

Financial Costs
  Internal (administrative)
  External (costs to clients)
	Mission Achievement:
	  Move welfare clients to
	  independence

	• Economically
	• Psychologically
	• Socially
	Reduce future welfare costs to taxpayers

Unintended Negative Consequences
  Alienating clients from programs
  designed to help
  Extending welfare dependency
	Unintended Positive Consequences
	  Shift cultural norms toward
	  independence

	Client Satisfaction
	Treat clients with respect
	Meet client needs
	Engage client aspirations
Social Costs of Using State Authority Rationing of services	Justice and Fairness
	Protect individual rights
	Impose obligations fairly
	Provide access for all welfare clients
	Offer extra help to neediest clients (?)

Figure 4.7. Public value scorecard for Jeannette Tamayo and Project Chance.

THE LEGITIMACY AND SUPPORT PERSPECTIVE
Progress and Planning for Jeannette Tamayo and Project Chance

Mission Alignment with Values Articulated by Citizens:
Focused organization on providing clients a chance for independence
Develop measures of value consistent with citizens' aspirations

Inclusion of Neglected Values with Latent Constituencies:
Seek balance between support, protection of rights, and obligations given to welfare clients
Provide extra help to neediest clients

Standing with Formal Authorizers:
Statutory Overseers in Executive Branch
  • Rationalized contracting system to "guarantee" contractor performance
  • *Produce evidence of cost-effectiveness of Project Chance*

Standing with Key Interest Groups:
Treat contractors responsively and fairly
Demonstrate cost-effectiveness of program to taxpayers
Demonstrate respect for clients' rights and equal opportunities for clients to welfare advocates

Media Coverage:
Monitor coverage to discern implicit values and explicit critiques

Standing with Individuals in Polity:
General Citizenry and Taxpayers
  • *Engage citizens in deliberative surveys on attitudes toward welfare-to-work programs*
Clients
  • *Survey clients on experiences with contractors*

Position of Enterprise in Democratic Political Discourse:
Provide accurate information about costs and performance to enrich public's understanding of the values at stake

Engagement of Citizens as Co-producers:
Involve client peer groups in assisting progress toward independence

---

THE OPERATIONAL CAPACITY PERSPECTIVE:
Progress and Planning for Jeannette Tamayo and Project Chance

Flow of Resources to Enterprise:
Sustained flow of government resources by meeting demands for accountability
Sustain flow of charitable resources to partners by aligning with funders' aims
Build public support through enriched public discussion of values and capacities

Operational Policies, Programs, and Procedures:
Organizational Learning (for network of providers)
  • *Explore heterogeneity of client population*
  • *Refine different methods for different client groups*
  • *Seek robust methods that work for all client groups*
  • *Adapt and experiment with the Ladder and the Scale as method for recognizing value creation*
Internal Resource Allocation
  • Exploited contracting system to shift resources to "high performers"
Performance Measurement and Management Systems
  • Used contract system to create uniform standards for performance
  • *Develop measures to distinguish hard core from marginally disadvantaged*
  • *Develop and encourage use of the Ladder and the Scale as method for recognizing value creation*

Organizational Outputs:
Ensure that all clients are treated with respect
Ensure an appropriate balance between support and obligations for clients

that would allow the agency and the public to explore what could actually be produced against all definitions of public value.

The failure to create a suitable public value account is compounded by a flawed operational capacity perspective that does not seem to recognize how much of the operational capacity needed to produce the desired results lies with the clients and their families. Herr's research made it clear that these actors play a crucial role in the value chain as coproducers of the desired results. From the operational capacity perspective, that meant three things. First, it meant that in trying to create a level playing field for Project Chance contractors, it was important to develop and use a measure of the private capacities the clients themselves brought to the program—otherwise, the providers' incentives would shift from finding ways to help clients make the transition to developing methods that would allow them to find the clients easiest to boost over the bar that Tamayo had set. Second, it meant that programs would have to find ways to address the motivations and engagement of clients, and to help them clear a path in their private lives for the pursuit of independence. Third, it meant that to ensure that all clients had the opportunity to make progress, it might be necessary to have special programs for the hard-core client population that were operated and compensated on a different basis.

Beyond the issue of coping with a heterogeneous client base, Project Chance needed to understand that it was at the beginning, not the end, of an effort to explore the production possibility frontier. Performance contracting in a competitive market can help reduce costs in the short run by giving one provider a competitive advantage over another, and in the long run by stimulating providers to create innovative approaches to the work. If Tamayo had understood that she was at the beginning of this exploration, she might have concentrated a bit more on the potential for long-run cost reduction and performance enhancement through innovations in helping the entire client population, or particular segments. She would have written contracts that supported research, experimentation, and innovation, as well as short-run operational performance. She might have been particularly interested in providers who were engaged in research that could help the field as a whole rather than the individual provider.

These comments suggest that a significant value-creating opportunity was lost in this collision between the new outcome-oriented management and the old process-oriented management. The apparently technical debate about performance measures could have been allowed to break out into a wider political and philosophical discussion about the public values at stake in Project Chance, and how performance with respect to those values might be measured. The question of whether the overall performance of Project Chance was best served by ignoring or taking account of differences among welfare clients that affected both the cost of helping them make change and the benefits (reckoned in both utilitarian and deontological terms) of doing so also could have been raised. The issue of whether the state's long-run interests in creating a welfare-to-work industry would be better served by a contracting system that provided incentives and access to public or private funding for innovation and research also went unaddressed. Viewed from this perspective, Tamayo's commitment to a simple idea of performance contracting and quick adoption of a particular form of measurement may have reduced rather than increased the public value of Project Chance. Again, it is not that systems that promote public value recognition and production are not useful; it is that simplistic ideas about how to use these systems often do harm rather than good.

A complete public value scorecard for Tamayo might have looked something like Figure 4.7.

5

Diana Gale and the Seattle Solid Waste Utility

Using Transparency to Legitimize Innovation and Mobilize
Citizen and Client Coproduction

Diana Gale and the Garbage Overhaul

In January 1987 Diana Gale became director of the Solid Waste Utility
for the city of Seattle.[1] She was a new kind of director for the utility, not
only the first woman appointed to the post but the first director without a technical engineering background. Equipped with a PhD in urban
planning and a strong understanding of policy analysis and urban politics, her task was to roll out a new system for dealing with the two thousand tons of solid waste the city and its surrounding areas produced
each day.

Gale's new system—designed to reduce both the economic and environmental costs of solid waste management—required changes in
how the city's employees and contractors handled the trash. But it
also required changes in the habits of the citizens themselves. Some
changes were big—requiring citizens to put different types of trash
(such as recyclables and yard waste) into different kinds of containers,
for instance. Others were smaller and perhaps harder for citizens to
remember—such as the requirement that garbage bins be placed three
feet from the curb.

In addition, the city redesigned the way in which it asked residents
to pay for garbage collection services. Residents accustomed to having
their trash removed directly from their backyards now had to pay a
premium for that service. New fees were established for yard waste,
backyard service, and even for larger cans. Residents had to consider
their needs, pocketbooks, and how much work they were willing to do

on their own in making decisions about the level and kind of service they wanted from the city's garbage collectors.

It was trial by fire for Gale. She had no prior experience managing a large operating agency. Her previous position was director of the City Council's central staff of analysts. She was experienced in managing complex policy development processes, not in managing an operating agency that had daily contact with the city's entire citizenry. But it was up to her to guide the residents of Seattle and her organization through these major changes.

Background: The Solid Waste Crisis in Seattle

Seattle's public utilities were part of a long and proud tradition of technically strong, professionally based public services that had started in the progressive era. Reflecting the widespread view that managing solid waste was primarily a technical problem, the Solid Waste Utility was lodged within the city's Engineering Department. Resident ratepayers provided virtually all financial support to the utility. Prices charged to residents for garbage collection were set by the Seattle City Council but had been low and stable for many years. Although, strictly speaking, the Seattle Solid Waste Utility was not constituted as a tax-supported public monopoly, virtually all citizens relied on the utility for the safe, legal, and efficient disposal of their garbage. The system operated inexpensively, conveniently, and mostly invisibly. The citizens of Seattle did not have to think much about solid waste—a strong bureaucracy was doing the work for them.

Then, on Thanksgiving Day, in 1985, a methane gas leak at the Midway landfill forced the evacuation of eleven families from their homes. The sight on the evening news of the families hauling half-baked turkeys to motel rooms revealed the degree to which Seattle's solid waste management system was pressed to the limit. For the first time in generations, Seattleites had to pay attention to garbage.

While the methane leak created a public sense of immediate and unforeseen crisis, those in city government were aware that it was just one sign of the persistent deterioration of Seattle's trash disposal systems. In the early 1980s, the two landfill sites on which the city had long relied were filled to capacity, closed, and capped. To meet its interim needs, the city contracted for the temporary use of a disposal site owned by the surrounding King County, but neither future access to this site nor future prices were guaranteed. Seattle needed a more permanent solution to its growing solid waste problem—and quickly.

A New Plan

Naturally the technocrats at the Solid Waste Utility were not without ideas about a more permanent plan for handling Seattle's solid waste. The front-runner at the time of the methane leak was a proposal to construct a city-owned "waste to energy plant" (basically an incinerator), but taxpayers who were concerned about the cost of the plant and environmentalists who were concerned about the environmental consequences of burning tons of garbage in Seattle joined together to force a reconsideration. In October 1987, at the direction of the Seattle City Council, the utility began an in-depth study of the city's "waste stream." At the end of nine months, the utility had concluded that with the right set of programs and financial incentives, Seattle could recycle up to 60 percent of its trash and send the rest not to an incinerator but, via rail, to a landfill in arid and rural eastern Oregon. This solution improved upon the incinerator scheme, since it was less costly, more protective of the environment, and less divisive within the community (which would otherwise have to find a site for the incinerator). To make the plan work, however, the city would have to achieve unprecedented levels of solid waste recycling. That, in turn, meant that both garbage collectors and residents would have to make significant changes in their solid waste handling habits. In effect, the new plan would ask residents of Seattle not only to pay attention to garbage collection, and to pay higher prices for it, but also to work on their own to facilitate the process of collecting and disposing of trash.

To minimize the chance of major disruptions, the planners divided the implementation of the plan into two stages. In phase one, the Solid Waste Utility would ask Seattle residents to sign up for a voluntary program of free curbside recycling. Phase two was more ambitious—all residents would be required to choose a particular level of garbage collection from a menu of options, each with its own price and its own limitations, and each with its own requirements for residents to organize their trash for easy collection and recycling.

Under the new plan the basic deal between the Solid Waste Utility and its citizen ratepayers was going to change considerably. Citizens would have to make choices about the levels and kinds of services they wanted and could afford. And, to reap the benefit of free recycling pickup, they would have to become active participants in the handling and sorting of their trash. Residents who wanted to stick with the comfortable, accommodating old system (no sorting recyclables, backyard pickup) would have to pay a premium. Those willing to separate recyclables and yard waste from other kinds of garbage and haul their trash cans to the curb would pay considerably less for their service. This phase, which would impose new burdens on citizens, would take effect in January 1989.

Diana Gale's Strategic Calculation

Gale had two years to shepherd her agency and the residents of Seattle through this complicated set of changes. To many, Gale's lack of administrative experience appeared to be a handicap. But Gale quickly understood that she had two tasks before her. On one hand, she had to use her administrative powers and tools to help employees and public contractors implement a series of systemic changes. Here her lack of administrative experience and technical expertise could have been problematic. On the other hand, she had to find the means to help hundreds of thousands of Seattle residents understand and accept the new system with all of its associated rates and fees, as well as mobilize them to sort through their garbage and become reliable cogs in the machinery that handled Seattle's solid waste. For this kind of political or community mobilization task, her experience in orchestrating complex policy development processes would serve her well.

This second task captured a great deal of Gale's attention. She knew it would be a struggle to get Seattle's citizens to pay attention to something as mundane as garbage. She knew that there would be lots of errors, slips, and confusion along the way. And she knew she was asking the Seattle citizens both to pay more and get less than they had in the past. She would need citizens to be tolerant and patient even as she asked them to accept new burdens. To meet the political mobilization challenge, Gale needed to speak to Seattle's citizens at different levels, and in different capacities. To manage relations with the citizens who authorized this innovation, she needed a narrative that would help citizens understand why they were being asked to accept the burdens of the new system. The story had to be simple, endorsed by persuasive leaders, widely understood, and repeated ad nauseam at each point that citizen support—both political and operational—seemed to falter.

She also needed a more detailed information campaign that would simultaneously explain to Seattle citizens what they needed to do to act as effective coproducers in the new voluntary recycling system and build momentum for their engagement by tracking the number of citizens who were signing up. If she could show that most citizens were supporting the program, those citizens who were not could be painted as the problem—not the norm.

Finally, in order to show that she too was doing her part in the renovation of Seattle's system of solid waste collection and disposal, she needed to speak to citizens as clients of the utility. She needed a system for hearing and responding to individual complaints, and then using those complaints to identify and address larger flaws in the system. A compelling story about a city mobilized to face a problematic reality and the information and transparency that would give the story life and urgency would be Gale's keys to creating a public consciousness that everyone was in the effort together.

The Solid Waste Utility had no tradition of marketing new policies and programs to citizens, or enlisting their cooperation as coproducers. It had only limited and traditional experience in responding to complaints. In any case the kind of large-scale public relations campaign that would give Gale maximum control over the utility's message was both unaffordable and likely to be met with public suspicion. In light of this, Gale recognized that she would have to supplement the utility's marketing campaign with the skillful use of the inevitable media attention given to any public official managing a complex governmental innovation that affects the basic routines of city life.

Gale's prior experience with the media told her that it would be no easy task to get the word out through the press. "When you're a bureaucrat," she said, "you're incredibly vulnerable because you stand to absorb public disdain for government. There's basically a negative attitude toward government in the press. There's a tendency for the press to jump on small mistakes you make. You're easy to criticize. It's easy to trigger negative feelings about the bureaucracy, no matter how high-minded and public-spirited a job you think you're doing." Despite this, Gale knew she had no choice but to embrace the media. Even though she could not control it, nothing else provided the free publicity and the opportunity to engage citizens in the work she needed them to do. If part of her problem was to make an issue of garbage collection so that individuals would take some ownership, then even bad stories, as painful as they would be, might help her achieve her goals.

Developing a Public Relations Capacity and Campaign

Within a few months of starting at the utility, well before the recycling campaign had started in earnest, Gale had retained a consulting firm (O'Neill and Associates) to conduct market research on recycling and the utility's public image through citizen focus groups. She also hired a public relations firm (Elgin Syferd) to help develop a strategy for considering public opinion about "disposal options." Both firms concluded that the utility needed to improve its public image. The consultants advised Gale to "get a logo, get colors, get an image, have a personality." Toward that end, Gale negotiated with the mayor and the City Council to hire Ginny Stevenson as a full-time public relations specialist. Stevenson's job, Gale said, was "to get on a friendly, first-name basis with reporters."

Gale did not believe, however, that all information should be channeled through Stevenson. If all the top policy-making officials at the utility were "open and knowledgeable," Gale figured they could all become important spokespeople for the utility's efforts. To help her top lieutenants become accustomed to dealing with the press, she invited them to spend two days with her under the tutelage of two former television anchorwomen who exposed them to what Gale called "aggressive video and radio taping" toward the goal of "helping us deal with difficult, controversial questions." To aid in this task the Elgin Syferd public relations firm provided pointed questions to help officials learn not to be defensive, no matter what the provocation. The message that Gale and the consultants aimed to get across was, "Don't let the press become an adversary. You want it to be a friend. You're not a victim. You, too, can handle the press."

The Recycling Campaign

In the fall of 1987, having laid the groundwork for good working relationships with the media, Gale undertook a series of initiatives designed to ready the public for the shift to voluntary curbside recycling. She saw the recycling initiative (phase one) both as an important end in itself and as a way of helping the utility achieve public acceptance of and cooperation in the pursuit of longer-range goals. Gale explained: "We weren't so naïve as to think the public would easily buy an incinerator or anything else from us. We knew we had to have a 'win' in order to make the kind of massive service delivery changes we'd be proposing. The 'win' was going to be recycling. We knew [from the market research] that recycling was a popular idea because of its association with environmentalism, and that if we could show how aggressively we were doing it, we would gain some credibility for doing things that were less popular. In a sense, you could say we wanted to put money in the bank of public opinion."

The Solid Waste Utility set out to make the campaign for curbside recycling a long-playing, ubiquitous part of the news, the political discourse, and the civic culture of Seattle. Months before announcing the particulars of the recycling program, the utility had convened a series of roundtable discussions with 150 "key decision-makers" (business and community leaders as well as members of the press) to participate in the shaping of solid waste policy. Stevenson noted, "We wanted to reach out and have an open process. We didn't even think it mattered if everyone came so long as they knew about it."

Once the recycling program was fully fleshed out, the utility took the offensive in explaining it to the media, holding a "background briefing" for reporters to provide detailed information and to answer questions about logistics—when households would get their new recycling bins, which materials were acceptable and which were not, and so on. Officials emphasized that under the new program, separated recyclables would be collected without extra charge. Since citizens paid for waste removal by the can, this meant a household that turned two cans of trash into one can of trash and one can of recyclables could help the environment and also save on its trash bill.

Gale and other top utility officials also visited the editorial boards of the city's two newspapers. "You always want to appear to be in control when you deal with the press," said Gale. "So, we went to the editorial boards at the moment of our highest control—and that was before we started!" Gale visited Seattle talk radio shows, where she presented a self-deprecating image—accepting the moniker of "garbage goddess" with aplomb and admitting that her neighbors gave her a hard time about not recycling more herself. Due to these efforts, the recycling program became so popular that three utility officials—including Gale—were profiled in the press. She recalled with satisfaction her profile in the *Seattle Post-Intelligencer:* "There I was! Not a faceless bureaucrat but a real live person with children."

To serve their larger strategic purposes, Gale and Stevenson knew they had to keep the garbage story alive. "We wanted to keep the story going," says Stevenson, "not only because it was a good story, but because every story got us more recycling sign-ups." There was a "media event" to announce the advent of plastics recycling. The utility produced an array of visually witty explanatory material about recycling, noteworthy for the logo of the "Recyclettes," anthropomorphic bottles, cans, and newspapers making their way down a green brick road to the recycle bin. The most powerful tool the utility discovered was a "recycling watch" that made the percentage of Seattle households participating in the voluntary program a feature of the city's daily news. When the proportion of residents taking advantage of recycling hit 50 percent, the mayor personally delivered the bin to the "50th percentile" household. Both major newspapers donated ad space to mark the occasion. As news coverage prompted more residents to sign up, the utility began sending officials and recycling contractors to street fairs and other community events.

Gale had gotten the attention of Seattle's residents. More important, she had gotten their commitment and their labor. In January 1989, eleven months after curbside recycling went into effect, the *NBC Nightly News* did a story on Seattle's program, cementing Seattle's new reputation as the recycling capital of the United States. It was a fortuitous deposit for Gale's bank of public goodwill—and it came at a time when she really needed it. Two months earlier, the Solid Waste Utility had begun making some major withdrawals.

New Garbage Rates and Service

Stevenson and Gale received the phase one win they wanted. They had strengthened the public profile and reputation of the Solid Waste Utility and made strides toward building the commitment of Seattle's citizens to participate in the solution of the city's solid waste crisis, even if that participation cost them something. But Gale now faced a bigger challenge in preparing citizens for phase two—the "new garbage rates and services." In phase two all current ratepayers would have to sign up for their preferred level of garbage service, at a given price. They had to estimate how much they could and would recycle and how many cans of nonrecyclable garbage they would put out and determine whether they would haul it to the curb or pay a 40 percent premium. The private contractors who picked up the garbage would supply the official barrels. Leaves, grass clippings, and other yard waste would have to be put out and paid for separately. On weeks that residents had extra trash that would not fit into their barrels, they could buy a "trash tag"—a sticker for sale at local convenience stores—to affix to a plastic trash bag. And so on. There were many new rules to learn, new charges to consider, and choices to be made.

Well in advance of the implementation date, utility officials again held background briefings for the press, complete with poster-sized versions of the sign-up card that each household would use to choose its rates. The utility promised explanatory mailings and display ads in all the newspapers. Seeing that these efforts might not be enough, the utility also sounded a new theme. In a series of televised public service announcements, Gale urged Seattle residents to "please be patient." That phrase became the utility's tagline. Gale publicly acknowledged that it was unlikely that the system would be fully functional within the first six months of operation. "Complaints were going to be coming," said Gale. "We expected them. Getting complaints would not mean there was something wrong with the plan." At the press briefing, she asked for understanding and assistance in explaining the particulars to Seattle's citizens. The utility also armed all the city officials they deemed likely to receive letters and phone calls about the new system (the so-called need to know officials in the mayor's office and the Seattle City Council) with information so they would be ready to answer basic questions and respond to complaints.

Still, on more than one occasion, disaster seemed imminent. Political disagreements about the particulars of the new rate structure held up the distribution of sign-up cards. By the time residents received their cards, they had less than a week to make their choices and send them back. It was not entirely clear to customers that they would need to request specifically not to be billed for yard waste. On November 15, 1988, some thirty thousand phone calls jammed the utility's lines. The press turned on the utility. A *Seattle Times* columnist pointed out that the theoretical impossibility of switching rate choices within the first year amounted to "garbage rate prison."

The utility responded with as much openness as possible. Gale summed up her policy for dealing with criticism: "The best defense is no defense. . . . Just do a better job." The utility relented on its hard-and-fast sign-up deadline. Rather than be dismayed about the criticism, the utility leadership saw that even negative press coverage provided customers with crucial information about the new system. One story in the *Post-Intelligencer,* headlined "People Are Really Confused," featured a detailed question-and-answer format that explained many of the issues that had people swamping utility phone lines.

Unfortunately, sign-up problems were just the beginning. A whole new crop of problems arose starting on January 1, 1989, when the new rates and service actually took effect. Just as utility officials had hoped, major explanatory articles about the new plan again appeared in the city's daily newspapers. And, as they had hoped, the coverage was linked to the recycling win. The *Seattle Times* reported, "Seattle is ringing out the old year as a national leader in garbage recycling and ringing in the new year with a revamped rate structure and new list of collection services." Despite the detailed explanations and favorable context, however, operational problems were legion. Contractors were slow to distribute the regulation trash bins, leaving residents uncertain about what they needed to do to ensure that their trash would be picked up. Many of the immigrant workers hired to collect the trash were unable to read routes written in English, and thus they failed to show up at the appointed time and place. Many trash pickup days had been changed, and thousands of residents were no longer sure when to bring their trash to the curb. Those who had slept through phase one were suddenly signing up in droves for recycling, and there were not enough bins ready for delivery. Thousands of questions and complaints continued to flood the utility. The "need-to-know officials"—including the mayor himself—took on some of the extra burden of answering citizen complaints, but they could not staunch the flood.

Nature refused to cooperate. Snowstorms in February and March shut down the city, stopping deliveries of cans and recycling bins. With the onset of spring, residents put out yard waste in unexpectedly large volumes. The confusion peaked in April 1989. Gale went directly to the home of one of her contractors to demand expedient delivery of bins. The utility asked the City Council to provide emergency funds to help staff its phone systems, inspiring two rather different reactions in news headlines: "City Acts to Reduce Complaints about Garbage Pickup" and "$198,000 Bill to Field Garbage Complaints." The utility continued to provide in a weekly bulletin all the relevant facts about the progress of implementation to all "need-to-know" city employees. Stevenson kept up a steady flow of information to the news media. Gale explained, "It's one of Ginny's responsibilities to come up with something good for reporters. You can never assure yourself of good press or cover up messes, but if you can give them stories on a continuing basis, you will get a little slack. And they'll be willing to come to your press briefings."

Still, a series of news stories about individuals (many of them elderly or disabled) whose best efforts to get their trash picked up had failed battered the utility, which estimated it had a hard core of some three hundred residents who were being regularly overlooked for one reason or another. Gale sent a number of utility officials to personally investigate a sample of twenty or so problem cases, an initiative she called the "account executive program." In the cases where households that were paying a premium for backyard trash pickup had been overlooked by trash collectors who had difficulty reading their routes in English, the utility quickly created color-coded route maps.

Because other households were overlooked for a variety of reasons, Gale's strategy was simply to improve the utility's capacity to respond to individual complaints. Sometimes, however, the media could respond more quickly. A July 1989 article in the *Times*, entitled "Raising a Stink: Household Battles City Over Garbage Pickup," told of one resident who had not had her trash picked up in seven weeks, despite an alleged twenty calls to the utility (which had a record of only two calls). The utility immediately investigated, and the *Times* followed up its story with a report that explained the woman had been missed because she had not had a regulation garbage can. Rather than point her finger, however, Gale told the newspaper, "[I]t was a real shock. I regret that this has happened to her." The woman who had complained was quoted as saying "I want to jump up and down for joy" now that her garbage woes were behind her. The utility had refunded her for the time during which her garbage was not picked up.

Less than two weeks later, a reporter from that customer's neighborhood newspaper, the *Queen Anne News,* wrote, "Despite early problems in its implementation caused by a flood of early sign-ups, the city of Seattle's new garbage and recycling program is picking up support from Queen Anne and Magnolia residents." A week or so later, at the National League of Cities recycling conference, Seattle announced the sign-up of the city's one hundred thousandth recycling household. It seemed as though the worst of the utility's public relations nightmare was over, and while Gale and her staff remained vigilant, their anxiety began to ease.

A Citizen's Defense

In May 1989 a sharply critical newspaper column spurred a response in the utility's defense that led Gale and others to believe the public might be coming around to their side. Because calls continued to come in by the thousands, the utility had launched an automated system for dispensing basic information, recording complaints, and queuing up calls with live agents. *Times* columnist Don Hannula complained: "Hello, Solid Waste, may I talk to a humanoid? . . . Tricky devils. Know what they did? They got rid of all the humans in the office. Nobody down there now but computerized tape recorders. . . . Since the system went into effect, it has been handling between 1,500 and 4,000 calls a day for everything under the sun. On one day there were 500 missed collection complaints. That's how many people had the patience to wait and leave their complaint on a tape recorder. . . . How are people describing the 'streamlined' system to me? They're portraying it in terms befitting the utility. It's garbage."

The next day the *Times* ran a citizen's response in its letters section: "The *Times* continues to print stories about people having difficulty with [trash] service changes. It is inevitable, with these sweeping changes over the past year, that there will be some problems. I think that under the circumstances, the service has done a pretty good job. . . . If people want to have a meaningful conversation with a human, I hope they can find someone else to call besides the Solid Waste Utility. In the meantime, if they forget to pick up the trash, I am more than willing to talk to their tape recorder."

Public-Sector Marketing and the Mobilization of Legitimacy, Support, and Coproduction

As the manager of the Seattle Solid Waste Utility, Gale had to confront the problematic reality that the local landfills were maxing out, with no end in sight to Seattle's steady stream of solid waste. As urgent as this situation was to the professionals inside the Solid Waste Utility, it took a trash-related public relations crisis to bring political urgency to the utility's problems. The image of families forced to abandon their homes and half-cooked Thanksgiving turkeys woke citizens up to the challenge the city faced. In an instant the methane leak accomplished what years of talk could not in terms of building a political will to act.

Fueled by this crisis, the city plunged into several years of deliberation and planning that ended with a mandate for a significant innovation in the way that the Seattle community, aided by the Seattle Solid Waste Utility, would handle its garbage. That innovation called for the Solid Waste Utility to find a way to reach unprecedented levels of solid waste recycling. To understand the challenge Gale faced, it is helpful to review her situation in terms of the strategic triangle as well as the other cases examined so far.

With respect to the public value Gale sought to produce, the task was relatively straightforward. For both health and aesthetic reasons, her agency had to take the two thousand tons of solid waste that Seattle citizens generated each day and dispose of it in a way that was convenient for citizens, affordable for ratepayers, and protective of the health of both the population and the natural environment, and it had to find a way to do all that at a relatively low cost to the government. The system also had to consider fairness in terms of who received the benefits and who paid the costs of the plan. Trade-offs were likely to be necessary among these various dimensions of value, but the architects of the recycling plan believed it offered significantly more value than the alternate plan of building an incinerator. The only concern was that the broader public could not yet fully see the implications of the plan in terms of convenience for citizens and costs facing ratepayers.

With respect to legitimacy and support, Gale had the strategic advantage of a clear mandate for the change she was supposed to implement. All she had to do was find the means for implementing that change. In this respect her position resembled both William Bratton's and Anthony Williams's. But while Bratton and Williams had both arrived in their offices after a political campaign had been waged and an election won on the issues that concerned them, Gale faced a citizenry that had not yet been as fully engaged in the issue, and whose support remained untested. This was particularly problematic because the success of Gale's initiative depended crucially not only on citizens' tolerance and support but also on their active engagement in producing the desired result.

With respect to operational capacity, Gale's situation resembled Jeannette Tamayo's in some fundamental ways. Like Tamayo, Gale ran an agency that delegated much of its value-creating work to private contractors, and she was responsible for ensuring not only the performance of each individual contractor but also that the system as a whole worked in a coordinated way and steadily improved its performance as an industry. And, like Tamayo, Gale's overall success depended on engaging the clients of her contractors in the work necessary to achieve the desired outcome. The critical difference between Tamayo and Gale was that Gale sought to engage the entire citizenry of Seattle, while Tamayo focused only on a small segment. Moreover, Gale was trying to manage a top-down innovation in the performance of the system as a whole all at once rather than waiting for the system of contractors to produce innovations in incremental steps.

Ultimately, two critical facts characterized the particular strategic challenge that Gale faced. First, she was managing a public enterprise that had regular, frequent transactions with virtually every resident in her jurisdiction. The impact of Gale's agency on the quality of individual life was huge, immediate, and conspicuous. No household or business could go very long without having an encounter with the Solid Waste Utility. If the encounter did not go well—if collection was missed, or garbage was spilled—residents would notice and complain. In these respects Gale anchored one extreme of public management.

Second, Gale was managing a number of major innovations in her core operating system.[2] At the back end of the disposal system, as the local landfills began to fill, close, and leak noxious gases, the city scrambled to find an affordable and environmentally friendly new home for Seattle's ever-growing mountain of trash. At the front end of the system, Gale had to convince the residents and businesses of Seattle to take more responsibility for managing their garbage.[3] She made use of social and political pressure as well as economic incentives to encourage recycling.[4] And she sought simultaneously to standardize the system to allow collectors to optimize performance along their routes and to offer Seattleites a menu of different services at various prices.

Major changes always threaten the reliable, smooth operation of a system, but the fact that Gale's innovation required millions of individual residents and businesses to change their behavior multiplied the risks dramatically. Indeed, the fact that the innovations would *increase* the burden on her clients created the third important feature of Gale's situation. If she could convince the residents and businesses of Seattle to accept the burdens she imposed, she would succeed. If she could not, she would fail. It is one thing to implement an innovation that promises better service to individuals at a lower cost; it is quite another to implement an innovation whose benefits are general and hard for individual clients to see (reduced economic and environmental costs in aggregate), and whose costs are quite specific and easy for individuals to notice (sorting their own garbage, new premiums for services).

Thus Gale seemed set up to fail on many counts. It seemed unlikely that the satisfaction of her clients would improve as a result of the changes she implemented, or that the citizens of Seattle would applaud her handling of a solid waste crisis that was not particularly visible in their day-to-day lives. And it seemed quite possible that a whole new system that depended on the cooperation of large numbers of potentially disgruntled individuals would grind to a halt. The carefully constructed response to the city's solid waste crisis could have quite easily crumbled under the weight of the new burdens being placed on the city's residents and businesses, but it did not.

The explanation for Gale's success seemed to lie in the way she chose to manage her relations with the citizens of Seattle and, more particularly, in the way she organized the public relations and information campaign to help citizens understand and adapt to the requirements of the new system.[5] Gale knew that in her pursuit of public value for Seattle's citizens, she could not afford to ignore the need for legitimacy and support.

One way to interpret the case is to say that Gale succeeded primarily by lowering citizens' expectations about what they should expect from a government agency—hence the importance of the call to "please be patient." But one could also say that Gale succeeded in engaging citizens in the problem of handling mountains of solid waste, and in doing so, she mobilized them to help with the task and think of themselves as partners with their government to achieve the desired result. Instead of being disgusted with the rotten service, citizens learned to contribute their fair share and to endure the frustrations without too many complaints. In short, in exhorting citizens to "please be patient," Gale asked them not only to forgive the Solid Waste Utility but also to think and act like citizens who could see the full set of consequences of the public policy initiative that they had (under the auspices of the City Council) authorized.

It is axiomatic in politics and public administration that government cannot easily ask an independent-minded public to tolerate reduced levels of service and increased frustration. The common assumption, rooted in hard experience, is that when government cuts back services or asks citizens to make bigger contributions to the public good, citizens will resist by showing their displeasure at the polls. Yet Gale seems to have succeeded in persuading citizens not only to accept losses in service quality but also to take more responsibility in achieving public goals. Given that many of the important challenges in public management involve inflicting losses on citizens and mobilizing them to take more responsibility for their own health and welfare, Gale's experience might have wide resonance and application. The lesson other public managers could learn from Gale's use of performance information in particular is that she understood that she was gathering information about the performance not only of her own agency and its contractors but also the wider political community of Seattle as it adjusted to the changes in solid waste management. She had to know how many citizens were signing up for recycling, and she used that information to pressure more to do so. She had to know whom her communication strategy was reaching, and to what effect. She had to use her performance information to engage her partners—hundreds of thousands of Seattle residents, as well as the handful of private contractors who picked up the garbage—in the story of what they were trying to accomplish together, how well they were doing, and who was not doing their part. She had to track and aggregate complaints and acknowledge when the utility failed to live up to its end of the bargain. Her performance information had to facilitate a wide, easily accessible, continuing public discourse about the performance not only of her agency but the community as a whole. It had to provide both a compelling story about why the utility's policy choices were sound and necessary and an accurate description of how ordinary citizens were squaring up to the changes Gale was making.

Because this kind of complex communication challenge is not ordinarily viewed as an important part of a public manager's responsibility (even though it often turns out to be critical for the manager's performance), Gale did not have much tried-and-true knowledge about how to proceed. As a result, she did not go as far as she could have in formalizing her information systems, but the case points to where a more rigorous public value scorecard could have become a device for animating public engagement in a complex task requiring adjustment and/or sacrifice on the part of each individual. This kind of performance and measurement challenge confronts those interested in public education, public health, and public security, as well as those interested in solid waste disposal. A public value scorecard can accommodate these challenges by including information on the degree to which citizens supported Gale's efforts in both the political and operational spheres, as well as information about the outcomes of the joint enterprise.

Understanding Gale's Strategic Calculation: The Arrows of the Strategic Triangle

Looking at Gale's work through the lens of the strategic triangle and the public value scorecard will help clarify why Gale focused so much attention on her public relations strategy, how she developed and managed that strategy, and how performance measurement could and did support her efforts to engage the Seattle community in the collective effort to deal with solid waste. It will also help broaden and deepen our understanding of both the legitimacy and support perspective and the operational capacity perspective because Gale's public relations strategy was designed simultaneously to build legitimacy and support among Seattle residents (expressed in terms of tolerance for implementation confusion and errors) and to build operational capacity (by instructing and motivating citizens to become active participants in the process).

As noted in Chapter 2, one key feature of the strategic triangle is that it focuses managers not only on the ultimate production of public value but also on the conditions that allow them to produce public value—that is, legitimacy and support from the wider political authorizing environment and operational capacity sufficient to produce the desired results. Managers tend to want to hold the *political* side of management apart from the *administrative* and *operational* sides of management, but the second core idea of the strategic triangle, symbolized by the arrows connecting its three points, is that the three realms marked out by the triangle are irrevocably interconnected. Each realm can be distinguished for purposes of analysis and diagnosis. We can explore different substantive conceptions of public value through public value accounts. We can take a broad, independent look at the landscape of the political authorizing environment from the legitimacy and support perspective and wonder what political forces might be mobilized as part of a broad strategy to improve value-creating performance. We can evaluate processes, policies, and partnerships from the operational capacity perspective and consider how to improve overall production processes. But in the end a strategy works only when it successfully integrates these three realms—when the public value proposition can command legitimacy and support, and when there is sufficient operational capacity to create that value.

The necessity of connecting the points of the triangle has been mostly implicit in the background of each case discussed in this book. The cases in Chapters 3 and 4 drew attention to the links between conceptions of public value and a political basis of legitimacy and support, on one hand, and the links between conceptions of public value and the development and deployment of operational capacity, on the other.

The Crucial Links between Legitimacy and Support and
Operational Capacity
However, Chapters 3 and 4 focused only on two of the three arrows in the strategic triangle. We have largely ignored the *key link between mobilizing political legitimacy and building operational capacity.* Focusing on this particular connection in light of Gale's problem points to a largely neglected problem in contemporary public management.[6] To many public

managers the link between building legitimacy and support, on one hand, and operational capacity, on the other, is the simple idea that effective advocacy for a public agency and its mission in the authorizing environment can be expected to generate a more consistent and more generous supply of resources to a given agency.[7] This notion assumes that the goal of engaging with the authorizing environment is to obtain more resources for the agency and ignores the normative and practical importance of seeing the challenge of political management in terms of embracing accountability and aligning public agencies with political aspirations rather than imposing one particular view of what constitutes public value.[8] Ensuring this alignment is a central function of the legitimacy and support perspective of the public value scorecard.

But there is a link between building legitimacy and support and creating operational capacity beyond the flow of assets from the authorizing environment to public agencies. Remember that the strategic triangle focuses attention not simply on *organizational* capacity but overall *operational* capacity. When much of the operational capacity needed to achieve a desired result lies beyond the boundary of a given agency, public managers have to find a way to animate and guide the contributions of external agents.[9]

There are really only three mechanisms that managers can use to shape activity beyond the boundaries of their organization. The public agency can (1) buy the operational capacity it needs through grants and contracts, (2) use its public authority to require or compel private actors to contribute to public purposes, or (3) rely on some kind of public spirit in which private agents recognize their role and duty and choose to do it without being paid or ordered to do so.

It is useful to make distinctions among paying individuals to contribute to public purposes, requiring them to perform a duty for public purposes or calling on their public spirit to make voluntary contributions to public aims; in practice, however, these different means for motivating individuals are often combined. We contract with nonprofit welfare-to-work organizations hoping to get a little extra performance from organizations that are morally committed to the aims of the program. We pay people to join the army (and sometimes draft them into military service) but imagine that many join for patriotic reasons. We require citizens to pay their taxes and fine litterbugs but hope that powerful social norms will cause individuals to pay taxes and avoid littering without direct compulsion. We pay individuals a nickel to return an empty bottle but hope that the payment is mostly a reminder of what they should do as a matter of duty anyhow. All this becomes particularly important when a public agency is trying to engage large numbers of atomized individuals (rather than organizations) in its production process. This is actually quite a common part of public management. The government has to persuade individuals to buckle their seat belts, get vaccinations, and quit smoking. It has to promote voluntary compliance with the tax laws, discourage littering, and convince individuals to help prevent forest fires—and so on. In these cases public managers need to build legitimacy and support in the authorizing environment not simply to secure resources, and not simply to give them bargaining leverage with organizations that they need as partners and coproducers in achieving desired results, but also to give them the moral authority to mobilize a kind of social movement or political campaign that can sweep up millions of individual citizens in an effort to accomplish public goals.[10]

It is this particular challenge that Gale faced. Her case makes it self-evident that the political work of building a movement that engages large numbers of individual citizens and clients as coproducers of public value represents an essential managerial strategy for building the operational capacity to accomplish her agency's mission. While this work takes the form of political mobilization and might therefore be seen as a process of building legitimacy and support, it should be clear that such efforts can also be shown as efforts to build operational capacity beyond the boundary of a given organization and distributed widely across the population.

Individuals in the Strategic Triangle and Their Different
Relationships to Government
To see even more clearly how the mobilization of legitimacy and support plays a key role in building operational capacity to deliver results in situations where the required operational capacity lies distributed across many independent individuals, it is useful to step back and see where individuals fit into the imagery and conception of the strategic triangle.

Figure 5.1 reproduces the image of the authorizing environment first presented in Figure 2.6. When this diagram was introduced, it was

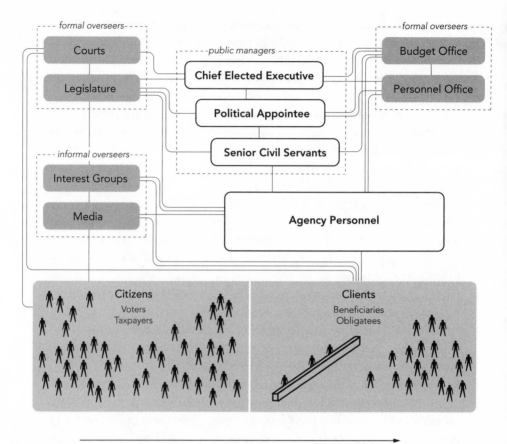

Figure 5.1. The authorizing environment, with individuals.

intended to show how many different social actors had interests in the performance of public organizations and were in positions to formally or informally call public managers to account for their performance. It did not sharply distinguish between social actors who were already organized into collectives from the individuals whose desires and motivations provided the energy for collective action, and whose values formed the basis for the overall evaluation of social conditions. Figure 5.1 seeks to draw a sharper distinction between these two kinds of social actors. The bottom level of Figure 5.1 consists of individual as opposed to collective actors.

Figure 5.1 also distinguishes among individual actors according to their legal, moral, and practical standing to call the agency to account for its performance and judge the value of what it produces. The individuals on the left side of the bottom of the figure—the individuals we typically describe as citizens, taxpayers, voters, and so on—*authorize* and *finance* a government enterprise. Their decisions to tax and regulate themselves to achieve a given purpose provide public agencies with the legitimacy and support they need to sustain themselves. The individuals on the right side—clients of public agencies (both beneficiaries or obligatees)—generally have less standing as agents of accountability and arbiters of public value. Again, there are many reasons individual citizens thinking on their own and deliberating together to define the public value they would like to produce collectively might focus on protecting the rights, serving the needs, and satisfying the desires of individual clients. But the ultimate arbiter of public value must always be a collective of individuals thinking more or less like citizens rather than clients.

While individuals (standing in different relationships to government) can be distinguished from one another with respect to their relative influence as arbiters of public value, they can also be distinguished with respect to their role in the material production processes of government. Figure 5.2 presents an image of the value chain linking operational capacity to the production of public value that shows individuals alongside collectives and organizations as potentially vital partners and coproducers of public value as well as clients (both types).

Table 5.1 presents a simple way of thinking about the complex roles that individuals in different positions and different frames of mind end up playing in the strategic calculations of a public manager. Individuals, in their roles as citizens, voters, and taxpayers, show up as important arbiters of public value in a public manager's authorizing environment. Individuals in their roles as partners, coproducers, and clients (both beneficiaries and obligatees) show up as an important part of the production process that links the use of public assets to the achievement of publicly valued results.

Measuring the Satisfaction, Support, and Engagement of Citizens
in Public Enterprises
If the support and engagement of individual citizens are strategically important to public managers like Gale in both the legitimacy and support

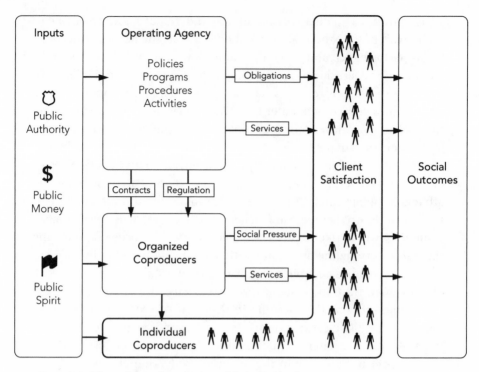

Figure 5.2. The public value chain, with individuals.

perspective and the operational capacity perspective of the public value scorecard, then it becomes important to measure the level of individual support as well as to find the means to increase it. The natural approach is to rely on surveys. And, as observed in Chapter 4, public agencies seem to be making increasing use of surveys to gauge the satisfaction of citizens and clients with government operations.

Until recently much of the survey work on individual satisfaction with government was carried out without reference to the crucial distinctions between citizens and clients, and between different kinds of clients (service recipients and obligatees). Questionnaires directed at random samples of the general population have been treated as essentially similar to questionnaires asking government clients about their encounters with public agencies when these different kinds of surveys actually address individuals in two quite different capacities. The former essentially engages them as citizens—perhaps as taxpayers—but

Table 5.1.   Individuals in different roles vis-à-vis government.

	Contribute legitimacy and support to public value propositions	Create operational capacity as coproducers of public value	Act as arbiters of public value
Citizens	***		***
Voters	***		***
Taxpayers	***		*
Partners/volunteers	*	***	
Client beneficiaries	*	**	*
Client obligatees	*	**	*

Note: Asterisks represent relative weight of each type of individual in making contributions to government.

not particularly as clients, while the latter asks individuals about their experiences as government clients.

More recently some surveyors have recognized the distinctions between citizens and clients and developed instruments that address individuals in these different capacities. For example, the Accenture Institute for Public Service Value, a research and development center for the promotion of "high performance in public service delivery, policy, and governance," has held forums to ask citizens living in cities across the world about their satisfaction with government as citizens, as taxpayers, and as "service users" (clients). In the user role individuals wanted easy access to high-quality, individually tailored services. In the citizen role they became more interested in equal access to services and the achievement of broad social outcomes. The responses they gave as citizens differed significantly from those they gave when addressed as clients.[11]

Political scientists also have been developing the art of "deliberative polling" as a device for eliciting the values of citizens rather than clients. This method begins with a traditional opinion poll asking individuals about their views of a public policy, but then it (1) provides respondents with information about the policies being evaluated, and (2) gives them an opportunity to discuss the issue with other citizens. Here, too, individuals' views change as a consequence of being better informed and having discussed the issue with their fellow citizens.

The fact that individuals can, through relatively small interventions, be encouraged to think like *citizens* rather than *clients* raises both the normative question of which valuations—those of socially conscious citizens or self-interested clients—should be the focus in guiding policy decisions and the practical question of when and whether efforts to determine individual satisfaction with government should focus more on citizen-like preferences or client-like preferences.

As emphasized in Chapter 1, however, many clients of public agencies receive obligations and duties—not services. In order to get individuals to contribute to the overall public good, the government puts its tax dollars and legal authority into getting clients to stop using drugs, sort their recyclables, pay their taxes, and find suitable employment. Because obligation encounters involve asking clients to do things they would likely prefer not to do, the goal is not to make clients happy but to secure compliance at the lowest possible cost in terms of tax dollars, force expended, and residual grumpiness on the part of the obligatee. But, paradoxically, it is for precisely this reason that government ought to be interested in satisfying obligatees. Regulatory and enforcement agencies have learned that an important part of their job is to provide advice and assistance that enables and encourages those who would like to comply with their obligations to do so. Thus many duty-imposing agencies strive to provide a high level of service to those who would like to meet their obligations. They have learned that compliance increases when obligatees are treated with courtesy, respect, and fairness. The legitimacy of government depends in no small part on the experiences that individuals have when public agencies use their power to impose duties. It is for these reasons that some police departments, for example, now survey those who are stopped, cited, or arrested, as well as those who have requested services. While the police cannot expect individuals in these positions to *like* the experience, they can try to make the experience as fair and respectful as possible and in doing so help reduce the cost of securing compliance, maintain the perceived legitimacy of government, and protect the rights of individuals.

Addressing and Engaging Individuals as Citizens, Ratepayers, Coproducers, and Clients

To succeed in her ambitious plans, Gale could not afford to limit her attention to those authorizers who occupied formal oversight positions or had already organized themselves into collective interest groups; she had to address and engage the individual residents of Seattle. And she had to address them in their different capacities as authorizers, clients, and coproducers.

It is worth noting here that for a public enterprise the Seattle Solid Waste Utility has several characteristics typical of private enterprises. It is financed by fees paid by users rather than general taxes. Private companies under contract to the city carry out garbage collection. But this apparently commercial transaction between citizens who paid to have their trash collected and private waste management companies is set inside a wider public framework. Laws and ordinances require citizens to find some effective means for dealing with their garbage and prohibit them from allowing their garbage to accumulate, burning it, or simply dumping it on someone else's property. The public utility maintains control over the private providers through contracts specifying certain levels of service. And the City Council rather than the market sets the fees, which are paid to the public utility rather than to the providers, allowing elected public officials to deal with some equity issues through cross-subsidies—setting prices a bit above cost for businesses and below cost for low-income residents. Thus Seattle citizens participate in the governance and operation of the Solid Waste Utility partly as clients (both beneficiaries and obligatees) and partly as citizen authorizers who use public authority and money to create the demand and the supply for recycling and other solid waste management services and to organize the system's financing.

Gale knew that she would encounter individual Seattleites as authorizers. She knew she was accountable to them in the usual ways that managers of public utilities are accountable to citizens, voters, and taxpayers. As voters, they might use their power at the polls to express their frustration over the withdrawal of benefits that they had grown accustomed to having. As citizens, they might worry about whether the system was organized not only to strike the right balance among the different dimensions of value at stake but also to ensure that everyone do their fair share and receive their just due. They might even be concerned about the degree to which the system encouraged the development of a kind of public spirit that helped all Seattleites feel both proud of and responsible for the civic accomplishment of an important public purpose.

Speaking to an audience of citizens, Gale's public relations task was to keep putting the changes she was making in a larger narrative context. She had to remind citizens of the overall context: the nature, scale, and urgency of the problem they were trying to solve together; why the proposed initiative was the best of all available options; the legitimacy of the processes that built the policy; and the success and problems they would face together in implementing the proposed policy. To the degree that citizens wanted to ensure high-quality service to clients, Gale also had to be able to talk about the aggregate experiences of clients and respond to questions about instances of particularly egregious service. She had to be able to talk generally about the costs and inconveniences of the system and to reassure people that the costs were being kept low and were fairly distributed across the population. In essence she had to be an advocate for the public value of the policy as a whole to the individuals who authorized it as citizens but were now experiencing it as both citizens and clients.

For her clients and ratepayers, Gale had to be concerned with the concrete transactions in which the utility engaged each day. She had to make the transition to the new service relationship as easy, predictable, and understandable as possible. She had to show concern and sympathy with regard to the fact that in the new client relationship, clients were expected both to do more and to pay more for some services. She had to track client satisfaction, both to learn about the average client experience and to hear and respond to the most unfortunate experiences with apologies and solutions that would prevent such events from happening in the future.

Finally, for her coproducers, whose willingness to work with the new system would be the decisive factor in its success, Gale had to think about how to motivate and inform them so that they could effectively participate in the production process. She had to provide information that was both simple and complete. She had to be sure that the equipment they needed in order to comply was available—and so on.

Calling a Public into Existence

Like all public managers, Gale faced a public that seemed divided by its different positions and interests vis-à-vis the solid waste management system she sought to establish. The good news, however, was that these different positions and interests did not create distinct differences among groups of individuals but, rather, existed within each individual! Most individuals in Seattle were simultaneously ratepayers, coproducers, voters, and authorizers of the initiative. Gale thus had an opportunity to take advantage of this fact to build a broader public consciousness in the collective public and in the mind of each individual that could recognize the value of, and take some responsibility for, the new system.

To the extent that she could organize her grassroots communication strategy to encourage the adoption of this perspective, she would be following the guidance of the American philosopher John Dewey. In his inquiry into the existence and nature of the "public," Dewey argued that only by recognizing the consequences of private interactions on those not directly involved in them could a public begin to understand and act on its own interests.[12] He conceded that there were many factors that threaten to "eclipse" a public, many of them related to the particular interests of individuals accustomed to thinking and acting only on behalf of themselves. According to Dewey, the only thing that can help individuals shift to a perspective where they recognize their interdependence and their moral and legal rights and obligations to one another is "the improvement of the methods and conditions of debate, discussion, and persuasion."[13] While Dewey was not specific about who was responsible for organizing that debate, he seemed to invite any citizen or anyone seeking or authorized to lead the public to embrace the role. Finally, Dewey suggested that in order for a public to become "alive and flexible as well as stable [and] responsive to the complex and world-wide scene in which it is enmeshed" rather than "broken, inarticulate, and faint," it must "possess the local community as its medium."[14] Thus while one could see Gale's public relations strategy as simply an effort to lower client expectations during a period of transition, one could also see her as acting to improve communication in order to help transform the individuals in her local community into a public that could understand and act on its own interests with respect to its system for solid waste management.

This picture of managerial ambition may seem hopelessly utopian, yet it is surprising to see how close Gale seems to have come to making it a reality. For the most part, the citizens of Seattle seemed to go along with the program. They did not throw Gale out of office. They embraced the recycling program. They even put up with the new burdens imposed on them and the new rate schedule. And, when one citizen was willing to stand up for the Solid Waste Utility publicly—to acknowledge that "under the circumstances, the service has done a pretty good job"—Gale finally had reason to believe that she had brought around at least one Seattle resident to a citizen's perspective.

A Comparison to the Private Sector:
Marketing and Public Relations

A private-sector executive would likely think about the task that Gale faced as a marketing problem.[15] She had a new set of policies and programs to "sell" to a public that was not sure it wanted to buy them. As a public manager, however, Gale could only take this perspective with a few caveats.

The Trouble with Marketing

There has always been some anxiety about the idea of marketing in a public-sector context.[16] Even in the private-sector context, marketing is often seen as inherently manipulative and deceitful.[17] To the degree that the normative justification for market mechanisms depends on individuals making rational choices in their own interests, and to the degree that marketing techniques take advantage of human weaknesses in decision making, marketing techniques seem to undermine the integrity of market mechanisms that are supposed to ensure the efficient and effective allocation of resources to meet the genuine wants and needs of individuals.[18]

When the techniques are brought into the public sector, the sin is compounded. The normative justification for public action in a liberal society also depends on individuals being able to make rational choices about the purposes that are worth taxing and regulating themselves to accomplish, and the means that will be used to accomplish the desired goals. But citizens often find themselves in very weak positions to assess proposed public policies. They have less expertise and less information than the experts who are designing the policies. They cannot always see accurately into the decision-making process. They are vulnerable to propaganda about the necessity of a particular policy, its efficacy, or the absence of alternatives.[19] They can be panicked into agreeing with a government-nominated choice. If the government were to become a skilled marketer, the quality of the public's choices would be compromised, and with that, democracy itself.

Marketing as Listening and Responding Rather than Manipulating

As described earlier the aim of marketing is to get individuals to demand something that they do not really want or need. The important interests are the company's interest in making profits and the government's interest in staying in power and persuading citizens that they should do what the government wants rather than the other way around.

But more often the real aim of marketing in the private sector is less to persuade individuals to buy something they do not want and more to find out what they do want.[20] Many marketing efforts are designed to operate as a high-fidelity receiver of individuals' desires rather than as an amplifier announcing to them what they should want to buy.

If the goal of marketing is to listen and respond rather than to talk and persuade, then many of the moral objections to marketing go away. Instead of a device that allows powerful producing organizations to impose their will on hapless individuals, marketing becomes a device through which individuals can communicate their desires to producing organizations, which are then able to respond with products that satisfy those desires.

In the public sector the idea of marketing as listening rather than advocating basically amounts to consulting with citizens about what they would like from government. Since this is an essential function of democratic government to begin with, there are plenty of arguments for doing so—and undertaking such efforts more frequently, at a higher level of detail, and in more intimate interpersonal settings than voting booths.[21] Once viewed as citizen consultation, the idea of marketing in the public sector may be, if Dewey is correct, an important way to call a public into existence and help it become articulate about what it wants.

Marketing Strategies

In response to the general question of what customers want, many marketing techniques have been developed. Private-sector marketers find ways to segment their market—to recognize diversity among individuals and to design both different messages and different products and services to appeal to the various market segments.[22] Marketers also find and exploit particular information and product distribution channels that help them reach the different market segments.[23] And they work to develop a brand identity that both sustains and generalizes the appeal of a corporation across the wide range of products offered.[24]

This kind of marketing has become so important in the private sector that the brands that these strategies have helped develop are considered major assets to a company—as important as the company's products and services and the production processes that ensure consistent quality in those products and services. Companies have begun to measure the success of these marketing strategies as a routine matter.[25] Indeed, it is this kind of performance information that fills out the "customer perspective" of Kaplan and Norton's "balanced scorecard."[26] For all these reasons, private-sector managers have long invested in sophisticated marketing campaigns, sought to measure their results, and built information systems that continuously monitor their relations with customers.

Similarly, I argue in this book that public managers should take seriously certain forms of marketing and citizen engagement in their strategic thinking and use the legitimacy and support perspective of the public value scorecard to record actions taken to strengthen relations with their formal authorizers, the informal authorizers who have organized themselves in interest groups, and the mass of individual citizens, voters, and taxpayers in whose name much public action is undertaken. As noted earlier, many public agencies, under pressure to become more customer oriented, have become accustomed to surveying their clients. But they have been a bit more uncertain about how to monitor and manage their relationships with client obligatees, particular authorizers such as congressional committees or interest groups, or the broad group of citizens who are simultaneously authorizers, clients, and coproducers.

Public Relations versus Marketing

In the private sector the idea of marketing to customers has always been distinguished to some degree from the related activity of "public relations."[27] While marketing focuses primarily on customers, public relations focuses on a broader array of organizational stakeholders, including potential investors, local communities, government, and the wider political and social community.[28] The goal of public relations strategies is not to learn what customers and potential customers want but, rather, to build a climate of at least tolerance and, at best, widespread enthusiasm and support for the company. Having a good name in the court of public opinion gives companies a broader "license to operate."[29] It is one thing to try to operate in a world in which every move your company makes is subject to close scrutiny and general suspicion and quite another to operate in a world where most everyone assumes that your company is doing a public good.

In public relations, as in marketing, it is important to identify the particular social actors with whom a company wants to maintain good working relationships, such as politicians, local community leaders, and potential critics, but also particular individuals, organizations, and agencies in positions to give or withhold particular kinds of authorizations or to speak publicly for or against a company's initiatives. Most of these are actors with whom a company is likely to have frequent, ongoing dealings.

Businesses have increasingly come to rely on relatively simple performance measurement systems to track the strength of their relationships with both customers and stakeholders who can shape their license to operate. Those systems are often described as "account management systems."[30] Such systems originally grew out of efforts to manage the marketing efforts of firms. Firms identified the particular organizations to whom they would like to sell, and salespeople were given the responsibility for doing what they could to strengthen the relationship with these key accounts. In principle the same systems could be used for managing accounts with the stakeholders who showed up as potentially important in shaping a given company's license to operate. In all cases the aim is to build a climate of legitimacy and support for the particular actions of a company, or its reputation in general.

Performance Measurement Systems to Support Marketing and
Public Relations Campaigns
As these marketing and public relations functions became fundamental to the design and execution of the basic strategies of private-sector companies, performance measurement and management systems were developed to monitor these functions as well as production processes and financial transactions. In turn, the performance measurement and management systems that guided the marketing and public relations functions were integrated into the wider performance measurement and performance management systems that allowed companies to execute value-creating strategies. These systems allow them to monitor their standing with past, current, and future customers—key indicators of their current strategic position and their ability to earn profits for their shareholders in the future, as well as evidence of how successful past marketing campaigns have been. Management systems make marketing divisions accountable for success in building the company's brand

and improving its standing with potential customers. They also make advertising agencies under company contracts accountable for hitting specific marketing goals.

More recently, private companies have begun to gather even more information about the performance of particular public relations efforts in order to assure managers and shareholders that they are getting value for the money expended on these activities. Much of this information concerns the many stakeholders who create the broad social context in which the company operates. There are accounts for those who make public statements and judgments about a company's social performance as well as for the firm's customers. Companies create, maintain, and measure these accounts in an effort to sustain their broader legitimacy in increasingly complex environments.

Marketing and Public Relations in the Public Sector

Viewed in this way, marketing and public relations may seem more ethically acceptable and practically useful to public managers than they first appear. It is crucial for public managers to see that the fundamental task of marketing and public relations is not to try to impose their will on clients and authorizers but to get close enough to the clients and the authorizers to learn what they would like to see their public agencies produce—to listen, consult, and understand rather than to talk, dominate, and deceive.[31] To build more responsive organizations, public managers have to rely on sympathetic, respectful engagement rather than on elaborate or defensive justifications.

The idea that there are two separate functions—one that focuses on individual customers and another that focuses on the collective stakeholders who have interests in what organizations do and some capacity to shape their conduct—seems to resonate with the idea that public managers ought to have a strategy for dealing with individual coproducers and clients, on one hand, and authorizers, on the other.

Marketing to Individual Coproducers and Clients

The goal of "marketing" campaigns directed at clients might be just to provide information about the availability of a given public service and where to obtain it, but often the goal of such campaigns is also to alert potential clients to the conditions and requirements for accessing the

service—who is eligible for what benefits and what kind of documentation they must provide to demonstrate their eligibility. Other times
marketing campaigns are designed to remind individuals of their obligations, motivate them to meet those obligations, and provide them
with the information they need to fulfill their obligations.

In making this pitch public agencies often make paternalistic
arguments—that individuals ought to comply for their own good and
that their better selves would want them to eat more healthily, drive
less recklessly, and live in right relationships with others.[32] Other times
they argue that individuals should accept certain obligations as part
of their duty as citizens and see them as a fair and efficient distribution
of the work necessary to achieve social results that they would value
both as individuals and as members of the broader public.[33] In either
case they are trying to align themselves with the positive aspirations of
citizens so that the citizens can reconcile themselves to the necessity of
doing their duties and perhaps even muster some enthusiasm for making a contribution to the public good (according to the degree of public
spirit they possess).

Public Relations with Authorizers and Citizens

The goal of the communications strategy with respect to the broader set
of organizational stakeholders—the public relations campaign—is to
cultivate a general attitude of support and legitimacy for the public
agency and its work. At a minimum, the public relations strategy seeks
the tolerance of an agency's stakeholders for its current operations and
future plans. If possible, the agency would like its stakeholders to presume that it is well motivated and competent, and that it could and
would avoid inflicting gratuitous harm on those with interests in what
the organization does. The agency could make an effort to garner more
support by initiating and maintaining reasonably well-oiled processes
of deliberation and consultation that would allow it to anticipate and
respond to issues before they become big problems. Ideally, the agency
would like its public relations strategy to ensure steady support for
what it is trying to accomplish and broad faith in its organizational values and capacities.

Ordinarily when public managers look out into their authorizing environment, they are most apt to focus their attention on a relatively
small number of officials who have the formal authority to give direction,

provide resources, and call them to account for their performance through official channels. Following this example, Gale would have looked up the bureaucratic chain of command to the head of the engineering division and the mayor of Seattle. Standing between her and her superiors in the executive branch, she would have seen a multitude of staffers and officials who oversaw her financial and personnel operations. Gale also would have to pay attention to the City Council, which set the rates for solid waste collection. Much of the focus and energy of public managers' political management efforts goes into managing relationships with this handful of intermittently attentive representatives of the people.

But experienced public managers also understand that for most practical purposes, the political authorizing environment includes a much larger number of social and political actors—who constitute, in some sense, a variety of "market segments." Many of these actors are organized in interest groups that use their political resources (size, legal position, expertise, media contacts, the general appeal of the values they seek to protect, etc.) to advance their interests through lobbying and other forms of advocacy. Navigating all of these currents of pluralist politics is the usual challenge of political management.

In this particular case, however, as we have observed, the political oversight Gale would face would be much broader than this ordinary kind of scrutiny. Because so many individual citizens would be involved in the implementation of the new system, political oversight would extend well beyond the shaping of the policy mandate into the implementation period, keeping Gale in the glare of intense public scrutiny in various public forums, large and small and formal and informal.

This fact dramatically increased the relative importance of two parts of the authorizing environment that can sometimes be ignored: the media and grassroots public opinion.

Of course, the media are always present in democratic governance, and their implicit threat to make an issue of anything that seems to affect the public interest gives them standing to create problems for elected officials and public executives of all kinds. Moreover, they use their latent influence not only to raise issues but also to shape the way citizens see the issues and the ways in which public officials react. While much occurs in the realm of public policy that is not deemed worthy of media attention, Gale did not doubt for a second that the media would be "all over" the implementation of the solid waste program.

Similarly, the grass roots are always present with the latent potential to shape the success of a given policy. But, again, because this policy depended on the grass roots not only to cooperate but also to do additional work, their involvement was crucial.

In short, Gale's efforts to manage her authorizing environment would have to be even more "political" than usual, in the sense that she would have to reach more broadly and more deeply into the political community of Seattle. Gale would not be playing inside baseball with elected officials or negotiating a complex deal among interest groups; she would be engaging in a continuing and broad public discussion about how her plans seemed to be working. Thus she would have to pay more attention than most public managers to both the media and the grassroots citizens of Seattle. She would have to figure out a way to manage the utility's relationships with these key pieces of the authorizing environment and a way to monitor her agency's performance with regard to those relationships.

Marketing and Public Relations in the Public Sector: The Role of Free Media
Giving these communications functions standing and influence in public agencies—treating public relations and marketing as differentiated and strategically important activities—often involves creating special departments and building special expertise. Unfortunately, this is often both expensive and politically unpopular. Consequently, many public managers are left with only a strategy for interacting with the free press to advance their public relations goals. They cannot afford their own marketing and public relations efforts.

Among the most interesting elements of Gale's practices as a public manager were (1) her immediate grasp of the critical strategic importance of a strong marketing and public relations campaign and (2) her temerity in building the utility's capacity to manage that campaign by hiring a full-time public relations specialist and preparing her staff to take advantage of the free publicity that would come their way.

To develop her own public relations capacity, Gale expended some political capital to get funding to contract with public relations firms that would assess the utility's current standing with the public and lay out a plan for building its brand and inspiring public confidence. Additional funds were necessary to enact the recommendations of the consultants, rebrand the Solid Waste Utility, hire Stevenson full time to manage public relations, and design and print the forms and public mailings that kept citizens apprised of the coming changes. Though she could oversee and control the details of this public marketing campaign, she could not be sure whether Seattle residents or the media would respond well to the fact that she was mounting this effort or to the particular form it took.

However effective her own public relations campaign would prove to be, she knew that she also had to develop some kind of strategy to manage her relations with the free press, and to use media attention to advance the goals of helping Seattle citizens understand and act to support her mandated initiative. Ideally, the media would keep the changes at the utility on the front page, communicate a sense of urgency and accomplishment in building Seattle's collective capacity to respond, and provide detailed and accurate information about what individuals needed to do to participate effectively.

But as nice as that might be, what Gale really needed was coverage that—positive or negative—helped her achieve the utility's goals. She needed coverage that engaged individuals in the story of how Seattle was or was not succeeding as a community in achieving the desired results. From that perspective, negative stories could often be as useful as positive stories as long as they were about the joint effort of the utility and the citizenry to deal with their mutual problem. The utility's job was to be the most conscientious citizen, working for and with the citizens of Seattle, and doing its part as energetically and competently as possible to achieve the results.

To help communicate that message, Gale decided not to use her new public relations capacities to centralize all public relations for the utility and insulate the rest of the organization from the press. On the contrary, she used these capacities to widen and decentralize the public relations campaign across the organization. She used them to ensure that her key managers were ready, willing, and even eager to speak with the press. She judged that the public relations strategy would be much more effective if everyone in the organization, from top managers to frontline workers, understood that their conduct toward all stakeholders and clients—not just the media—was part of the overall public relations strategy. This strategy guaranteed not only that there would be more individuals engaged with clients and stakeholders in encounters designed to strengthen legitimacy and support but also that the overall message of common cause, urgency, good-faith effort, and responsiveness to problems would come across more authentically as reporters and stakeholders found that attitude everywhere throughout the agency.

Toward this same end, Gale established her own personal profile as someone who was eager to do the job right and not defensive about protecting herself or the work of her agency. She communicated through her statements and actions that each citizen complaint, as well as each bit of negative press, was an important issue in itself and an occasion to comment on and improve the performance of the system as a whole. She tried to tell a story through her actions about the relationships she wanted to create in managing the implementation of the new solid waste management system: the community was all in this together, and she and her agency were doing their best to protect and advance the broad public values at stake in this initiative while minimizing the inevitable errors and correcting them as quickly as possible; if they kept at it, they would soon have a world-class solid waste management system of which they could be proud. All they had to do was "be patient" and pitch in and do their part!

Using Measures of Public Relations Performance to Produce Public Value

Once public managers have acknowledged the strategic importance of communications functions, it should be obvious that they need to develop performance measures to track these efforts and then integrate the measures into their broad performance management system. This is one of the primary reasons the public value scorecard includes a legitimacy and support perspective. The John James case in Chapter 3 illustrated the importance of building a stronger, more substantively aligned relationship with one key oversight body in the legislative branch. Gale's case, however, reveals how much that concept needs to be widened, particularly when a public agency is trying to mobilize a group of clients into voluntary coproduction activities. A legitimacy and support perspective might have helped James understand that while the State Department's Division of the House Appropriations Committee might have been the single most important piece of his authorizing environment, many other social actors—all of whom could benefit from the same close attention that he gave to the legislative committee—were in a position to call him to account, give him guidance, or provide him with legitimacy and support.

Similarly, if James had kept in mind that he too had a strategic problem in mobilizing a large number of Minnesota citizens to pay their taxes, he might have enlarged his legitimacy and support perspective to include marketing campaigns designed to mobilize individuals to pay their taxes by clarifying what they needed to do and showing that compliance rates were high and/or increasing in order to deter taxpayers from concluding that no one else was paying their taxes, so they did not have to either.

Principles for Mobilizing Legitimacy and Support for Public Agencies
If we were to combine these two cases, what might we conclude about the potential value and practical means for developing a legitimacy and support perspective of the public value scorecard? Gale's focused management of the utility's public relations efforts earned her some significant strategic rewards: she succeeded in sustaining grassroots authorization for dramatic changes in the utility's solid waste management processes even through a predictable set of mishaps; she built the coproduction capacity she needed among clients to make the changes work; and she may even have helped build some sense of civic responsibility, accomplishment, and virtue. To reap these benefits, Gale had to keep in mind some key principles for public-sector marketing that should guide all public managers making similar efforts:

- In mobilizing legitimacy and support, public managers have to address two quite different audiences: authorizers and clients. Success in speaking to these two different audiences and encouraging them to play their appropriate roles in both defining and creating public value often requires public managers to help individuals begin to integrate their roles as citizens and clients of the agency.
- Although the authorizing environment includes influential individuals in various formal positions, it is still essential to include the voices of citizens and clients who do not have much

power over the agency as individuals. Client surveys and account management systems can help temper the powerful influence of politicians and established interest groups.

- The clients of public agencies include both beneficiaries and obligatees. The marketing message will be different for these different kinds of clients, but one consistent thrust of the marketing message should be to encourage all clients to think a bit more like citizens.
- Whether they are receiving services or obligations or some combination of the two, clients play important roles as coproducers of social outcomes. Their active cooperation and effort are usually essential for achieving the social outcomes public managers are responsible for producing. The marketing effort has to focus on motivating and enabling clients to contribute to the public good.
- Public agencies need two somewhat different things from authorizers and clients. On one hand, they need tolerance, support, and authorization for the actions they take. On the other, they need active participation in transforming social conditions. The marketing strategy needs to focus not only on particular audiences but also on the particular things that the agency needs from the different audiences.
- The communication strategy designed to build support and operational capacity from stakeholders and clients must be based on listening, consulting, and deliberating rather than on telling, directing, and asserting. Without this commitment, the effort looks like propaganda, making it both ethically unacceptable and practically ineffective.
- There must be some organizational infrastructure in place for developing and executing a successful communications strategy and ensuring that there are performance measures in place to track both the state of relationships with stakeholders and clients and the impact of particular communications campaigns.

Account Management Systems for Public Agencies
In addition to these general principles, public managers might be able to improve their ability to build legitimacy and support from their collective authorizers by developing a formal account management system

that lists the particular social actors with whom they seek to maintain a relationship, assigns responsibility for maintaining those relationships to particular organizational units, and monitors the state of the relationship. If mobilizing legitimacy and support is an important part of building the operational capacity to get the job done as well as figuring out what the job should be in the first place, and if the required legitimacy and support comes from particular actors with particular interests, it makes sense to build a list of those actors and to manage the agency's relationship with them.

Gale may not have made a full-fledged effort to develop an account management system, and she certainly did not work as hard to develop her relationship with a particular legislative authorizer as James did, but she did spend a great deal of time cultivating her relationships with key individuals in the media. She also created the capacity to respond quickly and nondefensively to individual "horror stories," taking each story as a valid indicator of a performance problem, resolving the problem as quickly as possible, and using it as a basis for improving the average performance of the agency. To show the organization's commitment to resolving these matters, she created an "account executive program" that assigned a team of utility managers to personally investigate a sample of citizen complaints. The aggregate record of her response to these individual stories became an important part of a narrative that persuaded citizens that she and her agency were doing their part, and trying to improve.

When it became apparent that part of her problem lay with the individual contractors and their ability to live up to the service levels the citizens had signed up for, rather than relying on the bureaucratic mechanisms of contract accountability to improve their performance Gale made personal visits to her contractors, asking them to commit to firm deadlines for distributing trash barrels and publicizing their commitments in "The New Garbage Services Weekly Bulletin." She put them on the spot as agents who were failing to do their duty in what was a general public campaign as well as a particular contractual obligation. None of the private contractors wanted to be seen as the thing that was impeding the success of an initiative that depended on contributions from so many. Gale also adjusted her own fixed deadlines and policies to accommodate complaints from citizens who were trying to keep up and play their designated role in the new system.

Of course, there are risks in focusing a great deal of organizational attention on "accounts" with key stakeholders. An agency focused on sustaining itself and increasing its budget could use an account management system to identify a small coalition that would sustain the organization in its current activities, thereby defeating both a proper kind of democratic accountability and the potential for accurately identifying and producing public value. The agency would not only cease producing certain dimensions of public value, but also would fail to engage in the deliberative process that would guide it to an accurate value proposition and help create citizens willing to help pursue that value.

But this becomes a risk only if the agency keeps its account management system secret and uses it for these narrow purposes. If the agency publicizes the various accounts it recognizes and manages and the state of its relationship with its various accounts, other members of the public can act to change that set of accounts if it seems too narrowly focused and self-interested. Individual citizens who have interests in the actions of the agency but do not feel adequately consulted can ask to be recognized as an account. Other citizens, or representatives of civic interests (reporters, civic associations, etc.), can review the accounts and speak out when they seem to omit important stakeholders. Though we often assume that it is in the public's interest to protect public agencies from external influence, becoming transparent with regard to the actors that make claims on a public agency could increase and balance the number of stakeholders to whom it feels accountable. It would make transparent what is now largely invisible and formal what is now largely informal.

Similarly, if the agency used its account management system not just to build support for its current activities but also as a device for becoming more widely and explicitly accountable, and for orchestrating a broader process of deliberation about its purposes, its performance, and the kind of help it needs from citizens, then the system could strengthen both the democratic accountability and the performance of the agency. Like many managerial devices, then, an account management system can produce good or bad results depending on how it is used. The potential for misuse should not prevent public agencies from experimenting with these or other managerial systems borrowed and adapted from the private-sector context.

Getting on a Roll: The Mutually Reinforcing Processes of
Public Commitment

Finally, it is worth noting that developing and using information about how individual citizens are reacting to new challenges and burdens placed on them can become not only a record of success in some marketing campaigns but also a powerful instrument in producing the success. There is something very powerful about a process that begins with an appeal to individuals to make voluntary contributions and then keeps track of the rate at which individuals step forward to meet that appeal. Individuals do not want to be seen as shirkers or free riders. When there is a public task to be done, and some individuals step forward to do it, others will come along to avoid the shame of failing to do their fair share. The more individuals who sign up, the more obligation others will feel to do the work as well, and the more visible this process becomes, the greater the social pressure will be to join.

Gale's celebration of the growing number of households taking part in the recycling campaign is a perfect example of a strategic use of this mechanism. The public daily tally of citizens signing up for the recycling campaign provided both a record of Gale's success in persuading individuals to join in the effort and an impetus for more citizens to take part. This public accounting of enrollments made the contributions of recycling households highly visible. The households lagging behind the trend began to pay attention and to request their own recycling bins.

This kind of marketing campaign takes advantage of the theory of "social norms" and the process of "norming."[34] In the world of charitable fund-raising, for example, research has found that although there is an expectation (norm) that those whose income rises above a certain threshold ought to give some of that money back in the form of charitable donations, a general lack of information about actual behavior inhibits giving. This has led some to propose a voluntary public registry of donations that would track what proportion of their income individuals gave, thereby strengthening and clarifying the norm.[35]

Individuals may insist on their autonomy, but there is a powerful human drive to be part of the norm. Offering accurate information often changes the perception of the norm, which can alter the norm itself. When researchers corrected high school and college students' inflated perception of how common drug and alcohol abuse was among their peers, they found that providing accurate information about drug and alcohol use strengthened the hand of the many who were not abusing alcohol and drugs against the few who were.[36] It is as though a small minority sets the norm until data show that the norm is really quite different.

Thus to bring the public along, Gale associated the new solid waste strategy with well-documented general public support for recycling. She made signing up for and participating effectively in this effort an important act of citizenship. In order to mobilize legitimacy and build operational capacity, she used measures of enrollment in the recycling effort as a device to build momentum for the effort and pressure citizens to sign up. She celebrated milestones not in terms of the work of the utility and its managers but in terms of the grassroots efforts around recycling and the quality of citizenship those efforts seemed to embody. Like a Community Chest publicizing the fraction of community members that have made contributions, the American Red Cross using a publicly visible thermometer to show what fraction of the community has joined its blood drive, or a fund-raiser working a crowd of potential donors, Gale used the sign-ups as a device for changing the norm in the community. When she presented evidence that many others were making a contribution, it became harder for those not yet mobilized to sit on the sidelines.

Summary

Traditionally, we have looked askance at government-financed public relations and media campaigns. We have worried that such efforts will be used for nothing more than propaganda purposes, or that their major impact will be to insulate government operations from public criticism. But the Gale case suggests that a well-crafted public relations campaign might play a crucial role in supporting rather than defeating democratic governance.

To craft an effective communications strategy designed to call into existence a public that could understand and act in its own interests, Gale had to attend to four key segments of her authorizing environment: the public officials with formal authority over Gale and the Solid Waste Utility; the established interest groups that sought to influence those officials through well-worn channels; the media; and the grassroots citizens who were simultaneously authorizers, payers, beneficiaries, and volunteer workers in the wider public effort.

Gale needed at least continuing tolerance or support from each of these pieces of the authorizing environment in order to move confidently to produce public value. Without that continuing support, she would lack the moral, legal, and practical basis for continuing her effort. From some of them, however, she needed something more than mere authorization and support; she needed action that would materially contribute to the solution of the solid waste problem.

Efforts to impose new duties on citizens and clients generally do not work very well in democratic societies. Most citizens of democratic

---

PUBLIC VALUE ACCOUNT for Diana Gale and the Seattle Waste Utility

PUBLIC VALUE ACCOUNT	
Use of Collectively Owned Assets and Associated Costs	Achievement of Collectively Valued Social Outcomes
Financial Costs	Mission Achievement
Internal (administrative)	Manage solid waste reliably,
External (to ratepayers)	conveniently, and safely
	Protect the natural environment
	Client Satisfaction
	Provide choices in level of service
Social Costs of Using State Authority	Justice and Fairness
Co-production burdens on citizens	Ensure equal access for citizens
	Ensure fair pricing

Figure 5.3. Public value scorecard for Diana Gale and the Seattle Solid Waste Utility.

THE LEGITIMACY AND SUPPORT PERSPECTIVE
Progress and Planning for Diana Gale and the Seattle Solid Waste Utility

Mission Alignment with Values Articulated by Citizens:
Aligned mission closely over long run with low cost, environmentally
sound waste disposal

Inclusion of Neglected Values with Latent Constituencies:
Built tolerance for inevitable service problems in the short run
Restore demand for service convenience and reliability in the long run

Standing with Formal Authorizers:
Maintained support for policy and tolerance for problems

Standing with Key Interest Groups:
Maintained support for policy with environmentalists
Maintained responsiveness from contractors

Media Coverage:
Created internal capacity for marketing and media engagement
Built relationships with media

Standing with Individuals in Polity:
General Citizenry
- Built understanding of policies through marketing campaign
- Built tolerance for implementation problems through press relations
Clients
- Created system to respond to client needs and complaints
Ratepayers
- Provided choices in service levels

Engagement of Citizens as Co-Producers:
Engaged clients effectively in co-production of solid waste management

---

THE OPERATIONAL CAPACITY PERSPECTIVE
Progress and Planning for Diana Gale and the Seattle Solid Waste Utility

Flow of Resources to Enterprise:
Financial Revenues
- Secured emergency funds from city council to staff phone systems
Public Support/Popular Opinion
- Generated public enthusiasm for recycling program

Human Resources:
Training/Professional Development
- Built staff competence in press relations
- Authorized staff engagement with public and media
Public Volunteer Efforts
- Engaged clients in coproduction of solid waste management

Operational Policies, Programs, and Procedures:
Quality of Operational Performance
- Responded quickly to operational problems as identified through
complaints/media
Organizational Learning
- Created systems to distribute containers and implement new rate schedules
and routes
Performance Measurement and Management Systems
- Monitored sign-ups for recycling to spur increased participation
- Created "account executive program" to resolve problem cases
- Streamlined complaints system
- Used transparency to drive performance

Organizational Outputs:
Quantity of Outputs
- *Increase reliability in collections*
Quality of Outputs
- *Increase convenience in collections*

societies would prefer to act as clients—and particularly client beneficiaries who can make self-interested claims on government at the level
of both policy and operations. Yet government is not only in the service
delivery business and is not only interested in satisfying individual citizens. It often imposes duties on individuals as well as provides services.
And it often needs both those who receive services and those on whom
duties are imposed to shoulder the burden of helping it achieve publicly
valued outcomes that might be different from individual satisfaction.

To allow such efforts to succeed, and to allow such complex production systems to actually work to deliver the desired results, public
managers have to find ways to speak to the individuals who constitute
the public in their different roles as citizens and taxpayers; as clients
who receive benefits and/or obligations; and as individual coproducers of
collectively valued results. Public pressure to motivate individuals to contribute to public purposes works only when those individuals on whom
burdens are imposed can be persuaded, or have the chance to discover
together, that the burdens are legitimate. And the only way to legitimate
the government's use of public pressure and influence—whether lodged
in formal authority or informal exhortation—is to explain why it is
necessary and to show that it is being used according to widely shared
ideas about what would be just and fair as well as efficient and effective. It also helps to be able to show those who are resisting that many
others have accepted the necessity of assuming new duties, and that
those who are still resisting have become part of the problem rather than
the solution.

Gale seemed not only to understand that a successful effort to build
and sustain legitimacy and support from Seattle's residents for the solid
waste policy was key to the success of the effort but also that the key to
building that legitimacy and support was maintaining a close and responsive relationship to her political authorizing environment—not
just the political elites to whom she was directly accountable but also to
the citizens acting in their different roles as authorizers, clients, and coproducers. Getting her message out was only a small piece of her strategy
for communicating with her authorizing environment. She had to keep
communication lines open and flowing both ways between the utility
and the media and between the utility and the public. By making her
agency and its work a subject of public conversation, and by addressing
the individual citizens of Seattle in their different roles, she helped the

individuals of Seattle become *citizens* of Seattle who were joined in an effort to manage their solid waste. Only by thinking and acting in this way did she succeed in engaging the citizens in a policy created by the people (as authorizers), for the people (as clients), and of the people (as coproducers).

In these ways Gale's actions make a significant contribution to our understanding of how to develop and use a public value scorecard that focuses attention on the actions needed to build legitimacy and support and operational capacity at the grassroots level of citizens and clients. She fills a hole in our usual thought about strategic management in the public sector by having us concentrate on the task of building an effective public relations and marketing campaign that addresses citizens in their distinct roles as authorizers, payers, coproducers, and clients of public enterprises. And she reminds us that succeeding in these tasks can not only sustain legitimacy and support for a chancy enterprise but also effectively mobilize the decentralized capacity necessary to produce the desired results. Figure 5.3 presents an image of how a public value scorecard might have helped guide Gale's actions—and how the same actions that tended to the legitimacy and support perspective produced important results that registered in the operational capacity perspective.

———

6

Duncan Wyse, Jeff Tryens, and the Progress Board

Helping Polities Envision and Produce Public Value

Duncan Wyse, Jeff Tryens, and the Oregon Benchmarks

In July 1995 Oregon's statewide Progress Board invited Jeff Tryens to fly from his home in Maryland to interview for the position of staff director.[1] The Progress Board had been created in 1989 to translate a wide range of statewide public policy goals into a set of measurable benchmarks. Duncan Wyse, the founding director of the Progress Board, had kept the enterprise going for half a decade in the face of significant political controversy and strife. By 1995, he felt he had paid his dues and so stepped aside to become head of the Oregon Business Council, leaving a vacancy to be filled.

Only upon arriving in Oregon for the meeting did Tryens discover that the Progress Board was poised to lose its funding in just two years' time due to a "sunset" provision written into the law that created the agency in 1989. Late in the 1995 session, the Republican majority in the state legislature had decided to let the board dissolve. The Progress Board and the Oregon Benchmarks would have disappeared then and there had the legislature not approved a budget for the agency for the next two years in a routine action earlier in the session.[2] Democratic Governor John Kitzhaber effectively overruled the legislature's decision, reauthorizing the board via an executive order and giving it a two-year reprieve. Bob Repine, Republican cochair of the Joint Ways and Means Committee, recalled, "I advised [Tryens] not to sell his house in Maryland."

The Origins of the Oregon Benchmarks

The Oregon Benchmarks were a set of broad concepts and specific measures that sought to capture the economic, social, and environmental health of the state. Each broad concept (e.g., "exceptional people" or "outstanding quality of life") came with a set of measures thought to be valid indicators of the state's progress with respect to a particular concept of value. Each indicator came with a set of short-term and long-term targets specifying how much progress the state wanted to make on that indicator.

This measurement system was the by-product of Democratic Governor Neil Goldschmidt's sweeping and energetic strategic planning initiative, called "Oregon Shines," undertaken in response to the economic recession of the early and mid-1980s. The recession had affected the entire nation, but it hit Oregon and its forest products industry especially hard. Oregon Shines was a broad effort to consult with business groups and other players in the state economy to determine what business and government could do to revitalize the economy.

Oregon Shines

Governor Goldschmidt reached out to Wyse, a policy analyst living in California, and asked him to return to his home state of Oregon and lead the "Oregon Shines" planning initiative. Wyse and his colleagues established sixteen committees, made up, collectively, of about 180 business, labor, education, and government leaders. One group of committees reviewed the issues that affected all businesses in the state, while another group focused on the issues critical to Oregon's largest or most rapidly growing industries. Each committee reported directly to the governor with its initial findings and then went back and refined its recommendations. The final committee reports formed the basis for a single strategic plan, shaped at the Economic Development Department and in the governor's office.

In May 1989 the final Oregon Shines report concluded that Oregon was at a critical crossroads. With appropriate investments and policy choices, Oregon could become a high-tech, high-wage player in the international economy, even while preserving a healthy natural environment and shoring up public services. To chart a positive course, the report concluded, Oregon needed to do several things:

- increase the skills of its workforce so it would be "measurably the best in America by the year 2000, and equal to any in the world by 2010";
- preserve the state's natural environment and uncongested communities and market them "to attract the people and firms that will drive an advanced economy";
- cultivate an "international frame of mind . . . that distinguishes Oregonians as unusually adept in global commerce";
- contain the costs of doing business in Oregon—especially in the areas of workers' compensation rates, unemployment insurance, and energy rates; and
- invest in public facilities and services that would attract new firms to the state.

A recurring concern in the Oregon Shines citizen planning sessions, however, was how to implement a plan of such sweeping scope. To avoid the risk that the report would merely gather dust on a shelf, Wyse and his fellow planners advocated the creation of a special entity to serve as the steward of the state's strategic vision: the "Progress Board."

Establishing the Oregon Progress Board
In the eyes of its creators, the principal mandate of the Progress Board was to translate the Oregon Shines strategic vision into a set of specific goals, or benchmarks, and to monitor the state's progress toward those goals. The board was to have a small staff, no formal role in the biennial state budgeting process, and, in fact, "no power per se," said Wyse. Its influence would derive from the reputation of its members, the degree to which social actors in the state bought into the vision set out in its abstract goals and concrete objectives, and the degree to which the governor owned it and relied on its work to guide his administration. Even the most optimistic supporters of the Oregon Shines process thought that both the continued development of the benchmarks and the effective use of the benchmarks in animating and guiding the Oregon polity on a path toward prosperity lived or died based on the active support and participation of the governor. Wyse's first task, then, was to convince the governor to become the active chairman of the Progress Board.

In early internal meetings, Goldschmidt agreed to the idea but evinced little conviction or interest. When the Oregon Shines report was released to the public, however, and Goldschmidt suddenly faced a raft of questions about "what happens next," he became an enthusiastic booster of the Progress Board and the benchmarks and decided to establish the enterprise as a statutory body of the state. Because Goldschmidt was a Democrat and the Democrats controlled both the House and the Senate by a healthy margin, convincing the state legislature to go along with this idea was a relatively easy affair. In the summer of 1989 the legislature voted for the board to be created immediately, to propose a set of benchmarks to the legislature for approval in 1991, to provide a progress report every two years, and to sunset in 1995.

Shortly after getting the Progress Board up and running, Goldschmidt decided he would not run for reelection in 1990. To Wyse, now executive director of the Progress Board, this was a potential disaster. Oregon Shines and the Progress Board were strongly identified with Goldschmidt. The Progress Board was still a fledgling organization, just beginning the process of translating the Oregon Shines report into a set of benchmarks. At first, Wyse remembered, "I just thought we were dead."

The board's members came to the rescue. "This was the power of the Board—we had the right folks," said Wyse. Two Republican board members approached the leading Republican candidate for governor, Attorney General Dave Frohnmayer. Ed Whitelaw, a prominent Democrat on the board, approached the Democratic candidate, Secretary of State Barbara Roberts. Both Frohnmayer and Roberts promised full support for the effort if elected.

Creating the Benchmarks

Roberts was elected governor in November 1990 and, in a gesture of bipartisan goodwill, quickly appointed Frohnmayer to the Progress Board. In January of that year the Progress Board had created six steering committees to develop an initial list of benchmarks. These preliminary recommendations were presented to the public in twelve statewide meetings, attended by approximately five hundred people. At the end of the year, Governor Goldschmidt invited Governor-Elect Roberts to attend the final two monthly meetings of the Progress Board before it was to send its recommendations to the legislature. "I think he wanted to preserve the legacy," Roberts recalled. "So many good government ideas go with the office holder, because every politician seems to want to have their own legacy. *My invention.*" Roberts found it easy to resist this tendency, though, because "I could see its value, particularly for the long term. And—potentially—I thought I'd have more chance of changing things [through the benchmarking initiative] than through any government process I'd ever been involved with."

Themes
Early in 1991, with Roberts's input and her promise to give the Progress Board a prominent place in the new administration, the board sent the legislature a proposed list of 158 benchmarks, divided into three broad categories:

- *Exceptional People* included benchmarks for increasing the stability of home life, giving youngsters a healthy start in life, improving school performance, increasing levels of educational attainment, improving overall citizen health, and promoting equal opportunity and social harmony.
- *Outstanding Quality of Life* included benchmarks for improving air and water quality, preserving natural amenities, maintaining uncongested roadways, restoring and maintaining affordable housing, reducing crime, increasing access to health care and child care, and increasing citizens' community involvement.
- *Diverse, Robust Economy* included benchmarks for maintaining a strong manufacturing sector, increasing employment and per capita income levels, reducing the cost of doing business in Oregon, improving air transportation service to Oregon, improving road and telecommunications infrastructure, increasing research and development work, and maintaining or slightly increasing the state's overall per capita tax level (while reducing reliance on the property tax).

Setting Priorities, Choosing Target Goals, and the Problem of Limited Data
In addition to the master list of 158 benchmarks, the board created two short lists containing the benchmarks it deemed most important. "Lead"

benchmarks related to urgent problems "in which we must see progress in the next five years." "Key" benchmarks were those deemed "fundamental, enduring measures of Oregon's vitality and health."

One of the board's early dilemmas—and one that would later prove controversial—concerned the setting of benchmark goals. Should the goals be based on the ideal society it wanted to see? Or should they be based on some kind of "realistic" appraisal of what might be done given limited resources and other constraints? The board was not entirely consistent in setting its benchmark targets, but by and large it chose to "aim high," especially with the twenty-year goals.

The board also had to grapple with the limited availability of data to measure the benchmarks. Where possible, it provided for each benchmark historical data from 1970 and 1980, "baseline" data from 1990, and goals for 1995, 2000, and 2010. But a problem arose when the board wanted to create a benchmark for which no data existed. It did not have the resources to research the state's performance on more than a handful of benchmarks. Thus, as explained in its 1991 report to the legislature, "For this inaugural set of benchmarks, the Progress Board has elected to establish some benchmarks where data is not currently available in order to suggest priorities on data collection needs for the future."

Politics, Benchmarks, and Budget Cuts

In the 1990 election the Republicans had gained control of the House of Representatives for the first time in twenty years. Though "we didn't need to particularly, politically," Wyse recalled working "incredibly hard to bring the Republicans in" for the 1991 session. In fact, the idea of establishing clear and concrete goals with quantifiable measures had a natural appeal to Republicans, who tended to advocate for greater public-sector accountability. In retrospect, however, some Republican legislators suggested that the appearance of bipartisan support was a bit misleading. Many legislators never focused much attention on the project. "It had bipartisan support because no one knew what it was," quipped one former legislator. In any event, after the 1991 legislative session, the Progress Board and benchmark experiment were to become ensnared in Oregon's broader political—and partisan—crosscurrents.

In 1992, anticipating the need to cut the following year's state budget by as much as 15 percent, Governor Roberts resolved to use the benchmarks as a guide to setting priorities in the budget reductions.[3] She directed all state agencies to develop base budgets at 80 percent of their current levels but permitted them to add back up to 10 percent for programs linked to any of the Oregon Benchmarks. If agencies could demonstrate that their programs were linked to one of the seventeen "lead" benchmarks, they could restore funding above the 90 percent level. Agency administrators were quick to respond. The benchmarks documents "became *dog-eared* while those agencies searched for things in the benchmarks that applied to their work," recalled Roberts.

The sudden rise in the stature of the Oregon Benchmarks within state government had some unforeseen consequences. To be "in the game," each state agency and every special interest group had to have a benchmark. The Progress Board was inundated with petitions for the addition of new benchmarks. In 1992 and 1993 the number of benchmarks increased from 158 to 272. Within each benchmark as well, the number of items for measurement increased. Thus while in 1991 the "drug-free babies" benchmark had measured the number of infants whose mothers used illicit drugs during pregnancy, the 1993 version included separate measurements for the consumption of alcohol and the use of tobacco as well.

Roberts and the board were lenient about approving new benchmarks. "A group would come in and say, 'What about us?'" Roberts recalled. "Well, that's not a good way for people to feel—that their state doesn't think they're a priority. So a reasonable benchmark, on a subject they cared about, was not an unreasonable thing to add to the benchmarks. I mean, the benchmarks served a number of purposes." At the same time, Roberts and the board members understood that the only benchmarks that would receive concerted attention from the board—special studies, working groups, or priority in the state budget-making process—fell within the subset of benchmarks that the Board had designated as a high priority. (These lead and key benchmarks were renamed in 1993 "urgent" and "core," respectively.) Among these high-priority benchmarks, the number regarded as "urgent" jumped from seventeen to twenty-seven between 1991 and 1993, and the number regarded as "core" increased from thirteen to eighteen.

A New Political Landscape

The legislature approved the expanded list of benchmarks by a wide margin in 1993, but this time the vote was not unanimous. Evident was an undercurrent of dissatisfaction, especially among Republican lawmakers. Some legislators complained that agency directors and special interest groups used the benchmarks against them, saying, "You adopted such-and-so benchmark, calling for the eradication of such-and-so problem in 20 years. If you're serious about that, you must appropriate such-and-so dollars to fund my project." In addition, two legislators on the Joint Ways and Means Committee criticized the benchmarks as being too broad in scope to serve as an effective means of guiding and assessing the work of state agencies.

In Oregon's 1992 election the Republicans had retained control of the House and the Democrats of the Senate, but only by a slender 16 to 14 margin. After the 1994 election, the Democrats lost the Senate decisively; the Republicans controlled both Houses, although Democrat John Kitzhaber won the governor's seat. The incoming Republicans, many from the rural parts of the state, tended to be more conservative on social issues and more critical of government in general than their predecessors. In Oregon, as elsewhere, the partisan divide deepened. Democrats found the first legislative session under the new balance of power, in 1995, quite rancorous by Oregon standards.

Kitzhaber supported the Progress Board and the Oregon Benchmarks, but both were lower in his scheme of priorities than they had been for Roberts. More worrisome, the board was due to "sunset" in 1995. To continue as a statutory agency, the board would have to win reauthorization from the legislature.

Fate in the Balance

In conjunction with the Oregon Business Council, the Progress Board had made a concerted effort to reengage Oregon citizens in the state's strategic vision and the benchmark project in 1993. Over a three-month period, the two organizations set up twenty-nine community meetings across the state. These new meetings attracted about two thousand citizens (compared to about five hundred in the 1990 sessions). "But," Wyse said, "we didn't get the newly elected legislators to come to these. We weren't hooking in with them." The meetings did not serve to reinforce the legislature's "ownership" of the Progress Board and the Oregon Benchmarks program.

The bill to reauthorize the Progress Board for another four years easily passed the Joint Ways and Means Trade and Economic Subcommittee and was referred to the Ways and Means Committee. At this point, however, the Republican leadership decided that the bill would have to pass through the gauntlet of the Republican Caucus. While Wyse had calculated that in the legislature as a whole the board had enough support for the bill to pass, he was far less sanguine about its prospects in the Republican Caucus. Wyse decided to hedge his bets. The Progress Board's budget appropriation—a small part of the agency budget for the Department of Economic Development—existed in a separate bill from the act to reauthorize the Progress Board. "I figured— let's get our budget through. You've got a budget, you're going to be in operation, whether you're an official state agency or not. The governor can always create it by executive order," said Wyse. So Wyse and the Progress Board sat quietly by, while the reauthorization bill languished in the Ways and Means Committee, and waited for the budget process to take its course. "If it becomes a big issue and you lose, you lose everything," said Wyse. "I just didn't want to lose everything."

The legislature did approve a budget that included funding for the Progress Board and the Oregon Benchmarks project. Wyse had hoped that once they realized the budget was in place, the Republican lawmakers would quietly approve the reauthorization, but when several caucus members voiced their opposition, no one was willing to go to bat for the program. After a vote, the Republican leadership recommended that Governor Kitzhaber disband the board. Kitzhaber responded that he intended to keep the program alive via an executive order. This move "made the legislature a little angry," recalled Senator Neil Bryant, but the fate of the Progress Board had never been a do-or-die issue. As one observer put it, "Nobody was going to go back and try to undo the budget at that point." Thus the Progress Board had a two-year reprieve; to survive, the initiative had to win over a legislature now dominated by legislators who were indifferent to hostile toward the program.

Jeff Tryens Hears the Criticisms
When Jeff Tryens toured the state of Oregon in 1995, he heard concerns about the Progress Board and the benchmarks from both Democratic

and Republican legislators. Democrats tended to explain the Republican opposition to the Progress Board as a matter of partisanship—hostility to a program with Democratic roots. For their own part, many Republican legislators said they found the benchmarks "irrelevant." Senator Randy Miller called them "slightly above meaningless" and argued that the information in the Progress Board's biennial report was available through other sources. "We're funding something that tells you what everybody already knows," he said. Others liked the Oregon Benchmarks project in principle but believed that, by 1995, it had gone astray. Most of the criticisms that Tryens heard tended to fall into the following categories.

A Democratic Program with a Democratic Agenda. As a program originated and sustained by three Democratic governors, the benchmarks were seen as a Democratic initiative. Republican legislators believed too many of the benchmarks reflected a liberal social, environmental, and political agenda. Senator Bryant argued that the Democrats "used the benchmarks to try to sell social programs." Some legislators also noted that the Progress Board had never included any culturally conservative Republican, nor any member who represented Oregon's agricultural and ranching interests in debates on environmental matters.

Too Many Benchmarks. The Republicans were concerned that the proliferation of benchmarks between 1991 and 1993 had trivialized the whole notion of the benchmarks and rendered them unworkable. Said Tryens, "The criticism I heard over and over was, 'You've got too many benchmarks. We're measuring ridiculous things.'" Even the Progress Board members themselves had only passing familiarity with benchmarks that were neither "urgent" nor "core." Only a small number of the benchmarks had prompted coordinated efforts to meet the benchmark goals. The vast majority existed only on paper. By 1995 approximately fifty benchmarks still lacked complete data or clear goals.

Unrealistic Goals. Some legislators objected to the utopian goals of many benchmarks and argued that they led to endless calls for increased state spending and failed to offer any real guidance to state agencies or any other entity. For example, the teen pregnancy goal—eight per thousand—was a lower rate than had been achieved anywhere in the country. Tryens acknowledged that there was an arbitrary quality to some of the benchmark goals. "There isn't a strategy attached to each one that says, 'This is how we're going to achieve that target and how much it's going to cost.'"

No Agency Accountability. The decision to use the benchmarks in the 1993 budget-cutting process led many state agencies to claim that they were working toward some of the urgent or core benchmarks. In fact a number of state agencies claimed to be working on the same benchmarks, but no system was in place to coordinate their efforts, nor to assess their performance vis-à-vis the benchmark goals. "They should show us what's working, what's not working—where to invest our money," said Bryant. In addition, the state's 140 agencies were inconsistent in how seriously they took the benchmarks, and in the degree to which they used them in their strategic planning processes.[4]

Democratic Suspicions. Amid these criticisms, Democrats began to worry that the Republicans wanted to use the benchmarks to fuel an antigovernment attack. Some legislators "see this as a tool to measure state agency performance, but that's not really what it's intended to do," said Bill Wyatt, chief of staff to Governor Kitzhaber. "Agencies are understandably worried that they're going to be measured against objectives over which they have very little control." Democrats feared that Republican legislators would use the inability of state agencies to meet farflung benchmark goals as a hammer to pound at state government. Said one prominent Oregon Democrat, "There are people who are antigovernment—and many of those exist in my state today, as they do across the country. They want to measure government to prove government is failing."

Refreshing the Mandate

Tryens tried to learn from all he had heard. He took particular note of an observation by Republican Senator Stan Bunn. Not all Republican legislators were unalterably set against the Progress Board, said Bunn, but the board had no champions in the Republican Party either. Thus Tryens "set out to find two powerful, supportive champions" among the Republican legislators. He set his sights on two legislators he had met during his prehiring visit—Bob Repine, cochair of the Joint Ways and Means Committee, and Neil Bryant, who drove many of the major policy bills in the Senate. "They were critics, but constructive critics," said Tryens. "In my mind, they were both winnable." Winning them over, however, would require addressing their complaints—and that meant building the political support to make some major changes.

The first was to update the Oregon Shines strategic plan. Between 1989 and 1995, Oregon's economy had made a dramatic recovery. On the other side of the ledger, however, many Oregonians, especially in rural areas, had not benefited from the economic boom at all. Housing costs, juvenile crime rates, and student drug use were escalating. Metropolitan areas were becoming more congested. Tryens wanted to amend the original Oregon Shines plan to address these shifting conditions.

In addition, Tryens suggested to Governor Kitzhaber that he appoint a task force "to reassess the entire process from top to bottom" through a series of community meetings across the state. Tryens recommended that a number of business leaders be appointed to the task force. He brought in one of Oregon's most prominent corporate leaders, utility executive Fred Buckman, to head the forty-five-member Oregon Shines Task Force. At the beginning of the process, Tryens bluntly told the task force that the decision to continue Oregon Shines, the Progress Board, and the Oregon Benchmarks project was an open question.

> I was really up front with everybody, including my legislative critics, that this was the chance to say, "No." To say, "Yeah, it's been a great run, but guess what? The economy's recovered. Maybe we don't need a strategic economic plan anymore."
>
> I said to them at the first meeting—and this sort of became a famous line—"I haven't sold my house in Maryland yet, and I'm completely willing to go home if you don't think this is a worthwhile enterprise for us to continue. At the end of this process, I'm going to ask you to vote in secret about whether or not you think Oregon Shines and the Progress Board and the Benchmarks are something we should continue to support, so please keep that in mind through the process."

Changing the Benchmarks

In the end the Oregon Shines Task Force reaffirmed the importance of retaining a statewide strategic vision. As written in the task force's final report, "Oregon Shines II: Updating Oregon's Strategic Plan," in

January 1997, "The pace of change keeps most of us focused on the present, even in the midst of a major economic and social transformation. The Oregon Progress Board's responsibility is to remind us of our shared vision, monitor our progress in achieving measurable goals, and bring choices to our attention." The new, revised version of the state's strategic plan continued to emphasize improved education and training. But while the original Oregon Shines focused on luring out-of-state businesses to come to Oregon, Oregon Shines II emphasized the development of local Oregon businesses to compete in the global economy. The new version also emphasized preventive approaches to social problems such as crime and drug use and the development of stronger, more supportive community networks.

The task force also helped Tryens pare down the benchmarks. "What I was able to take back to the legislature was 92 benchmarks [down from 259 in 1995], [and] a big-time sign-off from the business community. . . . We released the thing at a school to make the point that education was still the key to this. We had all the top state officials there. The governor was there. We got lots of coverage on the release. We'd been able to do what the legislature really wanted us to do, which was make the benchmarks more manageable." In terms of making the benchmark goals more "realistic," the Progress Board settled on a compromise, agreeing to establish more modest targets in 2000 but to preserve the idealistic targets for 2010.

Linking Benchmarks to Performance
Tryens also took several steps toward aligning the activities of state agencies with the benchmarks. The Progress Board created a "Benchmark Blue Book" that clarified which state agencies had "signed up" for which benchmarks. This gave legislators a tool for demanding some accountability from the agencies during budget season, if they chose to exercise it. In addition, the Blue Book was a potential aid to agency administrators, who could see which other agencies were working toward a given benchmark, paving the way for the easier sharing of information and resources.[5]

Tryens also began to put forward a new vision of how agencies might work with benchmarks, intended to address the gap between the sweeping nature of the benchmarks and the limited purview of any single state agency. The idea, he said, was to use "tiered indicators." A task force of agency representatives and other interested parties, created to tackle a given benchmark, could first break down that large benchmark—for example, reducing juvenile crime—into a set of interim indicators and goals—for example, reducing the number of youths carrying handguns. For each indicator, one agency would take responsibility for collecting and providing data to the team. The next step was for the agencies or interested parties to take responsibility for pursuing a specific subset of these interim goals, both through specific agency-controlled projects and activities and through the influence of the agency in areas beyond its direct purview.[6]

These efforts to align the activities of state agencies with the benchmark goals were crucial in maintaining the support of the legislature. Still, winning approval for the reauthorization legislation in 1997 required one last effort. At the urging of Senate President Brady Adams, Tryens met personally with each of the thirty state senators. In the spring of 1997 both the House and Senate approved the reauthorization of the Progress Board—this time without a sunset clause. There were still a few dissenters, but overall support for the measure was strong and secure. The bill was approved by a vote of 17 to 4 in the Senate and 39 to 9 in the House. "For me, that was the positive culmination of two years' work. That meant I had achieved what the Board wanted me to do when I set out, which was to get the legislature back on board," Tryens said.[7]

From Organizational Accountability to Political Leadership

The champions of public value recognition in this case—Duncan Wyse and Jeff Tryens—started from a much weaker position and (paradoxically) sought to use performance measurement systems for much more ambitious purposes than the managers whose work we have analyzed in previous chapters. Wyse and Tryens were staffers loosely connected to the governor's office—neither line managers themselves, nor explicitly connected to any executive authority. They did not have formal authority over any public agencies, let alone the private companies and nonprofit service providers whose performance could contribute to the goals they were measuring.

Yet the benchmarks they established, monitored, and published reached much more broadly across the social landscape than any other measurement system we have yet considered. The broad aspirations captured in the Oregon Benchmarks framework encompassed not only the work of all of Oregon's state agencies but also the businesses that shape the Oregon economy and the nonprofits that work alongside government in pursuing and sometimes defining public purposes. It follows that the benchmarks could not exist only or even predominantly for the purposes of calling public agencies to account for their performance. The benchmarks had to have a use above and beyond measuring government performance. The question is what that use might be.

The natural tendency is to think first of the potential administrative uses of the benchmarks. Such a measurement system, disconnected from direct executive authority, could not be expected to drive performance as powerfully and directly in a particular direction as the performance measurement systems that William Bratton or Anthony Williams established, or even Jeannette Tamayo's performance contracting system. But they could nonetheless play an operational role in animating and guiding social and government action that would materially alter social conditions. They could, for example (at some risk to their political future), be a tool to help governors make resource allocation decisions among different government agencies. They could also be a tool for legislators and governors to gather empirical data about the degree to which government seemed able to produce desired results. Given a strong enough social and political commitment to these goals, the benchmarks could even provide a broad framework that invited powerful social actors outside of government—beyond the direct management of legislators and governors—to make contributions to specific benchmarks according to their abilities and inclinations. In all these ways the benchmarks had the potential to strengthen the capacity of the society to deliver on its most important aspirations.

A second possible answer to the question of what purpose the Oregon Benchmarks project served is that it was a performance measurement system that served as a public value account for an entire polity—not just a single public agency, or even state government as a whole. Like any public value account, it could serve as a political tool for engaging a polity in defining its common goals, as a basis for animating and guiding the polity's capacities toward reaching the goals, and as an instrument for learning about what public value could be produced in the future. Because the context of Wyse and Tryens's enterprise is so different from anything we have previously considered, it is worth a quick review of how establishing a public value account for a whole polity could do this strategic work.

If Wyse and Tryens were trying to build a public value account for an entire polity, it seems likely that some of the greatest benefits and risks would lie in its potential as a "political tool"—political not in the sense of political partisans using the benchmarks for their political purposes (though they did), nor in the sense of particular agencies and interest groups using the benchmarks to justify additional resources for their preferred purposes (though they did), but in the sense that the benchmarks could be used for the purposes John Dewey suggested: to help call into existence a public that could understand and act on its own interests, both independently and through the agency of government. From this point of view, what was valuable about the Oregon Benchmarks was less that they created a tight performance framework in which government agencies could be called to account for their performance and more that they helped create a statewide political community focused on the task of defining and pursuing a very broad but also quite specific vision of the good and just society in which they would like to live. The benchmarks became a kind of mirror that could reflect back to Oregon citizens an image of what they were trying to accomplish and how well they were doing.

As important, perhaps, using the benchmarks would require the polity as a whole to keep revisiting the question of what it was trying to accomplish, and to do so at a level of specificity and concreteness that would begin to create a certain kind of mutual accountability that spread across it rather than stayed within the boundaries of government operations. This would enable the polity to become much more self-conscious about the public value it sought to achieve, how its conceptions of public value might be changing, and what actual experience was teaching it about what was possible to do. Changes in the set of benchmarks would reflect judgments about what the polity thought was important. Observed performance with respect to the benchmarks could instruct the polity about what seemed possible to do. Annual confrontations with these commitments and results might help keep alive a public that understood and acted on its own interests.

As Wyse and Tryens doggedly and skillfully worked to make the Progress Board an enduring institution that could continuously improve the benchmarks as a measurement system that would both enable and create the occasion for powerful, independent actors to reflect on their contributions to a shared vision of a good and just society, they (like all the other managers we have seen) had to find some way to build legitimacy and support for the purposes they had in mind. That meant gathering and sustaining political support not for any particular substantive conception of public value *but for the idea that performance measurement itself can be a useful tool of governance.* Their basic public value proposition seemed to be that a system of performance measures—even when thrust into the middle of intense ideological/partisan conflict, even when constantly vulnerable to political rejection, and even when disconnected from a structure of authority that can demand accountability for performance—can help a political community define and pursue public value.

If Wyse and Tryens had their own public value scorecard, the legitimacy and support perspective for the efforts to create public value through the Progress Board and the benchmarks would probably focus on four different kinds of political work.

First, they would have to do the work of building support for the general idea of performance measurement as a tool of governance and for their particular institution as the best place to develop and use a performance measurement system.

Second, they would have to facilitate the process of accommodating many different political concerns and demands in the particular dimensions of value to be included in the benchmarks and organizing those concerns and demands in a representation of public value creation for Oregon.

Third, in order for the benchmarks to have some impact on the performance of both government and private agencies, they would have to find a way to attach political pressure to the measures without using direct, formal authority and/or to align their measures with the executive powers of the state.

Fourth, they would have to continually adapt the performance measures to the will of the people as expressed through regular elections or through special consultative processes that invite citizens to participate in the process of setting clear goals for both government and private agencies.

In this case analysis I consider whether a performance measurement system not tightly linked to a structure of executive authority could have any practical use. If the primary practical utility of a performance measurement system depends on being tied to some authority that could hold others accountable for achieving particular results, the answer must be no. If, however, it is possible that some practical utility derives from the inherent appeal of the values that the performance measurement system pursues and monitors, and that a kind of mutual accountability can arise when a public states explicitly what it wants and expects for and from each of its members, then perhaps the answer is yes. Viewed from this perspective, this case naturally extends the logic from the Diana Gale case that said performance measurement systems could be used to help call into existence a public that can act on its interests, despite a public manager's minimal direct authority over the actions of individual actors.

I then look at how the architects of the Oregon Benchmarks sought to anchor the benchmarks in the real institutional structures and contemporary politics of Oregon in order to elevate and inform the political discussion about Oregon's future and to enhance the state government's ability to shape that discussion. This requires them not only to build an institutional platform for developing and using the system but also to build and refresh the political mandate for using performance measurement as a tool of governance. I also note and discuss how the concept of performance measurement itself acquires an ideological significance that creates political conflict about its forms and uses.

Finally, I look closely at the substantive properties that allow a performance measurement system to survive and be useful even in the midst of political tumult and change, and how public managers can use a system as broad as the benchmarks to focus attention on performance issues that measurement systems designed around single organizational missions usually ignore.

Beyond Agency Accountability: Using Performance Measurement to Mobilize a Polity

For the most part the public managers considered so far have been running single public agencies with specific missions and purposes.[8] Those missions and purposes have included the delivery of services and obligations to clients and the achievement of collectively desired social outcomes. The managers of these agencies have relied primarily on measures that already existed, or could easily be created. Thus Bratton wanted to use the New York City Police Department (NYPD) more effectively to reduce crime; John James wanted the Minnesota Department of Revenue to collect taxes more honestly, fairly, and efficiently; and Tamayo wanted her contractors to help welfare clients move toward increased economic and social independence.

Gale was similar to the managers described previously in that she had a fairly narrow purpose and responsibility: introducing an innovation in handling solid waste that would reduce the cost to government and do more to protect the environment. What made her situation different was the degree to which her success depended on engaging large numbers of individual residents of Seattle in the process of managing solid waste. Her performance measures had to focus not only on organizational outputs, client satisfaction, and desired social outcomes but also on residents' enthusiasm for the initiative and the character of their contributions to the effort.[9]

Williams's position and commitments make an even sharper contrast with agency managers like Bratton and James. He was similar in that he had executive authority and sought to use performance measures to demand accountability and create more public value, but his formal authority was spread across many different organizations, and the dimensions of performance he monitored were much wider—not only for the government as a whole but also for each agency. In the wider scheme each agency was seen as not having its own particular mission but also a more general duty to help other agencies solve problems in the society that had political salience.

The biggest difference, however, was that Williams sought to go beyond the use of performance measures for managerial purposes. He initiated a broad process of consultation with citizens of Washington, D.C., that focused on the development of goals that went beyond improved service delivery. He sought an "identity of purpose" between the aspirations of citizens and the performance of their government. In this respect Williams acted similarly to former Oregon governors Goldschmidt, Robert, and Kitzhaber (Kitzhaber was reelected for a third term in 2011). The technical and managerial process of developing performance measures became an occasion for a wider effort to galvanize a broader public into a cohesive whole and to use the political power generated to mobilize the entire polity, not just those managing government agencies, to make its particular contributions to the cause.

Governors as Chief Executive Officers; Benchmarks as a
Performance Measurement System

Both management analysts and practitioners might be tempted to view the Oregon Benchmarks simply as a performance measurement system that the state's governors can use to call the agencies and actors under their authority to account. In this conception the management of a state amounts to a scaled-up version of agency management. The governors are the "chief executive officers" (CEOs) of a state, and the benchmarks are the measurement system underpinning their performance management system. Just as Bratton applied Management 101 principles to the NYPD, the benchmarks gave the governors of Oregon the necessary tools to do the same for state government, and perhaps even for the broader set of public and private actors whose actions helped or hindered progress toward the benchmark goals. But there are two basic problems with framing the story of the Oregon Benchmarks in these terms.

The Limits of Gubernatorial Authority and Influence. First, it would be a mistake to assume that a state governor has effective managerial control over the assets and actions necessary to achieve the benchmark goals. Even when the stakes are high and the ends sought are vital, governors in democratic societies are simply not in a position to command and control the actions of all the relevant social and economic actors in the state.[10] They cannot command industry to produce certain kinds of jobs, or CEOs to act in civic-minded ways. They cannot even necessarily get local school boards to do a better job of guiding children to become economic contributors and conscientious citizens. They are, for better or for worse, as much *under* the control of powerful private actors as they are in control *over* them. Apart from their authority over government agencies, their financial control over contractors, and their regulatory control over private agencies, governors can only invite, convene, encourage, engage, and hope that some commitments and capacities for collective action will emerge.

Even within the scope of their direct authority over state agencies, however, governors find it hard to exert precise managerial control.

Roberts was able to use the benchmarks to prioritize spending decisions, and the system did seem to give her some leverage in tough budgetary decisions, but it did not seem to give her much power to hold those particular agencies that claimed they would contribute to benchmark goals accountable for their success in doing so. Nor did she use her office to help create a sense of interdependence in operations that could overwhelm the stovepipe mentality of Oregon's public agencies.

Tryens, responding to Republican criticisms that it made no sense to pay government money to produce reports on conditions in the state that could not be used to drive government performance and make resource allocation decisions, finally led an effort to link the benchmarks to particular agencies, publishing the "Benchmark Blue Book" that made these links explicit. Further, where several agencies shared responsibility for achieving a given goal, he created cross-organizational "teams" and gave one agency responsibility for collecting data on the shared goal. In principle such teams and their measurement systems allowed the state to manage government problem-solving efforts that cut across organizational boundaries. But there were no specific requirements that they do so.

Thus the management system that Oregon's governors had to rely on to help drive both private and public actors to make contributions to the future of Oregon depended more on the political arts of persuasion and encouragement than on the muscular sinews of money, authority, and accountability.

The Contestability and Transience of Political Aspirations. The second error would be to imagine that the purposes that one sitting governor sets out as the aspirations of the citizenry as a whole will be complete, go uncontested, and stay steady over time. In winning an election a governor earns the right and the responsibility to pursue a particular vision of a good and just society and is free to develop performance measures around that vision in an effort to steer the government (and the rest of society) in that direction.

But elections do not mark the end of the political discussion about the ends and means of government; they simply punctuate the discussion for a brief moment before it begins anew. Throughout their terms in office, governors will face challenges from political opponents in legislatures and elsewhere. Some of those challenges will focus on large questions of political ideology concerning the ultimate goals of the political community and the role of the state in helping define and pursue those goals. Some will focus on fairly large matters of public policy such as tax rates, the quality of public education, the amount and kind of assistance to be given to laid-off workers, or the appropriate uses of public parks. Some will focus on very small matters, indeed, that could hardly have been anticipated in a campaign. And there is always a good chance that in a few years' time, someone else will be sitting in the governor's office committed to advancing a somewhat different set of values to be expressed through government operations.

These observations suggest that if a particular vision (represented in a particular set of benchmarks) becomes too closely tied to a particular governor, then that vision and the performance measurement system built around it will not be viable as a stable, long-term framework for monitoring social progress. It will be seen as a partial view— held by one temporarily dominant political faction—that ignores other important values. When political tides turn, the framework will be sacrificed at the altar of partisan politics.

Solving a Paradox in Public Value Accounting

These observations shine a light on the basic paradox that has been lurking in the shadows of public value accounting: to ensure that a public value account has political legitimacy, the account has to be closely tied to democratic politics; but because the political authorizing environment is constantly surging with conflict and change, no measurement system can last long. Yet somehow the Oregon Benchmarks held up for years during a period of intense political and ideological dispute. During those years it continued to function as a kind of framework that could hold, reflect, and give some content and precision to the swirling political debates occurring at both the ideological and policy levels. How was such a result produced? What did Wyse and Tryens do to sustain the framework as a vital perspective on Oregon's condition and aspirations?

The answer seems to be that Wyse and Tryens did the hard political work of building legitimacy and support for the general idea of a public value account that could, to some degree, stand outside and above particular governors and the clash of partisan, ideological politics. This did not mean that they could ignore sitting governors or the

pressures of partisan politics. They knew that these powerful actors
and forces had to be engaged if the benchmarks were to have any
standing and relevance in the Oregon polity and the Oregon state government. But they also knew that if they yielded entirely to the preferences of those actors, the benchmarks would soon be eliminated, or
turned directly to partisan purposes. They needed to find some anchor
for the system in the shifting sands of partisan politics that could sustain
the framework over time so that it could continue to have some influence over collective thought about what constituted public value, and to
accumulate evidence about the degree to which the Oregon government
could act as an effective agent of the Oregon polity's aspirations.

One might suspect that such a strategy would have little chance of
success. In today's world the force of partisan, ideological politics seems
much more powerful than the force of a cultural commitment to some
kind of rationalism and honesty in government. But in assessing the
prospects of this approach, it is useful to look back in time. At the turn
of the twentieth century the progressive movement gave birth to many
institutions that encouraged rationality in government that survive today. Many of the formal mechanisms of accountability that we rely on
to keep the government from stealing or wasting money and to ensure
that public officials are technically qualified for their positions were
created during the progressive era.

A more recent and perhaps especially relevant example is the development of the measurement system that came to be called the "national income accounts." In the 1930s and 1940s the idea that a society
would spend the necessary money and face the political risks associated
with developing an accurate picture of national economic activity and
output must have seemed as outlandish as the idea of building measurement systems to capture the economic, social, and governmental
performance of a polity. But that very important and complex system
was nonetheless constructed, and it is now routinely used in shaping
political debate.

Against that historical backdrop, the fact that Wyse and Tryens's
strategy kept the benchmarks alive for nearly two decades, spanning
a very contentious period in Oregon politics, does not seem quite so
surprising, and perhaps it offers some hope for the long run. The benchmarks respond to a line of reasoning with a long historical pedigree
that views politics and government as instrumental in helping society

define and achieve collective aspirations and expects that government and its various managers will be called to account for their performance.[11] This view ultimately seems to require the development and use of a performance measurement system that not only names the values to be achieved but also measures how well the public and the government (acting as the public's agent) are performing with respect to those values.

This basic reasoning keeps surfacing in the swirling eddies of democratic political discourse. It is this bit of flotsam that could support the kind of politics that relies on rational debate and discussion, aided by facts about performance, in the processes of democratic government. Wyse and Tryens had to recover whatever political strength could be mobilized for this idea—to turn the bit of political flotsam into a raft that both hard-nosed businessmen and committed political activists (on both the left and on the right) could climb aboard and steer toward improved government performance.

Each time it seemed that the Progress Board and Oregon Benchmarks had lost their political mojo, Wyse and Tryens were able to regain some ground through one of two means. First, they found ways to align the procedural and substantive goals of the benchmarks more closely with the concerns of those who had recently been elected. Second, they were able to shake things up a bit by going outside the process of electoral politics to convene a wide public conversation about the vision for Oregon's future and government's role in realizing it, and to use that conversation to develop a broader and deeper set of expectations for and demands on state government operations. Thus it seems the progressive era ideal of a government that can act rationally on the basis of facts to define and pursue agreed-upon public purposes is not entirely dead, and that it can be roused from the grave to support a sustained effort to measure social conditions and government's efforts in seeking to transform them.

The Goal of the Progress Board and the Oregon Benchmarks

Viewed from this perspective, what Wyse and Tryens seemed to be developing was not simply a public value account that governors could use to animate and guide the actions of the state's public agencies to implement their policy goals. It was, in addition, a relatively comprehensive, precise, and durable framework to capture a rough political agreement within the state's polity about the kind of society it would like to become. Because achieving that vision required private as well as public actors to act, the framework had to link the vision to the actions of private corporations, small businesses, churches, and civic organizations, as well as to the agencies of state government. As the Oregon Shines Task Force explained at the end of its review of the Progress Board, "The Oregon Progress Board's responsibility is to remind us of our shared vision, monitor our progress in achieving measurable goals, and bring choices to our attention." Of course, the "us" the task force had in mind was not the task force or the current administration but the Oregon public. The citizens of Oregon, distributed across many different structural positions, were being summoned to act and to be accountable to one another for achieving a shared vision of the future of the state.

Securing an Institutional Base and Building a Political Constituency for the Use of Performance Measurement in Politics and Management

The architects of the Oregon Benchmarks faced a problem that none of the managers seen in previous cases did: they needed to develop the very institutional platform from which their performance measurement enterprise would operate. The fact that the benchmarks were a performance measurement system concerned with the actions of private as well as public actors raised questions about exactly what kind of institution the "Progress Board" ought to be. The fact that both the vision of Oregon's future that the benchmarks embodied and the ways in which that vision would be used to call social actors to account were sure to encounter intense political partisanship meant that those creating the system had to carefully consider what kind of institutional platform would be best suited for the work, and where the political support for sustaining such an enterprise might best be cultivated.[12]

Choosing an Institutional Position for the Progress Board
As the Oregon Shines campaign came to an end, the governor faced questions from those he had recruited to the cause about what came next, and what kind of institution could carry on the work of that initiative. What kind of institution could take responsibility for constructing and refining a set of performance benchmarks linked to the Oregon

Shines report, and, ultimately, for publicizing progress made toward those goals in a way that could motivate and guide action?

One option would be to create an organization that operated as a staff arm to the governor's office. In this arrangement the governor could use the benchmarks to hold operating agencies directly accountable for their performance against the benchmarks.[13] This approach works best in terms of the private-sector analogy that views the governor as the CEO of the state. But, as noted earlier, because the governor cannot control actors outside of Oregon's public agencies, committing himself to benchmarks that required significant contributions from private actors would leave him exposed. He would create performance expectations that the state government could not meet. Further, because political aspirations encounter resistance and change over time, if the benchmarks were too closely identified with a particular administration, the next administration might feel obligated to disown them.

A second option would be to create an agency within the executive branch responsible for developing and maintaining the performance measurement system but to distance it from the governor's office by making it a public agency with its own independent board. This setup risks weakening the influence of the benchmarks by disconnecting them from the direct formal authority of the governor but increases the chance that they would survive changes in governors and come to be viewed as a more institutionalized piece of government.

A third possibility would be to create a civic organization outside of state government whose mission was simply to provide facts on the state of the Oregon community to be used for any and all purposes nominated by interested social actors in the state. This position would keep the organization out of the treacherous tides of partisan politics. And, it could invite all citizens of Oregon into a process of envisioning their future without the "help" of partisan politics and their grand political ideologies. The weakness of this setup is that the measurement system might lack the authority to collect the data it needs and fail to connect with any political currents that could galvanize action from those whose contributions were needed to achieve the goal.

Establishing a Semi-Independent Agency in the Executive Branch
At Duncan Wyse's urging the governor's office decided the second option, a semi-independent agency in the executive branch, would be the

best platform from which to carry on the work of the Oregon Shines initiative. As the leader of the initiative, Wyse wanted to pursue the vision of a bright Oregon future through a durable institution in the Oregon government that would outlast the tenure of any particular governor. He saw the benchmarks as a vital way to inform and support the Oregon political community in its deliberations about public value. Wyse and his colleagues in Oregon Shines hoped to build a statewide commitment to a shared vision of a good and just Oregon, and to make pursuing and reflecting on that vision routine not only in partisan politics and state elections but also in budget politics, regulatory politics, and local community politics. They wanted to create a device that would keep the objective state of the Oregon union in view not just when big decisions had to be made but on a day-to-day basis as both big and small decisions were made within and outside of government.

Ultimately, in service of these aims, the choice was made to establish the Progress Board as a public agency closely linked to the governor's office, but not directly within it. Figure 6.1 offers a picture of both the institutional position of the Progress Board and the scope of the Oregon Benchmarks.

In this diagram the Progress Board is closely linked to the governor's office and to the lines of authority that link governors to execu-

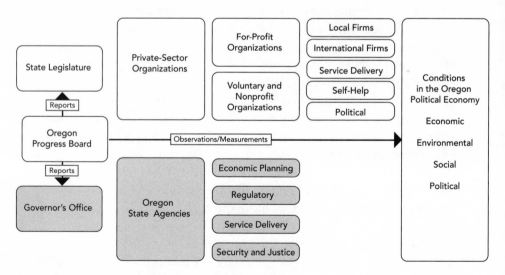

Figure 6.1. The scope of the Oregon Benchmarks.

tive branch agencies. But it is also engaged with the legislature and the wider public discourse about what would constitute a good quality of individual and collective life, and what government should be doing to help the public reach those goals. This structural position allows the board and the benchmarks to perform the important functions of a public value account: helping to animate, guide, and evaluate the operations of government agencies; facilitate and strengthen a collective discussion about social and material conditions; and generate ideas about what both government and private institutions could do to improve those conditions.

Linking the board and the benchmarks to the governor's office provides the governor with a tool that can perform two important functions. First, it serves a political function by allowing a governor to convene a wide public discussion of the specific goals the government he or she leads should pursue. Second, it serves a managerial function by allowing the governor to use the benchmarks to challenge the performance of government agencies. By combining these two efforts, the governor can create what Williams described in Chapter 2 as an identity of interests between citizens and their government—at least for a time.

While the Progress Board's position offered Oregon governors a tool for engaging legitimacy and support, its position outside the governor's office left its leaders with significant political work to do. Wyse and Tryens had to work to engage and sustain the governor's participation, even as they sought to supplement the governor's effective authority and influence over social actors who were the natural constituency of the governor's political competitors.

But the separation from the governor's office also created an important opportunity for the Progress Board to make itself useful to the Oregon public as well as to the state's governors. Wyse and Tryens were able to run the Oregon Progress Board not as a staff serving a sitting governor but as a bipartisan agency operating in the storm of government's unending partisan battles. Indeed, an excellent bipartisan agency working to develop a frame of specific performance measures that can both capture and inform contentious political debates can be the public's last hope for ensuring some continuity of purpose in democratic government.[14]

Sustaining the Political Constituency for the Oregon Benchmarks

Creating the Progress Board as an institutional platform for the Oregon Benchmarks gave the initiative a chance to make a difference, but the board would not survive and the benchmarks would not be effective in guiding civic and governmental action without continual surges of political commitment to refuel the initiative. Because the Progress Board itself had no executive authority, all of its effective influence would have to come from its capacity to generate the support of the public and the elected representatives who direct government action and have some degree of authority over private actors in the for-profit and non-profit sectors. For most of the period described in the case, the Progress Board's most important sponsors were Oregon's governors. The Progress Board and the benchmarks would never have been born if Governor Goldschmidt had not seen them as a good answer to the question of "what comes next" following the political success of the Oregon Shines campaign. The Progress Board and the benchmarks would have fallen into obsolescence and disuse if Governor Roberts had not found them useful in sustaining focus on Oregon's economic progress and prioritizing government spending at a time when budget cuts were needed. And, when Governor Kitzhaber cooled on the Progress Board and the benchmarks, they became less effective, and politically vulnerable.

But the case also makes clear that the political support of the governor was probably necessary but not sufficient to ensure either the short-term or long-term survival and usefulness of the system. Governors could change. The political ideologies they represented could change. So the challenge was to root the effort in even stronger soil than the enthusiasm and commitment of a powerful but temporary gubernatorial sponsor.

It is testimony to the quality of Wyse and Tryens's leadership that instead of continuing the strategy of rooting political support for performance measurement in the increasingly barren soil of the governor's office, they both moved to cultivate new sources of support in Oregon's changing political landscape. When Republicans registered gains in the state legislature in 1990, Wyse reached out to the new legislators for support, or at least tolerance. When the Republicans continued to make electoral progress in 1993, Wyse created a new consultative basis for the Oregon Benchmarks but later regretted not reaching out to the new crop of elected legislators. And when Tryens arrived in

1995 and found the program dangling by a thread, he returned to the original basis for the Oregon Benchmarks: the business-led "Oregon Shines" initiative that focused both the Oregon business community and the Oregon state government on rebuilding Oregon's economy. In going back to the original idea that led to the creation of the Progress Board, Tryens was able to refresh the political mandate for performance measurement and recommit an old constituency (the business community) to the task of improving economic and social conditions in the state.

Even with the support of the business community, Tryens saw that where Wyse had enjoyed support from an enthusiastic Democratic governor and a Democrat-controlled Congress, he would have to knit together a broader constituency—drawing in Republicans as well as Democrats in both the legislative and executive branches. To secure this new political base Tryens had to make the system more responsive to the concerns of the emergent Republican leadership. The Republicans wanted a tighter connection between the benchmarks and the performance of state agencies, fewer goals, priorities that reflected new challenges in Oregon's economic environment, and goals set at levels that agencies could achieve with existing resources.

In making such changes, Tryens ran the risk that the Oregon Benchmarks would become a political football—a device used for partisan advantage rather than an enduring institution that could lend coherence and focus to a sustained political and governmental purpose. To be useful and reliable for citizens, public value accounts need to seem objective and consistent over time rather than easily manipulated for short-term political advantage. Tryens also ran the risk that changes in the system would render previous investments worthless and weaken the performance of the system as changes were instituted.

While most authorizers could agree in principle that it was a good idea for Oregon to have a set of benchmarks to identify and measure the state of the state, continuous political and financial support for the development, maintenance, and use of the system was far from assured. Only when Tryens recognized that he needed to root the benchmarks in a new "Oregon Shines" initiative (Oregon Shines II) that mobilized support from the business community, and only when he adapted the system to make it useful to Republican legislators as well as Democratic governors, was the continuation of the benchmarks (temporarily)

assured. The efforts of Wyse and Tryens to generate and sustain political support for a performance measurement system in general, and for
a particular version of a public value account appropriate to a particular
political context, underscore the point that creating a powerful performance measurement system in government requires a great deal of political work and, further, that a crucial part of that work is constructing
a measurement system that works for the politicians who want to use
it. But the discussion earlier in this chapter and elsewhere also makes
it clear that a primary reason to develop a public value account is to
challenge politicians to think about the values they would like to see
achieved by and reflected in the government operations they command, and to speak about their purposes in terms that can be defined
and measured.

Partisan Politics and Political Ideology in Defining and Recognizing Public Value

What is remarkable about the Oregon Benchmarks case is that the chosen institutional arrangement, as well as the diligent political work and
leadership of Wyse and Tryens, kept the system alive and allowed the
benchmarks to gain some standing as a reflection of Oregon's collective
thought about what sort of polity it would like to be, even when the issues under debate involved some of the broadest and deepest questions
of political ideology. Indeed, the case centers on the role that contentious partisan politics play in shaping discourse about the overall political economy of Oregon. The political community uses the benchmarks
to debate large ideological questions about social welfare, justice, and
the role of the state in promoting social welfare and justice. The central
tension in the case is whether the benchmarks can continue to be helpful in revealing the substantive values at stake over a period of dramatic
political and economic change—whether they can continue to hold this
debate without collapsing in a heap.

The Partisan Character of the Oregon Benchmarks as a Governing Tool and a Substantive Ideal

It is sometimes said that there is no Republican or Democratic way to
pick up the garbage. The underlying claim is that performance measurement need not become a partisan political issue; that it is funda-

mentally a technical, objective issue; or, less ambitiously, that there are many aspects of government performance on which we can all agree. Yet in this case many social and political actors seem intensely interested in the question of whether the Progress Board and the benchmarks are a Democratic or a Republican idea both as an instrument of governing and as a substantive conception of a good and just society.

At the political level the Progress Board looks like a Democratic idea. It was initiated by a Democratic governor at a time when the Democrats also controlled both Houses of the state legislature. It was sustained by Democratic governors even as they were losing power in the legislature. If political sponsorship determines whether an idea is Democratic or Republican, one would have to conclude that the Oregon Benchmarks were a Democratic idea.

At the substantive level, however, the Oregon Benchmarks have a distinctly Republican character, for two reasons. The first is that the Oregon Shines initiative elevated economic development over other concerns that Oregonians might have had—including, perhaps, environmental protection and equal opportunity for all. The Progress Board seemed to adhere to an idea that has, since the New Deal, generally been associated with Republican rather than Democratic political ideology— namely, that the role of government was to do what it could to support business and keep Oregon economically competitive rather than regulate business to keep it from doing harm to the community. Since economic development is an important public value, an important goal of government should be to support the business community's efforts to build a strong economy.

The second seemingly Republican feature of the benchmarks is the general idea that government should be held accountable for its performance, and that its performance should be assessed objectively. Both Democrats and Republicans have suspicions about the motivations and capabilities of government. Democrats generally worry that public policy will reflect the interests of the powerful rather than the disadvantaged, and that the government will fail to meet social needs, or protect important rights. Republicans generally worry that elected politicians will curry favor by promising more than the government can afford and delivering less than it could if it had more commitment to efficiency and less to political posturing. But the regular, persistent demand that government account for its use of money and what it actually accomplishes has been generally associated more with Republicans than Democrats. Republicans like to point out that public spending cannot be justified simply by the attractiveness of the cause; it has to be justified by performance. If a goal cannot be practically realized, it should not be pursued, regardless of its urgency or general appeal.

The Ideological Issues Incorporated within the Oregon Benchmarks
The competitive political process cannot help but turn any government-sponsored effort to construct a broad vision of a good and just society into a debate between competing political ideologies, and so it was with the Oregon Benchmarks. The benchmarks became not only a partisan issue in themselves but also a framework within which contending partisan visions of a good and just society could be nominated and debated or advanced or set aside. Their development and evolution seem to reflect incremental shifts in the political ideology of Oregonians as a political community. To see the case in these terms, let's briefly review the history presented in the case, and the particular way in which objective conditions in the state and prevailing political forces shaped the construction of the benchmarks.

Having made a campaign promise to lead an "Oregon comeback" after the economic recession of the mid-1980s, newly elected Democratic Governor Neil Goldschmidt launched the Oregon Shines campaign to create a new strategic plan for the government of Oregon. With the active support and participation of the Oregon business community, Oregon Shines set out to understand how Oregon's economy could stay competitive and grow in the context of the emergent global economy, and what government needed to do to support the state economy. This focus on economic development as the key to the future of the state and the central task of government represented a particular ideological position—one that might tend to favor a small government over a large one, and a prosperous society even at the expense of some kinds of environmental or social justice. Concerns that Oregonians might have about the implications of this approach for the state of the environment or social justice seemed to be swallowed up by the demand for an economic turnaround.

One could argue that economic development—increased wages, increased prosperity, wider economic opportunity—is the essence of "public value," and Oregonians may have agreed that their best chance for better health, education, or environmental conditions lay in taking both private and public action to improve the performance of the state economy. In this case it would make perfect sense to focus on improving Oregon's economy, develop a set of measures to help define and achieve the conditions under which the economy could grow, and assign part of that task to government. If sustained economic development is important in itself and the key to success in achieving other social goals, the benchmarks need do no more than measure the necessary means for economic development.

But focusing on economic growth as both the most important end for the Oregon community and government to pursue and the most important means for pursuing other goals risks overlooking or subordinating some other important dimensions of public value. Perhaps other aspects of individual and collective life also needed to be protected or emphasized even as Oregon concentrated on improving its economy. These concerns ultimately did find their way into the political discussions sponsored by the Progress Board and into the benchmarks themselves. As the benchmarks developed during Roberts's administration, they began to expand their concerns beyond creating favorable conditions for businesses to the wider economic, social, and environmental conditions that Oregonians wanted to realize in their state.

Table 6.1 compares the recommendations in the Oregon Shines report with the benchmarks the Progress Board submitted to the legislature. With Roberts's input, the Progress Board combined the benchmarks into three broad clusters: Exceptional People; Outstanding Quality of Life; and Diverse, Robust Economy, presented in that particular order. This framework seemed to shift the priorities of the Oregon Shines era, reversing the relationship between economic development, on one hand, and social needs, on the other. Education and health showed up not just as conditions that would attract business to the state and allow it to be more productive but as desired ends in themselves. In the three themes that emerged, not only did "Exceptional People" and "Outstanding Quality of Life" precede the economic theme, but equal opportunity also seemed to precede growth in the vision of a "Diverse, Robust Economy."

As Table 6.2 shows, however, many of the specific objectives included in the Oregon Shines framework could fit comfortably in the categories that Roberts created. The only difference lies in what is

Table 6.1. A comparison of the objectives of Oregon Shines and the Oregon Benchmarks.

Oregon Shines	Oregon Benchmarks
Exceptional people	
	Increase the stability of home life.
	Give children a healthy start.
	Improve school performance.
	Increase levels of educational attainment.
	Improve overall citizen health.
	Promote equal opportunity and social harmony.
Outstanding quality of life	
	Improve air and water quality.
	Preserve natural amenities.
	Maintain uncongested roadways.
	Restore and maintain affordable housing.
	Reduce crime.
	Increase access to health care and child care.
	Increase citizens' community involvement.
Diverse, robust economy	
Increase the skills of Oregon's workforce so it will be measurably the best in America by 2000, and equal to any in the world by 2010.	Maintain a strong manufacturing sector.
Preserve the state's natural environment and uncongested communities, and market them to attract the people and firms that will drive an advanced economy.	Increase employment and per capita income levels.
	Reduce the cost of doing business in Oregon.
Cultivate an international frame of mind that distinguishes Oregonians as unusually adept in global commerce.	Improve air transportation service to Oregon.
Contain the costs of doing business in Oregon—especially in the area of workers' compensation rates, unemployment insurance, and energy rates.	Improve road and telecommunications infrastructure.
	Increase research and development work.
Invest in public facilities and services that attract new firms to the state.	Maintain or slightly increase the state's overall per capita tax level (while reducing reliance on the property tax).

Table 6.2. Oregon Shines recommendations matched to the three themes of the Oregon Benchmarks.

Themes of the Oregon Benchmarks	Oregon Shines recommendations
Exceptional people	Increase the skills of Oregon's workforce so it will be measurably the best in America by 2000, and equal to any in the world by 2010.
	Cultivate an international frame of mind that distinguishes Oregonians as unusually adept in global commerce.
Outstanding quality of life	Preserve the state's natural environment and uncongested communities, and market them to attract the people and firms that will drive an advanced economy.
	Invest in public facilities and services that attract new firms to the state.
Diverse, robust economy	*All of the above, plus:* Contain the costs of doing business in Oregon.

viewed as a super-ordinate goal and a subordinate goal. Just as we saw that Tamayo and Toby Herr might have been able to reach agreement on measures (since Tamayo's could be fitted into Herr's), so the Oregon Benchmarks could go forward even though the framing of the major goals and objectives—so important to ideological discussion—had changed.

The benchmarks expanded further when Governor Roberts, under pressure to reduce the state budget, invited state agencies to commit to particular benchmark goals in exchange for smaller cuts to their budgets. That invitation led to a proliferation of goals. As many different factions added their particular ideas of what constituted an important dimension of value in Oregon life to the benchmarks, the goals increasingly became a representation of the full range of aspirations that the Oregon political community had for the state and provided a justification for continued government spending in support of important social goals.

All this was happening in the midst of a major political challenge to what had been a solid Middle Left consensus (with Goldschmidt more to the middle and Roberts more to the left) from a strong Right insurgency.

The incoming Republican legislators, focused on reducing the size and scope of government, ran directly into a benchmarking system that they believed was being used to justify broadening rather than controlling the scope of government.

Aspirational or Realistic Goals?

The question of whether the benchmarks would consist of aspirational or realistic goals persisted in the background of this political conflict.[15] Two different ideas about the role that the benchmarks could play in animating and guiding the Oregon community and the Oregon government toward the creation of public value were at stake in this decision. The benchmarks could either function as declarations of intent—purely political (though not necessarily partisan) statements about how Oregonians would like to live and what they were committed to achieving as a community and through their government—or as devices for holding particular public managers and agencies accountable for their performance (with real consequences for their standing if they failed to hit their targets) and as best guesses at what the government was realistically able to do.

At the political level, aspirational goals could help inspire the body politic and commit the government to achieve great things. Realistic goals, in contrast, could keep citizens' expectations about what the government might be able to do grounded and reasonable. At the operational level, aspirational goals could inspire heroic efforts but also could defeat any real sense of accountability, while realistic goals could create a strong sense of accountability but risked setting performance expectations too low to motivate and inspire significant improvements. Democrats seemed inclined to view the benchmarks more as a record of government commitments than as a reliable mechanism for holding governmental actors accountable for performance. Accordingly, they tended to favor aspirational goals. The benchmarks represented an attractive vision of the future and a constant goad for action. Republicans, however, skeptical about the possibility of achieving aspirational goals and concerned about the political implications of committing to such goals, wanted to use the benchmarks to hold government agencies accountable and to test the feasibility of particular goals and objectives—not as tempting visions of a utopian society that could encourage government to grow in size and scope. The Republican leadership in the

Oregon legislature preferred to start by fixing a budget constraint and then pushing agency managers to make as much progress as possible toward the more modest benchmarks with those resources.

This tension forced a dialogue between the two parties that resulted in a benchmark system that included both aspirational and realistic goals. The Democrats' impulse to set aspirational goals was countered by their fear that the Republicans would use failures to meet aspirational goals as evidence that the goals were unrealistic and ought to be abandoned. The Republicans' impulse to set realistic goals was countered by their fear that they would appear less exacting than the Democrats in insisting on high levels of performance. Neither side got to win the partisan debate, but the potential result of this dialogue was improved understanding on both sides of what was really possible for government to do in the pursuit of Oregon's (shifting) vision of what constituted a good and just society.

Thus partisan conflict did not crush the benchmarks. Under Tryens's leadership, the system survived, at least partly because both Democrats and Republicans could use it to point to and emphasize the values they wanted to express. The benchmarks helped shape and discipline the ideological argument about the proper role of government underlying the partisan debate. They provided a framework that could hold and account for all the values at stake in this question, allowing Oregonians to see the concrete value issues lying beneath the ideological conflict. The Oregon Benchmarks channeled the ardor of citizens who held particular values and brought those values to the attention of members of the political community who might have otherwise discounted those values.

The economic recession focused many Oregonians on the virtues of having a strong economy and using government to encourage a strong economy. But once Oregon Shines had laid out a vision of government as a supporter of economic development, it became clear how limited an ideal for a good society and a good government that vision was, and some of the old environmental and social concerns were revived with new benchmarks. When that vision was deemed insufficiently responsive to economic realities and the general idea of limited government, the framework changed again. But it changed around a core set of values, and a core set of measures, and the public could see which values were being added and subtracted or elevated or subordinated in that framework.

When a set of core public values can be nominated and held in the consciousness of a political community at the same time, a political discussion that would otherwise rely on broad strokes and ideological caricatures can become more precise, comprehensive, and balanced. Similarly, when the benchmarks provide data on what has been accomplished at current levels of effort, the discussion can become grounded in facts about what seems possible to do through government and social action. Over time, a public value account like the Oregon Benchmarks, scrupulously developed by skilled custodians, allows that transformation in the overall quality of the political discussion to occur.

The Public Value Account as a Flexible, Politically Responsive Hierarchy of Goals and Objectives

As noted in Chapter 2, if political aspirations are both highly heterogeneous and highly dynamic, and politics will not be disciplined to stay at the policy level but instead swing freely from large ideological issues to much smaller operational details, then a performance measurement system that could stay closely connected to political interests would have to have some unusual properties. It would have to be simultaneously rigid enough to be a consistent and objective standard over time and flexible enough to accommodate differences in changing aspirations, and changing social conditions. It would have to be subject to negotiation yet firm enough to guard against partisan political manipulation. It would also have to be able to focus attention on the widest ideological issues as well as on the values at stake in narrower policy and organizational issues, and even on some very small operational issues that seem linked more to processes than results. And there would have to be mechanisms that guaranteed the quality of the data highlighted by the account.

Chapter 1 showed the difficulty of creating a public value account that could both capture the many different dimensions of value a public agency can produce *and* express the overall performance of the organization in a simple story and a simple set of aggregate measures. Both Chapter 2 and this chapter show that this problem is compounded when the challenge is to identify the values produced by general units of government such as a city (Williams) or a state (Wyse and Tryens).

Instead of continuing to strive for that unattainable simplicity, I recommended in Chapter 1 creating a comprehensive public value account with a detailed set of performance measures to describe and illuminate the value-creating activities of the agency. But that advice can sacrifice simplicity and coherence for an illegible complexity. The real challenge is to find a way to organize the irreducible complexity into a more coherent narrative.[16]

To accomplish the sleight of hand that would allow managers to sustain a simple narrative and a simple idea of purpose while acknowledging the wide variety of purposes and effects that real organizations pursue and produce, managers often seek to arrange their many complex objectives in a *goal hierarchy*. The purpose of the hierarchy is to establish a coherent relationship between the broad, simple narrative of what the public wants to accomplish (captured in the terms at the top of the hierarchy) and the many different and more concrete events that the narrative seems to require or entail (captured at lower levels of the hierarchy). At the philosophical and conceptual level, setting out a hierarchy of goals can start either at the top or the bottom. Starting at the bottom might mean writing down all the dimensions of public value that could be important to someone in the authorizing environment and gradually working up to the agency's broadest mission. Starting at the top might mean beginning with the broad mission and working down to the particulars of operational and process values. While it is natural to think of arraying a set of goals in a kind of goal hierarchy, those who build such hierarchies often do not pay close enough attention to a key question: What is the logic that ties the goals at the top to the objectives at the bottom?

The Different Logics of Goal Hierarchies
What makes the challenge of constructing a goal hierarchy more an art than a science is that there are several different logics that may determine which concepts of value should be at the top of the hierarchy and which at the bottom, and how different dimensions of value should be grouped together in coherent sets. In developing a goal hierarchy it helps to be self-conscious about the different logics because they require different kinds of knowledge in their construction, and they have different implications in their use.

The Logic of Ends and Means. The most commonly invoked principle is that the goals at the top of the hierarchy describe the *ultimate ends* to be pursued, while those at the bottom describe the *preferred means* to be used to achieve those goals. Thus a high-level goal for Oregon could be to promote the long-term economic development and global competitiveness of the state's economy. Lower-level objectives judged to be important means for achieving this goal could be achieving a low tax rate on business, a favorable regulatory environment, and a highly educated workforce.

Given the current commitment to focus government attention on outcomes over processes, ultimate ends seem to belong at the top of the hierarchy. It is those ends that give meaning to the more particular activities clustered at the lower rungs of the hierarchy. The processes and activities that contribute to the ultimate end only have meaning and value insofar as they help bring the desired outcomes into existence. This is the logic that Progress Board member Ed Whitelaw summed up as "Policy 101. There's where we'd like to be. Here's where we are. Here's how we get from here to there."

The Logic of the Long Run and the Short Run. Closely related to the logic of ends and means is the idea that goals that can only be realized in the *long run* belong at the top of the hierarchy, with goals that can be achieved in the *short run* below. For instance, the state of Oregon cannot create a highly educated workforce overnight, but it can remove some outmoded regulations that slow the process of business development relatively quickly.

Initially, the logic of short-term objectives and long-term goals seems straightforward, but there are some subtleties in this conception that are worth noting. The first concerns the question of whether, in talking about the short or long run, we mean (1) the time frame within which action is to be taken (and costs incurred) or (2) the time frame within which valued results will be achieved. Many important results in government are consigned to the long term not because the government delays action but simply because it takes a long time for the desired results to occur. When Oregon sets a benchmark for "drug-free babies" or "readiness to learn" among kindergarteners, it does not expect to see immediate economic benefits. It makes a short-term intervention and then has to wait a full generation for the results of that intervention to appear.

Alternatively, effects of government action show up in the long term because producing the effects requires sustained efforts by the government. This was a central issue seen in Chapter 4: Tamayo was hoping that a single intervention would produce a reliable effect that showed up in both the short term and the long term; Herr thought that it would take a sustained effort over a long period of time to produce small (and sometimes fleeting) effects in the short term that would ultimately accumulate to produce a valuable long-term effect.

So when talking about whether a goal should be considered short term or long term, it matters whether the time frame for the goal refers to taking the action or to the anticipated results. Some actions are taken in the short term and produce their ultimate valued effects in the short term. More typically, actions taken in the short term produce ultimately valuable effects only over the long term.

The second subtlety has to do with the effect of bringing the long term into view on the capacity of a goal hierarchy to create a sense of accountability and urgency. When goal hierarchies define goals and objectives that are far in the future, two good things happen. The first is that the long-term goals stay on everyone's mind. The second is that taking a long-term view makes it easier to imagine various possible paths toward those long-term goals. For example, knowing that a well-educated workforce would strengthen the economy, and knowing that children born to teenage parents are less likely to achieve academically, the Oregon Progress Board created benchmarks for teen pregnancy rates—a value that might not have seemed relevant to the board's mission without taking the long-term view.

But this kind of "blue sky" thinking often comes with a price: the loss of a sense of urgency and specificity in the day-to-day work. If everything is geared toward the long run, and many different methods look like possible routes to the long-term goal, then both accountability and focus in the short term may suffer. We will know where we want to be tomorrow but feel less committed to the actions today that will get us there.

The third subtle issue in the logic of the long term and the short term has to do with the degree to which decisions about when to initiate certain actions are tied to changes in the environment. Often an action that could reasonably be delayed in the logic of ends and means gains urgency (i.e., priority in the logic of the long and short term) because something changes in the agency's environment. An opportunity appears that will disappear if not exploited immediately.[17] A threat appears that if not dealt with now could result in catastrophic losses. In such situations it makes sense to take actions that would have been delayed in the logic of means and ends and give them immediate priority as short-term objectives.[18]

While the logic of the long and short term has these complexities, using this logic (as well as the logic of ends and means) helps managers understand and review the connections between today's actions and tomorrow's results. Some efforts that start out on a very small scale grow to a larger scale over time. Things that did not seem possible at one point in time later become possible—partly as a result of actions taken today and partly as a result of independent changes in the environment. Cultural values can change, and aspirations once shared among a few can be gradually embraced by many, providing both the impetus and supply of resources that can transform conditions. Or, public agencies can experiment and find a new means for accomplishing goals the public thought it might never reach. Because there is some chance for these kinds of growth and development to occur, it is not unreasonable to treat long-term goals as aspirations rather than specific commitments for which people could actually be held accountable—despite the current pressure to make public agencies accountable for the achievement of ultimate ends.

The Logic of Greater or Lesser Importance. Goal hierarchies can also be built on the basis of a logic of greater or lesser importance and priority. And, often, this logic also parallels the idea of ultimate ends and intermediate means, and the long and short term. Presumably, the important things to achieve are the ultimate ends that will take a long time to achieve. But the fact is, some means, maybe even some that require short-term action and deliver short-term results, are very important and urgent in themselves or as a necessary first step to allow subsequent actions to be effective. Thus a goal at the bottom of a hierarchy based on ends/means or the long/short term might be at the top of a hierarchy organized on the logic of greater or lesser importance.

The Logic of Abstract Ideal to Concrete Reality. One last way to think about the logic of goal hierarchies is to think of the goals at the top of the hierarchy as inspirational and abstract rather than specific and concrete. In Oregon the three goals at the top of the hierarchy are cast in abstract, inspirational language ("Exceptional People"; "Outstanding Quality of Life"; "Diverse, Robust Economy"). Objectives lower down in the hierarchy are cast in much more concrete, pedestrian, and limited terms, such as "increasing the number of major domestic and international cities served by non-stop flights to and from any Oregon commercial airport" and "increasing the percentage of Oregon telephone lines that can transmit data reliably at medium speeds."

To many, the abstract language at the top of goal hierarchies is problematic. Such large and encompassing ideas quickly become useless in their vagueness—and impossible to measure in concrete terms or numbers. The Oregon Benchmarks, however, indicate that this is not always true. The board found ways to measure some important aspects of those long-term, abstract ends. The converse also turned out to be true. Some of the benchmarks associated with the concrete, short-term means for achieving the ultimate goals turned out to be difficult to measure—not so much because they were intrinsically difficult to measure, but because no one seemed interested in making a concerted effort to do so. Even by the end of the case, Tryens was still carrying on his books benchmark goals that had no measurement system to back them up!

By the logic of abstract and concrete, lower-level goals would not necessarily be a causal means for achieving some desired end (in either the short or the long term) but simply more concrete descriptions of what the more abstract, encompassing goals and aspirations at the top of the hierarchy mean. Thus instead of seeing the relationship of overall economic welfare to low levels of unemployment as causal, it can be seen as *definitional*. What we *mean* by economic welfare is that, at least in part, all those seeking a job can get one.

The difference between seeing the relationship between higher- and lower-level goals as the difference between ends and means and between abstract concepts and concrete descriptions of conditions that give meaning to the abstract ideas is the type of *test* used to decide whether a lower-level objective can be seen as subordinate to some higher-level idea. In the case of ends versus means, the test is empirical: *Does the lower-level objective ultimately produce the higher level result?* In the case of abstract concepts versus concrete instantiations of the concept, the test is conceptual: *Is the lower-level concept an example of what we mean by the broader concept?*

Key and Lead Benchmarks. The designers of the Oregon Benchmarks appeared to struggle with these different logics in creating their performance measurement system. It was a relatively easy matter to develop a long list of benchmarks to describe conditions in Oregon corresponding to broad notions of a good and just society. In fact, they created so many that they quickly realized that they would need to both organize the benchmarks into broader categories and somehow prioritize them. Their choice to identify certain benchmarks as "lead" and others as "key" combined several of the different logics described previously.

"Lead" benchmarks seemed to be those deemed both important and achievable in the short term. The case does not make clear, however, why particular lead benchmarks were deemed important: Were they valuable ends in themselves, or were they essential for realizing other goals? Nor was it clear why these were achievable in the short run: Did they produce effects quickly, or did they take advantage of fleeting opportunities?

"Key" benchmarks similarly confused the logics. Key benchmarks were considered "fundamental." But were they fundamental in the causal sense that nothing important could be accomplished without achieving them? Or were they fundamental in the sense that nobody would think anything important had been accomplished unless they were achieved?

The Progress Board later tried to clean this up by changing the words they used to describe the different benchmarks. "Lead" benchmarks became "urgent"; "key" benchmarks became "core." But those terms failed to clear up the underlying ambiguity. "Urgent" certainly suggests short term, but under some definitions it could also mean important. "Core" suggests both causal significance and normative weight and gravity. So it seems that the designers of the system did not really succeed in working out the underlying logic of their goal structure.

The designers of the Oregon Benchmarks struggled to construct a system that could help Oregon achieve several different, apparently conflicting goals. On one hand, the desire for a system capable of capturing both the full range of effects that government action could have, and the full range of interests and values that Oregon's citizens might bring to their evaluation of those effects, pushed them to include a large number of measures. On the other hand, the desire to use the measures to focus attention on and call the government to account for its performance in a simple and meaningful way pushed them to limit the number of benchmarks or to group them into larger categories.

Similarly, they wanted a system that could focus on the long term and present an inspiring vision of Oregon's future, as well as a system that could call a large number of public managers and agencies to account for concrete activities. They wanted a set of measures that laid out a persuasive path to the future with all the causal steps neatly delineated, but they would also be flexible enough to allow them to exploit unexpected opportunities and react to sudden threats.

One could look at these requirements and conclude that no fixed system of measurement could meet all these goals simultaneously. Yet one could also observe that all these requirements are appropriate. Consequently, one might conclude that the best hierarchy of goals and objectives was not one that fulfilled any one of these functions perfectly but, instead, one that succeeded in helping a polity think, act, and learn as it accumulated experience. That would mean developing a system that could use all of the different logics in constructing a tolerably useful set of measures, understanding that it would be inadequate for some purposes, and would have to change over time as circumstances changed. As important as it is to be self-conscious about the implications of relying on one kind of logic versus another, it is probably better to evaluate goal hierarchies in terms of their practical utility than their intellectual purity.

Practical Use of the Oregon Benchmarks

The effort to take a very broad view of conditions in the state had practical implications for the state beyond the performance management task of linking benchmarks to particular agencies and activities and using them to call agencies and their managers to account. Those who created the benchmarks and those who fought to have their concerns represented in the performance measurement system understood that the structure of the benchmarks would have an impact on the government's understanding of its role and responsibilities. When the benchmarks reached out to make public agencies accountable for broad social outcomes, agencies had to shift operational perspectives and practices to recognize the complex ways that different organizations contributed to broad purposes, and how their actions might be better coordinated. A more subtle effect of the benchmarks was to give new prominence to the idea of a government engaged in prevention as well as reaction.

Using the Benchmarks to Reorganize Government Operations and
Focus on Problems that Cut across Organizations

Because the benchmarks focused attention on social conditions rather than on organizational missions, they highlighted the question of how well government's current organizational structure was adapted to achieve the desired social outcomes and invited Oregon's public managers to "map backwards" from the benchmarks to the actions their agencies could take to contribute to the desired outcomes.[19] Since many different organizations' actors—public agencies, public agency subunits, and private actors outside the boundaries of government—offered a piece of the solution to any given problem, public agencies would have to learn to work in partnerships that combined bits and pieces of various organizations in "networks of capacity."[20] Government structures that divided the responsibility, resources, and capabilities of government into "silos" were not well suited to meeting the benchmark goals. Public agencies needed to find ways to outperform their existing structures and boundaries.[21]

The usual way to organize a "network of capacity" is to organize various coordinating forums around particular problems to be solved. At a minimum these forums could allow agencies to share information about what each agency was doing to address a particular problem. With more information about what other agencies were doing, each agency could adjust its own operations to fit more precisely within the whole.[22] Somewhat more ambitiously, these forums could be used for negotiations and deal making among agencies sharing responsibility for particular objectives. More ambitiously still, the forums could become formal planning processes—even allowing different agencies to pool and redistribute their resources to create a more effective allocation of effort across all the agencies, programs, and activities involved. Executives and overseers at the state level could shift their focus from holding each agency accountable for its performance with regard to its mission to include accountability for agencies' contributions to the collective effort to achieve certain outcomes.[23] And if none of these particular institutional arrangements worked, a governor could decide to appoint czars or program managers to take the responsibility for coordinating the actions of different independent agencies, effectively creating a government-wide authority attached not to an organization or a particular bundle of assets but to the solution of a particular complex problem.[24]

The benchmarks' focus on problems to be solved and social outcomes to be achieved rather than organizational missions forced public managers to think about how they were organized and how they operated, creating opportunities for improved performance. This shift from an accountability system that makes managers responsible only for their own organization and its mission to one that makes them accountable for transforming social conditions alongside many other organizations complicates the task of government management but also makes it more goal oriented and more flexible in its approach to achieving the desired social results.[25]

Using the Benchmarks to Focus Government on Prevention
The benchmark goals also tended to shift the attention of government slightly toward preventive rather than reactive methods for dealing with problems. Generally, public agencies are accountable for making appropriate responses to problems when they appear—not dealing with problems before they arise.[26] Police departments react to criminal incidents. Child protection agencies react to instances of abuse and neglect. Environmental protection agencies react to instances of pollution. Once the accountability system is tilted to focus attention on the solution of problems, however, public agencies start to think about how they can become more proactive and shift their efforts to prevent certain problems from occurring in the first place.

In distinguishing among *primary, secondary,* and *tertiary* prevention efforts, the public health community has developed a framework for thinking about the prevention of health problems that can help public managers in other spheres think about the social problems they are trying to solve.[27] Primary prevention focuses on reducing the likelihood that a problem will occur in the general population—ensuring access to clean water, providing mosquito nets to prevent malaria, or offering flu vaccinations. Secondary prevention focuses attention not on the general population but on those individuals who are at particularly high risk of experiencing a specific harm—providing prenatal care in needy populations or offering needle exchange programs for drug addicts. Tertiary prevention typically consists of trying to mitigate the harms once they have occurred.

Much government intervention falls into the category of tertiary prevention: the government waits for a problem to appear and then tries to deal with the problem. Think of this as the "whac-a-mole" approach. In contrast, the public health community often seeks to intervene before the problem appears within a given population.

When accountability shifts from procedures to be followed to problems to be solved, government agencies start to notice that they are engaged primarily in mole-whacking and wonder whether they could do better by making more secondary or primary prevention efforts. This often forces agencies to look at much larger populations and wider sets of conditions than they had previously considered.

To many, the shift toward multiagency preventive efforts seems good in itself. It seems self-evident that an ounce of prevention is worth a pound of cure. But whether primary and secondary prevention is really more valuable than tertiary prevention is an empirical question. If the preventive efforts are ineffective, or if the effective interventions are so expensive that they cannot be spread widely over the population, then one might have to deliver several pounds of prevention to compensate for a pound of cure.

There is the additional problem that as the government's attention shifts to primary and secondary rather than tertiary prevention, its scope widens considerably. Ideologues opposed to big government will surely raise objections when the government begins to operate in situations and with populations that have not yet evidenced the problems the government is trying to solve. One of the main reasons government reacts to problems rather than seeks to prevent them is that this policy limits government activity to situations and populations where government intervention is clearly warranted. If government begins to involve itself in situations and with populations that do not yet have particular concrete problems, then one clear boundary line between government and society becomes significantly more blurry.

Even worse, because efforts to intervene in situations before they become measurable problems are based on hypotheses about what will eventually occur, government will inevitably make mistakes of two types. Sometimes it will intervene in situations that seem to require action but really do not, wasting public money and infringing on individual liberties without due cause. Other times, government will fail to intervene when or where it should have, failing to provide the kind of prevention that it was trying (at some cost in terms of money and the infringement of privacy) to provide.

This shift to primary and secondary prevention in addition to tertiary prevention, then, acquires a certain Left/Right political valence. The Left, feeling more of an urgency to solve social problems, more confidence in government's ability to address them, and an increased willingness to spend government money and authority to alter social conditions, will tend to see the shift toward prevention as a value-creating step. The Right, feeling much more suspicious of government, less hopeful about government's capacity to engineer social conditions in desired directions, and less willing to spend government money and authority on quixotic efforts to deal with problems that do not yet exist, will tend to see the shift toward prevention as a worrisome expansion in the size and scope of government.

While both the Right and the Left will have their views about the wisdom of shifting to a prevention-oriented approach, neither really has the requisite knowledge to say how primary and secondary preventive efforts may best be combined with tertiary prevention efforts to minimize a particular problem at a minimal cost. Only by experimenting with different kinds of preventive efforts and measuring the results can we learn what is possible to achieve. And, to the extent that the shift toward a problem-focused approach encourages more thought and experimentation about preventive actions, and to the extent that a performance measurement system captures the real experience of a society in reaching prevention objectives, both the Right and the Left should applaud these developments.

Summary

I have presented the Oregon Benchmarks case as yet another case in which public managers seek to develop and use a complex performance measurement system to improve government performance, but several features of the Oregon Benchmarks make this case particularly interesting to those interested in creating public value accounts to improve government performance.

First, the case reveals the potential for using public value accounts not only to drive the performance of public agencies but also to facilitate a broad political discussion about the kind of society in which the citizens of a particular political community would like to live. And it suggests that this is possible even in the context of sharp and continuing partisan ideological fights.

Second, the case reinforces the idea that public value accounts have to be linked to political interests to give the measurement systems the weight they need to drive performance. But the case also suggests that in order to secure legitimacy and support for a public value account, the account cannot be rigid, fixed, and narrow; rather, it must be flexible, adaptable, and broad. This means that public value accounts have to be capable of adding new elements, jettisoning old elements, and changing the ways in which the smallest elements of the system (particular measures constructed to measure particular dimensions of public value) can be combined in goal hierarchies.

Finally, this case is a reminder that focusing on social outcomes rather than on organizational performance tends to make public managers think about their work in different ways. Instead of thinking of themselves as running organizations with fixed, largely reactive missions, they can begin to see themselves as running organizations that make contributions to a variety of public purposes, and thus can act preventatively as well as reactively. Their freedom to manage their organizations for public purposes larger than their immediate mission increases and with that the overall potential for improved government performance.

In sum, the Oregon Benchmarks case describes a public value account that focuses on social learning more than on government accountability. It asks bigger questions and invites more people into the discussion than the systems that were previously examined. It changes the discussion about public agency performance from performance with regard to established missions to performance with regard to contributing to the solution of social problems that cut across organizational missions. It does all this in the context of continuing a partisan struggle that challenges but does not destroy the performance measurement system. Changing the framework to keep it politically responsive allows it to survive tough political challenges. To some, the changes look like the politicization of what should be an objective, technical system, but these changes could also be taken as evidence of social learning. If the system helps the political community keep learning not only about what it would like to achieve but also about the best methods, or what is and is not feasible, then the Oregon Benchmarks can light the path ahead not with the distant glow of hope but with the bright light of real experience objectively documented.

7

Harry Spence and the Massachusetts Department of Social Services

Learning to Create Right Relationships

Harry Spence and the Professional Learning Organization

In 2001 Lewis "Harry" Spence became the commissioner of the Massachusetts Department of Social Services (DSS).[1] After five years on the job, in an interview with the *Boston Globe Magazine,* Spence spoke briefly about the experience of returning to his home state of Massachusetts after his previous position as deputy chancellor of operations in the New York City Department of Education: "I came back with a deep appreciation for the politics and civic life of Boston. New York has a brutal, dog-eat-dog political and civic life. . . . When I was in New York, I said to my wife, 'Why do I work where I have to be involved in fighting constantly when I don't relish fighting?' "[2]

Ironically, as DSS commissioner, charged with ensuring the safety of the eleven thousand children in the DSS system and overseeing the investigation of the hundred thousand-plus reports of child maltreatment filed each year, Spence was speaking from one of the most besieged positions in public management. He had taken on daunting tasks before. In addition to his position at the Department of Education, his background included stints as receiver for both the Boston Housing Authority and the bankrupt city government of Chelsea, Massachusetts. In these roles Spence had gained a reputation for "imposing order, including previously disfranchised groups, and leaving the place, while not completely cured, considerably better off."[3] Spence also brought with him to the DSS some unconventional ideas about how to cope with the chorus of demands for accountability. "He's always thanking people . . ." a lobbyist for the New York City Board of Education told the *New York*

Times. "He'll be the first person to apologize for a screw-up. . . . It's very disarming."[4]

Spence's surprisingly low-key management style at the DSS rested on a strong commitment to using performance measurement for organizational learning. He sought a fundamental shift that would take the DSS from a rigidly hierarchical "industrial" accountability model to a more collaborative "professional" model of accountability that depended on learning through communication and self-reflection at and between every level of the organization. Although he had plenty of critics, he made a strong case that this was the only way to improve the system's performance.

Negotiating the Terms of Accountability

The nature of child welfare work presents unique challenges for managing the DSS. Spence described the three-way tug-of-war of expectations from the wider child welfare community and the general public as a "Bermuda Triangle" for DSS managers:

> The public insists that DSS work to prevent atrocities to children, and there's zero tolerance for failure. Countering that first expectation is another that mandates that we support families (with minimal intervention) to improve their parenting in order to keep children safe. But these two expectations are in complete contradiction, since we cannot ensure safety while maintaining our distance with vulnerable families. There is also a permanency expectation from the community. People believe that the outcomes for youth in the child welfare system should not be any worse than for other children. . . . All three have some reasonable and appropriate element to them, but when each is made absolute, it is what I call the Bermuda Triangle of child welfare.[5]

The Culture of DSS

Tragedy is an inevitable feature of DSS work. There are no fail-safe methods for social workers to begin with, but taking into account the typical caseworker's average training time (about one month) and staggering caseload (as many as eighteen families to monitor continuously), it is surprising that more lives are not lost or destroyed. The heavy responsibilities of the DSS, the inevitability of caseworker error, and the constant scrutiny and attacks from the public have traditionally made for a punitive and hierarchical organizational culture where social workers perform their duties in isolation and fear, and their primary dealings with upper management involve inspection and often disciplinary action. The political pressure on top managers to produce a scapegoat when tragedies occur means that those social workers often take the fall, regardless of the quality of their judgment or their work.

Spence noted early on that there were few opportunities for collaboration and learning about case practice, and that "sticky" communication on both individual cases and general practice led to failures in case management. The "indoctrination of all workers in a highly autonomous and isolated model of case responsibility . . . continues to impede communication and information flow."[6]

Spence's two immediate predecessors at the DSS had attempted to improve the organizational culture in two very different ways. In the mid-1990s Commissioner Linda Carlisle focused on improving data collection and using the data to build a system grounded in compliance with central office guidelines. Loosely following the Compstat model, Carlisle used her comprehensive data to convene forums with caseworkers, investigators, and midlevel managers and to hold them strictly accountable for their performance on a number of process and output measures (the number of nonemergency complaints investigated within ten days, the number of subsequent assessments completed within forty-five days, etc.).[7] The adversarial nature of those proceedings and the disconnect between the activities being measured and the results that caseworkers sought to produce left workers in the field feeling deeply alienated from a leadership that seemed to put numbers and bureaucratic compliance ahead of the welfare of the children that those numbers represented. In fact, sensing that there might be something amiss in Carlisle's DSS, the Massachusetts House Post Audit and Oversight Committee conducted a ten-month investigation that found that "the state's child welfare agency is so concerned with concluding investigations quickly rather than thoroughly that it leaves vulnerable children at risk." The committee noted that the DSS was distorting its numbers to make caseloads look manageable, and that caseworkers were "pressured by managers to backdate reports, and to cut corners by not interviewing all the people familiar with a child's circumstances, such as doctors, teachers, and siblings."[8]

Carlisle was replaced by Jeff Locke, who sought to repair the deep division that had developed between the field and the central office during Carlisle's term, often by allying himself with the field. He was frequently quoted as saying that more important than compliance is that "you've done the right thing by the child." "The skill of our social workers is to exercise their professional judgment," Locke told a reporter from the *Boston Globe*. "We ask them to make assessments on the safety of a child. An assessment is an educated guess. Most often, we're right. But the process almost compels the fact that sometimes we're going to be wrong."[9] These efforts restored a sense that the commissioner, and therefore the department, valued casework and caseworkers. However, as the compliance-oriented data collection system waned, the staff responsible for establishing it began to resign, leaving numerous vacancies and reducing the capacity of the central office to carry out its performance measurement and oversight functions. While the organization was glad to get out from under the thumb of what seemed like an arbitrary demand for bureaucratic performance, the lack of guidance or standards from the central office left the agency vulnerable to charges that it was failing to demand, recognize, and produce high-quality performance. "[In the past] social workers [were] too often tied to their computers, doing a lot of busy work that may help [data flow] to the central office, but which doesn't necessarily help kids," Locke explained. It was this system that Locke sought to change by reducing the reporting burdens on caseworkers. "The downside is we may lose some data, but I'll do without the data to know a child is safe."[10]

A New Philosophy

Spence believed that the performance management systems that the previous commissioners had devised were less effective than they could have been because DSS leadership had been asking the wrong question. Instead of asking "How do we get out of trouble?" they should have asked "How do we run an efficient and effective organization that focuses on long-term strategies *while in trouble*? In fact, how can we use 'trouble' to continually learn and improve our practice?"[11]

Part of the difficulty seemed to spring from a failure to produce a coherent "statement of the nature of [DSS] child welfare practice"[12] and to provide consistent and predictable guidelines for caseworkers to follow. He hoped to redefine, and in some ways to define clearly for the first time, the goals and values of the DSS, organizing the agency's beliefs and practice around a "family-centered" approach:

Family-centered child welfare practice begins with the recognition that children who are abused or neglected are already traumatized by the time the child welfare system intervenes to protect the child. It recognizes further that removal of the child from its home of origin is itself also a traumatizing event. . . . Recognizing that children who grow up with so much trauma are at very high risk for homelessness, substance abuse, family violence, mental illness and criminality, family-centered practice works to ensure a child's safety in a manner that minimizes further traumatization and maximizes opportunities for healing. Family-centered practice looks to community resources to assist families with supports that can enable them to restore a safe environment for their children. It enlists the assistance of extended family in creating a safe place for the child, whether in the family of origin or in out-of-home placement. . . . It pursues permanency, in either the family of origin or in an adoptive family, as quickly as possible. . . . Family-centered practice recognizes further that the role of family does not end at the point a child turns eighteen [and] . . . focuses on nurturing family or family-like networks from the moment a child enters care.[13]

Spence hoped that this statement of DSS values and goals would serve as scaffolding—providing a conceptual frame and a shared vocabulary for everyone in the organization to use in thinking and talking about the work, and in making decisions in casework. Spence believed that this was the essence of a professional organization and the key to empowering caseworkers, and that empowered caseworkers would ensure accountability and performance. "You have the ethical standards, the agreed-on professional standards about how we operate," he said. He thought this set of standards would help the organization move beyond the culture of fear and resentment that decades of punitive, hierarchical management had created. "You're constantly creating a culture," Spence added. "You're reinforcing it through professional development, but it's not fundamentally through regulation and enforceability by punishment."[14]

With input from central office leadership, regional and area directors, and regional clinical staff, Spence developed the following six core practice values:

child-driven
family-centered
strength-based

community-focused
committed to diversity and cultural competency
committed to continuous learning

DSS leadership also stated that the department intended to support continuous learning through the use of outcome data and open acknowledgment of error, to help staff at all levels develop self-reflective practice, and to replace worker isolation with collaboration. Finally, Spence emphasized that he intended to maintain a consistent agenda throughout his tenure and to focus on initiating and maintaining long-term strategies.

Unfortunately, Spence's inauguration as commissioner had coincided with a fiscal crisis in the state. Suddenly, Spence was forced to cut unprecedented numbers of social workers from a system he had not yet had the chance to fully understand.[15] He described the experience as "blindly hacking away with remarkably little sense of what the result would be," and he openly admitted that some of the layoffs were mistakes.[16] He consciously used the fiscal crisis and the difficulties it presented to point out that competence does not mean error-free work. He reminded workers that not sharing and discussing problems will threaten the organization, while exposing and addressing them will help strengthen it. He wrote a letter to the staff acknowledging the emotional impact that the cuts were having on the organization. He hoped to foster a sense of openness, to touch on the social and emotional aspects of the work, and to let his staff know that they could trust him even during this period of instability. He intended to keep the organization focused on long-term strategies and learning. "Firefighting is the enemy of a learning organization," he said.[17]

Restructuring Internal Accountability
Recognizing the DSS leadership's history of indifference toward the particulars and challenges of casework, Spence aimed to flip the customary ratio of time the central office spent on politics and administration (80 percent) versus substantive issues and improving practice (20 percent). He sought to affirm the importance of casework by traveling to area offices around the state, where he participated in casework and problem solving. In some respects this move made a virtue out of a necessity. Spence came to the DSS with no direct experience

in child welfare work. Immersed in casework, he was able to identify three essential components to the art of social work: "An open and sensitive emotional connection to the family and child," a "habit of self-reflection," and a "supportive DSS community of self-reflective practitioners."[18]

In an effort to soften the organization's rigid hierarchy, Spence endeavored to shift the locus and spread the responsibility of organizational decision making. He incorporated senior staff from the central office and the twelve regional directors and regional counsels into an "executive staff" that met regularly to review data and discuss all aspects of practice and performance. He also organized central office staff into project management groups (PMGs) responsible for key improvement initiatives around topics such as family networks and diversity. The PMGs were required to meet at least every other week "to map out detailed work plans for each of our improvement processes, and to define schedule, phasing, and workload requirements to achieve our goals."[19] Each PMG then provided these plans to the executive staff, which made the ultimate decisions. For the regional directors, whose previous responsibilities were primarily administrative and budget related, this was a new and, for the most part, welcome role. "Regional directors had their legs cut out from under them lots of times," Spence said. "We really saw this as building their role."

The breaking down and reconfiguring of internal working relationships and organizational hierarchies went hand in hand with a new structure of accountability. The customary way of enacting accountability had been simply to fire the social worker responsible for any case that went badly awry. Spence was not willing to take such drastic measures against caseworkers whose cases, due to bad luck or "conscientious" error, had tragic outcomes.

> I said I'll defend error. I will never defend negligence or dereliction of duty. But I will defend error because if I didn't, I should be fired at the end of every day. I don't know anybody who's had a perfect day yet. . . . The other thing we enunciated was accountability is not at the lowest level; it's at the highest level. Historically it had always been at the lowest level. . . . And we said exactly the opposite. You move up the chain all the way up and the highest level of failure is the point where the accountability occurs. . . . If [the newspapers] have a scalp, they're satisfied . . . [but] the public is being duped completely because

the fraud is it's far more likely the commissioner is covering his own ass
by blaming somebody than [it is] that that worker is guilty.

As always, Spence emphasized the implications of these ideas for
every level of the organization:

1. Commitment to continuous self-reflection must start at the top
   and characterize the work of every level of the organization.
2. The best forum for learning about and exploring self-reflection
   at the "Practice Point" [where social workers connect with
   individual families] is in examining our relationship with our
   colleagues and coworkers.[20]

Spence also broke down the boundary that divided the DSS from
its clients and constituents, inviting clients and other stakeholders to
participate in consultative and review processes that continuously examined the practices of the agency. Following a 2004 statewide "Listening and Learning Tour" that sought to gather feedback from families
and community members as well as staff, Spence organized ninety
participants (40 percent area office staff, 40 percent parents and community members, and 20 percent regional and central office staff) into
work groups to plan around the six core practice values and to make
recommendations for policy, procedural, and legislative changes. These
groups met at least monthly for over a year.

Putting all these changes into practice was a relentless daily challenge for everyone involved. Spence explained, "You have to start making the boundary between public and private much more permeable,
and that's very threatening to people. People want to say, 'You own my
technical skills as my employer. My character is my character.' . . . And
I always say, 'Fine, as soon as you stop bringing your character to work,
I'll stop working on it.'"

The biggest innovation Spence made in support of his vision of a
more thoughtful and professional working environment for the DSS
was "teaming." For the first time, caseworkers shared the responsibility for individual cases. They made home visits and carried out supervisory duties in teams of two or more. "The truth of the matter is
peer-to-peer learning is always more powerful than hierarchical learning," Spence said. He wanted the DSS to benefit from strong peer-to-peer

accountability. "Each of us is responsible for pushing the other to do the best work they can do," he explained. "That's accountability."

Given the high stakes in child protection, neither the public nor the DSS want to acknowledge that they do not always know how best to "do right by the child." Spence saw that denying this reality, however, did not serve anyone:

> The insistence on knowing is a constant source of terror. . . . Nobody ever talks to anybody, and the first thing we need to realize is that the biggest protection against error is constant discussion. . . . In an industrial organization, disagreement is disobedience and disloyalty; in a professional organization, disagreement is the ground of clinical thinking. So you have to build a culture from one that has punished disagreement to one that does exactly the opposite—one that rewards disagreement, as long as disagreement is done conscientiously and as a shared problem-solving process. . . . As soon as you talk about multiple viewpoints and how every viewpoint is partial, you start opening up the possibility that, "I can live with my not being perfect." Over time, we got more and more explicit that we're not very useful to families when we say we know exactly what to do because who knows exactly how to raise children? There isn't a known technology, so we have to be able to say to families, "No, we don't know everything."

Spence set up the Teaming Advisory Board, which included DSS staff as well as some outside experts. Hoping to follow a model established by another state, the board searched for examples around the country and quickly discovered that no other states used teaming in child welfare work. The board secured funding from the Casey Foundation to implement the teaming initiative and in 2003 sent out a request for proposals to all of the state's area offices. They received ten proposals. Their original plan was to approve only one or two, but the board ultimately approved seven in order to gather more evidence about effective approaches.

After only six months, team workers who had joined the initiative with some doubt expressed relief at being able to share the analysis and decision making on their cases as well as the actual work tasks. Because child welfare work tends to come in waves, teaming allowed the DSS to provide more resources for the initial demands of the case and then to allow the flexible transfer of resources around the team in response to emergencies. The workers involved in the eight original initiatives conveyed tremendous excitement and enthusiasm. In fact, although Spence himself had planned to write the "convergence document" about what the DSS could learn from the eight models, the eight original teams asked if, together, they could be the ones to distill the important principles that DSS staff should learn from their work. They planned to send the convergence document to the entire organization and to solicit comments and reactions before developing the final model. Other units in the original eight offices began to adopt teaming, and many of the other area offices wanted to implement it. Child welfare organizations in other states began to contact Spence about adopting the DSS' approach to teaming.

To his surprise, Spence quickly realized that families preferred working with teams to having individual caseworkers. Spence had imagined that families might feel overwhelmed when confronted by multiple workers at once, but he began to understand that what actually overwhelmed families was the autocratic nature of the decision-making process. Before teaming, the family's fate had depended on the judgment of one person. For families, teaming reduced the terrifying sense of dependence on one person.

Managing External Political Accountability

Spence knew that the changes he was making would be hard for those who were not involved to understand and value. Citizens and their elected representatives already had a view of what the public had a right to expect from the DSS: zero errors. They would hold the agency and its employees strictly accountable for observed outcomes. Spence's insistence on acknowledging tragedy, pointing out the crucial difference between negligence and bad outcomes, supporting the staff, and focusing on continuous learning and improvement over the long run did not fit neatly into the familiar paradigm.

To create room for this new kind of accountability, he had to build external support—particularly with the legislature. Shortly after his appointment, Spence began a series of letters to the Massachusetts legislature describing—and preemptively defending—his reforms to the DSS and his ideas about how legislators could hold the DSS accountable for its performance in a productive way. The letters emphasized the difficulty and trauma involved in child welfare work and the importance of supporting workers in their practice, and it specifically condemned the punitive accountability system.

Spence's first letter to the legislature, sent in 2002, focused on how his overall approach to managing the DSS—building a professional learning organization—would serve the children of the state: "I am certain that if we can establish . . . a culture of continuous learning, and can discard an antiquated accountability system that is based on the fiction that error can be eliminated, we can make the Massachusetts Department of Social Services the best child welfare system in the nation. If we do, we will far better protect and heal the thousands of victims of child abuse and neglect in this state."[21] It also explained why reforms to guide and support social workers would be necessary: "If we are going to ask them to improve the quality of their decision-making and of their interactions with families, we must provide them with ongoing staff development of the highest quality, and make them feel less isolated, more supported, and safer in making their inherently risky decisions."[22] The letter went on to describe the six core values and how they would support communication and casework at the DSS.

In another letter, sent in 2005, Spence sought to enlighten the legislature about the importance of changes that supported the "art of social work" and reduced the isolation and "secondary trauma" that social workers often experience. "Fostering emotional openness and the habit of self-reflection are not conventional organizational tasks," he acknowledged. "But child welfare work is not conventional work."[23]

He reinforced his point by using the example of changing accountability systems in medical practice.

> The public and the medical profession have come to understand that [a punitive] system of public accountability actually reduced safety for patients, rather than increasing it. In place of this error- and blame-based system of public accountability for hospitals, health care specialists have introduced a system based on continuous review and improvement of practice. This system recognizes that negligence needs to be sanctioned, but that ordinary human error is a fact of existence. The task of hospitals, and other similar care-giving institutions, is to create a culture in which it is safe to identify and acknowledge error, in order to do the organizational learning necessary to reduce the chance that inevitable future human error will result in harm to a patient.

Like the historic approach to hospital fatalities, the public account-ability system for child welfare actually reduces the Department's abil-ity to make children safe [because] . . . it teaches the Department and its staff to be risk-averse, to deny error and to engage in classic compli-ance and "CYA" ["cover your ass"] activity that actually impedes the development of organizational learning and systemic improvement that would increase children's safety. . . . The myth that human error can be eliminated actually perpetuates human error by preventing the creation of a culture of continuous improvement and learning.

It is my hope that, with your support, we can put in place in the De-partment a set of diagnostic performance measures and self-assessment practices for each Area Office that will support continuous improve-ment in practice. Once in place, those structures offer the public an al-ternative to its customary accountability system: in the event of a death or other breach of safety for a child, a determination would be made whether the event had occurred as a result of negligence. If so, the ap-propriate personnel action would be taken. But if not, then the burden would be on the leadership of the Department and of the particular Area Office to demonstrate not that there is "error free" practice, but rather that the Department and the Area Office are taking systematic and appropriate steps to improve practice, reduce error, and establish systems that diminish the likelihood that the inevitable error will lead to harm to a child.[24]

Using Data for Mutual Accountability

Spence's learning model of accountability would not have been possible without the availability of outcome data, and he viewed the new em-phasis on outcome measures over process measures as a much-needed paradigm shift in child welfare services. Spence believed that the focus on compliance that characterized the DSS and other child welfare agencies in the 1990s served only the organizations and not the children in their care. "The fury about this procedural stuff—what I call the in-dustrialization of child welfare, which was a classic strategy in the nine-ties generally . . . was to protect the department," said Spence. "So now if we can dumb down the work to a series of definable tasks, then when the high profile case hits, we hold up the list and say, 'Look, we did everything. Not our fault.' . . . A professional organization is only pos-sible now because we have outcome measures. Absent outcome mea-sures, I [the Commissioner] have to constantly tell [caseworkers] how to do the [work]."

By the time Spence took office, changes in federal guidelines had required child welfare agencies in every state to collect and report outcome data showing increases and reductions in permanent placements, time spent in foster care or group homes between placements or family reunifications, and the occurrence and recurrence of abuse and neglect in homes and foster care. In Massachusetts a computer system called "FamilyNet" not only produced the required outcome data at many different levels of aggregation but also allowed immediate access to every case file in the system. This gave the DSS an unprecedented capacity to connect quantitative outcome data with the rich qualitative data in individual case files. "If you look at repeat maltreatment numbers for Attleboro, on exactly the same system you can pull up every single individual case," Spence explained. "It forces on you the recognition that .072 means Johnny and Mary and whoever. . . . The outcome data is linked in a very powerful way to how the worker experiences the work. . . . So you can connect the numbers back to kids, to a real kid and a real family."

FamilyNet also made DSS data—both outcome and process numbers—transparent throughout the entire organization. Every area office received a book with data on over a hundred performance measures for itself and every other area office. Process measures remained important, but Spence wanted to use them "less for accountability than . . . for diagnostic [purposes]. The whole issue is, 'I'm not doing as well on this outcome: Why?' Then we need to do tons of work building hypotheses about why and then measuring whether or not [there is improvement]."

Critical Incident Case Reviews

Ideally, the information systems and the new forms of accountability would shift DSS culture and day-to-day practice toward improved average performance. But, given the inherent limitations of child protection methods, these changes could not prevent every tragedy or insulate the DSS from the media firestorms that would surround those incidents.

Despite the scope and sincerity of Spence's efforts to improve the DSS, the media launched a new attack on his leadership with every high-profile case of child abuse in Massachusetts. At the end of his tenure, the *Boston Globe* published this brief time line of newsworthy occurrences under Spence's leadership:

2002

July 2: LaVeta Jackson kills her 3-year-old son and 6-year-old daughter and is then shot to death by police. DSS had returned custody of the children to her in June.

August: Spence places a caseworker and the manager of the Whitinsville office on administrative leave for failing to aggressively investigate a Warren home where children were allegedly raped and beaten for 11 years.

2004

Sept. 20: Paul P. Dubois is found guilty of murdering a DSS worker in Provincetown in 1996. The investigation involved a custody dispute between Dubois and his former wife, who was awarded custody of their two children.

2005

March 6: Dontel Jeffers, 4, is allegedly beaten to death by his foster mother 11 days after DSS places him in the foster home.

2006

Jan. 17: DSS gets permission from the Supreme Judicial Court to withdraw life support from 11-year-old Haleigh Poutre, who is in a coma after an alleged beating by her adoptive mother and stepfather. A day after the ruling, Haleigh begins breathing on her own, and DSS says she is emerging from her vegetative state.

Dec. 13: Rebecca Riley, 4, dies of a prescription drug overdose, and her parents, who were under DSS supervision, are charged with first-degree murder.[25]

At DSS the incidents described fall within a broader category of cases where the safety of a child or a caseworker is in immediate jeopardy. These cases are called "critical incidents." The DSS commissioner has to confront every critical incident and find a way to deal with its particulars and its larger implications both internally and externally. As commissioner, Spence tried to tread the hazy line between tolerating and defending caseworkers' errors and taking a strict punitive approach without seeming arbitrary or inconsistent. Rather than engaging in the usual investigation and ritual sacrifice that followed high-profile cases, Spence's executive staff developed an organizational learning process around critical incidents. "We just went in and we ran these learning forums, and at the same time or shortly after we would do the investigations," Spence explained. "We talked about, 'Okay, what are the implications for practice?' And then we wrote up a whole series of

'Here's what our learning is from this.' [Then we'd] share it with the whole area office, and we'd send it out to everybody, so they'd actually see learning from it."

This new approach was an adjustment for the regional office directors who had always played the role of executioner in the old regime. "I remember talking with the regional director about going to the area office to meet with the staff around this case," said Spence, "and the regional director said, 'But if you're a regional director the only reason you can go into an area office is to punish somebody.'"

Continuous Quality Improvement

All data that the DSS collected were meaningless without a formal monitoring system. With this in mind, in 2003, Spence set up oversight bodies to convert the data into practice improvement, establishing continuous quality improvement (CQI) teams to help improve practice at the clinical, managerial, and systemic levels. The DSS leadership asked each of the twenty-nine area offices to develop a CQI committee that would include representatives from outside the DSS (e.g., school superintendents, local mayors, government officials, and members of foster families, adoptive families, or client families).

Each office also put together a staff CQI team charged with analyzing data and using that analysis to develop and test hypotheses about strategies for practice improvement. The teams were told to consider three options in thinking about how to respond to weaknesses and failures in the system: program development (establishing an initiative to deal with a problem); professional development (training); and practice and policy development (improving practice and designing policy). A broader oversight body, the Statewide Steering Committee, was responsible for evaluating the DSS' progress in meeting its stated goals, reviewing the regional and area office CQI teams' reports, and recommending systemic changes.

Spence's aim was to develop a capacity for innovative thinking and organizational learning in each area office, starting at the team level. Ultimately, he wanted "area office CQI discoveries to drive central office priorities for delivering resources and supports to the field, in order to expand learning and capacity in each area office."[26]

Child Welfare Institute

All of these reforms pushed harried social workers to start thinking of themselves and their coworkers as professionals working together in a collegial environment challenged to reflect on and improve their performance as their most important objective. To support that transition, Spence had acted early to invest in professional development for social workers. In 2002 the DSS partnered with Salem State College School of Social Work to establish the Child Welfare Institute (CWI), a professional development training program for DSS staff.

Supplying workers with important and relevant information about their field helped reduce their anxiety about making mistakes and, in turn, allowed them to learn how to be more effective in developing relationships with families and assisting them in making positive changes.

Quality of Service Reviews

The last phase of Spence's practice improvement strategy, developed specifically to support peer-to-peer learning around casework, joined staff from central, regional, and area offices in a collaborative effort to select strategies and fix problems through a quality of service review (QSR). A team of staff representing each of the three tiers of the organization would go into an area office and pull up a set of twenty cases—either at random or pertaining to particular areas of practice—and review those cases, talk to people involved, and then provide feedback to the whole office about the quality of the casework. For example, a QSR team was sent to the Attleboro office to investigate high levels of repeat maltreatment. Looking deeper into the data revealed that repeat maltreatment occurred mostly among families with caregivers suffering from severe substance abuse problems. The QSR team suggested hypotheses for how best to address this problem through programming, professional development, and changes in policy and practice.

Learning Forums

Spence intended the continuous review of quantitative and qualitative data that CQI and QSR made possible to lead to more formal, department-wide learning forums where area directors would not only share what they had learned but also turn that learning into strategy for future practice. Spence explained, "Learning forums are not unlike Compstat because, in the end, what you want is for every area director to be able to articulate the strategy for practice improvement that they are pursuing within their office."

It was important to Spence that the DSS avoid its old pattern of reacting to a problematic case with sweeping policy changes. "There's a wonderful saying in child welfare which is, policy is the scar of the last error," he said. "The tendency in governmental organizations is to say, 'Whoops! Write a policy!' And most of the time it's right for the one situation and wrong for 99 others, so you have to actively propose resisting the policy reaction. This is not fundamentally about policy. It's about situated problem solving."

In the education world from which Spence came, studies showing that the only sure route to improved problem-solving skills is knowledge and experience of the context of a given problem have caused educators to teach "situated problem solving." Spence saw the policy reaction in government as being just as unhelpful to social workers as teaching generic problem solving to students, and far more damaging.

Still, because of the political pressure on child welfare agencies, even those that avoid the policy reaction often fail at "situated problem solving." Spence cited a study in Connecticut showing that the rate at which children were removed from their homes following high-profile cases went up 30 percent. The reason for this trend may be obvious, but it takes discipline, knowledge, and experience on the part of a child welfare agency to avoid it.

Fallout

In May 2007 Spence was one of many agency directors to be replaced under Deval Patrick, the new governor of Massachusetts. Looking at the list of high-profile cases that erupted over Spence's tenure, many in the media were quick to conclude that he had it coming. The names and photographs of the children who had slipped through the cracks in the system—Haleigh Poutre, Dontel Jeffers, and Rebecca Riley— explained it all. Asked if Spence's leaving came as a surprise, a reporter for the New England Cable News network replied that it wasn't and that Spence had been under fire for some time. The reporter went on to cite an incident where a minister had filed a report on himself for molesting his own nephew and the DSS had failed to act on the call. Ironically, Spence described this case as the one "critical incident" in his six and a half years at the DSS where the initial investigation led back to one social worker's apparent negligence. At the investigation's conclusion, however, that social worker kept his job. Hospital records showed that he had been admitted the same day, in cardiac arrest. "You think you finally have the case; you finally have the guy who just dropped it," said Spence, "and he was having a heart attack!"

Navigating the "Expert Slope" in Public Management

Protecting children from abuse and neglect at the hands of their caretakers is surely one of the most difficult public tasks—the sort of task that has been described as a "wicked problem," or an "impossible job." One could also think of it as the "expert slope" in public management—the kind of challenge that really separates the good skiers from the not so good.[27] The job makes extraordinarily heavy demands not only on those who dare to lead and manage child welfare agencies but also on the caseworkers who confront on a daily basis the complex circumstances that surround the abuse and neglect of children, on the families who are asked to honor their duties toward their children, and on the contractors and foster families who manage the care of at-risk children and families.[28] It could even be seen as making heavy demands on those in positions to oversee the agency's operations and to call it to account on behalf of the citizens who have given the agency extraordinary powers, and no small amount of money. The challenge for them is determining how best to hold an agency accountable when it is all but certain that significant problems will arise. When inevitable mistakes occur, overseers will have to decide whether they are looking at an impermissible failure of the public agency at the managerial or operational level, or at a tragedy that the agency simply could not anticipate or prevent.[29] The subtlety and complexity of this work mock those who would like to solve important public management problems with the tenets of Management 101.

Indeed, any effort to manage a child protection agency by holding agency staff strictly accountable for their performance against some kind of simple bottom line runs into all the conceptual and practical difficulties facing public agencies that have been explored in these pages:

- The public value that a child welfare agency produces must be assessed against numerous distinct dimensions of public value— each with its own particular meaning and importance.
- The agency uses not only public funds but also public authority to protect children from harm.
- The transactions between the agency and its clients include not only service encounters but also obligation encounters of the most deeply sensitive nature.
- The ultimate public value produced is not judged by the clients the organization serves and obliges but by citizens and their elected representatives.
- These authorizers can only judge the agency against some imperfectly articulated idea of the valuable outcomes they hope the agency can produce and the values they hope the agency will reflect in its operations.
- The public values that the agency seeks to advance include practical, utilitarian concerns (such as improving the welfare of children over the short and long term) as well as important deontological values tied to protecting right social relationships between parents and children, parents and society, and society and children.
- Because the political authorizing environment that sets out the terms of accountability is unsettled, dynamic, and contentious, the systems designed to capture the agency's performance are always in development rather than firmly established. Neither agency managers nor those who oversee them can take for granted their current structure of accountability; they have to create a suitable structure of accountability jointly through philosophical, political, and technical deliberation.
- The agency creates public value over long time frames, and at many different points along a complex value chain that trans- forms inputs into organizational activities and operations, transactions with clients, and, ultimately, social outcomes. The agency incurs costs long before the ultimate desired social outcomes can be achieved, or the desired social benefits accrue.[30]

The system that actually produces (or fails to produce) public value relies on the resources and the actions of many social actors outside the scope of a public manager's direct control.[31]

An Impossible Job?

While all of these features are generally typical of public-sector operations, it is rare that they are all present to the degree that they are in child welfare in general, or the Massachusetts DSS in particular. Moreover, some additional special features of child welfare agencies seem to make the challenge of developing public value accounts and using them to satisfy demands for accountability and to guide and improve performance particularly fraught with political controversy, technical difficulty, and managerial challenge.

Compelling and Exacting Values at Stake

First, the public values at stake in the performance of child welfare agencies are among the most urgent and sensitive that the public faces. As citizens, we urgently want to protect vulnerable children from the abuse and neglect of caretakers. We want to do so for practical, utilitarian reasons—we want the kids to be happy, we want them to grow up to be resourceful citizens, and we want to avoid the trouble and expense they could cause if they do not. We also think that children have a right to protection and care—if not from their parents then from society at large—as a matter of justice and fairness. We think that parents ought to care for their children and refrain from harming them through abuse or neglect as a matter of duty and obligation.

These concerns line up on the side of intervening in family life when there are allegations of abuse and neglect. But other compelling and sensitive values line up on the side of avoiding intervention. As a practical matter, we would prefer that parents pay the price of caring for their children. We know that the alternative is expensive—and often not very effective in raising children. As a matter of justice and right relations, we want to protect the rights of parents to raise children as they deem appropriate, particularly in situations where different cultures seem to have much different ideas of good parenting. For utilitarian as well as justice reasons, then, we want to keep the parenting responsibility on those whose duty it is, and on those who are in the best position to provide it.

To show how compelling and exacting the standards are in child protective services, Figure 7.1 sets out one conception of what the public value account for such an agency might be. There is no dimension of public value that can be set aside as even temporarily unimportant; each dimension requires serious and rigorous attention. Each sets a level of performance that cannot easily be compromised. In this sense child protection is truly a "wicked problem."

Technical Challenges and the Inevitability of Errors of Two Types
The tangle of philosophical values is problematic enough. But the challenge of child protection is also technical and operational. One could boil down the core operational capacities and technologies of a child welfare agency to the set of policies and procedures on which the agency relies to perform five specific functions:

- identifying possible cases of abuse and neglect;
- investigating complaints and more generally diagnosing the conditions under which vulnerable children are being raised;
- making predictions about whether abuse and neglect will continue in the future;
- devising methods for monitoring conditions and providing families with services designed to prevent future instances of abuse and neglect; and
- deciding when the future welfare of the child demands as a matter of prudence the temporary removal of the child from the custodial setting and the permanent termination of the custodial rights (and responsibilities) of the parents.

If these policies and procedures are robust, reliable, efficient, effective, just, and fair, the organization can be expected to perform well, but as long as difficulties exist in any of these processes, the agency will always be "in trouble."[32] Simply to list these core tasks is to suggest precisely how difficult the task is, and how unreliable the established policies and procedures are.

The difficulties begin with the very first step: trying to locate cases of abuse and neglect.[33] The usual practice of government is to avoid looking for problems—particularly if efforts to find the problems would require breaching boundaries of individual privacy. Thus government

PUBLIC VALUE ACCOUNT for Harry Spence and the Massachusetts DSS

PUBLIC VALUE ACCOUNT	
Use of Collectively Owned Assets and Associated Costs	**Achievement of Collectively Valued Social Outcomes**
Financial Costs	Mission Achievement
Internal (administrative)	Protect children from abuse and
External (costs to families)	neglect by parents and other
	caretakers
	Provide safe, long-term homes for
	at-risk children
	Ensure positive long-term outcomes
	for children in system
Unintended Negative Consequences	Unintended Positive Consequences
Family break-ups	Adoptions by caretakers unable to
Relocation of children	have children of their own
	Client Satisfaction
	Treat clients with respect
	Engage and support caretakers
Social Costs of Using State Authority	Justice and Fairness
Intrusions into families	Give all children in system an equal
Relationships structured by court	chance to succeed as adults
orders	Protect parental rights
Terminations of parental rights	Enforce parental duties
	Treat cases equally
	Respect cultural differences

Figure 7.1. Public value account for Harry Spence and the Massachusetts DSS.

services are typically less *proactive* than *reactive;* they wait for some clear indication that a serious problem exists, or that someone's rights are being violated before intervening in private lives. Most often, the person who raises the alarm is the person experiencing the problem. But in the case of child abuse and neglect, the usual system does not work. Often the only witnesses of the problem are the perpetrators of abuse and neglect. The victims are hidden from view and voiceless, invisible to the government.[34]

Even when someone raises an alarm that abuse and neglect might be occurring, it proves difficult to determine whether the allegation is credible. And even when the DSS can get a picture of the form that abuse and neglect have taken in the past, it is difficult to make reliable predictions about whether that pattern will improve or worsen in the future. And even if the DSS can make good predictions about the future, caseworkers may not know exactly what they should do to alter the family trajectory in desirable directions. And, most difficult of all, the DSS has to decide when the public interest would be better served by removing a child from a family and seeking a permanent, alternative placement than by continuing to support and supplement the existing familial arrangements.

Because the procedures on which the DSS and other child welfare agencies rely to discover and respond to child abuse and neglect are imperfect, DSS employees inevitably make decisions that produce bad results. There are signs of abuse and victims of abuse that the schools and hospitals the DSS relies on as the first line of defense never see. This produces an error described in operations research literature as a "false negative": the system that exists to identify abuse and neglect reports no problem when, in fact, there is a problem. The system also nominates cases that turn out to be innocuous. This produces a "false positive": the system identifies an instance of abuse or neglect when, in fact, there was no instance. Table 7.1 lists the errors of both types that can be made at each stage of DSS processing.

Adding to the difficulties, these types of errors can occur at any point in the casework process. Caseworkers might decide that they can safely leave a child in the care of a parent, without knowing that the violent boyfriend who was the original source of the problem is about to return home, exposing the child to danger. This too is a kind of false negative. In another case the DSS might judge a single man with an ag-

Table 7.1.   Two types of errors in child-protection case processing.

	False positive	False negative
Identifying cases of abuse and neglect	Identifying a case where there is none	Missing a case that exists
Investigating complaints	Seeing danger where there is none	Missing a dangerous condition
Predicting future trajectories	Wrongly predicting a negative outcome	Wrongly predicting a positive/acceptable outcome
Monitoring conditions and making interventions	Sustaining interventions when they are not needed	Stopping interventions too soon
Deciding whether to terminate parental rights	Terminating parental rights when the child would have been safe in the parents' care	Leaving the child in the home where abuse and neglect will continue

gravated assault rap and a sixty-hour workweek as being unable to care for his children, when in actuality he was a temporarily overwhelmed but an otherwise capable father who failed to pack his daughter's school lunch one too many times—a false positive.

The vast majority of these errors occur not as a result of any individual's stupidity or maliciousness but because we simply do not know how to make completely reliable predictions about human behavior. The fact that errors are inevitable in child protection is what prompted Spence to observe that the work of the DSS is not to avoid or get out of trouble but to keep on working conscientiously while in trouble. This commitment led him to begin creating internal processes that use the inevitable errors and the agency's responses to those errors not only to increase the agency's knowledge about how to reduce errors in the future but also to sustain and reaffirm their commitment to doing so. The best way to deal with the terrible impact of errors on DSS clients and DSS personnel is to find in the response to the errors a hope that the organization can keep improving its performance. To do that, the agency has to own rather than reject its errors.

To own up to and create a capacity to learn from these "errors," however, the organization has to make a crucial distinction between bad outcomes, on one hand, and negligent performance, on the other. The "errors" described earlier might be best described as "bad outcomes": the agency, acting through an individual caseworker, had a choice to make; it made the choice, and the result was bad. But the observed bad result could have occurred as a result of at least three different circumstances: (1) a caseworker was negligent or incompetent and failed to apply a known and proven procedure that would have worked in that particular case; (2) a caseworker applied a known and proven procedure to the particular case, and it produced a bad result; (3) an experienced caseworker, relying on professional expertise and discretion, properly recognized that an existing procedure would not work in this case, adapted the established procedure to the particular circumstance, and still got a bad result.

Among these possibilities, only the first is clearly a negligent error for which the caseworker is culpable. The second simply reveals the limitations of the agency's knowledge and should focus the organization's attention on its existing policies and procedures rather than on the actions of the caseworker. The third represents a potentially helpful response on the part of the caseworker that, had it worked, might have helped improve agency performance, but because of the limitations of professional knowledge, it resulted in a bad outcome. While the tradition of the DSS was to find a scapegoat to assuage the general anxiety associated with encountering the limits of the organization's knowledge, Spence saw the "conscientious errors" that produce bad outcomes—whether through application or thoughtful adaptation of established procedures—as occasions for sustained organizational learning and improvement and the reaffirmation of professional values.[35]

Confusion about Accountability Systems for Learning Organizations

Spence's recognition that "conscientious errors" were inevitable led him to develop an accountability system that would not only tolerate such errors but also use them as a basis for improving organizational performance and searching for better methods. The difficulty, however, was that this kind of accountability system ran afoul of an entrenched, unhelpful general idea about the best way to guarantee high performance in public agencies that we first encountered in Chapter 4.

This entrenched idea insisted that the right way to run high-performing, error-free organizations was to develop reliable policies, procedures, processes, and technologies that could not only guarantee consistent treatment across individual cases but also ensure that the organization could produce the desired results. Caretakers accused of abuse and neglect would get consistent treatment from the DSS, and that treatment would guarantee the desired results because the procedures laid out the right and effective actions to be taken. The procedures embodied the professional knowledge of the DSS, and that was sufficient to get the job done. Obviously, if there were such clear and reliable procedures, the task of managing the DSS would be relatively simple. Management could establish a tough policy of zero tolerance for errors and demand exacting compliance with existing policies and procedures, confident that if those procedures were followed, good and just results would occur. If there was a problem in performance, the right way to fix it would be to rewrite the policy manual and insist on ever more exact compliance with the rules that told frontline workers how to do their job.

To Spence, however, this standard bureaucratic approach had two closely related problems. On one hand, Spence was not sure that all the professional knowledge his organization needed to perform well was contained in the existing policies and procedures. In fact, he saw many of those policies and procedures as a sad history of responses to previous crises—the "scar of the last error," as he put it—rather than as the embodiment of real professional knowledge. He worried that there was not enough existing professional knowledge to allow caseworkers to perform excellently and without errors. If he hoped to improve performance over the long run, the key would be to do a much better job of capturing and codifying professional knowledge to be used in the future.

On the other hand, embracing the standard bureaucratic approach meant "dumbing down" the complex and messy human drama of casework to a set of standard policies and procedures. Spence's work with housing had taught him that "the varieties of human misery outstrip any taxonomy which I can create, and regulations are just taxonomies. They're just bin systems. . . . The next case that walks in your door confounds your bin system."[36] Even if it were possible to identify all the complex situations that caseworkers face and make policy out of current understandings about the best way to handle those particular circumstances, doing so would effectively freeze the development of the "art" of casework.

Understanding that bureaucratic accountability was a counterproductive approach for the DSS, Spence sought to create an organization that was accountable not primarily for compliance with unreliable policies and procedures but for learning how to improve its practices. He believed that through the pursuit of learning, his organization could harness all the motivation and control traditionally associated with the idea that management should insist on strict compliance with established policy.

To see the DSS as a learning organization, however, ran hard against the public's accustomed ideas about what government agencies should do. The public tends to think that if a government organization does not know how to do its job, then there must have been an error in the policy process that created the organization. Public agencies should know what they are doing. If they do not, then the government should never have gotten into that business in the first place. It is morally wrong and practically foolish for the government to gamble with taxpayers' dollars and clients' lives and fortunes when it does not know how to guarantee the desired results.

Some citizens become even more alarmed when public agencies start doing the things they need to do in order to learn how to do their work better. By definition, learning involves trying something different—departing from the standard to test alternative approaches in order to improve performance. Citizens worry that an organization wandering around in search of solutions will do a lot of damage without much benefit. It might treat similarly situated individuals differently, violating the principle of horizontal fairness. Worse, it might try a novel approach that results in a less desirable outcome for a particular client or the broader public than the standard approach would have produced. While some might think the effort was worthwhile inasmuch as the organization learned what did not work, others will condemn it as a waste of public dollars, and a clear case of government incompetence results.

Of course, in certain exceptional cases, citizens and their representatives may tolerate or even encourage some exploration. How else to get beyond government's notorious commitment to the one-size-fits-all solution? Citizens and their representatives might also accept the idea that some established professional practices might have to be tested to ensure that they work as intended, hence the common call to determine and implement "best practices" and the rise of evidence-based medicine, policing, and social work.[37] They might also understand the potential for systematic experiments to develop new methods for dealing with old and intractable or new and emerging problems.[38] So there is some constituency for a flexible, innovative government as well as a reliable, predictable government.

But when public agencies actually start doing these things—when they try to become the kind of flexible, innovative learning organizations that could effectively meet today's challenges—they often stumble over the question of how a learning organization can be called to account for performance. The usual systems of government accountability do not really know what to do with adaptation and experimentation, whether carried out at the caseworker or the organizational level.

Using Authority Efficiently, Effectively, and Fairly

Beyond the tangle of competing values, the technical challenges of the task, and the difficulty of developing administrative systems that can strike the right balance between demanding adherence to current professional standards and searching for more reliable and robust methods, child welfare agencies face (in spades) a problem that we have seen in some of our other cases as well: they must make the most scrupulous use of their public authority.

Child welfare agencies routinely exercise coercive public authority. The law requires professionals in positions to see evidence of child abuse and neglect (such as pediatricians, social workers, and school nurses) to report suspicious cases to the DSS. Caseworkers show up uninvited to interview individuals and observe conditions in private homes. Agencies initiate criminal and civil cases against parents and others who assume legal responsibility for children. Most pressingly, the power to remove a child from a home hangs heavily over every relationship between child welfare agencies, at-risk children, and their caretakers.

As with any public agency, and all other things being equal, the DSS should endeavor to use as little state authority as possible. As noted in Chapter 1, the use of public authority shifts the normative framework for assessing its performance to concerns about individual rights, treating individuals with fairness and restraint, and the proper role of the state in defending rights, imposing responsibilities, and advancing more practical goals. The public and the courts will insist that the DSS not trample the rights of parents and children. The public wants the DSS to use the minimum authority and money necessary to restore "right relations" within families on a permanent basis.[39]

The public also wants the DSS to use its authority in ways that land lightly on the shoulders of its client obligatees—to exercise restraint and respect the dignity and rights of obligatees, perhaps assuring them that there are legitimate reasons for imposing a duty or sanction on them, and that they were fairly selected for the burden.[40] Ideally, the DSS would gently remind citizens of a duty they knew they had, and would wish to follow as a service to the wider community. In accepting the burden the obligatee would get the benefit of protecting his or her status as someone who wanted to live in a right relationship with his or her fellow citizens.[41]

Performance Management Systems for High-Stakes Learning Organizations
Spence, like all of the public managers discussed in this book, encountered challenges at each point of the strategic triangle in his efforts to help his organization create public value. In trying to locate the important public values at stake in DSS operations, he had to understand the "Bermuda Triangle" of expectations for child welfare services and find a way to integrate those conflicting values into the evaluation of his agency's performance without becoming lost at sea. He had to convince an anxious authorizing environment that his novel system of internal accountability was preferable not only for his employees but also for children and families. And he had to find a way to build the operational capacity of his own organization and its many partners and coproducers despite a notoriously dysfunctional organizational culture and a round of brutal budget cuts.

But while the case touches on all points of the strategic triangle, Spence invested most heavily in developing operational capacity at the DSS. A well-developed operational capacity perspective might have helped guide him in his efforts to create an organization that strove simultaneously to meet external demands for performance and develop the internal systems that would make it accountable for learning (as well as compliance with policies and procedures).

Three Models of Internal Accountability
As DSS commissioner from 1993 to 1999, Carlisle focused on creating a tough internal accountability system rooted in a performance measurement system that allowed the central office to exercise close control over operating units of the department. On first glance her approach

resembled Compstat in form and spirit. She collected and published performance data much more frequently than past commissioners, and she used the data to hold midlevel managers (as well as frontline workers) accountable for their performance. But while Compstat focused on a social outcome (reduced crime), Carlisle's performance reviews focused principally on organizational outputs and compliance with operating processes and standards. Her system did not focus accountability on the relative safety of children but instead on whether required investigations were completed within the appropriate amount of time, and whether certain specified levels of contact with each family were maintained. This approach, which tended to reinforce a strict status hierarchy, had unfortunate consequences for the system's capacity to motivate and guide caseworkers. It alienated them from the experience of performing meaningful and valuable work. The disconnect between what the caseworkers valued and the basis on which their performance was being evaluated undermined the legitimacy of the management system and, by extension, the central office.

Because Carlisle's system did not focus on outcome measures, it also failed to give any indication of whether individual caseworkers and the broader agency were ultimately producing anything of value, or whether and how current policies might be improved. Without a way to link activities and outputs to outcomes, there were fewer opportunities to learn. And while overseers could be reassured that the DSS was being led by a hard-nosed, no-nonsense manager, Carlisle's system offered neither the legislature nor the broader public a full account of the public value the DSS was creating. Her account did not measure ultimate outcomes or client satisfaction and included only some measures of output and activity that the public valued intrinsically.

Coming in on Carlisle's heels, Commissioner Locke countered the backlash from frustrated midlevel managers and caseworkers with an easing up on process and organizational output-oriented accountability. He gave caseworkers more discretion in carrying out their work, relying more on his staff's sense of professional responsibility and less on their fear of punishment to produce valuable results. This "do right by the child" ethos may have been a relief to workers in the field, but it left the agency defenseless against the political firestorms that attended the all-but-inevitable errors or bad outcomes when they occurred. And, without some top-level attention focused on performance and results—measured either in outcome or activity terms—it became easy for both particularly good and particularly bad practices to go unnoticed and unremarked upon. This apparent disinterest could reduce morale and undermine efforts to learn as easily as an overly controlling system. Commissioner Locke could still rely on the professional training and commitment of his workers, and the personnel system that recruited them and screened them for the work. But without a well-maintained system to track action and results and provide feedback to employees, Locke's ability to build the operational capacity of his organization was severely hampered.

Spence chose a different path. He arrayed and dissected the tangle of values to be advanced through and reflected in DSS operations: protecting children from abuse and neglect; creating safe but also permanent and (ideally) familiar home environments for children; protecting not only the rights of children to be free of abuse and neglect but also the rights of parents to maintain their family's privacy and raise their children as they saw fit; and, finally, maximizing the efficiency and effectiveness of the DSS on a restricted budget. He focused not just on valued outcomes but also on values attached to the means used to get the outcomes—an approach to casework that was "child-driven, family centered, [and] strength-based." He used not only quantitative outcome measures but also qualitative data to help the DSS search for better methods of accomplishing desired results. Instead of using performance failures as an occasion for finding a scapegoat, he used them as an occasion for analysis and reflection throughout the organization. Instead of limiting his attention to conversations with midlevel managers, he went deeper and wider into the organization, reaching out to the caseworkers who knew the real conditions in the families that the DSS hoped to help and did the day-to-day work. Instead of relying principally on top-down accountability and control, he emphasized mutual accountability, particularly peer-to-peer accountability among individual caseworkers with shared desires to do a good job and to improve as professionals. In these respects he distributed his attention across the different elements of the public value scorecard.

For the purposes of this discussion, we could imagine that the management systems previously described represent three different ideas about how to create internal accountability. The first model comes from the bad old days of public bureaucracy, when government employees, drilled on policies and procedures, answered to the next level in the chain of command for reliably adhering to those policies and procedures. Carlisle's system did not manage to move the DSS too far from this compliance-based model. It did, however, result in the creation of a strong information system that could produce quantitative data about organizational outputs and link the data to individual case files.

The second model comes from professional organizations like universities and hospitals, which rely on the selection and training of personnel to create a professional culture that motivates employees to perform well in pursuit of personal pride, satisfaction, and virtue, with less reliance on supervision and oversight. In such organizations, policies and procedures function more like guidelines than rules, and frontline workers are expected to use their professional discretion to make the best response to the unique circumstances they confront. Locke seemed content to follow this model but lacked either the personnel systems or organizational culture to support it.

Between these two poles, various models have begun to find their way from the private to the public sector. These models hold midlevel managers (and, through them, frontline workers) accountable for achieving desired results but give them some freedom to experiment with different methods and place a greater emphasis on reflecting on practices and using errors constructively to improve future performance.[42] Spence looked to build performance management systems somewhere in this middle ground.

The Simple Analytics of Internal Accountability Systems

At root, these performance management systems are different combinations of five basic elements that characterize all internal accountability systems. These elements mirror the four components of principal-agent accountability relationships that were outlined in Chapter 3, but they add a crucial fifth consideration: the forums developed to allow and encourage organizational learning.[43]

1. Assignment of Accountability. Does the system divide up responsibilities, tasks, and assets so that accountability is assigned separately to each individual manager and employee? Or, does the system hold individuals jointly and severally accountable for

achieving an overall result? Are individuals accountable for helping one another? Do they feel personal responsibility for the performance of the organization as a whole?

2. Focus of Accountability. Where along the value chain are individuals' responsibilities concentrated? Does the system emphasize controlling assets to ensure proper stewardship? Compliance with prescribed policies and procedures? The quantity and quality of the organization's outputs? The satisfaction of the organization's clients? The achievement of the public's desired outcomes? Or, does it focus on a thoughtful analysis of how inputs are converted into public value?

3. Information Systems to Support Accountability. What particular information does the organization systematically collect and use in the performance measurement systems that will allow it to assess and discuss the performance of managers and employees? Is the system essentially a closed system that will allow only certain kinds of data into discussions about performance, or is it flexible and open to new information that managers and employees would like to add? Are the data only quantitative, or can qualitative data be introduced? Do they come only from organizational records, or can anecdotal ideas, observations, and ideas be introduced? Does the organization operate exclusively or primarily with a fixed, formal system with only a few data elements, or does it try to develop and make use of a data-rich environment?

4. Sanctions and Rewards to Make the Accountability Real. How does the organization respond to reviews of managerial or employee performance as revealed in the performance measurement system? Are there real consequences for good and bad performances that resonate in individual managers' lives? Are there rewards for good performance as well as punishments for bad? Are the sanctions big or small in the lives of those being sanctioned? Are the sanctions perceived as fair to individuals and legitimate in terms of serving an appropriate organizational purpose, or are they seen as arbitrary?

5. Forums to Make Accountability Useful for Organizational Learning. Finally, what sort of dialogue and discussion grows out of the organization's performance measurement and management systems? Is it a one-way process in which top managers

use performance information as an objective basis for judging comparative performance, or is there a two-way conversation in which an effort is made to understand why good or bad performance occurred without assuming that the answer lies in the motivation, effort, and competence of the manager or employee? If it is a two-way conversation, how rigorous is it in seeking out the causes of success and failure? Is the conversation private or public? If it is public, is it simply public within the organization, or does it include clients and overseers from outside the organization?

It should be clear that within this standard frame of accountability, one can construct many different organizational systems that create different kinds of accountability. Table 7.2 shows how some of the systems examined in this chapter arrange these elements of accountability. Which approach a manager chooses is partly a function of how the manager understands the motivations and capacities of his or her staff, how much the manager believes in the efficacy of existing policies and procedures, and how the manager understands the relationship between the people and the task.

Compliance bureaucracies assume that they cannot count on the capacities and motivations of managers and employees, that existing policies and procedures are reliable methods for achieving desired results, and that the best form of accountability is to insist on compliance with existing policies and procedures. This is what Spence describes as the "industrial model" of organizational management. As noted in Chapter 4, such a system can work reasonably well if policies, processes, and procedures have been technically well designed to achieve the desired results, if most of the variables that affect progress toward desired results are under the control of the public agency, and if the client population and material conditions with which the agency works are generally homogeneous and stable. If any of these conditions are not present, however, the organization will have trouble adjusting to and performing in variable and changing conditions.

In the professional association model, accountability and control systems proceed on the opposite assumptions: the real strength of the organization lies precisely in the motivations, skills, and knowledge of its managers and employees; the existing policies and procedures of the

Table 7.2. Different forms of accountability and performance management systems.

	Compliance model (Carlisle)	Pure professional model (Locke)	Learning model (Spence)
Assignment of accountability	Individual	Individual	System (and individual)
Focus of accountability	Policies, processes, and procedures	Professional credentials and commitments	Professional credentials and commitments; reflective practice
Information systems to support accountability	Process indicators; compliance audits	Negative outcomes	Process measures; process reviews; outcome measures; outcome reviews; negative outcomes
Sanctions in accountability	Negative sanctions for failure to hit targets		Protection from "conscientious error"; support for development
Forums for discussion and learning	Top-down control; strict liability		Frequent, team-led discussion of practices supported by central office

organization are not sufficient to guarantee desired results; and workers should share accountability for interpreting and modifying existing policies and procedures in particular as well as in general circumstances. Accountability is not absent in such organizations; it simply changes its form. The accountability is for the conscientious pursuit of improved performance rather than compliance with policies and procedures. Such management systems tend to work best for organizations confronting highly variable conditions. Their success, however, depends crucially on having systems that can (1) attract, select, and train highly motivated, skilled, and committed individuals and (2) build and sustain a professional culture committed to performance and learning without the need for too many extrinsic rewards and penalties.

Somewhere between these extremes lies Compstat—and the many public-sector performance management systems it has inspired. Compstat started with the kind of tight accountability and discipline associated with both old-fashioned bureaucracies and the bottom-line ethos of private firms. It assigned responsibility for performance to particular individuals in the organization. It called them to account for improved performance and sanctioned them for failure to meet performance standards. But as Compstat developed at the New York City Police Department and other police departments and was adapted by other kinds of public agencies in various "org-stat" and "citistat" management systems, it began to depart from the compliance model. It encouraged managers to experiment and innovate—either to deal with particular unique problems or to find more powerful general methods. Instead of generating a one-way discussion in which top management questions the commitment and methods of subordinate managers, the system shifted to a broader deliberation in which top-level managers, midlevel managers, and members of the authorizing environment were invited to think about how stubborn problems could be solved.

What remains unclear about Compstat and its imitators is how the leadership style and administrative systems have evolved to support the professional development and learning side of the performance management system. On one hand, insofar as the whole system increased the sense of responsibility and agency among midlevel managers, invited them to use their own imaginations, and encouraged a two-way discussion about what should be done, it had some features of a professional, learning organization. On the other hand, to the extent that the system focused on punishing bad performance, and remained suspicious of the motivations and capacities of the professionals who staffed the organization, some potentially important features of a professional learning organization were compromised.

Making a Difference in Performance

To repeat a point made in Chapter 2, given a certain stock of resources, a performance management system can help an organization improve its performance in two ways. The system could drive those in the organization to work harder—to pour greater, more conscientious effort into their work. Or, the system could help the organization work smarter—improving its methods through experimentation, testing, and learning.[44] Some—maybe many—of these improvised methods might perform less well than standard methods, but some of those methods might also succeed and point the way toward improved performance.

Both "industrial" and "professional" accountability models make particular assumptions about how operating organizations become smarter. Industrial models assume that organizations have a core technology, or perhaps a few core processes that they use over and over again to achieve their goals. To reduce crime, a police department arrests or threatens to arrest individuals who break the law and relies on the basic methods of patrol, rapid response, and retrospective investigation to accomplish that goal. To protect children, a child protection agency investigates allegations of abuse and neglect, develops service plans to help families avoid future incidents, and determines when it is necessary to move a child to a safer living environment. Embedded in these core processes are thousands of particular policies and procedures designed to ensure that the organizations can carry out these core functions reasonably well. From this perspective, working smarter means making a top-down change in the core operating technology that creates a productivity gain across the board.

Professional models tend to think that an organization's success depends on a large number of individual responses to an equally large number of circumstances. In a very heterogeneous and dynamic task environment, the general methods designed for the last decade's average case might not work for the particular case now at hand. More precisely, the old procedures might provide a basis for beginning to think about this week's case, but there is room for experimentation and potential improvement in adapting the old general methods to the new particular case. If the particular cases are small-stakes, and the improvised adaptation is nothing too radical, then de jure or de facto discretion can accommodate the variability of cases.

Though we often assume that most public agencies are stuck in the "industrial model," these innovations, which tend to come from the bottom rather than the top, happen often in many public agencies. The problem is that many go unexploited and unacknowledged by top managers or the broader authorizing environment. This lack of recognition from the top is a pity, because sometimes these small innovations, when accumulated, can become the basis for significant improvements in organizational performance. Sometimes an improvised small solution turns out to be the solution for cases that come up not once in a thousand days but once every ten days, indicating that the organization needs to recognize, test, and codify this particular innovation. And sometimes the improvised small solution reveals something important about how the overall core operations of the organization might change so that the daily practice of everyone in the organization can improve.

The distinction between large, top-down programmatic innovations and the bottom-up accumulation of small improvements can be likened to the private sector's distinction between production line organizations and job shops.[45] In a production line organization, the company is built on a core production system that both enables and constrains what it does. In one vivid example, Burger King could only meet the challenge from McDonald's quarter pounder (which was a thicker version of its standard burger) by creating the whopper (which was a wider version of its standard burger) because Burger King's core production process relied on burgers moving along a conveyor belt that fixed the amount of time heat could be applied to the burger. It could not make a thicker burger without leaving it very rare, or running it through the conveyor belt twice. Because McDonald's put its hamburgers on a grill, it could vary the cooking time and make a thicker burger.[46] Production-line organizations make certain commitments in the way they organize their standard production process. They retain some capacity to customize, but only around the edges of their standard process.

Job shops, in contrast, are all about customization. Each new task that shows up is a fresh design problem—a challenge to the existing methods of the organization. Architecture firms, business consultancies, and firms that make customized machine tools are all job shops. Of course, such firms rely on what they have learned from their past experience and usually start with some basics that seem to come up over and over again. But they do not assume that the current task is exactly, or even very much, like the old task. Instead, they assume that to perform well they might have to invent some wholly new methods, or combine old methods in new ways.

In reality, production-line organizations and job shops anchor different ends of a continuum. Hospitals, schools, police departments, and child protection agencies all combine these features. They have basic methods that work for all cases, basic methods that work for well-understood varieties of cases, customized methods that deal with novel circumstances, and new methods that occasionally revolutionize the basic methods. All of these organizations have some basic knowledge about how to do their work, but their knowledge is incomplete (both in the sense that they do not know how best to deal with the novel circumstances they encounter and in the sense that they might not yet have discovered the best way of dealing with the usual cases). Because their knowledge is incomplete, they have to become learning organizations as well as performing organizations. And the learning part of the organization sometimes has to challenge the performing part of the organization.

Performance management systems can drive organizations toward improved performance if they produce increased effort with the same stock of resources, or if they help the organization develop and use more effective methods (whether this means major changes in core technologies, the development of new methods for more or less particular tasks, or a large number of small adaptations that improve performance in individual cases but hold few lessons for general management).[47] An effective performance management system would motivate a workforce both to work harder and to experiment and innovate conscientiously (i.e., work smarter).

Professional, Peer-to-Peer Accountability for the DSS

As he thought about how to improve the DSS' performance, Spence considered the various accountability models described earlier. The complexity of the tasks that DSS caseworkers faced made Spence wary of the industrial model. In his view the route to improved performance was not through the reliable execution of existing policies and procedures but, instead, through the conscientious efforts of caseworkers to diagnose the unique conditions of each situation and tailor their interventions accordingly. Those on both sides of the encounter would judge this kind of response more effective because it seemed both attuned to the client's particular circumstances (a made-to-order intervention works better at a technical level than a one-size-fits-all intervention) and more respectful of the client. Spence thought that respect for the assistance being offered might in itself be an active ingredient in the effort to restructure the relationship between caretakers and children. All of these considerations led him to believe that caseworkers would do better work if they were encouraged to follow their own judgment (shaped through professional training and experience and guided by past policies and procedures as a codification of good past practice) rather than feeling compelled to follow existing policies and procedures. This seems to have been the thinking behind Spence's commitment to teaming. Peer relationships rather than bureaucratic control would motivate caseworkers to work a bit harder for the sake of professional satisfaction, to develop technically superior interventions for particular circumstances, and to engage clients in working toward happier and healthier caretaking relationships.

As in the case of Project Chance, the risks of embracing the professional model (relying on the clinical judgment of individual caseworkers) over the industrial model (adhering to policies and procedures) begin with the variability that relying on this kind of discretion would inevitably introduce into DSS conduct vis-à-vis clients. Spence thought that such variability would be beneficial, since it created both the prospect of improving performance in individual cases in the short run and finding better methods for dealing with a broad class of cases over the long run. If, however, the people of Massachusetts thought it was important for the DSS to behave consistently with respect to its clients to ensure a certain kind of fairness in its operations, then encouraging caseworkers to use their discretion conscientiously could be seen not simply as a risk but as a degradation of the performance of the agency on at least one dimension of value (horizontal fairness).

Solving the Problem of Accountability, Discretion, and Learning
As noted earlier in this chapter, these issues make the use of professional discretion simultaneously a potential virtue and a potential problem. If reliable and responsible workers are given some degree of de jure discretion and prove themselves to be well motivated and competent in the use of that discretion, then public agencies can do more just and effective work. To get this desired result, however, agencies have to monitor workers as they use their discretion. Without oversight, there is too much room for mischief to creep into agency operations. Moreover, there is no way for the organization as a whole to learn from the exceptions. Observing, and then discussing, the use of worker discretion is necessary to ensure that the case genuinely was an exception that presented unique challenges and could not be handled just as well by existing routines. Discussing the basis for making exceptions to the rules also presents an opportunity to improve the quality of the improvised response, since it would draw on the expertise of several rather than just one. Finally, open discussions about the handling of individual

cases would create an occasion for reflection and learning in the organization. For all these reasons, discussion would be important as a condition that encumbered the use of discretion.

The need for discussion presents an important question: Who should participate in that discussion? One possible answer is that caseworkers should have the discussion with their bureaucratic superiors, perhaps even the top management of the organization. This is the best answer, given two conditions: (1) bureaucratic superiors have superior knowledge and judgment and (2) the need for making adaptations is relatively rare. If, however, bureaucratic superiors are not uniquely knowledgeable, or the need to adapt standard practice comes up often, then peer consultation might represent the best way to keep workers accountable for the use of discretion.

Spence judged peer consultation to be much more important than consultation along hierarchical lines. He thought that peers were more likely to have useful substantive information. He thought caseworkers could absorb advice and criticism from one another more easily than they could from their bosses. And he thought that lessons learned would spread more quickly through the organization. These essential beliefs informed his ideas about how to structure accountability and measure performance at the DSS. He envisioned and built processes to encourage rippling discussions across the organization that would simultaneously celebrate professional discretion, call it to account, and improve its substantive quality over time. He was willing to sacrifice the appearance of tight accountability for a kind of mutual accountability that could draw the best performance out of caseworkers.

This seemingly looser form of accountability could work well for an agency under enormous pressure to produce zero errors, for two reasons. First, it would allow the organization to tailor its response to cases as needed and would give it a chance to learn and systematize its knowledge over time. Second, it would have far greater potential to engage the hearts and minds of workers than an industrial, compliance-based system. Precisely because organizational hierarchies and rules fail to capture the complexity of the tasks and undermine caseworkers' initiative, morale, and sense of responsibility, Spence decided to cast his lot with professional, peer-to-peer accountability. Peer discussion works for all the reasons the industrial model does not—it allows for complexity, maximizes the chance to cope with it in the short run, and helps individuals who are facing overwhelming problems to do so with the right mix of confidence and humility. It also seems to create the conditions under which the organization can learn most quickly and effectively from its own operating experience.

Spence's goal was to create a learning organization that could win tolerance for inevitable errors in the short run by promising steady improvement over the long run. Orchestrating the continuing series of performance-oriented discussions that would push this agenda throughout the organization meant simultaneously shifting both the organizational culture and the administrative systems on which the DSS relied to structure and organize its working relationships and methods.

Looking to Private-Sector Learning Organizations

Perhaps we should not be too surprised that public managers have been gravitating toward more complex performance management systems that favor creating professional accountability for conscientious work over either a rigid bureaucratic model that demands compliance with policies and procedures or a ruthless performance-based model that demands the achievement of outcomes without too much concern for the means used. Many private companies have been moving in this direction over the last several decades as well.[48]

One of the powerful forces that sparked this change was the growing recognition of the importance of innovation in business. This began with the recognition that what distinguished companies that were successful over a long period of time was not their ability to do one particular thing well (though it was important for them to "stick to their knitting" and focus on doing one or two particular things very well at any given time) but their ability to adapt to the changing conditions in their markets.[49] This meant developing new products or new features for old products, or taking advantage of new technologies to improve their production processes, and so on. The only way that a firm could consistently make above-average returns in a dynamic, competitive market was to constantly develop new products and processes that took advantage of temporary niches in the market where above-market returns could be realized.[50]

This general insight was followed by a focus on CQI—a set of managerial devices through which employees working in production and service activities were encouraged to examine their own work practices and make suggestions for improvement.[51] These practices provided employees with direct and timely access to top-level managers and cut through the ordinary bureaucratic processes of making and reviewing proposals that moved so slowly that no frontline employee had much incentive to offer an idea for improvement.[52] CQI brought the shop floor directly into the executive suites so that necessary changes could be made quickly and reliably—not just in one location but throughout the firm.[53]

The focus on innovation in process, product, and competitive positioning also moved business authors and scholars to recommend collecting and using a much denser body of information to help companies operate more efficiently and reposition themselves more effectively. Robert Kaplan and David Norton's argument, that firms should pay attention not only to financial measures of performance but also to the customer perspective, the operational perspective, and the learning perspective, is just one example of this trend.[54] The private sector came around to the idea that the really important managerial questions were about the future. The future would be built on a strategic vision that was itself built on information about what customers wanted and how operations could be made better and more consistent over time. In order to plan for the future, and to monitor investments made to exploit the potential opportunities, companies needed lots of nonfinancial information about the market environment and about its own operations. Firms needed data-rich environments if they were going to remain innovative in their thought and dynamic in their operations.[55]

To create organizations that could move quickly to exploit new market niches, private managers had to maintain strong methods for monitoring financial performance. Increasing shareholder value remained the fundamental imperative for business and the core accountability framework that kept everyone focused on performance, but the pursuit of future financial performance required firms to look forward (into future costs and revenues), outward (into the markets), and inward (at their own production processes).[56] The firms that would succeed would be those that could move most quickly to exploit new opportunities and stay in the niche the longest.

To speed up the rate of innovation at all levels, firms invited more individuals to nominate ideas for action. The process of imagining and developing innovations shifted from the top of the organization to the middle and bottom—the people who were closest to both customers and production processes and who would, in any case, have to embrace any proposed innovation from the top.

CQI and learning models also altered the basic structure of individual accountability. Individual employees at the managerial and operational levels remained accountable up through the hierarchical chain of command, but their accountability began to extend outward as well. They became accountable to their bureaucratic peers and their customers as well as to their bosses. And there was a general sense that accountability between the top and the bottom of the organization was mutual rather than hierarchical. Bosses were understood to have responsibilities to subordinates, as well as the other way around, and accountability to a boss could be trumped by accountability to the customer, to peers, or to the wider set of values that a company was trying to reflect and produce in its operations.

In these respects Spence was following the advance guard of private business when he developed his management philosophy for the DSS. It was important for him to keep everyone's attention on the value to be created, and to keep pressing for improved performance—but it was a mistake to imagine that improved performance lay only in following existing policies and procedures. In fact, improved performance probably lay in exploring new possibilities in producing old products and services as well as developing new products and services that could serve existing goals more effectively. To make this possibility a reality, Spence had to engage caseworkers in the search for improved performance. The task was not simply to get workers to give their time and their fidelity to existing policies and procedures but to engage their minds.[57] And to engage their minds, Spence had to find a way to engage their hearts as well. He thought the best way to do that was to hold open a vision of what could be accomplished and to give them a prominent role in imagining and executing that vision. The administrative control systems had to be adapted. They needed not only to provide a certain amount of tension and accountability but also to support efforts to improve performance on all dimensions rather than to coerce or bully workers into doing a good job.

So even as the virtues of a kind of crude bottom-line accountability were being pressed on public agencies as the solution to their performance

problems, business was migrating toward a different model of accountability. The new kind of accountability was not any less exacting. Financial information continued to be reported and used in the evaluation of particular lines of business and particular managers. But the
new model sought to create a kind of accountability that was broader
and more demanding than the old one. The employees of the organization would be responsible for the future as well as the present. They
would be responsible for the nonfinancial as well as the financial. They
would be responsible for being thoughtful and innovative as well as
reliable. They would be asked to commit their minds and hearts to continuous improvement rather than simply producing a consistent product. And the measurement and management systems that could support
this work more closely resembled the learning model of accountability
that Spence tried to create than the cartoon of accountability for which
Compstat is so often mistaken.

Creating Organizational Conditions for Professional Accountability
Trying to build an organizational culture and a performance measurement system that could turn the DSS into a learning organization was
a lot to take on, and Spence took care to develop and promote particular conditions and working relationships within the agency. The list
that follows, which enumerates these conditions and working relationships, could serve well as a rudimentary operational capacity perspective for Spence's putative public value scorecard. Each condition
could be supported with empirical performance data (mostly gathered
through surveys) that would help guide the execution of Spence's strategy for the DSS.

- a widely shared vision of the organization's mission and values,
  and a collective determination to act in the furtherance of and in
  accordance with those values[58]
- shared leadership and decision making
- leadership based less on control and more on guidance and
  support
- working relations that emphasized teamwork, cooperation, and
  the sharing of knowledge, information, and responsibility
- an internal culture that supported acknowledging error as a
  means to learning and improvement

- continuous reflection, inquiry, and learning at all levels of the organization
- an emphasis on the development of long-term, sustainable strategies rather than quick fixes to problems

This list, in addition to serving as a set of goals to be pursued and measured in the operational capacity perspective of a public value scorecard, can also be seen in the context of the considerations about how best to structure the internal accountability of the DSS described in the analytic schema developed earlier for characterizing different kinds of accountability and performance management systems. We can locate Spence's particular system of accountability in that schema by seeing what particular choices he made with respect to each consideration.

Spence's choices began with a less sharp focus on assigning specific responsibility to particular individuals. Individuals were invited to take responsibility for their actions, but their individual responsibilities seemed to have less sharp boundaries than in the classic compliance bureaucracy, or in the Compstat-inspired models that created strict accountability for outcomes rather than process. The responsibilities assigned to caseworkers were not theirs alone; others were expected to contribute. And their specific responsibilities were not limited to their particular caseloads; caseworkers were expected to contribute to the success of others in their casework as well. As members of "teams," individuals were "severally and jointly," as well as individually, held accountable.

Similarly, the focus of each individual's joint and several responsibilities extended all along the value chain, from inputs, to activities, to social outcomes. Everyone was supposed to be accountable not only for reliably executing existing procedures but also for evaluating how well those procedures worked to achieve desired outcomes, recognizing errors, and developing new and better procedures. The emphasis on learning meant that all the information in the organization—the information held in the heads of experienced professionals as well as the information held in records or summarized in information systems—had to be available for examination.[59]

To make this collegial, future-oriented approach work, the central office had to relax its sanctioning system. The agency used fewer extrinsic rewards and punishments and did not necessarily tie what sanctions it applied to specific performance measures. The expectation was that the relaxed sanctioning system would allow individual officers in the organization to feel more free to confess error and to work collaboratively.

Finally, Spence's performance management system sought to create a broad, continuous conversation across all levels of the organization about performance and how it might be improved at both the individual and organizational levels.

The Information Side of Accountable, Professionalized Learning Organizations

On the basis of this analysis, Spence seemed to embrace a professional model that depended primarily on professional motivations and commitments to ensure performance. But given the importance and sensitivity of child protection, the public would not tolerate a system with no external, top-down controls and no way to decide who or what was at fault when errors occurred. To create a professional organization with enough top-down accountability to meet the public's demands for accountability, Spence had to build a performance management and measurement system that combined the virtues of a value-oriented, Compstat-style management system with those of a professional organization that relied primarily on professional motivations and capacities continuously reinforced and developed through peer-to-peer learning processes. His success in doing this would depend a great deal on the culture he fostered at the DSS and the attitudes and practices he managed to instill in his managers, contractors, and caseworkers. But it would also depend on the structure of information that he built to document and allow the exploration and review of the organization's operations.

There may be many variations among different learning organizations in the methods they use to influence organizational culture and to collect and use data, but all learning organizations are different from the usual performance management systems that still pervade the public sector.

- Learning organizations focus on outcomes but also pay attention to processes, seeking to improve them. (How else can they learn what works and what does not?)

- Learning organizations rely on formally established performance measurement systems but also make other, more ad hoc efforts to gather information, including the widespread use of individual case material. They try to use what they have learned in the past to ensure consistent high-level performance but also deliberately encourage and evaluate variability in operations.
- Learning organizations call their workers to account, but sanctions are less automatic and more open to discussion about the merits and shortcomings of individuals' performance.
- Learning organizations believe that knowledge lies at the bottom of organizations as well as at the top, and they develop methods of consulting the bottom to benefit from that knowledge.
- Learning organizations do not want to give up a sharp focus on performance, reliability, and zero tolerance of errors but think that the best way to approach these goals is to focus on continuous learning and improvement.

To provide the information infrastructure to support this kind of accountability, Spence developed a variety of performance measurement systems that focused relentlessly on the quality of the organization's casework. Improving casework was the point of the various processes he created to support reflection and critical discussion inside the organization: the critical incident case reviews that focused the organization's attention on bad outcomes and what, if anything, could have been done to prevent them; the continuous quality improvement teams that searched for improved methods of handling more ordinary cases; the Child Welfare Institute that trained caseworkers; and the quality of service reviews and learning processes that systematically engaged caseworkers in and across regional and area offices in working together to improve performance. All of this activity relied on detailed information about families, about state interventions in families' lives and relationships, and about the outcomes of those interventions. Quantitative and qualitative data on both outcomes and processes were the basis for a multitude of professional discussions among peers about whether each member of the organization was doing her or his best to advance the overall goals of the organization. While no small amount of accountability ran through such a system, it very much differed in character from what Spence viewed as the industrial model of accountability. If Spence had been working with a public value scorecard, the development and use of this alternative system of accountability would have been a critical part of his operational capacity perspective.

Of course, there are significant risks in embracing this form of accountability. There is the risk that organizations will become so absorbed in learning and talking about possibilities that they will forget to perform—that having finally made a commitment to focus on achieving outcomes, they will fall back on focusing on their internal processes and their own development. There is the risk that softening hierarchical accountability and encouraging conversation between top-level managers, midlevel managers, and workers will weaken the voltage that strict, top-down accountability runs through the organization. To Spence, however, these risks seemed worth taking in exchange for the possibility of getting a more wholehearted and conscientious effort from his organization, and the potential benefits that could come from continuously adapting to new and unique circumstances and learning from errors.

Structuring External Accountability: Coping with the
Political Demands for Zero Errors
The choices Spence made about how to structure the internal accountability of the organization seem reasonably well suited to the difficult task that he and the DSS faced. But while he may have chosen the performance management system that was most likely to animate and guide the DSS (and its partners, coproducers, and clients) toward enhanced public value creation, it was not at all clear that the system of internal accountability he had created would pass muster with the agency's many overseers.

In fact Spence faced a very significant strategic risk in committing his organization to the particular form of internal accountability that he judged was best designed to achieve its mission. Spence knew that some very bad incidents involving abused and neglected children would occur during his tenure, and that the public reaction would be to look once again at the adequacy of DSS policies and procedures, and the degree to which management was able to insist on and get compliance with those policies and procedures. That was the model of accountability that the public expected to find in the department. When it was discovered that Spence had a much different kind of management system, there was the risk that this difference would make him look incompetent. The likelihood was that no one in the external authorizing environment would spend much time thinking about what form of accountability might work best for the DSS but would go immediately to whatever model overseers took to be the best general form.

Spence found himself caught between the public's desire to demand zero defects in DSS operations and insist on strict accountability and his own understanding that the demand for compliance was not the best way to improve performance—even in the short run, let alone the longer run. He fully understood that the public would hold his agency strictly responsible for any performance failure that occurred. If a child were killed, maimed, or seriously injured by his caretakers, or starved, degraded, and psychologically abused on a daily basis, the DSS would be called to account for that failure. This would be true even when it had no prior knowledge of the case but especially if it had once heard of the particular case or was providing to the case some kind of service and continuous oversight.

Spence also fully understood that the DSS could not operate without bad results that would have to be accounted for as performance failures. He lacked sufficient money and authority, and sufficient knowledge, about how to use the money and authority he was granted to guarantee that no child in the Commonwealth would be victimized. He could not expect to be given additional resources, or to suddenly develop superior methods for finding cases, intervening with families, or knowing when to stop making the effort with a given family. All he could do was work with what he had to try to improve his performance. To do that he had to be able to motivate his workforce through their professional aspirations and to develop their professional skills while simultaneously holding them strictly accountable for their performance—a task that was made easier by the assumption that they were all motivated to do a good job, and it was only their unreliable methods that threatened performance.

Spence saw that he would need to create some space within the organization where errors could be identified and discussed honestly and openly and experiments could be conducted with new methods to see if performance could be improved. Facilitating these discussions meant making an explicit distinction between the bad results that occurred from human negligence, on one hand, and the bad results that came from the limitations of existing technologies and human judgment, on the other.

It is hard for the public to accept that even operating at peak performance and using the best current systems for producing desired results, the DSS might fail to protect every child in Massachusetts from serious instances of violence. Given all we have learned about the importance of embracing external accountability for reaching ambitious goals, it is somewhat counterintuitive that Spence might have had to soften or reduce the public's expectations about the agency's accountability, making it accountable not for perfect performance but for constant improvement—a very different, and perhaps more reasonable, goal in this and many other public-sector operations. Like John James at the Minnesota Department of Revenue, Spence had to find a way to capture the attention of his overseers and help them understand the nature of the work they had asked him to do before the glare of performance failures put him on the defensive. He had to hope that the politicians would hold steady in the terms of accountability that they had negotiated with him when the shit hit the fan.

If Spence had been relying on our model of strategic management in government, and had built a public value scorecard to focus his own and his organization's attention on the work necessary to execute and sustain a value-creating strategy, the scorecard's legitimacy and support perspective would have raised the vital question of how best to manage his external accountability. It would also have encouraged him to identify the steps he needed to take to reduce this strategic risk.

In the actual case, Spence, following a less ambitious approach than James, decided to engage his overseers in a dialogue through a series of open letters addressed internally to his own staff but also to the legislature and the governor. In these letters he tried to create a shared understanding of the nature of the work that the DSS does, and the form of accountability that he believed would work best for the agency. The letters aimed to get everyone used to the idea that a system of accountability (and performance measurement) should be designed to improve performance over the long term as well as the short term and to engage the staff's professional commitments rather than simply command their time and energy. It should focus on outcomes. It should insist on accountability for conscientious casework, not just for outcomes or compliance with existing policies and procedures. The performance management system that supported the DSS' work would include all the federally mandated data but also a sustained conversation among peers that would keep the pressure on for performance but also allow creativity and learning. Spence had to persuade his authorizers that even though this system looked less "tough" and exacting than a system rooted only in quantitative measures of compliance with policies and procedures, it might actually be more demanding and exacting than the usual systems and, in any case, might allow greater opportunities for learning.

This campaign to mobilize the support of the external authorizing environment for the new form of accountability that Spence was creating worked up to a point. Nobody in the external environment tried to stop him, and he heard some mutterings of support. Yet, despite his best efforts, as soon as a bad incident occurred, Spence found himself under enormous pressure to go back to the old way of doing things—to serve up a scapegoat in the form of a caseworker who did not follow policies and procedures that would have ensured effective performance. To his credit, Spence resisted this pressure and continued developing a learning organization. But there was a price to be paid, and the price was paid in the form of diminished political support, leaving Spence vulnerable when a new governor took office. He might not have had to pay this price if he had not only seen the importance of taking action to build legitimacy and support but also had used a public value scorecard to monitor the impact of his efforts to win over the legislature or, more broadly, to help the wider public understand the nature of the problem as Diana Gale did. This would have required a much larger public relations effort, but in the end it might have given Spence a greater chance of surviving to carry on his good work.

Summary

Spence entered the DSS as a neophyte in the world of child protective services. He was not a professional social worker imbued with the values and knowledge of the profession that he sought to lead to improved performance. He knew just enough to be confident that his organization

PUBLIC VALUE ACCOUNT for Harry Spence and the Massachusetts DSS

PUBLIC VALUE ACCOUNT	
Use of Collectively Owned Assets and Associated Costs	Achievement of Collectively Valued Social Outcomes
Financial Costs	Mission Achievement
Internal (administrative)	Protect children from abuse and
External (costs to families)	neglect by parents and other
	caretakers
	Provide safe, long-term homes for
	at-risk children
	Ensure positive long-term outcomes
	for children in system
Unintended Negative Consequences	Unintended Positive Consequences
Family break-ups	Adoptions by caretakers unable to
Relocation of children	have children of their own
	Client Satisfaction
	Treat clients with respect
	Engage and support caretakers
Social Costs of Using State Authority	Justice and Fairness
Intrusions into families	Give all children in system an equal
Relationships structured by court	chance to succeed as adults
orders	Protect parental rights
Terminations of parental rights	Enforce parental duties
	Treat cases equally
	Respect cultural differences

Figure 7.2. Public value scorecard for Harry Spence and the Massachusetts DSS.

THE LEGITIMACY AND SUPPORT PERSPECTIVE
Progress and Planning for Harry Spence and the Massachusetts DSS

Mission Alignment with Values Articulated by Citizens:
Sought balance in "Bermuda Triangle" of child protection values

Inclusion of Neglected Values with Latent Constituencies
Build public tolerance of bad outcomes and conscientious errors
Engage public support for social workers handling "wicked problems"

Standing with Formal Authorizers:
Sent letters to legislators proposing new terms of accountability
Increased transparency of operations
Sustain engagement to secure commitment to new terms

Standing with Key Interest Groups:
Aligned goals of DSS with dominant expert views in child welfare

Media Coverage:
Increased transparency in agency's approach to crises
Engage media in understanding and explaining new terms of accountability

Standing with Individuals in Polity:
General Citizenry
• *Help citizens understand and accept new terms of accountability*
Clients
• *Survey clients about experience of services and pressures to meet obligations*

Engagement of Citizens as Co-Producers:
Develop role of citizens as reporters
Develop potential role of citizens as support to families

THE OPERATIONAL CAPACITY PERSPECTIVE
Progress and Planning for Harry Spence and the Massachusetts DSS

Flow of Resources to Enterprise:
Financial Revenues
• Absorbed major budget cuts
Public Support/Popular Opinion
• *Build more support for mission among citizens by shaping expectations*

Human Resources:
Status of Workforce
• Built morale by reducing isolation, increasing support to caseworkers
Training/Professional Development of Staff
• Built competence through professional development efforts
• Gave new responsibilities to midlevel managers
Performance Measurement Systems for Individual Accountability
• Maintained accountability through transparency and peer-to-peer learning

Operational Policies, Programs and Procedures:
Quality of Operational Performance
• Maintained existing policies and procedures as guidelines
• Established six core practice values for casework as a set of professional standards to guide caseworkers
Organizational Learning
• Involved entire organization in reviews of existing policies and procedures
• Used "critical incidents" to evaluate performance of system, not individuals
• Initiated team model for casework to reinforce culture of reflection, learning, and mutual accountability
Performance Measurement and Management Systems
• Used qualitative data to supplement and elucidate quantitative data
• Maintained regular performance reviews
• Used performance data as basis for discussion, not reprobation

Organizational Outputs:
Quality of Outputs
• Reduced clients' fear of arbitrary decisions in casework through teaming
• *Improve capacity to coordinate services to families*
• *Improve cultural competence in diagnosing conditions and developing plans*

would be held to a very high, exacting standard of performance, that some failures would be inevitable, and that these errors would generate public outrage. The first question before him was how he could construct an internal accountability system that could align the inherent difficulty of the work with exacting external demands for performance and the caseworkers' own aspirations in a management system that could not only sustain the organization's best efforts in the short term but also challenge it to improve over the longer term. The second question was how he could sustain support from his political authorizing environment for a system intended to do all this that was so different from the familiar (albeit dysfunctional) DSS accountability system.

Spence saw that the DSS confronted complex problems without the luxury of well-developed, codified procedures for producing reliable and effective solutions. Without reliable processes to enforce, he could have turned to outcome measures as the basis for establishing accountability and ensuring results. But because the procedures were unreliable, it was hard to tell when looking at a bad outcome whether it was the result of a failure to follow procedures that would have produced a good result or the unintended and unfortunate result of precisely following the procedures. And without the flexibility to experiment with new procedures, the organization would remain locked forever in its cycle of failure.

To escape this fate, Spence decided to develop and use the DSS' information and performance measurement systems to create an organization focused on continuous learning and improvement. A key part of that effort was committing the organization as a whole to conscientious, self-conscious professionalism in its work. In his mind that essentially cultural objective was not inconsistent with measurement and accountability; rather, measurement and accountability would be central to achieving it. What was different from the usual systems of accountability was that Spence's performance management system relied on a combination of qualitative and quantitative data, individual cases and aggregate statistics, and processes of peer accountability to create a constant internal discussion about the practice of casework and how it might be improved. In addition, when inevitable tragedies occurred, though they would be examined closely to discern any caseworker's negligence, the investigation, carried out through open discussion, would treat the tragedy as an occasion for the organization to learn about the strengths and weaknesses of its procedures. Ultimately, Spence built a performance measurement and management system that held DSS employees accountable not primarily for results or processes but for maintaining a kind of professional conscientiousness that revealed itself in the continuous review of both employees' daily activities and the terrible tragedies that occurred in the course of their work. He hoped that the focus on "good work" would improve performance not only in the short term but also the long term.[60]

Figure 7.2 presents a public value scorecard for Spence and the Massachusetts DSS.

Conclusion

It has been a long journey from William Bratton's efforts to energize the New York City Police Department (NYPD) and focus it on reducing crime to Harry Spence's attempt to turn the Massachusetts Department of Social Services (DSS) into an accountable and conscientious organization capable of learning and improving under enormous pressure. This book opened with the case of Compstat because that particular story has so often been held up as an example of how introducing the private sector's disciplined commitment to producing bottom-line value to public-sector organizations could bring much-needed energy and focus to government performance. According to the conventional interpretation, if public managers would only measure their agencies' performance in terms of some kind of bottom-line value and create management systems that hold everyone in the organization accountable for increasing the bottom line, as Bratton did, they could dramatically improve performance.

But, on review, this simple story quickly became complicated. It became clear that there were critical differences in the practical and normative contexts in which private and public managers work. While the arbiters of value in the private sector were individual customers whose choices to buy or not buy their products made companies accountable for value creation, the arbiters of value in the public sector were citizens, taxpayers, and their elected representatives rolled up into a collective that defined the social outcomes it wanted to achieve with public dollars and authority. While the private sector could rely primarily on voluntary transactions, the public sector often relied on the coercive power of the state, which brought into play concerns about justice and fairness as well as efficiency and effectiveness. While the private sector could rely heavily on financial measures to gauge value production, the public sector had to rely on specific nonfinancial measures of incommensurable values—and so on. Each of these differences in context required a significant adjustment in the way that public managers would need to think about the value they were creating and how to measure it. The simple private-sector model would not easily "go through" in this different context.

Equally important, it became clear that the simple story of strict accountability for bottom-line performance did not capture the most advanced and sophisticated uses of performance measurement and management systems in the private sector. To be sure, bottom-line financial accountability remains an important part of the performance measurement and management systems that private managers use to meet external demands for accountability and to create and impose organizational discipline. But it has also become clear that many for-profit private enterprises rely increasingly on different performance measures and different internal mechanisms of accountability. Many rely on "balanced scorecards" as performance measurement and management systems that can drive the execution of forward-looking strategies for improving their financial performance. They develop accountability systems that create room for innovation and creativity in learning organizations. And some even experiment with double and triple bottom lines that account for their performance with respect to the achievement of nonfinancial goals deemed to be socially valuable.

These complications pointed the way toward a somewhat different idea about how performance measurement and management systems could be used in the public sector, suggesting that the legend of Compstat might be due for reconsideration.

Rethinking the Legend of Compstat

Perhaps the legend of Compstat has taken root not because it is true but because the story appeals to a particular set of ideological ideas or political prejudices. Suppose that the features typically associated with Bratton's success (hard-nosed, bottom-line management) were not the only or even the most important features that allowed the system to survive, or to spread as a managerial practice in policing and across the public sector. Suppose that Compstat evolved from Bratton's notion of earning the "profit" of reduced crime for the citizens of New York City to an idea that public agencies should be accountable for producing the full set of results that citizens value. Suppose that as the system evolved, it improved in its capacity to improve organizational performance not only by driving it toward desired outcomes in the short term but also by helping political communities and police departments learn what values they really wanted to achieve and what methods would help them do so. Suppose that the best iterations of Compstat as a system of internal accountability that could drive performance ultimately took on many of the features that Spence tried to develop in the systems he constructed to support learning and to animate and guide the DSS in the short and long term.

If these speculations were true, those holding up Compstat as an ideal of "bottom-line management" in the public sector would have to consider the possibility that public agencies need more nuanced measurement and management systems—systems that could help them learn what citizens and their elected representatives want and expect them to do and how well current operational methods are working with respect to those desires and expectations, while simultaneously supporting and encouraging innovation to build operational capacity and strengthen working relationships with their partners and coproducers. To investigate these speculations, we have to look a bit more closely at the Compstat model as it was first conceived and as it developed through use in New York City and the many other police departments that took it up.

Accountability Makes Organizations Work Harder

One common explanation for the success of Compstat is that Bratton motivated the NYPD's precinct commanders through a kind of ultimatum: work harder at their jobs or lose them. At least one of the principal architects of Compstat, Jack Maple, thought that this was among the most crucial outcomes of Compstat. "I know something about the police that you don't," Maple once told me. "They don't work very hard." If precinct commanders could be motivated to work harder and, in turn, get the patrol officers and detectives working harder, Maple figured, the effective supply of officers on the street would go up substantially.

The other explanation for Compstat's success is that the system worked not only because it got precinct commanders and the department as a whole to work harder but also because it caused the organization to work smarter. This, too, is part of the familiar interpretation of Compstat. But there are two quite different versions of this story.

More Effective Methods of Policing

One says that Compstat succeeded because it required or motivated the NYPD to embrace new, more powerful general methods of policing. At least three different ideas about new police strategies could explain Compstat's success.

The War against Grime

One idea is that Compstat committed the NYPD to a specific idea about how best to reduce crime that had been set out in James Wilson and George Kelling's influential article, "Broken Windows: The Police and Neighborhood Safety." The theory had been dubbed the "war against grime" because it encouraged the police to focus special attention on minor disorder offenses.[1] This reversed a long-standing professional practice that had focused police departments throughout the United States on serious crimes such as murder, assault, rape, robbery, and burglary and had given less attention to public nuisance offenses such as public drinking, noise violations, and loitering.[2] The old practice of focusing on serious crimes had been justified in part for its presumed efficiency: it seemed to make sense to focus resources on the most serious crimes.[3] But the practice was also part of a commitment to fairness. Because enforcing disorder offenses typically required officers to use their individual discretion in proactive police methods, this was the arena where much police corruption and racial discrimination occurred. It followed that keeping the police away from this activity would therefore help the police avoid racial or class discrimination or corruption.

The justification for reversing this policy lay in three slightly different arguments. The first was rooted in a finding that the public feared minor offenses more than serious crimes.[4] If police were expected to reduce fear as well as (serious) crime, focusing on the minor offenses would help the police enhance the psychological experience of security.[5] Once police departments began to focus on minor offenses for these reasons, they discovered a new reason to focus on minor offenses: rates of serious crimes also seemed to decline.[6]

The second and third arguments for enforcing minor offenses grew out of two different explanations for this unexpected result. One was that reducing fear had allowed law-abiding citizens to reclaim the public spaces that had become dangerous, and that this made the spaces safer.[7] (This was the original "broken windows" theory.) The other explanation was that a focus on minor offenses allowed the police to arrest dangerous individuals and intervene in dangerous situations before serious crimes could occur. As the head of the New York City Transit Police, Bratton had shown that a crackdown on fare-beaters in the subway seemed to produce a reduction in subway robberies—perhaps because the fare-beaters were about to engage in robbery as well as fare-beating.[8] By a similar logic, if the police arrived at a scene where noisy youth were congregating, they might be able to prevent that situation from escalating into a knife or gun assault.

Real-Time Crime Information
Threaded through the rhetoric and reality of Compstat, however, was another theory about a second general method for controlling crime. Maple insisted that the police needed real-time information on the character and location of reported crimes. With this data they would be able to identify crime hot spots or general patterns in criminal offending and use this data to deter and control crime more effectively.[9]

Maple's enthusiasm for giving police real-time information about crime patterns was nothing particularly new in policing. In the 1930s police departments connected phones, cars, and radios to build the capacity to respond rapidly to crime calls. If the police could get to the scene faster, they might be able to stop crimes in progress. If the police suspected in advance that crimes might take place in a particular location and time, they could engage in "directed" rather than random patrols.

By the time of Compstat, however, this simple idea had evolved. The mapping of real-time information about crime spikes and hot spots allowed the police to be more inquisitive about causes and points of intervention, and more imaginative about plausibly effective tactics. As

Maple said, "The beauty of the map is that you can ask, 'Why is this happening?' 'What is the underlying cause?'" That could, in turn, stimulate a more thoughtful approach to policing that focused on crimes as problems to be solved rather than incidents to be handled through investigations and arrests.[10]

Department-Wide Strategies for Dealing with Specific Crimes

A third change in operational methods that observers of Compstat could claim helped the NYPD work smarter as well as harder was the command staff's development and promulgation of department-wide strategies to deal with the most significant crime issues facing New York—illegal firearms, youth violence, the drug trade, domestic violence, police corruption, auto-related crime, and the disorder offenses that undermined citizens' sense of safety on the roads and in public spaces.[11] In some sense these strategies moved toward the development of more specific interventions tailored to particular bursts of criminal activity that broke out in the city as hot spots or crime spikes.

Yet we can treat them as general, top-down strategies for three reasons. First, each strategy covers a very broad class of crimes. The strategies themselves are more specific than patrol and investigation, but they are still very broad. Second, the strategies were developed at the top of the organization and distributed through the department as recommended approaches. While they were presented as suggestions and guidelines, a risk-averse precinct commander who wanted to protect his professional reputation would be wiser to rely on these strategies than invent one anew. Third, and perhaps most important, the strategies had a lot in common; each seemed to emphasize increasing the proactive efforts of the police to make direct contact with the community. In effect, the seven different strategies all seemed to amount to one basic strategy: get the police onto the streets and into the faces of citizens.

The Core Crime Control Strategy of Compstat

In fact, looking across all the supposedly different substantive strategies of policing associated with Compstat—the war against grime, the use of real-time crime data, the development of recommended strategies to deal with specific high priority crimes—one finds a common core. The core idea was that instead of waiting for trouble to occur, the police should engage citizens proactively on the basis of their suspicions.

To students of police history, this was hardly a new crime control strategy for policing. It was the re-creation of a well-known police strategy, common in the early sixties, that had been described as "aggressive preventive patrol."[12] The literature on this strategy made it clear that while this tactic could reduce crime, it also tended to decrease legitimacy and support for the police—particularly among minority groups—and it has often set the stage for urban riots.[13] But perhaps it was the return to this basic strategy of policing that produced the crime reduction that Rudolph Giuliani and Bratton heralded.

Compstat Created a Capacity for Situated Problem Solving

If the top-down general police strategies that seemed to emphasize the use of aggressive preventive patrol are not the essential secret of Compstat's success, however, there may be another, less obvious answer. Perhaps Compstat, as it developed over time, created the conditions under which the NYPD began to develop and learn from bottom-up improvisations for dealing with particular crime problems facing particular precincts. This view of Compstat is not discussed much publicly—perhaps because it complicates the simple and satisfying story of a demanding bottom-line management system driving an organization to work harder. But the question of whether Compstat evolved into a different kind of accountability system that engaged well-meaning professionals in formal and informal learning processes comes as no great surprise to the people who have actually taken part in or closely observed Compstat over the years, and across many agencies that adopted (and adapted) the system.

As police departments from cities around the world began adapting the legend of Compstat to more local conditions, they often began with systems that focused accountability on crime reduction, and many police departments responded with methods that looked a lot like aggressive preventive patrol. Many, however, sensing that there was more to be gained by engaging the lower ranks of the department in efforts to invent better approaches to particular problems, began transforming Compstat into a system that created accountability not only for doing but also for thinking and innovating.

If Compstat were to become a tool for thinking, inventing, and learning as well as control, the managerial systems associated with it had to create spaces where those responsible for controlling crime—precinct commanders in the first instance, but their subordinates and their peers in support functions as well—could begin talking about the conditions they confronted and how they might best be handled. Because these conversations were being carried out in forums created by and attended by those in positions of authority in the department, the discussions seemed to encourage and authorize creative thought that departed from existing policies and procedures in a more open-ended search for more creative solutions. Compstat had to be a forum in which a conversation about how the NYPD could best address specific crime problems could occur rather than simply an occasion for top brass to call out a precinct commander for his inability to bring down the crime numbers in his precinct.

To many who have watched the evolution of Compstat not only in New York City but throughout the country, Compstat began as a top-down accountability process and evolved into a process through which precinct commanders could consult with their bosses and peers about how to make an effective response to particular problems and enlist their help in making that response. From this point of view, Compstat begins to look a lot more like what Spence was trying to introduce into the DSS than it first appeared. Instead of being a success story about tough internal accountability, Compstat might be a success story about the use of performance measurement and accountability to develop and deploy a new professional culture of learning.

The Learning Perspective

Private-sector proponents of organizational learning have trumpeted the virtues of bottom-up learning and the organizational culture that supports it.[14] Given that so much of the information about how production processes are working to create value lies with those who engage in those processes daily, encouraging frontline workers to hone their skills and imagine ways they could produce more value or produce value more efficiently makes perfect sense.[15] Given that the natural human desire to learn can provide a strong motivation within a professional organization, creating chances for learning can increase the overall motivation and commitment of the organization. Thus the "learning and growth perspective" of Kaplan and Norton's balanced scorecard focuses on setting objectives and creating performance measures to track employee satisfaction, retention, and productivity, as well as employee suggestions made and implemented, the outcomes of implementing those suggestions, and the degree to which individual and departmental goals line up with the broader goals of the organization.[16] These are indeed important features of organizational performance worth tracking, and they have a rightful place in the operational capacity perspective of the public value scorecard as well.

But the public value scorecard has no such "learning perspective" because the very act of developing and using it should foster learning *at each point of the strategic triangle.* The learning that occurs at each point of the triangle, in turn, helps integrate the points of the triangle into a coherent strategy for a given context. As public managers make philosophical inquiries into the nature of the public value they produce, evaluating it from the point of view of both individual clients and the collective public, and bringing both utilitarian and deontological frames to bear, they begin to uncover both the true costs of their activities and the full spectrum of social benefits they are now creating, or could create in the future. As they look to their political authorizing environment in search of recognition for the value creation revealed in their public value accounts and support for the value creation envisioned in their public value propositions, they learn what the public and its representatives truly want them to produce with the public money and authority entrusted to them and help them become articulate, precise, and concrete about this. And as they turn their attention to the operational capacity necessary to produce the desired social outcomes, they learn what could be done to improve the internal processes that represent their organizational capacity, how the public might be engaged in coproducing the outcomes it seeks through the development of a broader operational capacity, and what values attach to the means they use in their production processes—including the important question of how the work is divided between the public and private actors on whom success depends.

Indeed, the journey through this book is itself a learning process. We have moved from the simple concept of a financial bottom line to the necessity of constructing a more complex accounting scheme that can capture the full set of values that public agencies produce and the financial and social costs that they incur along the way (the public value account).

We have moved from the idea that the only measures that managers need to effectively manage their organizations are those associated with a public value account that can reliably recognize value produced in the past to the idea that managers need a full set of performance measures that can also capture and guide the organization's execution of a forward-looking strategy for maintaining or increasing the value of its performance in the face of changing circumstances (the public value scorecard).

We have used the legitimacy and support perspective of the public value scorecard to consider how developing a public value account aligned with legislative concerns could help transform the relationship between one's organization and legislative oversight bodies and build legitimacy and support for a public agency.

We have employed the operational capacity perspective to see how efforts to ensure efficient performance through performance contracting highlight the importance of measuring performance all along the value chain, examining processes as well as outcomes.

We have seen how the challenge of engaging citizens in the coproduction of public value ties the development of operational capacity irrevocably to the building of legitimacy and support.

We have investigated whether a comprehensive public value account that embodies a vision of a good and just society can survive the twists and turns of democratic politics—including differing views about whether and how performance measures might best be used in government—and still help a polity both define and pursue public value over the course of a decade.

And we have looked at the heartbreaking challenge of dealing with inevitable failure in solving society's most "wicked problems" through an improved capacity to recognize and learn from the failures that the organization's measurement and management systems help reveal, diagnose, and ultimately seek to prevent.

The challenge to capture the valued effects of government in performance measures and to develop measures that can help public managers produce more value in the future is never just about recording the results of past practice against a past understanding of what constitutes public value. It is always part of a continuous learning process in which the public changes its mind about the public values it wants to see produced by and reflected in the actions of government organizations; in which the processes of building legitimacy and support for a given value proposition can be improved and strengthened through better deliberations; and where the mobilization of both external and internal operational capacities becomes both more comprehensive and more intelligently focused on the desired goals. From this viewpoint the most important contribution of performance measurement is not that it allows us to execute what we already know we want to do, and know how to do, more perfectly but, rather, that it helps us learn what we should do, and what is possible to do.

An inevitable part of the learning is failing against the measures that were established to help show and secure success. Learning how to acknowledge and learn from failure is a challenge that all public agencies and overseers must embrace once they are committed to effective performance measurement. Measurement does not only reveal success; it also exposes failure. What is hard for managers and perhaps even harder for their overseers to grasp is that both success and failure can be value-creating events if both managers and overseers have the courage to recognize the limits of current knowledge and imagination. Both create an opportunity to learn more. The best-designed management systems will facilitate and support that learning.

Preserving the Best of Private-Sector Thinking in a Different Context

From the outset the goal here has been to preserve the best from the private sector's extensive experience in using performance measurement to create organizational accountability and performance improvement as the concepts moved into the distinctive environment of the public sector. The caution was that the process of doing so would not be as simple as it first seemed, and that any hope or expectation that introducing performance measurement and management into the public sector would simplify the managerial process ought to be kept to a minimum.

And so it appears to be true. To get the most out of performance measurement and management in the public sector, some major adjustments have to be made not only from old public-sector practices but also from some of the simple ideas borrowed from the private sector. To see how the important core ideas can be maintained, and how they might have to be adjusted, consider how those who have read this book might answer the core questions that an unreconstructed advocate of simple bottom-line management in the public sector might put before them.

Question 1: Isn't it valuable and important to create a strong sense of accountability for performance in the public sector?

Answer: It absolutely is. But the problem has never been that there are not strong demands for accountability in the public sector. The problem is that both internal and external demands for accountability have been inconsistent and often focused on the wrong things.

The external demands for accountability come from a wide variety of authorizers and overseers who do not always agree on the definition of public value. Even if they can agree that there are many different dimensions of public value at stake in a given agency's performance, authorizers will still insist on performance with respect to the one value they deem most important. To deal with this problem, public managers have to keep making public value propositions to their authorizers and tailoring their public value accounts to fit the value propositions that garner enough political support to serve as reasonable guides for organizational performance. This process helps both authorizers and managers learn what values are at stake in a given organization's activities and the actions taken to produce those results.

When it comes to the methods that managers use to create internal accountability systems that will motivate their employees to work harder and smarter, simply specifying particular policies and procedures and demanding compliance with them are not enough. A strong public agency is one whose workers feel accountable to a professional calling that aligns with a politically viable strategic value proposition. Employees should feel accountable for performance with respect to the values named in that value proposition and measured in a corresponding public value account. They should feel accountable to their professional peers as well as their bosses. They should also feel accountable to the clients they both serve and oblige, and to the citizens in whose name they do their work.

In the end a proper accountability system for both external and internal purposes depends on having a strong conceptual and operational definition of what constitutes public value creation, with some kind of measure attached to each important dimension of public value.

The existence of such a thing is far from assured. On the contrary, creating a proper public value account takes a huge amount of external political work to bring differing conceptions of value into a workable alignment as well as internal managerial work to maintain and modify measurement systems and use them to hold employees accountable. In short, one has to do the hard political, philosophical, and technical work of developing a clear public value proposition and constructing a public value account to measure progress made with respect to that value proposition.

Question 2: Shouldn't we hold public agencies accountable for performance now rather than let them off the hook with promises about future improvement?

Answer: We absolutely should. Just as private-sector firms have to be accountable for what they delivered yesterday and today, so public agencies ought to be held accountable for current performance. But just as private companies have come to understand that their future value to their shareholders depends on their ability to exploit new technological possibilities and adapt to new conditions that appear in the world, so public-sector enterprises must be able to change and adapt. This means that public agencies should be called to account for not only for their current performance but also for the investments they are making to position themselves for improved performance in the future. Just as shareholders expect companies to make and implement plans for sustained profitability in the future, so citizens should expect public agencies to sustain and improve their level of public value creation in the future. If citizens find that a public agency that once performed well now lags behind the demands of its environment, they should increase the pressure on the agency not only to perform better now but also to make some kind of investment in increasing its capacity to improve in the future.

Question 3: Shouldn't public agencies be required to develop and use performance measures that can provide accurate information about their performance on a timely basis?

Answer: They absolutely should. Just as private-sector firms have to be accountable for providing accurate information to shareholders and investors about their financial performance, public agencies should be accountable for providing accurate information to citizens and their elected (and self-appointed) representatives. But, in developing such measures, citizens and their elected representatives must understand that a single measure of performance probably cannot capture the full value-creating performance of a public agency. There will be many different dimensions of performance that have normative significance to citizens and their elected representatives. Consequently, just as private companies have found it useful to report on many different dimensions of their performance, so public agencies will have to record and report their performance on multiple dimensions that cannot be made commensurate.

Public managers must also recognize that the statistical performance measures will not be the only basis on which their performance is evaluated. They will also be evaluated on the basis of isolated incidents that capture public attention, and they have to consider whether and how to incorporate this fact into an effective performance management system. Harry Spence specifically used "critical incidents" in his performance management system, presenting the events for both external and internal evaluation and treating them as occasions for the public and the agency to consider the values at stake in DSS activities, which of them had been advanced and protected and which lost and sacrificed in the particular incident, and how the practices of the DSS could have been adjusted to produce a different, perhaps more satisfactory (but not perfect), result. If performance measurement is about recognizing value, and if it is hard to get both public and organizational attention focused on defining and producing value, then the particular incidents and anecdotes that garner public attention become an important opportunity for orchestrating a conversation about value, performance, and what is reasonable to expect.

Question 4: Shouldn't public agencies focus on social outcomes rather than exclusively on their internal activities?

Answer: They certainly should. Just as it is impossible for a private-sector firm to judge whether it is creating value or not by simply looking at costs and operational activity without paying attention to revenues, so it is impossible for public agencies to determine or demonstrate how much (net) public value they are creating without knowing the degree to which they are producing the outcomes that justified the expenditure of public money and authority.

But the important question is whether in raising the importance of outcome measures, public-sector agencies can afford to reduce their efforts to monitor costs, processes, and activities. Because the public often values particular attributes of the process by which public agencies produce social outcomes, as well as the results, public agencies need to develop and use outcome measures, but they must also retain and perhaps improve methods for measuring costs and monitoring internal performance. The public would like to know that the process of providing services or imposing obligations was fair, efficient, and effective. It would like to know that public officials were conscientious in their decision making—particularly when the decisions produced unhappy results. And, as noted in Chapter 4, monitoring processes is also necessary for innovation and learning. Public agencies cannot learn from experience and experiments unless they know what they did to produce the results they got.

Question 5: Shouldn't public agencies become more responsive to the individual circumstances of their clients and adapt their performance to those particular circumstances?

Answer: They absolutely should. Just as private-sector firms learned to be accountable to their customers as well as their shareholders, so public-sector agencies should become more attentive and responsive to the clients they both serve and obligate. But in seeking to increase the responsiveness of public agencies to individual client circumstances, public managers have to remember that because they make use of public authority, they must always be accountable for the fairness with which they distribute benefits and impose burdens. The pressure to treat like cases alike and to keep the rules simple will force public agencies to work with a small number of "bin" systems that will likely do an injustice to the variety of individual circumstances. To overcome this limitation, public agencies may have to create a far more complex set of rules, or grant their workers more discretion to make reasonable adaptations. If the workers are free to use their discretion, the agency must develop the means to ensure that workers use their discretion conscientiously, such as regular reviews of the cases that provoked departures from standard procedures or complaint procedures that allow clients to speak up when they have been treated unfairly.

In addition, as important as clients are in the evaluation of public agency performance, public agencies have to remember that their views are not the proper basis for the evaluation of agency performance. The ultimate arbiter of public value is not the individual who receives a service or an obligation from the government; it is the collective citizenry that decides that it is willing to tax and regulate itself to achieve particular results through particular means that it finds both just and effective. One part of that evaluation may well be the satisfaction that an individual client experiences in service and obligation encounters with public agencies. But that is not the only, and probably not the most important, dimension of evaluation.

Question 6: Should public agencies be held accountable for the fairness with which they use public assets, and for using public assets to increase justice as well as material well-being in the society they seek to serve?

Answer: Yes, absolutely. By definition, public managers use assets that are collectively owned—both the money and the authority of the state. In fact, most of the money the state has to spend comes from the use of its authority. In a democratic society the use of public authority, and funds raised by the use of authority, has to be justified in terms of the common good, and the idea of the common good has to have room for some ideas of both justice and fairness. The ideas of justice and fairness pertain to the particular way in which government interacts with its citizens when it is operating as an agent of the common good: it has to treat like cases alike, treat cases that are judged to be different differently, and protect individual rights in the course of doing its work. But government also has to be an agent in the pursuit of the particular vision of a just society that is held among citizens. Among the rights that free societies created was the right to have individual ideas about what constituted a good and just society, and to pursue them through a variety of means. When, therefore, a democratic society decides to tax and regulate itself to produce a publicly valued purpose, the state has to see itself as enacting some idea of a just as well as a good society.

So there is much in the private sector's commitment to performance measurement and management that can be usefully imported into the public sector. The accountability created by value-oriented management is good both as a driver of improved performance and as a device that creates the right relationship between citizens and the public agencies we entrust with both our money and our freedom in hopes of creating a good and just society. The sense of urgency and focus that "bottom-line" accountability gives to managers and workers helps invigorate tired old bureaucracies. The focus on outcomes reminds us—as citizens, taxpayers, and clients—why we agreed to tax and regulate ourselves to pursue a given result and enables us to make more reliable judgments about the degree to which our collective aspirations can be achieved.

All of this is good. The problem is that even a carefully constructed public-sector version of the "bottom line" will not suffice to create useful performance measurement and management systems in public-sector agencies. Instead of relying on existing measurement systems to create a simple bottom-line summary of performance, public managers have to go through the demanding political and philosophical work of developing a reliable public value proposition, the complex technical work of turning that into a public value account, and the ultimate challenge of developing and using a public value scorecard that supports an integrated strategy for improving public-sector performance in both the short and long term.

What we have seen in this book is the example of able public managers pursuing the value that could come from using strong, thoughtful, and well-designed systems to measure and manage performance. They are the pioneers. The hope is that this book will encourage others to occupy the vast territory that these pioneers have staked out and to join them in pushing the boundaries of what public agencies can accomplish.

APPENDIX

NOTES

ACKNOWLEDGMENTS

INDEX

Appendix

A Public Value Scorecard for Public Managers

THIS appendix presents for reference the three basic components of the public value scorecard initially presented in Chapters 1 and 2: the public value account (Figure A.1), the legitimacy and support perspective (Figure A.2), and the operational capacity perspective (Figure A.3).

PUBLIC VALUE ACCOUNT	
Use of Collectively Owned Assets and Associated Costs	Achievement of Collectively Valued Social Outcomes
Financial Costs	Mission Achievement
Unintended Negative Consequences	Unintended Positive Consequences
	Client Satisfaction
	Service Recipients
	Obligatees
Social Costs of Using State Authority	Justice and Fairness
	At Individual Level in Operations
	At Aggregate Level in Results

Figure A.1. Public value account: general form.

THE LEGITIMACY AND SUPPORT PERSPECTIVE: General Form

Mission Alignment with Values Articulated by Citizens
(Link to Public Value Account)

Inclusion of Neglected Values with Latent Constituencies
(Link to Public Value Account)

Standing with Formal Authorizers:
Elected Executives
Statutory Overseers in Executive Branch (Budget, Finance, Personnel)
Elected Legislators
Statutory Overseers in Legislative Branch (Audit, Inspectors-General)
Other Levels of Government
Courts

Standing with Key Interest Groups:
Economically Motivated Suppliers
Self-Interested Client Groups
Policy Advocacy Groups
Latent Interest Groups

Media Coverage:
Print
Electronic
Social

Standing with Individuals in Polity:
General Citizenry
Taxpayers
Clients
   • Service recipients
   • Obligatees

Position of Enterprise in Democratic Political Discourse:
Standing in Political Campaigns
Standing in Political Agendas of Current Elected Regime
Standing in Relevant "Policy Community"

**Status of Key Legislative and Public Policy Proposals to Support
   Enterprise** *(Link to Operational Capacity Perspective)*:
Authorizations
Appropriations

Engagement of Citizens as Co-Producers *(Link to Operational Capacity Perspective)*

Figure A.2. Legitimacy and support perspective: general form.

THE OPERATIONAL CAPACITY PERSPECTIVE: General Form

Flow of Resources to Enterprise *(Link to Legitimacy and Support Perspective)*:

Financial Revenues Flowing to Public Agencies:
- Appropriations
- Intergovernmental grants
- Fees

Legal and Statutory Authorizations/Mandates

Public Support/Popular Opinion

Human Resources:

Current Status of Workforce
- Size
- Quality
- Morale

Recruitment and Selection Processes

Training/Professional Development of Staff

Compensation Levels

Advancement Opportunities

Performance Measurement Systems for Individual Accountability

Public Volunteer Efforts

Operational Policies, Programs and Procedures:

Quality of Operational Performance
- Documentation of current procedures
- Compliance with tested procedures
- Auditability of performance recording methods

Organizational Learning
- Evaluation of current untested policies
- Stimulation and testing of innovations
- Institutionalization of successful innovations

Internal Resource Allocation

Performance Measurement and Management Systems
- Investment in systems
- Use of systems

Organizational Outputs *(Link to Public Value Account)*:

Quantity of Outputs

Quality of Outputs
- Attributes that produce desired results
- Attributes that increase client satisfaction
- Attributes that reflect justice and fairness in operations

Figure A.3. Operational capacity perspective: general form.

Notes

Introduction

1. This simple aim has spawned a huge industry that focuses on the measurement of desired social outcomes. A leader in this field for many years has been Harry P. Hatry. His work has encompassed the fields of program evaluation, customer surveys, and performance measurement—all of the ways in which government has tried to give an objective, quantitative account of the results it was producing. See, for example, Joseph S. Wholey, Harry P. Hatry, and Kathryn Newcomber, eds., *Handbook of Practical Program Evaluation* (San Francisco: Wiley, 2010); Harry P. Hatry et al., *Customer Surveys for Agency Managers: What Managers Need to Know* (Washington, DC: Urban Institute, 1997); Harry P. Hatry, *Performance Measurement: Getting Results* (Washington, DC: Urban Institute, 2006).

2. See Michael Barzelay, *The New Public Management: Improving Research and Policy Dialogue* (Berkeley: University of California Press, 2001).

3. Albert Gore, *Creating a Government That Works Better and Costs Less: National Performance Review Status Report 1994* (Washington, DC: Dianne Publishing, 1994).

4. Mark H. Moore and Jean Hartley, "Innovations in Governance," *Public Management Review* 10, no. 1 (January 2008): 3–20.

5. See Alan A. Altshuler and Robert D. Behn, *Innovations in American Government: Challenges and Dilemmas* (Washington, DC: Brookings Institution Press, 1997).

6. George T. Milkovich and Alexandra Wigdor, *Pay for Performance: Evaluating Performance Appraisal and Merit Pay* (Washington, DC: National Research Council, 1991).

7. On the critical importance of strategy for private-sector organizations, and the methods used to conceive and execute strategy, see Michael E. Porter,

Competitive Strategy: Techniques for Analyzing Industries and Competitors (New York: Free Press, 1980); also see Robert S. Kaplan and David P. Norton, *The Strategy Focused Organization: How Balanced Scorecard Companies Thrive in the New Business Environment* (Boston, MA: Harvard Business Publishing, 2001).

8. Porter, *Competitive Strategy.*

9. The Nobel Prize–winning economist Kenneth Joseph Arrow demonstrated the theoretical impossibility of doing so in *Social Choice and Individual Values* (New York: John Wiley and Sons, 1951). As a practical matter, however, this process occurred, more or less satisfactorily, on a daily basis. Every time a publicly owned asset was committed to a particular activity and produced a particular effect, the problem that was theoretically insoluble was practically resolved. An explicit or implicit judgment was made as to the public value of that particular effort.

10. David Osborne and Ted Gaebler, *Reinventing Government: How the Entrepreneurial Spirit Is Transforming the Public Sector* (Reading, MA: Addison-Wesley, 1992).

1. William Bratton and the New York City Police Department

1. This case study is adapted from John Buntin, "Assertive Policing, Plummeting Crime: The NYPD Takes on Crime in New York City," John F. Kennedy School of Government, Harvard University (Cambridge, MA: The President and Fellows of Harvard College, 1999). Quoted material in cases not cited otherwise in this chapter is from this source.

2. James Dao, "Dinkins and Giuliani Split on Public Safety Issues," *New York Times,* October 11, 1993.

3. Poll data from a *New York Times*/WCBS-TV News Poll cited in the James Dao article.

4. James Q. Wilson and George Kelling, "Broken Windows: The Police and Neighborhood Safety," *The Atlantic Monthly,* March 1982: 78. George Kelling worked with Bratton in each of his principal assignments.

5. Buntin, "Assertive Policing," 7.

6. In Bratton's opinion, the Knapp Commission's focus on reducing corruption in the NYPD in 1970, and the changes made within the NYPD to implement its recommendations, had stripped police officers of many of the regulatory powers they had once enjoyed (such as the power to cite businesses for violating licensing codes). The deemphasis on "order maintenance" activities in the interest of avoiding corruption and racial discrimination had produced an unintended, harmful result: the police had lost control of the streets.

7. Manhattan, Brooklyn, and Queens were divided into north and south patrol boroughs.

8. Buntin, "Assertive Policing," 6.

9. In early 1994 Maple drafted *Police Strategy No. 1: Getting Guns Off the Streets of New York,* the first in a series of strategy papers focusing on topics such as youth violence, drug dealers, domestic violence, "broken windows" policing, auto crime, and corruption (see Buntin, "Assertive Policing," 10–11).

10. Ibid., 12.

11. Ibid., 17.

12. This is an application of a particular management technique. Gordon Chase, another aggressive New York City public manager from an earlier era, used this technique to drive the process of building a network of methadone maintenance clinics to deal with the city's heroin problem in the mid-1970s. See Mark Moore and Robert Svensk, "Methadone Maintenance: (B) The Entrepreneur's View," Case Study for Kennedy School of Government Case Program (Cambridge, MA: The President and Fellows of Harvard College, 1976), Case No. 66.0. More recently, this idea has appeared in the private-sector management literature that discusses the managerial utility of setting very ambitious goals. In "Building Your Company's Vision" (*Harvard Business Review,* September/October 1996), 73, James C. Collins and Jerry I. Porras recommended that every company set a "Big Hairy Audacious Goal" (BHAG) as "a clear and compelling unifying focal point of effort and a catalyst for team spirit." The business community has also used the term "burning platform" as shorthand for "the compelling business reason for making a change," or "the bad things that will happen to us if we don't change now" (Jeff Cole, "How Hot Is Your Platform?" http://www.sixsigmaiq.com/columnarticle.cfm?externalid=677&columnid=13, accessed March 4, 2009). The idea is that in order to introduce change to an organization, the leadership has to make a compelling case that bad things will happen if the organization does not make the change. See Paul R. Niven, *Balanced Scorecard Step-by-Step for Government and Nonprofit Agencies* (Hoboken, NJ: John Wiley & Sons, 2003), 48.

13. The precincts did send robbery figures to police headquarters every week; however, nothing much was done with those figures.

14. Since the department was divided into seventy-two patrol precincts, the twice-a-week meeting schedule meant that precinct commanders would appear for Compstat reviews about once every nine months.

15. Both the precinct commander and the head of the detectives' unit at the precinct appeared at these meetings.

16. The department also created an internal auditing team to make sure that crime numbers were not being manipulated.

17. Compstat tracked homicide, rape, robbery, burglary, felony assault, grand larceny, and grand auto larceny. It did not track arson.

18. These measures were meant to reward police for going beyond the usual practices of preventive patrol and "sticking their noses" more directly

into social life. Their target was individuals using and carrying guns, but since it was hard to know in advance who these were, they often intruded into the lives of others who were not using or carrying guns. They targeted suspected drug dealers, panhandlers, squeegee men, and the homeless, as well as known and suspected shooters. In the past such methods had been described as "aggressive preventive patrol." Now the tactics were described as "proactive policing" or, more colloquially, the "war against grime." Such initiatives were considered central to the "broken windows" theory of crime control.

19. At roughly every third Compstat meeting, executive officers, who were second in command in the precincts, stood in for their commanding officers. "We discovered some real stars that way," said Maple.

20. The figures cited for the country actually overstate declines in crime outside of New York City, since the city itself accounts for a significant proportion of the total number of crimes nationwide.

21. Crimes figures are taken from the FBI's Uniform Crime Index.

22. Unpublished report by Andrew Karmen, "An Analysis of Murders Committed in New York City in Recent Years," John Jay College of Criminal Justice, City University of New York, February 1996.

23. See William K. Rashbaum, "Retired Officers Raise Questions on Crime Data," *New York Times,* February 6, 2010. For similar instances of falsifying data in high-stakes testing in the public school system, see also Greg Toppo, "Atlanta Public School Exams Fudged," *USA Today,* July 6, 2011.

24. The figure for misdemeanor arrests was calculated from data cited in Alfred Blumstein and Joel Wallman, *The Crime Drop in America* (New York: Cambridge University Press, 2000), 225. All other statistics are from Buntin, "Assertive Policing," 23.

25. In *Terry v. Ohio,* 392 U.S. 1 (1968), the U.S. Supreme Court ruled that when a "reasonably prudent" officer "performing [the] legitimate function of investigating suspicious conduct" believed that his safety or the safety of others was endangered, in order to neutralize that danger, the officer could pat down the person believed to be armed and dangerous, regardless of whether there was probable cause to arrest that individual for crime. If the pat down turned up anything illegal, the officer could then make an arrest.

26. A single complaint could contain multiple allegations of police misconduct. The CCRB divided allegations of police misconduct into four categories: force, abuse of authority, discourtesy, and offensive language. Citizens could complain either to the NYPD or to the CCRB.

27. "Two of the three officers found guilty of misconduct after administrative trials in 1994 were sentenced to 10 to 15 days' loss of vacation and one to 10 days' loss of vacation" (*United States of America: Police Brutality and Excessive Force in the New York City Police Department,* Amnesty International [AI Index: AMR 51.36.96], June 1996, Sections 5.5, 2.9).

28. Statistics are drawn from the voluminous appendices of the *Civilian Complaint Review Board Semi-Annual Report, January–December 1998,* Vol. VI, No. 2 (City of New York: Civilian Complaint Review Board).

29. "Complaints against Cops Surge 135%," *Daily News,* April 23, 1996, 22.

30. Over half of the investigations (1,229) were cut short when callers withdrew their complaints, proved to be uncooperative, or could not be located. Of the 557 full investigations that were conducted, 225 complaints were found to be unsubstantiated; 111 were substantiated. (The remaining investigations were inconclusive.) The complaints that were substantiated by the CCRB were then passed on to the police commissioner for further review and possible disciplinary action, which could range from a letter of reprimand to an administrative trial.

31. The poll also found that 52 percent of New Yorkers believed Giuliani had done a "good" or an "excellent" job dealing with the crime issue, while 72 percent said the same of Bratton. See "Bratton Tops Giuliani in a Poll," *Newsday,* April 20, 1996, A4.

32. The analysis that follows was previously developed and published in a different form in Mark H. Moore, with David Thacher, Andrea Dodge, and Tobias Moore, *Recognizing Value in Policing: The Challenge of Measuring Police Performance* (Washington, DC: Police Executive Research Forum, 2002).

33. Bratton's innovation has spread widely in policing. The Compstat model has also gone beyond policing to other public agencies, and to entire jurisdictions. See Robert Behn, "PerformanceStat as a Search for Strategic Evidence," paper presented at the National Public Management Research Conference, Columbus, and the Annual Research Conference of the Association for Public Policy Analysis and Management, Washington, D.C., October 1–3, 2009, and November 6, 2009.

34. William Bratton, "Cutting Crime and Restoring Order: What America Can Learn from New York's Finest," lecture delivered at the Heritage Foundation, October 15, 1996.

35. Indeed, over time, an obsession with reducing serious crime had led the NYPD to ignore minor disorder offenses. Bratton, understanding that minor offenses had important consequences for citizens' sense of security, was committed to widening the focus of the NYPD to include reducing disorder and fear.

36. John E. Boydstun and Michael E. Sherry, "San Diego Community Profile: Final Report" (Washington, DC: Police Foundation, 1975), 25.

37. I realize that there is a lively public debate about the proper goals of a business enterprise. However, this discussion seems to make less powerful and consistent claims on managers than debates about the ends of public agencies make on public managers. See Sybille Sachs, *Stakeholders Matter: A New Paradigm for Strategy in Society* (New York: Cambridge University Press, 2011). But see also Michael Jensen, *Foundations of Organizational Strategy* (Cambridge, MA: Harvard University Press, 1998).

38. In economic theory, costs include the opportunity costs of resources used in policing rather than other potentially valuable government activities. They also include losses in welfare inflicted on particular individuals who would have preferred not to be regulated by the police, or taxed to support them.

39. The idea that the assets used by the police include both money and authority was set out in a report about the Philadelphia Police entitled *Philadelphia and Its Police: Progress Towards a New Partnership* (Philadelphia Police Study Task Force, March 1987). See also National Research Council, Wesley Skogan and Kathleen Frydl, eds., *Fairness and Effectiveness in Policing: The Evidence* (Washington, DC: National Academies Press, 2004).

40. Bratton did not seem worried about whether and how the NYPD should try to compete with these alternative private security arrangements. Nor is there any analysis of the success of the NYPD in expanding its market share in the market for security—core issues in any standard private-sector competitive strategy analysis. See Michael E. Porter, *Competitive Strategy: Techniques for Analyzing Industries and Competitors* (New York: Free Press, 1980).

41. An important strategic question in public policing is whether the police, acting as an agent for the public, should have any interest in the level, form, and distribution of private security efforts. They certainly act as if they have an interest. They have a practical interest in allowing citizens to exercise their right to self-defense and to take on some of the burden of defending themselves against crime. They are active in the regulation of gun ownership and enforcement of carrying laws. They have long assisted home owners and small businesses in security checks of their premises. They have struggled with the question of what priority to attach to calls from privately installed burglar alarms. They have supported neighborhood watch programs but resisted offers of assistance from the Guardian Angels and the Black Muslims in crime-ridden neighborhoods. The critical questions are (1) the degree to which private security is actually helpful in reducing levels of crime and fear; (2) the degree to which the public police can prevent vigilantism and protect individuals who become subject to private security activities; and (3) the degree to which the private security ameliorates or exacerbates inequality in the distribution of security in the society. There is also an interesting question about the degree to which the police and the public have an interest in whether private security arrangements take an individual or a collective form. Guns, alarms, and dogs deployed by individuals create a very different community experience than do neighborhood watches and patrols. For an example of the impact of community patrols on a hard-pressed inner-city neighborhood, see Francis Hartmann and Harvey Simon, the Kennedy School of Government case study, "Orange Hats of Fairlawn: A Washington, D.C., Neighborhood Battles Drugs" (Cambridge, MA: The President and Fellows of Harvard College, 1991).

42. Actually the bottom line quickly becomes a more complex subject—even in business. Business accountants track two bottom lines: (1) profit (the difference between income and expenses over a given time period), and (2) total assets and liabilities (the basis for a general ledger or balance sheet). Robert S. Kaplan and David P. Norton argued in *The Balanced Scorecard* (Boston, MA: Harvard Business School Press, 1996) that companies ought to manage their operations in more than financial terms—even though financial performance remains the touchstone of corporate performance. John Elkington argued in *Cannibals with Forks: The Triple Bottom Line of 21st Century Business* (Philadelphia: New Society Publishers, 1998) that firms should calculate a "triple bottom line" to measure the social and ecological impact of their activities.

43. N. Gregory Mankiw, *Principles of Economics* (Mason, OH: Cengage Learning, 2008), 268.

44. This is one of the fundamental ideas in welfare economics. Whether a market is efficient or not in allocating resources to production tasks is dependent on having some reliable arbiter of the value of what is being produced. In economic theory, that is assumed to be individual consumers making choices about how to spend their own money. If individual customers are allowed to spend their money in competitive markets in order to satisfy their wants, a market economy will tend toward efficiency both in the sense that it will produce what individuals (with money to spend) want, and that it will do so at a low resource cost (that is the beneficial result of competitive pressures in consumer markets). If one does not assume that individuals with money are the appropriate arbiter of the value of the economic system that uses the world's resources to produce products and services, the claim that markets will be efficient in producing individual or social value weakens considerably.

45. But see qualifications in the preceding note 44.

46. Some would argue, for example, that America paid a huge price in the 1960s and 1970s because it relied on a mistaken comparison between the failure to confront Hitler early in Munich and the apparent advance of "international communism" in Southeast Asia. See Richard Neustadt and Ernest May, *Thinking in Time: The Uses of History for Decision Makers* (New York: Free Press, 1986), 75–90.

47. Economic theory makes the consumer the important arbiter of value in market systems (see the preceding note 42 and note 49 that follows). Profitability is the primary goal of companies, in two senses. Practically, the owners of the company would like to make money as a matter of professional competence. Legally, companies have a fiduciary responsibility to those who hold stock or have otherwise invested in the firm. Societies understand that profits are a necessary incentive to motivate companies to create the products and services that individuals pay to consume (at prices higher than the costs of production). Over the long run, economic theory holds that competitive

markets will drive excess profits out of businesses, delivering the maximum value to customers. It is this story, plus the notion that there ought to be a reasonable return to capital as well as to labor, that justifies a distribution of the economic value created by a firm to its owners and shareholders as well as its laborers and customers.

48. Increasingly, public agencies rely on voluntary sources of financing, such as user fees that partially cover the costs of a given public service. For example, visiting national parks used to be free, but now there are entrance fees. There are also fees associated with securing licenses to engage in regulated activities such as expanding one's home or carrying a gun. Some public agencies also benefit from charitable contributions. However, for most, the majority of financing still comes from tax dollars or other kinds of public subsidies.

49. In economic theory, the idea that individuals are the appropriate arbiters of value is called the principle of "consumer sovereignty." This idea, often used in the context of efficiency and social welfare, is routinely challenged on the grounds that individuals do not always make choices in their own best self-interest. While this is plainly the case (e.g., with smoking, tanning beds, alcohol abuse, etc.) in contemporary times, suggesting that individuals are not the best arbiters of value invites criticism that one would prefer a paternalistic "nanny state" in which the collective, or the state, substitutes its judgment of what is good for individuals for the judgments of individuals. The point of using this logic here is to illustrate why the ideas of customers and markets have such a hold on our imagination. For an elegant treatment of this question by a Nobel Prize–winning economist, see Thomas C. Schelling, "The Intimate Contest for Self Command," *The Public Interest* 63 (Spring 1981): 37–61. For a philosophical treatment by a political theorist, see John Elster, *Sour Grapes: Studies in the Subversion of Rationality* (Cambridge: Cambridge University Press, 1983).

50. Public managers have to pay attention to bad things that their agencies produce as well as the good—whether those things come about intentionally or unintentionally. In economic theory, such unintended—and unpriced—effects would be described as "externalities," and their presence interferes with the smooth functioning of markets. See the "Thinking beyond the Current Mission: Unintended Consequences, Unexploited Opportunities" section in this chapter. See also Deborah Stone, *Policy Paradox: The Art of Political Decision Making* (New York: W. W. Norton, 1987); Donald A. Schön and Martin Rein, *Frame Reflection: Toward the Resolution of Intractable Policy Controversies* (New York: Basic Books, 1994).

51. As noted earlier, the bottom line in the private sector can refer to two different financial statements: balance sheets that express the net worth of a company by comparing existing assets against existing liabilities, and income statements that record financial activity in terms of expenditures (made and owed) and revenues (received and anticipated). For our purposes the income statement is the more important idea, so we will start with that as the analogue.

52. An important feature of valuing performance in the public sector is that both individuals who have encounters with public agencies and the broader public place value not only on the financial costs of production and the ultimate effects of agency activity but also on features of actions that public agencies take in producing those effects. For more on this, see Chapter 4 in this book.

53. See Robin Cooper and Robert S. Kaplan, "Activity-Based Systems: Measuring Costs of Resource Usage," *Accounting Horizons* (September 1992): 1–13.

54. See the preceding note 47.

55. See Harry P. Hatry, ed., *Customer Surveys for Agency Managers: What Managers Need to Know* (Washington, DC: Urban Institute, 1998); Christopher G. Reddick, *Politics, Democracy, and E-Government: Participation and Service* (Hershey, PA: Information Science Reference, 2010).

56. See Carol H. Weiss, *Evaluation: Methods for Studying Programs and Policies*, 2nd ed. (Upper Saddle River, NJ: Prentice Hall, 1998), for a classic discussion; see Joseph P. Wholey, Harry P. Hatry, and Katherine E. Newcomer, *Handbook of Practical Program Evaluation* (Washington, DC: Urban Institute, 2010), for a more recent account.

57. See the preceding note 50.

58. The mission of a public agency plays a critical role in its management. The current mission of the organization seeks to define what valued purposes or results a given agency is supposed to produce. Any effort to change an agency's mission would constitute a strategic innovation for the organization and would require high-level political legitimation. But organizational missions are often set at very high levels of abstraction, so that much discretion is left to managers in figuring out exactly what their mission authorizes or requires them to do. The discretion is not only with respect to the means to be used but also with the naming and prioritization of more concrete goals and objectives that the organization intends to pursue. On the importance of mission to public agencies, see James Q. Wilson, *Bureaucracy: What Government Agencies Do and Why They Do It* (New York: Basic Books, 1989), 25–26. See also Mark H. Moore, *Creating Public Value: Strategic Management in Government* (Cambridge, MA: The President and Fellows of Harvard College, 1995), 89–102.

59. For further discussion of this point, see Chapter 6 in this book.

60. Strategy is commonly thought of as the means an organization uses to achieve predetermined ends. In business, however, the concept of strategy is concerned as much with ends as with means. While the abstract goal—maximizing returns to shareholders (or stakeholders, see the preceding note 35)—remains constant, the "business" or "product" strategy, based on a review of existing markets and a given company's organizational capacities, may change frequently. Businesses define goals in light of internal capacity and external opportunity, while public agencies tend to work in the reverse order.

61. Like many public agencies, the NYPD also has a "values" statement: "In partnership with the community, we pledge to: protect the lives and property of

our fellow citizens and impartially enforce the law; fight crime both by preventing it and by aggressively pursuing violators of the law; maintain a higher standard of integrity than is generally expected of others because so much is expected of us, value human life, respect the dignity of each individual and render our services with courtesy and civility." http://www.nyc.gov/html/nypd/html/home/mission.shtml, accessed December 7, 2011. On the role of such statements in policing, see Mark H. Moore and Robert Wasserman, "Values in Policing," in *Perspectives on Policing* (Cambridge, MA: Kennedy School of Government Program in Criminal Justice Policy and Management, 1988).

62. See Wilson, *Bureaucracy.*

63. Ibid.

64. William Niskanen, *Bureaucracy and Representative Government* (New Brunswick, NJ: Aldine Transaction, 2007). See also Anthony Downs, *Inside Bureaucracy* (Boston, MA: Little & Brown, 1967).

65. Cost reduction is, of course, a value-creating activity—as long as the production of value can be maintained at the same level. That is captured in the simple idea that the goal of public management is to produce *net* public value, not *gross* public value. But cost reduction is also sometimes seen in more ideological and principled terms. The idea of "small government" is not simply about keeping the costs of government low. It is also the idea that the total size and reach of government should be limited as a matter of just relations between individual citizens and government: society should leave more to individual decisions than collective decisions as a matter of preserving liberty. In this view, cost reduction often becomes a valued end in itself.

66. It is often said that private managers have a simpler job than public managers because they have a simple, one-dimensional, easy-to-measure goal: maximizing profits. While the fact that both costs and valued results can be measured in financial terms does give private-sector organizations a greater capacity to measure and respond to net value creation, the idea of profit itself is a two-dimensional goal: managers have to concentrate on both increasing revenues and reducing costs. And, if we follow the advice of those encouraging corporations to embrace double and triple bottom lines, their goals become as complex and as difficult to measure as those in the public sector.

67. See Stone, *Policy Paradox*; also see Schön and Rein, *Frame Reflection.*

68. See the preceding note 50.

69. Mark H. Moore and Harvey Simon, "Rocky Flats: DOE Manager in an Environment of Distrust," Kennedy School of Government Case Study (Cambridge, MA: The President and Fellows of Harvard College, 1996).

70. See Moore, *Creating Public Value.*

71. General Electric took some of its support operations and turned them into outward-facing product lines, fundamentally changing the position of the organization in the economy. See Francis J. Aguilar, Richard G. Hamermesh, and Caroline E. Brainard, "General Electric Co.—1984," Harvard Business

School Case Study (Cambridge, MA: The President and Fellows of Harvard College, 1985).

72. See the preceding note 48.

73. David Osborn and Ted Gaebler, *Reinventing Government: How the Entrepreneurial Spirit Is Transforming the Public Sector from Schoolhouse to Statehouse, City Hall to the Pentagon* (Reading, MA: Addison-Wesley, 1992), chap. 6. For a critique of the customer orientation, see Moore, *Creating Public Value*; Henry Mintzberg, "Managing Government, Governing Management," *Harvard Business Review* (May/June 1996): 75–83; Joel D. Aberbach and Tom Christens, "Citizens and Consumers: A NPM Dilemma," *Public Management Review* 7, no. 2 (2005): 225–246.

74. I am indebted to my colleague George Kelling for noting and emphasizing the importance of this phenomenon (personal communication with author).

75. Insofar as most public agencies rely on tax dollars collected through the coercive power of government, the public always has an interest in the fair and just use of public resources.

76. In this process of rationing, public agencies can make two types of errors: wrongly deciding that an ineligible person is eligible (a "false positive"), or wrongly deciding that an eligible person is ineligible (a "false negative"). There are many causes for such errors, including negligence and mistakes on the part of the public agency, as well as clients misrepresenting themselves, or losing or forging documents. One can reduce the number of errors, but only at a cost that must be borne by the public agency or the client. This phenomenon shows up in Chapters 4 and 7 of this book as well, in somewhat different contexts. See Jerry L. Mashaw, *Bureaucratic Justice: Managing Social Security Disability Claims* (New Haven, CT: Yale University Press, 1983); Jeffrey Manditch Prottas, *People Processing: The Street-Level Bureaucrat in Public Service Bureaucracies* (Lexington, MA: Lexington Books, 1979); John Alford, *Engaging Public Sector Clients: From Service Delivery to Coproduction* (New York: Palgrave Macmillan, 2009).

77. William K. Frankena, *Ethics*, 2nd ed. (Englewood Cliffs, NJ: Prentice Hall, 1973).

78. I refer here to communitarian philosophy as well as utilitarian and deontological. See Amitai Etzioni, *The Moral Dimension: Toward a New Economics* (New York: Free Press, 1988).

79. Edith Stokey and Richard Zeckhauser, *A Primer for Policy Analysis* (New York: Norton, 1978), 270–273.

80. Ibid., 149–153, 262–266.

81. This concept is rooted in a third strand of normative political theory—communitarianism—that differs from both utilitarianism and deontology.

82. In *The Origins of Totalitarianism*, 2nd ed. (New York: Meridian Books, 1958), Hannah Arendt wrote that "To abolish the fences of laws between

men—as tyranny does—means to take away man's liberties and destroy freedom as a living political reality; for the space between men as it is hedged in by laws, is the living space of freedom," (446). By this logic, one could say that freedom is in essence the right for the democratic public to participate in designing the architecture of its own restraint. A similar sentiment appears in Gilbert K. Chesterton's *Orthodoxy* (Project Gutenberg, May 1994), book 130, chap. 7, http://www.gutenberg.org/cache/epub/130/pg130.txt. Chesterton wrote, "I could never conceive or tolerate any Utopis which did not leave to me the liberty for which I chiefly care, the liberty to bind myself."

83. See Robert B. Reich, "Public Administration and Public Deliberation: An Interpretive Essay," *The Yale Law Journal* 94, no. 7 (June 1985): 1617–1641; Jane J. Mansbridge, *Beyond Adversary Democracy* (Chicago: University of Chicago Press, 1983). This foreshadows the discussion in Chapters 3, 5, and 6.

84. This view was strongly and succinctly advanced by Ronald Reagan and Margaret Thatcher. In an interview Thatcher famously stated that "there is no such thing as society." See Douglas Keay, "AIDS, Education, and the Year 2000!" *Women's Own*, October 31, 1987, 8–10. A stronger philosophical basis is found in Robert Nozick, *Anarchy, State, and Utopia* (New York: Basic Books, 1974). While all liberal societies give prominence to the individual, they vary in terms of how narrowly they construct the public sphere.

85. John Dewey, *The Public and Its Problems* (New York: Henry Holt, 1927).

86. See Jane J. Mansbridge, ed., *Beyond Self-Interest* (Chicago: University of Chicago Press, 1990). See also James Q. Wilson, *Political Organizations* (Princeton, NJ: Princeton University Press, 1995). These ideas, however, can be traced to Adam Smith's *An Inquiry into the Nature and Causes of the Wealth of Nations* (London: Methuen & Co, 1902).

87. For a discussion of "smaller collectives" and their role in democratic societies, see Nancy Rosenblum, *Membership and Morals: The Personal Uses of Pluralism in America* (Princeton, NJ: Princeton University Press, 1998).

88. Kenneth Arrow, in *Social Choice and Individual Values* (New York: John Wiley and Sons, 1963), 22–33, demonstrated that it was impossible to aggregate individual preferences into a simple social utility function. While that is theoretically true, as a practical matter democratic societies act as though it were possible to a greater or lesser degree on a daily basis. Moreover, all public managers have to assume that there is some capacity to form a public purpose, otherwise they are without guidance as to what should be produced. If there is no reliable collective principle that can legitimately define public purposes, then it is hard to know how the public's agents should behave.

89. Importantly, those ideas of the good and the just could include the maximization of the individual well-being of each individual in the society—the basic welfare principle in economics. This is why utilitarianism must be seen as a form of ethical theory.

90. This is the realm of the voluntary sector perhaps, though there could be other explanations.

91. See Rosenblum, *Membership and Morals*. See also Amartya Sen, *Identity and Violence: The Illusion of Destiny* (New York: W. W. Norton, 2006).

92. John Rawls, *A Theory of Justice* (Cambridge, MA: Harvard University Press, 1971), 118–123.

93. On the social character of individual motivations, see Wilson, *Political Organizations;* Mansbridge, *Beyond Self-Interest.*

94. Moore et al., *Recognizing Value in Policing.*

95. See Stacy Osnick Milligan and Lorie Fridell, "Implementing an Agency-Level Performance Measurement System: A Guide for Law Enforcement Executives," Executive Summary (Washington, DC: Police Executive Research Forum, 2006).

2. Mayor Anthony Williams and the D.C. Government

1. This case study is adapted from the case "Mayor Anthony Williams and Performance Management in Washington, D.C.," by Esther Scott, written for Steven Kelman, Weatherhead Professor of Public Management, for use at the John F. Kennedy School of Government (Cambridge, MA: The President and Fellows of Harvard College, 2002). Quoted material in cases not cited otherwise in this chapter is from this source.

2. Vernon Loeb, "Required 'Accountability Plans' from DC Are Late, Incomplete," *Washington Post*, July 15, 1997, B3.

3. Michael Powell and Michael Cottman, "Williams Wins Mayoral Primary," *Washington Post*, September 16, 1998, A1.

4. Michael Cottman, "Hope for Change Pinned on Williams," *Washington Post*, January 2, 1999, A1.

5. Colbert King, "100 Days Are Not Enough," *Washington Post*, April 17, 1999.

6. Peter Perl, "Behind the Bow Tie," *Washington Post Magazine*, June 4, 2000, W6.

7. Powell and Cottman, "Williams Wins Mayoral Primary."

8. David Montgomery and Linda Wheeler, "New Mayor Has Many Roles to Fill," *Washington Post*, January 3, 1999, B1.

9. Eric Lipton, "Williams Sets Goals for Improvements," *Washington Post*, January 28, 1999, B1.

10. While it was not one of his short-term action plans, perhaps the earliest sign that "something was happening" came on March 10, when the city was socked with an unexpected snowstorm. When residents awoke that morning, the *Post* reported, they got another surprise: the roads had been cleared of snow. This was in marked contrast to 1996, when the city's aging snowplow

fleet was overmatched by a series of snowstorms in January, leaving many of the streets unplowed for weeks.

11. Michael Cottman, "A View from the Summit," *Washington Post*, November 21, 1999, C1. The top vote getters among the priorities were building and sustaining neighborhoods and strengthening children and families.

12. Two years earlier, the District's city council had passed legislation that made the reclassification possible.

13. When she arrived at the DMV, Newman says, she discovered that office supplies were scarce—ten employees, for example, would share a single stapler. One of her first acts as director was to give workers "individual goody packages" that included staplers, pens, tape dispensers, and other supplies.

14. A fourth division—alcoholic beverage regulation—was made a freestanding department in 2001.

15. District officials pointed out, however, that they had "ratcheted up" performance targets on 34 out of the 62 goals carried over from the previous year.

16. Carol Leonnig, "For District Voters, a Way to Keep Score," *Washington Post*, April 21, 2000, B2.

17. Carol Leonnig, "Williams Says City Achieved Most Goals," *Washington Post*, January 5, 2001, B9. Some residents pointed out, for example, that the scorecard for the Department of Public Works did not include a goal for trash pickup, which had been "a constant source of complaints."

18. "Another Term for the Mayor?" *Washington Post*, December 21, 2001.

19. All high-level public managers, whether elected chief executives like Williams, politically appointed public executives like Bratton, or senior civil servants with responsibility for making and executing government policies, are subject to various formal and informal systems through which the public and its representatives hold them accountable for their performance. But all also have the right and the obligation to nominate ideas for public value creation that include both ends and means of government action. Elected executives have wider discretion than those below them in the hierarchy and face daily political challenges to their legitimacy. They also have the final say over executive branch operations (as long as the legislatures or the courts do not intervene!). But both political appointees and career civil servants have important roles to play in nominating, legitimating, and pursuing value-creating opportunities. Throughout this book, I take explicit note of the particular position of the individuals who are trying to introduce and use performance measurement and management systems, and the protagonists will cover the range of such officials. This chapter provides a more detailed discussion of the distribution of responsibility for developing and using performance measurement and management systems among these three different kinds of senior public executives. (See the "Whose Work Is This?" section).

20. Performance *measurement* systems consist of information systems that recognize or capture data about overall performance (including, but not lim-

ited to, data collected on values in a public value account) or the performance of individual managers, units, or employees. Performance *management* systems tie performance measurement systems to organizational structures and processes (operating units, budget and resource allocation, personnel, etc.) to allow top managers to isolate the performance of individual managers, units, or activities in order to improve accountability and performance. See Harry P. Hatry, "Performance Measurement: Fashions and Fallacies," *Public Performance and Management Review* 25, no. 4 (June 2002): 352–358.

21. Robert S. Kaplan and David P. Norton, *The Balanced Scorecard: Translating Strategy into Action* (Boston, MA: Harvard Business School Press, 1996).

22. This is a quick survey of what will later be described as the "authorizing environment" of a public agency. I develop this concept systematically as I move through the book, particularly in Chapter 3.

23. See Mark H. Moore and Margaret Jane Gates, "Inspectors General: Junkyard Dogs or Man's Best Friend?" *Social Research Perspectives,* no. 13 (New York: Russell Sage Foundation, 1986). Somewhere in between the wider public's and the government's own audit and control agencies are independent citizen watchdog agencies (supported by charitable contributions) that check on government spending.

24. Chapter 3 focuses on precisely these circumstances.

25. Mark H. Moore, "The Simple Analytics of Accountability" (working paper no. 33.9, the Hauser Center for Nonprofit Organizations, Harvard University, 2006).

26. W. Lance Bennett, "Towards a Theory of Press State Relationships in the United States," *Journal of Communication* 40, no. 2 (June 1990): 103–127.

27. Martin Linsky, *Impact: How the Press Affects Federal Policy Making* (New York: W. W. Norton, 1988).

28. Archon Fung, "Varieties of Participation in Complex Governance," special issue, *Public Administration Review* 66, no. s1 (2006): 66–75; Erik Olin Wright, *Deepening Democracy: Institutional Innovations in Empowered Participatory Governance* (New York: Verso, 2003).

29. The courts are not routinely involved in the oversight of public agency operations, but they are sometimes called in when an agency seems to have abused its authority (at least in one case, but more commonly when a group of citizens can show a pattern of systematic abuse of authority). At that moment the courts take on a role with respect to the use of state authority that budget bureaus and audit agencies take on with respect to the use of state money: they seek to drive out improper uses of state authority just as the finance agencies seek to drive out improper uses of state money. For a general analysis, see David H. Rosenbloom, "Public Administration and the Separation of Powers," *Public Administration Review* 43, no. 3 (May–June 1983): 219–227. For an analysis of an example of this phenomenon, see Mark H. Moore, *Creating Public Value: Strategic Management in Government* (Cambridge, MA: Harvard University Press, 1995), 125–126.

30. Some personal professional experience is relevant here. Charles Bowsher, then the comptroller of the United States, once asked me to work with the General Accounting Office (GAO) to develop what he called a "general performance review" of individual federal departments. The idea was that while the GAO had long examined pieces of organizations—reviewing their financial accounts, reporting systems, and other managerial systems (personnel, strategic planning, etc.), and had even ventured into program and policy evaluation—it had never looked at the overall performance of an agency over time. Since there was no existing method for doing this, it would have to be invented, and it would be quite subjective—at least at the start. But a second problem proved even more difficult: it was hard to find anyone in the authorizing environment of government who was interested in receiving and acting on the report! This contrasts sharply with practices in the private sector, where much of the reporting and evaluation focuses on the long-term performance of an organization rather than its management systems, or particular products and services.

31. The "technical challenges" of developing performance measures are all the problems that must be overcome in order to translate a normative concept of public value into a set of valid and reliable measures at some suitable level of aggregation. To develop a valid measure requires one to find some concrete condition, event, or experience in the world that is reliably indicative of the value one wants to measure. This means working from a philosophical idea to an operational definition of that idea to a specific measure. For example, in policing, one could say that an important goal is to "hold offenders accountable for their crimes." One could then use the number of reported crimes cleared by arrest to measure the degree to which the police were successful in achieving this goal. Developing reliable measures requires one to learn how the measures chosen actually behave in the world. Do they fluctuate widely, even when conditions do not seem to be changing that much, or are they relatively steady, changing only when relevant conditions change? In the example cited previously, the reliability of the measure might be vulnerable both to police neglect in clearing multiple crimes committed by an offender once they had evidence on one crime and to their overeagerness in attributing crimes to an arrested individual who did not commit the crimes. Finally, to make use of measures they have to attach to a particular unit of analysis. It is one thing to measure the state of a polity, another to measure the performance of an organization, and quite another to focus on individual employees in an organization. For example, the statistic "crimes cleared by arrest" could be reported at the citywide level, the precinct level, or the individual detective level. For an excellent discussion of the technical problems in measuring educational performance, see Daniel Koretz, *Measuring Up: What Educational Testing Really Tells Us* (Cambridge, MA: Harvard University Press, 2008).

32. Personal communication with senior managers from the Los Angeles Police Department in the Kennedy School of Government's Senior Managers in Policing Program.

33. "Managerial work" differs from the political, philosophical, and technical work that managers must do to build a relatively accurate and useful performance measurement system. It is the work they must do inside their organizations to build the performance measurement systems and use them in managerial processes that create internal accountability and foster learning among the staff of the organization. Managerial work is what is required to transform a mere performance measurement system into a performance management system that can produce real changes in organizational behavior.

34. Throughout this book I will be working to develop performance management systems that support both accountability and learning. It is worth noting, however, that there is a potential tension between the goals of holding an organization accountable and helping it learn. Certain forms of accountability can actually prevent an organization from learning. For example, if organizations are held strictly and universally accountable for implementing existing policies and procedures, there is no way they can engage in innovations and experiments that could support their learning. They are locked into their current methods. Similarly, if managers are held strictly accountable for their performance in terms of results, but the desired results keep changing and no information is collected about the processes they are relying on to produce results, then both the motivation and the capacity to learn will go down. Efforts to combine accountability with learning are the central focus of Chapter 7 in this book.

35. I describe this work later and throughout subsequent chapters as the development and use of a "public value scorecard." While a public value account measures past and current performance with respect to the production of public value, the public value scorecard is a more complete performance measurement system to support a strategic performance management system that will focus a public agency on future performance and value creation.

36. For an insightful discussion of the collision between elected officials and senior civil servants at the federal level, see Hugh Heclo, *A Government of Strangers: Executive Politics in Washington* (Washington, DC: The Brookings Institution, 1977).

37. In this he is most like the governors of the state of Oregon who are discussed in Chapter 6 rather than the functional managers who are discussed in Chapters 3, 4, 5, and 7.

38. On the idea of calling a public into existence, see Mark H. Moore and Archon Fung, "Calling a Public into Existence," in *Ports in a Storm: Public Management in a Turbulent World*, ed. John Donahue and Mark H. Moore (Washington, DC: Brookings Institution Press, 2012). See also John Dewey, *The Public and Its Problems* (New York: Henry Holt, 1927).

39. I am paraphrasing a question that a participant in one of the Kennedy School's executive programs actually posed to me.

40. See the preceding note 30.

41. For a review of the impact of these measures, see James S. Bowman, "The Success of Failure: The Paradox of Performance Pay," *Review of Public Personnel Administration* 31 (December 2011): 369–395. Importing performance contracts from the private into the public sector has had some influence in requiring managers to live up to their espoused theory of professional managerial conduct. But, again, there are many ways that such instruments of managerial accountability can be blunted or rendered ineffective.

42. Mark H. Moore and Anthony Braga, "Measuring and Improving the Performance of Policing: Lessons of Compstat and Its Progeny," *Policing: An International Journal of Police Strategies and Management* 26, no. 3 (2009): 439–453.

43. These are fundamental ideas of governance for private-sector firms and public-sector agencies. On the private sector, see Michael C. Jensen, *Foundations of Organizational Strategy* (Cambridge, MA: The President and Fellows of Harvard College, 1998). On the public sector, see Woodrow Wilson, "The Study of Administration," *Political Science Quarterly* 2 (June 1887): 197–222. Also see Moore, *Creating Public Value*.

44. The idea of organizational slack was initially seen as a problem. See James March and Herbert Simon, *Organizations*, 2nd ed. (Cambridge, MA: Blackwell, 1963). Later it was viewed as a useful way to cope with environmental change and innovations. See Jay R. Galbraith, *Designing Complex Organizations* (Boston, MA: Addison-Wesley, 1973). Today it is seen as a variable that managers can use strategically to adapt to conditions in their environment. See Nitin Nohria and Ranjay Gulati, "What Is the Optimum Amount of Organizational Slack? A Study of the Relationship between Slack and Innovation in Multinational Firms," *European Management Journal* 15, no. 6 (December 1997): 603–611.

45. For a general discussion of the problem of organizational change and methods for overcoming obstacles, see David Collis, *Organisational Change: Sociological Perspectives* (London: Routledge, 1998); Marshall Scott Poole and Andrew H. Van de Ven, eds., *Handbook of Organizational Change and Innovation* (New York: Oxford University Press, 2004). For a more practical guide that includes lessons learned from Compstat, the use of the balanced scorecard, and other ideas in this book, see Jean Helms Mills et al., *Understanding Organizational Change* (New York: Oxford University Press, 2004).

46. For a discussion of the difficulties of helping an organization face a problematic reality from a position of authority, see Ronald A. Heifetz, *Leadership without Easy Answers* (Cambridge, MA: Harvard University Press, 1994).

47. The debate over the degree to which management can rely on workers to put out a good effort simply because workers enjoy their physical and mental duties has gone on for a long time. The argument in favor of relying more

on the intrinsic motivations of workers was set out forcefully by Douglas Mc-Gregor in *The Human Side of Enterprise* (New York: McGraw-Hill, 1960). Currently the debate often takes the form of compliance agencies versus commitment agencies. This issue is addressed in Chapter 7.

48. Peter Senge, *The Fifth Discipline: The Art and Practice of the Learning Organization* (New York: Currency Books, 1990).

49. This insight into managing organizational change, commonly invoked by business leaders like Jack Welch, is often called "the burning platform" argument. For a brief description, see Ken Embley, "The Burning Platform," *Policy Perspectives* 1, no. 1 (2005), http://www.imakenews.com/cppa/e_article 000368179.cfm, July 1, 2012. Also see Amir Hartman, *Ruthless Execution: What Business Leaders Do When Their Companies Hit the Wall* (Upper Saddle River, NJ: Pearson Education, 2004), 54, which includes a case study on how Jack Welch used a "burning platform" to help make General Electric "the most competitive company on earth."

50. This is very similar to the situation that the governors of Oregon confront, which is discussed in Chapter 6.

51. Moore, *Creating Public Value.*

52. See Malcolm K. Sparrow, Mark H. Moore, and David M. Kennedy, *Beyond 911: A New Era for Policing* (New York: Basic Books, 1992); Mark H. Moore, *Recognizing Value in Policing: The Challenge of Measuring Police Performance* (Washington, DC: Police Executive Research Forum, 2002); Mark H. Moore and Anthony Braga, *The Bottom Line of Policing: What Citizens Should Value (and Measure!) in Police Performance* (Washington, DC: Police Executive Research Forum, 2003); Mark H. Moore, "Alternative Strategies for Public Defenders and Assigned Council" (paper prepared for the Executive Session on Public Defense, John F. Kennedy School of Government, April 2001); Mark H. Moore and Gaylen Williams Moore, *Creating Public Value through State Arts Agencies* (Minneapolis, MN: Arts Midwest, 2005); British Broadcasting Corporation, "Building Public Value: Renewing the BBC for a Digital World" (London: BBC, 2004).

53. Kaplan and Norton, *The Balanced Scorecard.*

54. Ibid., 9.

55. For Kaplan's perspective on uses of the balanced scorecard outside of the private sector, see Robert S. Kaplan, "Strategic Performance Measurement and Management in Nonprofit Organizations," *Nonprofit Management and Leadership* 11, no. 3 (2001): 353–370. For a critique, see Mark H. Moore, "The Public Value Scorecard: A Rejoinder and Alternative to 'Strategic Performance Measurement and Management in Nonprofit Organizations' by Robert Kaplan" (working paper, the Hauser Center for Nonprofit Organizations, Harvard University, 2003).

56. Andrew W. Savitz, with Carl Weber, *The Triple Bottom Line: How Today's Best-Run Companies Are Achieving Economic, Social, and Environmental Success, and*

How You Can, Too (San Francisco: John Wiley and Sons, 2006). See also Mark H. Moore and Sanjeev Khagram, "On Creating Public Value: What Business Might Learn from Government about Strategic Management" (working paper of the Corporate Social Responsibility Initiative, Harvard University, 2004).

57. Robert S. Kaplan and David P. Norton, *The Strategy-Focused Organization: How Balanced Scorecard Companies Thrive in the New Business Environment* (Boston, MA: Harvard Business School Press, 2001).

58. Susan Colby, Nan Stone, and Paul Carttar, "Zeroing in on Impact: Helping Non-Profit Organizations Develop Strategic Clarity," *Stanford Social Innovation Review* (Fall 2004): 24–33.

59. The public value to be produced could be the same as the mission of the organization, but sometimes organizations are in a position to produce valuable effects that are not included in their mission. See, for example, the case of the librarian in Moore, *Creating Public Value,* 13–23. Also see the discussion of a public value account in Chapter 1 in this book.

60. See William Niskanen, *Bureaucracy and Representative Government* (Chicago: Aldine-Atherton, 1971); Anthony Downs, *Inside Bureaucracy* (Boston, MA: Little & Brown, 1967); Wilson, "The Study of Administration."

61. Often the highest strategic use of a managerial position and a particular organization depends not only on the deployment of assets held within a single organization but also on other organizations and individuals that the first organization can influence. For a discussion of the role of networks of organizations in dealing with public problems, see Stephen Goldsmith and William D. Eggers, *Governing by Network: The New Shape of the Public Sector* (Washington, DC: Brookings Institute, 2004).

62. Accenture Institute for Public Service Value, *Managing Current and Future Performance: Striving to Create Public Value* (Chicago, IL: Accenture, 2007), 7–8.

3. John James and the Minnesota Department of Revenue

1. This case is adapted from Michael Barzelay and Kirsten Lundberg, *The Executive Branch and the Legislature: Opening Lines of Communication in Minnesota,* Case Studies 991–994 (Cambridge, MA: Harvard University Kennedy School of Government, 1990). Quoted material in cases not cited otherwise in this chapter is from this source.

2. Many governments have something like the invest/divest concept—usually mandated. The most famous of these systems was called zero-based budgeting and was used in the federal government under President Carter. For a review of that experience, see Allan Schick, "The Road from ZBB," *Public Administration Review* 38, no. 2 (1978): 177–180.

3. None of the items on this list qualify as "outcomes" as defined in this book, but they are all related to achieving the broader outcomes the DOR seeks

to produce, such as the just and efficient delivery of services and obligations, the satisfaction of individual clients, and so on.

4. Of course, public managers may underestimate how much conflict lies beneath the surface of corporate governance. Shareholders may disagree about how long they are prepared to wait for financial returns, and how much risk they are willing to bear. There is even more debate about the best possible strategy for the firm to follow. And, as private corporations have assumed increased influence in shaping the individual and material conditions in which we live, and governments have become less active regulators, social movements demanding increased corporate social responsibility have made corporations feel some duty to avoid social harms and advance social goods within their powers. The question of how much responsibility corporations should assume, and for what, exposes corporations to public and political accountability. The board of directors, drawn into these conflicts, often probes more deeply into operations than public managers tend to imagine. But the idealized image of a board of directors that focuses on strategy and leaves operations to managers has a hold on managerial imaginations like James's.

5. Erwin Hargrove and John C. Glidewell, eds., *Impossible Jobs in Public Management* (Lawrence: University Press of Kansas, 1990). See also James Q. Wilson, *Bureaucracy: What Government Agencies Do and Why They Do It* (New York: Basic Books, 1989), 238, 249.

6. It is clear that Armajani for one holds this view, and he longs for this principle to be established in the working relationship between the DOR and the legislative committee. The distinction between policy and operations was first suggested by Woodrow Wilson in "The Study of Administration," *Political Science Quarterly* 2, no. 2 (1887): 197–222. It was essentially demolished by James Q. Wilson in *Bureaucracy*.

7. For a discussion of the idea of accountability in the public sector, see Mark H. Moore and Margaret Jane Gates, *Inspectors General: Junkyard Dogs or Man's Best Friend?* Social Research Perspectives No. 13 (New York: Russell Sage Foundation, 1986), appendix A. For a more recent abstract account, see Mark H. Moore, "The Simple Analytics of Accountability" (working paper no. 33.9, the Hauser Center for Nonprofit Organizations, Harvard University, Cambridge, 2006).

8. Richard Zeckhauser and John W. Pratt, *Principals and Agents: The Structure of Business* (Cambridge, MA: Harvard Business Publishing, 1985). But see also Jane Mansbridge, "A 'Selection Model' of Political Representation," *Journal of Political Philosophy* 17, no. 4 (2009): 369–398.

9. Zeckhauser and Pratt, *Principals and Agents.*

10. Ibid.

11. Professor Herman B. "Dutch" Leonard, personal communication with the author.

12. Robert Clark, "Moral Systems in the Regulations of Nonprofits: How Value Commitments Matter" (working paper no. 33.6, the Hauser Center for Nonprofit Organizations, Harvard University, Cambridge, 2006).

13. Some have suggested that there ought to be some kind of entitlement for citizens that would allow them to know what particular dimensions of value had been nominated as purposes for a public organization, whether governmental or nonprofit, and, further, that organizations should be required to capture and report data on their performance. For a wider discussion of the role of transparency in promoting democracy and governmental performance, see Archon Fung, Mary Graham, and David Weil, *Full Disclosure: The Perils and Promise of Transparency* (New York: Cambridge University Press, 2007). For the idea that nonprofit organizations should be required to produce auditable performance statements, see Herman B. Leonard, "Should Mission Statements Be Promises (And Should They Have to Be)?" (working paper no. 33.5, the Hauser Center for Nonprofit Organizations, Harvard University, Cambridge, 2006).

14. Wilson, "Study of Administration."

15. John Dewey, *The Public and Its Problems* (New York: Henry Holt, 1927).

16. In democratic theory the government acts as the agent of "the people." The aim is always to give "the people" the most effective control over the actions of government—whether government is engaged in service or obligation encounters, whether it is trying to achieve the good by helping individuals or producing aggregate social results, or whether it is trying to protect individual rights, impose individual duties, or advance toward a conception of a just society. The problem has always been how to enable "the people" to become articulate about what they want as a collective, and to ensure that the government acted to produce what they wanted. To many political theorists the desire to construct a clear delegation of public desire to governmental action leads inevitably to the desire to create parliamentary democracies in which the legislative and executive branches of government are tightly integrated. This avoids the hazard that there might be one public that spoke through the legislature and another public that spoke through the executive branch. Such systems give citizens acting as voters in elections structured by disciplined parties the best chance to exercise real influence over what happens in government. The difficulty, however, is that such elections can never fully legitimate government actions. There are too many government actions that never rise to significance in the elections. And the world changes too quickly to be sure that the decisions made at election time will be the ones the people want in the future. Recognizing this legitimacy gap, governments all over the world seem to be reaching out for more legitimation through transparency, complaint processes, and consultative processes. See Archon Fung and Erik Olin Wright, eds, *Deepening Democracy: Institutional Innovations in Empowered Participatory Governance*. The Real Utopias Project Series, v. 4 (London: Verso, 2006). See also Mark H. Moore and Archon Fung, "Calling a Public into Existence," in *Ports in a Storm: Public*

Management in a Turbulent World, ed. John Donahue and Mark H. Moore (Washington, DC: Brookings Institution Press, 2012).

17. Notably, the James case suggests that overseers might be able to reward public managers with something as simple as respect and praise. Many public managers identify strongly with their agency's mission and would be glad to know they were pursuing it effectively and appreciated for that. The only price overseers might pay in doing so is disappointing citizens and taxpayers who would like them to view the motivations and performance of public managers and agencies with unremitting skepticism.

18. Note, however, that some of the managerial work we are suggesting managers might do is precisely to overcome these conditions. On the political side we are hoping they might do some of the work of assembling a public that can become at least articulate, maybe even wise, about concepts of public value (see Moore and Fung, "Calling a Public into Existence"). On the technical side, we are hoping they might do some of the work of building the performance measures that can give real power to the implicit or explicit contract they have with the public who is ultimately the principal, and the appropriate arbiter of public value. That is the main purpose of this book.

19. Archon Fung, "The Principle of Affected Interests: An Interpretation and Defense" (working paper, Kennedy School of Government, 2010). This document is viewable online at http://www.archonfung.net/docs/articles/2010/FungAffectedInterests4a.pdf (accessed July 5, 2012).

20. Ibid.

21. It is here that one must face the inevitable question of whether the real democratic accountability systems accurately identify the important values at stake in governmental choices, and give them their proper weight. If one is a strong Democrat, the answer has to be yes, since a strong Democrat takes the view that the people are always right in the arbitration of value. But one does not have to observe democratic politics too closely to have doubts about the strong democratic claim. For this reason, it is useful to think that any real democratic accountability system can be usefully challenged from outside on the basis of philosophical arguments about the full range of values that are at stake in a given governmental decision or action. That is why public value is a philosophical as well as a political concept. It is also where political leadership might come in. Sometimes it will be the duty of the public official—elected, appointed, or career—to defend some plausibly important but neglected values. When public officials do this, they have to be worried that their conceptions might be wrong— that their views are idiosyncratic or self-serving. They also have to be willing to test their views in the authorizing environment. Ideally, they will do so in a way that enriches and strengthens the legitimacy of the democratic policy-making process by helping the participants see what is at stake.

22. Legislators and managers might share some responsibility for improving the process. John Dewey wrote, "The public is organized and made effective

by means of representatives who as guardians of custom, as legislators, as executives, judges, etc., care for its special interests by methods intended to regulate the conjoint actions of individuals and groups." In this way, if I may paraphrase Dewey, public officials can help to call a public into existence. *(*John Dewey, *The Public and Its Problems,* [New York: Henry Holt, 1927] 35*)*.

23. Malcolm K. Sparrow, Mark H. Moore, and David M. Kennedy, *Beyond 911: A New Era for Policing* (New York: Basic Books, 1992).

24. Lawrence W. Sherman, *Scandal and Reform: Controlling Police Corruption* (Berkeley: University of California Press, 1978).

25. Political scientists and historians often write as though there were a consistent politics of a given issue, or surrounding a given agency. The idea of an authorizing environment organized around particular dimensions of public value brings practical, operational significance for something that has long seemed an academic topic. For a method, see Richard E. Neustadt and Ernest R. May, *Thinking in Time: The Uses of History for Decision Makers* (New York: Free Press, 1986), chap. 6, 91–110. Also see Mark H. Moore, "What Sorts of Ideas Become Powerful?" in *The Power of Public Ideas,* ed. Robert Reich (Cambridge, MA: Harvard University Press, 1988), 55–84.

26. Mark H. Moore, *Recognizing Value in Policing: The Challenge of Measuring Police Performace* (Washington, DC: Police Executive Research Forum, 2002); Mark H. Moore and Anthony Braga, *The Bottom Line of Policing: What Citizens Should Value (and Measure!) in Police Performance* (Washington, DC: Police Executive Research Forum, 2003).

27. By some accounts, this shift in values produced a shift in performance, with the police focusing more of their attention on "not being corrupt" and less on being effective in reducing crime, reducing fear, and holding offenders accountable. This effect was highlighted by a police student of mine who described a time when he was a sergeant monitoring patrol officers in New York City just after the Knapp Commission filed its report on police corruption. He saw two patrol officers standing together on the street, approached them, and asked them what they were doing. Their response was "Nothing, sir, nothing!" He, of course, was hoping that they might be doing something that would advance the mission, while they thought it sufficient to say they were not doing anything that was corrupt.

28. The consequence was a dramatic increase in stops and arrests; see statistics cited in the case study in Chapter 1.

29. Sometimes the values can change dramatically. Described in Chapter 1 was how the mission of the weapons program of the U.S. Department of Energy went, in effect, from "build nuclear weapons as fast as possible without much attention to environmental contamination" to "stop building nuclear weapons and clean up the environmental mess." See Mark H. Moore and Harvey Simon, *Rocky Flats: DOE Manager in an Environment of Distrust,* Case Study 1314.0 (Cambridge, MA: Harvard University Kennedy School of Government, 1996).

30. Edith Stokey and Richard Zeckhauser, *A Primer for Policy Analysis* (New York: Norton, 1978), 273–277.

31. Martin Cole and Greg Parston, *Unlocking Public Value: A New Model for Achieving High Performance in Public Service Organizations* (Chicago, IL: Accenture, 2006).

32. Ibid., 77.

33. Ibid.

34. Hargrove and Glidewell, *Impossible Jobs in Public Management*. More recent discussions have focused on what have been called "wicked problems." See Brian W. Head, "Wicked Problems in Public Policy," *Public Policy* 3, no. 2 (2008): 101–118.

35. The effect of using a particular dimension of value as an occasion for inspecting one's production processes, and having that search reveal opportunities for improvement across all dimensions of value, is described in Mark H. Moore, *Vision and Strategy: Paul O'Neill at OMB and Alcoa*, Case Studies 1134.0–1134.2 (Cambridge, MA: Harvard University Kennedy School of Government, 1992). Paul O'Neill unilaterally committed the organization to dramatic improvements in safety. Shareholders and managers thought this would increase costs, but this search revealed many ways to improve not only safety but performance as well.

36. In Chapter 6 I explore the power of a public value framework created in Oregon to "hold" some of the more contentious fights in the state over a period of time.

37. Robert S. Kaplan and David P. Norton, *The Balanced Scorecard: Translating Strategy into Action* (Cambridge, MA: Harvard Business Review Press, 1996).

38. Morten T. Hansen, Nitin Nohria, and Thomas Tierney, "What's Your Strategy for Managing Knowledge?" *Harvard Business Review* 77, no. 2 (March–April 1999): 106–116. Data richness is particularly important when we start using performance measurement and management systems for learning as well as for accountability.

39. For a more precise analytic discussion of the idea of a production possibility frontier, see Stokey and Zeckhauser, *Primer for Policy Analysis*, 23–28.

40. It is hard for those who want to talk about improving public-sector performance to remember that a production possibility frontier is an *empirical phenomenon*, not a normative claim. The normative claim identifies relevant values of interest to be produced, and thereby it sets the axes of the production possibility frontier. But it is only empirical evidence from the performance of existing organizations that helps us properly identify what now seems to be the production possibility frontier. That evidence will often reveal some organizations that are performing worse on all dimensions than other organizations, and there will be room for them to improve without having to give up value on any dimension of performance. But where the true production possibility frontier

lies will always be a bit of a mystery—a thing to be discovered through trial and error rather than something that is known for sure in advance.

41. Social utility functions, not production possibility frontiers, describe which attributes of performance we value more than others (see Stokey and Zeckhauser, *Primer for Policy Analysis*, 33–43). It is much easier for societies to name things that they value and see if they can produce more of them than it is for them to construct social utility functions. For a method, see Ralph L. Keeney and Howard Raiffa, *Decisions with Multiple Objectives: Preferences and Value Tradeoffs* (New York: John Wiley, 1976).

42. Michael C. Jensen, *A Theory of the Firm: Governance, Residual Claims, and Organizational Forms* (Cambridge, MA: Harvard University Press, 2000).

43. This is the challenge of building an organization that can be accountable for innovation and learning as well as short-run performance using existing means (see Chapter 7). See also Mark H. Moore, *Accounting for Change: Reconciling the Demands for Accountability and Innovation in the Public Sector* (Washington, DC: Council for Excellence in Government, 1993).

44. See Keeney and Raiffa, *Decisions with Multiple Objectives*.

45. The insistence that an organization confront its failures or accept a new challenge can be considered a "problematic reality" to which the organization has to adjust. Helping an organization adjust to this reality requires a certain kind of skillful leadership. See Ronald A. Heifetz, *Leadership without Easy Answers* (Cambridge, MA: Harvard University Press, 1998).

46. William A. Niskanen Jr., *Bureaucracy and Representative Democracy* (Chicago: Aldine-Atherton, 1971).

47. George T. Milkovich and Alexandra K. Wigdor, eds., *Pay for Performance: Evaluating Performance Appraisal and Merit Pay* (Washington, DC: National Research Council, 1991).

48. Francis Aguilar, Richard G. Hamermesh, and Caroline E. Brainard, *General Electric Co.—1984*, Case no. 385315-PDF-ENG (Cambridge, MA: Harvard Business Publishing, 1985).

49. Introducing explicit performance contracts into the public sector has helped align the motivations of managers more closely with their overseers than their employees, and has focused managerial effort on reducing costs as well as increasing output. Still, these contracts typically focus more on achieving output targets within a fixed budget constraint than on optimizing the difference between costs incurred and results achieved, or reducing costs. See Milkovich and Wigdor, *Pay for Performance*.

4. Jeannette Tamayo, Toby Herr, and Project Chance

1. This case is adapted from Arnold Howitt and David Kennedy, *The Ladder and the Scale: Commitment and Accountability at Project Match*, Case 1076.0

(Cambridge, MA: The President and Fellows of Harvard College, 1990). Quoted material in cases not cited otherwise in this chapter is from this source.

2. As in the other cases discussed, the aims of a public program, or the public value that a manager seeks to create, can be represented in practical, utilitarian terms or in terms of some concept of justice. In this case the welfare-to-work program could be seen in utilitarian terms as a device for reducing future welfare payments or as an altruistic effort to help needy individuals. It could be seen in justice terms as an effort to give everyone an opportunity to gain economic independence as a matter of right. The focus on Project Chance invokes the justice frame more than it does the utilitarian frame, but behind the justice aim the utilitarian aims could also be accommodated.

3. For a discussion of performance contracting in government, see Gary L. Sturgess, "Commissions and Concessions: A Brief History of Contracting for Complexity in the Public Sector," in *Procuring Complex Performance: Studies in Innovation in Product-Service Management,* ed. Nigel Caldwell and Mickey Howard (New York: Routledge, 2011), 41–58.

4. As noted often in this book, many transactions with clients in the public sector have this mixed quality of being both a service and an obligation encounter. For a discussion, see John Alford, *Engaging Public Sector Clients: From Service Delivery to Co-Production* (Basingstoke, UK: Palgrave MacMillan, 2009).

5. For an evaluation of welfare-to-work programs, see Judith Gueron, Edward Pauley, and Cameran M. Lougy, *Welfare to Work* (New York: Russell Sage Foundation, 1991).

6. Toby Herr, Robert Halpern, and Aimee Conrad, *Changing What Counts: Re-Thinking the Journey Out of Welfare* (Evanston, IL: Center for Urban Affairs and Policy Research, Northwestern University Press, 1991), 8.

7. The use of the word "outcome" here is interesting and problematic. It is similar to the way that we want to use the idea of social outcomes in the sense that it defines states and conditions that are ultimately, intrinsically valued. But the idea of an outcome seems to suggest a result at a particular point in time that is permanent, when Herr's whole point is that reaching for and sustaining higher levels of economic and other forms of independence is a process that never stops. The real outcome Herr is after is the cumulative effect of striving for, reaching, and sustaining independence over many years. The outcome can be measured at any particular point in time, but it is not necessarily a permanent state until the person's life ends.

8. Herr, Halpern, and Conrad, *Changing What Counts.*

9. S. Anil Kumar and N. Suresh, *Production and Operations Management* (New Delhi, India: New Age International Publishers, 2006), 1–17.

10. Lynn Olson, Linnea Berg, and Aimee Conrad, *High Job Turnover among the Urban Poor: The Project Match Experience* (Evanston, IL: Center for Urban Affairs and Policy Research, Northwestern University Press, 1990), 1.

11. These figures, as well as information in the preceding paragraph, are drawn from Linnea Berg, *Job Turnover of Disadvantaged, Inner-City, Minority Workers over a One-Year Period* (Evanston, IL: Northwestern University Press, 1991).

12. Project Chance was dissolved in 1993. Project Match continued, however, and under Toby Herr's leadership eventually won the MacArthur Foundation Award for Creative and Effective Institutions.

13. For a critique of hierarchical government and the potential of more fluid networks, see Stephen Goldsmith and Donald F. Kettl, eds., *Unlocking the Power of Networks: Keys to High-Performance Government* (Washington, DC: Brookings Institution Press, 2009).

14. For the introduction of the idea, see David Osborne and Ted Gaebler, *Reinventing Government: How the Entrepreneurial Spirit Is Transforming the Public Sector* (New York: Plume, 1993). For a discussion about what sorts of things ought to be put out to purchase, see John D. Donahue, *The Privatization Decision: Public Ends, Private Means* (New York: Basic Books, 1989).

15. Sturgess, "Commissions and Concessions."

16. It is also worth noting that private-sector firms make heavy use of process measures, both when they are examining production systems to eke out efficiency gains and when they are trying to guarantee consistency in product quality. For example, the McDonald's Corporation does not monitor the performance of its restaurants in financial terms; it focuses on twelve characteristics of the combined product/service experience of a customer in its restaurants— whether the food was hot and fresh, whether the restaurant was clean, whether there was a place to sit down, whether the person assembling the order smiled when the bill was presented, and so forth. See David C. Rikert and W. Earl Sasser, *McDonald's Corporation (Condensed)* (Cambridge, MA: Harvard Business School Case Services, Case no. 9-681-044, rev. 2/82).

17. Robert S. Kaplan and Steven R. Anderson, *Time-Driven Activity-Based Costing: A Simpler and More Powerful Path to Profitability* (Boston, MA: Harvard Business School Press, 2007).

18. The concept of *allocative efficiency* focuses on the degree to which resources are allocated away from low-value uses toward higher-value uses. If we make more money selling oranges than lemons, we ought to allocate more resources to growing oranges. The concept of *technical efficiency* is that we use fewer resources to produce a particular product or service. In government management, planning, programming, and budgeting (PPB) systems were used primarily in hopes of increasing public value through *allocative efficiency*— the goal was to find the high-value government activities and push resources to them. Management by objectives (MBO) systems, in contrast, seemed to focus more on increasing public value production through the *technical efficiency* that would come from focusing on increasing the output of particular government activities given a stock of resources. Generally speaking, efforts to

increase value through resource allocation are more difficult than those that work on technical efficiency, because one can quickly and easily see whether one is getting more output per unit of cost (the goal of technical efficiency). In contrast, the question of whether there is more public value associated with expenditures on defense or Social Security is a much more difficult calculation. For the most part, this book is working on generating technical efficiency or productivity gains rather than on allocative efficiency. For a discussion of PPB, zero-based budgeting, and MBO, see Allen Schick, *The Federal Budget,* 3rd ed. (Washington, DC: Brookings Institution Press, 2007).

19. Ibid.

20. For a textbook treatment of compliance auditing, see Harold L. Monk, *Compliance Auditing* (New York: American Institute of Certified Public Accountants, 1998). For an analysis of the role of inspectors general in carrying out compliance audits, see Mark H. Moore and Margaret Jane Gates, *Inspectors General: Junkyard Dogs or Man's Best Friend?* Social Research Perspectives No. 13 (New York: Russell Sage Foundation, 1986). For evidence of the price that compliance auditing can exact, see John J. DiIulio Jr., ed., *Deregulating the Public Service: Can Government Be Improved?* (Washington, DC: Brookings Institution Press, 1994).

21. Moore and Gates, *Inspectors General.* For a classic discussion of the value and problems of "red tape," see Herbert Kaufman, *Red Tape: Its Origins, Uses, and Abuses* (Washington, DC: Brookings Institution Press, 1977).

22. Marshall W. Meyer and Lynne G. Zucker, *Permanently Failing Organizations* (Thousand Oaks, CA: Sage Publications, 1989). See also Mark H. Moore, "Policing: De-Regulating or Re-Defining Accountability," in *Deregulating the Public Service,* ed. John J. DiIulio (Washington, DC: Brookings Institution Press, 1994).

23. Jerry L. Mashaw, *Bureaucratic Justice: Managing Social Security Disability Claims* (New Haven, CT: Yale University Press, 1983).

24. Ibid.

25. For an introduction to process reengineering, see B. R. Dey, *Business Process Re-Engineering and Change Management* (New Delhi, India: Dreamtech Press, 2004).

26. It is worth noting that many government agencies do not have direct clients because they are focusing on materially altering conditions in the world directly. Think of road building, direct efforts to clean up the environment, or national defense. In these cases the government produces something without necessarily having to encounter clients directly. Most things that government produces do work through transactions with clients, but those transactions are often viewed as a means for creating ambient conditions in the society—not just in terms of transactions with clients.

27. For an example, see David Kennedy, *Patrol Allocation in Portland, Oregon,* Case Study 818.0, 819.0 (Cambridge, MA: Harvard University Kennedy School of Government, 1988).

28. Bradley T. Gale, *Managing Customer Value: Creating Quality and Service That Customers Can See* (New York: Free Press, 1994).

29. This work was pioneered by R. Edwards Deming; see his *Out of the Crisis* (Cambridge, MA: The MIT Press, 2000). It has been very usefully extended and applied to the field of medicine; also see Donald M. Berwick, A. Blanton Godfrey, and Jane Roessner, *Curing Health Care: New Strategies for Quality Improvement* (San Francisco: Jossey-Bass, 1990).

30. Core to liberal democratic theory is the idea that individuals are the only important arbiters of value. Those who support the idea of liberal democracies hold to that idea as a normative ideal as well as a brute empirical fact. But an important part of the theory of this book is based on three observations that complicate the simple idea that individuals are the only important arbiters of value in a liberal democratic state. First, as observed in the book, individuals play many different roles in a democratic society, among them citizen, voter, taxpayer, client beneficiary, and client obligatee. Second, the values and commitments of individuals playing these different roles are combined, with varying degrees of success, in the many different forms of politics that give guidance to and evaluate the performance of government agencies. Third, those managing for the public have no choice but to believe that the collective can become articulate in a way that would give them guidance. Ideally, this would mean some kind of deliberative assembly of citizens or their representatives in which the values of citizens as opposed to the other roles gained great weight.

31. There is an important sense in which this conception is illiberal. The dominant role of individuals is pushed aside to make room for a collective that is evaluating social conditions. One could argue that a fundamental tenet of a liberal society is that the idea of a collective should play only a modest role in the organization of society, and that individuals be accorded significant rights that allow them to defend themselves against collective claims and collective institutions like governments. But even libertarians have to acknowledge enough of an interdependent, collective life to need to establish a government, and then to imagine enough of a collective life to decide together that all of the "I's" should live in collective circumstances that privilege the "I's" over the "we's."

32. This shows up in the techniques used to value public activity. Benefit-cost analysis, based largely in economics with its relentless focus on individual valuation, wants to value public policies in terms of how each individual values the net effect on himself or herself as an individual, then sums over the individuals. Program evaluation, based largely in statistics, tries to evaluate public expenditures in terms of whether the program achieved the objectives intended. But to make that set of measurements, program evaluators have to assume some collective purposes. They find that largely in stated legislative purposes—a recognition of a collective arbiter of value and desired social outcomes. For a discussion of benefit-cost analysis and its ties to individual valu-

ation, see Edith Stokey and Richard Zeckhauser, *A Primer for Policy Analysis* (New York: Norton, 1978), 257–270. For a discussion of program evaluation and its ties to legislative or policy intent, see Carol H. Weiss, *Evaluation Research: Methods of Assessing Program Effectiveness* (Englewood Cliffs, NJ: Prentice Hall, 1972), 7, 27, 118.

33. Note that each of these ideas would reduce the net public value of the program. If operating costs were high, if the program could not consistently produce desired results, and if the benefits to the society arrived long into the future, the overall net benefit of the program would be less than if the opposite of these facts were true. Presumably, then, more citizens of Illinois would regard the program as not worth the effort—even if there were a strong commitment to giving folks a chance as a matter of justice.

34. For further discussion of the incentives that are created for program managers when confronted by a heterogeneity among clients that is not reflected in payments to them for their work, see the section later in this chapter titled "Heterogeneous Client Populations and Cherry-Picking."

35. "Technology" is meant in the economic and engineering sense of the material process that uses resources to produce a particular output that is thought to be en route to the creation of a socially desired outcome.

36. Mark H. Moore and Anthony Braga, "Sizing Up Compstat: An Important Administrative Innovation in Policing," *Criminology and Public Policy* 2, no. 3 (2003): 457–460.

37. The discussion in this paragraph is picked up again in Chapter 7 in this book.

38. Note that both possibilities could be true—Herr's methods, if used with other client populations, could prove more cost-effective than the methods used by other contractors, *and* her own costs could be legitimately higher because of her particular client population.

39. See Mark H. Moore, "Learning While Doing: Linking Knowledge to Policy Development in Community Policing and Violence Prevention in the United States," in *Integrating Crime Prevention Strategies: Propensity and Opportunity*, ed. Per-Olof Wikstrom (Stockholm: Swedish National Council for Crime Prevention, 1995), 301–331.

40. U.S. Government, *Federal Support for Research and Development* (Memphis, TN: General Books LLC, 2001).

41. The federal agency that is responsible for many mixed-use research projects is the Defense Advanced Research Projects Agency (DARPA). For an account of its activities and accomplishments, see Frederic P. Miller, Agnes F. Vandome, and John McBrewster, *DARPA* (Saarbrücken, Germany: VDM Publishing, 2010).

42. For a discussion of the obstacles to innovation in government, see Alan A. Altshuler and Robert Behn, eds., *Innovation in American Government* (Washington, DC: Brookings Institution Press, 1997).

43. Geoff Mulgan, *Ready or Not? Taking Innovation in the Public Sector Seriously* (NESTA Provocation 03, April 2007), http://www.nesta.org.uk/publications/provocations/assets/features/ready_or_not_taking_innovation_in_the_public_sector_seriously.

44. Jan Carlzon, *Moments of Truth* (Cambridge, MA: Ballinger, 1987).

45. Her practitioner's perspective also had an important implication for the way she thought about her interventions: when she found a great deal of heterogeneity in her client population and learned that many small things stood in the way of their success, she concluded that she needed a continuous, highly flexible response to individual clients and changing circumstances and not, for example, a large-scale intervention that altered the social or economic structures that contributed to those many small problems.

46. Herr's detailed focus on the individuals whose behavior and condition simultaneously constituted the problem she was trying to solve and the solution to the problem yielded an unexpected benefit. It produced images of her clients and their struggles that made them more human and thus more sympathetic than the politically entrenched images of "welfare queens" cynically exploiting an overly generous citizenry.

47. Indeed, one could view the conflict between Herr and Tamayo as a great opportunity to orchestrate some kind of public deliberation about the public values at stake in the operations of the welfare-to-work programs and to clarify the values that ought to be pursued through such efforts. For a discussion of techniques for managing this sort of activity, see James S. Fishkin, Robert C. Luskin, and Roger Jowell, *Deliberative Polling and Public Consultation* (Stanford, CA: Center for Advanced Studies in the Behavioral Sciences at Stanford University, 2002). For a discussion of the role of this kind of activity in strategic management in government, see Archon Fung and Mark H. Moore, "Calling a Public into Existence," in *Ports in a Storm: Public Management in a Turbulent World*, ed. John D. Donahue and Mark H. Moore (Washington, DC: Brookings Institution Press, 2012). Also see the discussion of the mobilization of citizens in Chapter 5 in this book.

5. Diana Gale and the Seattle Solid Waste Utility

1. This is an adaptation of the case "'Please Be Patient': The Seattle Solid Waste Utility Meets the Press" by Howard Husock (Cambridge, MA: The President and Fellows of Harvard College, 1991). Quoted material in cases not cited otherwise in this chapter is from this source.

2. For a general discussion of the problem of innovating in government, see Alan A. Altshuler and Robert D. Behn, eds., *Innovation in American Government* (Washington, DC: Brookings Institution Press, 1997).

3. In Great Britain the challenge of getting individual citizens to behave in ways that support public purposes is called the behavioral change prob-

lem. Whenever the government tries to do this, it is pilloried as the "nanny state." But the reality is that governments do have to find ways to at least keep individuals from doing harm to others, and sometimes to cause them to do good. Governments do this in part by organizing what we have called "obligation encounters" with citizens. But governments also try to do this by "marketing" behavioral change efforts. For a review of the problem, see Geoff Mulgan, *The Art of Public Strategy: Mobilizing Power and Knowledge for the Common Good* (New York: Oxford University Press, 2009), 197–217. For a discussion on the methods of reaching large numbers of individuals, see Janet A. Weiss, "Public Information," in *The Tools of Government: A Guide to the New Governance,* ed. Lester Salamon (New York: Oxford University Press, 2002), 217–255.

4. For a discussion of this problem in the context of promoting tax compliance, see Mark H. Moore, "On the Office of Taxpayer and the Social Process of Taxpaying," in *Income Tax Compliance,* ed. Phillip Sawicki (Reston, VA: American Bar Association, 1983), 275–291.

5. This is a classic example of what Ronald Heifetz describes as the problem of adaptive change, in which individuals are called on not only to change accustomed activities but also to take a loss and invent new forms of behavior. See Ronald A. Heifetz, *Leadership without Easy Answers* (Cambridge, MA: Harvard University Press, 1998).

6. See Mulgan, "Changing Minds and Behaviour" in *The Art of Public Strategy: Mobilizing Power and Knowledge for the Common Good* (New York: Oxford University Press, 2009), 197–217; Weiss, "Public Information."

7. Mark H. Moore, "Mobilizing Support, Legitimacy, and Coproduction: The Functions of Political Management," in *Creating Public Value: Strategic Management in Government* (Cambridge, MA: Harvard University Press, 1995), 105–134. See also James Q. Wilson, *Bureaucracy: What Government Agencies Do and Why They Do It* (New York: Basic Books, 1989); William A. Niskanen Jr., *Bureaucracy and Representative Government* (Chicago: Aldine-Atherton, 1971).

8. Moore, *Creating Public Value.* Also see Robert Reich, *Public Management in a Democracy* (Englewood Cliffs, NJ: Prentice Hall, 1990). The issue is also discussed in Chapter 3 in this book.

9. For an argument that this is becoming the norm in government rather than the exception, see Stephen Goldsmith and William D. Eggers, *Governing By Network: The New Shape of the Public Sector* (Washington, DC: Brookings Institution Press, 2004).

10. Moore, "Mobilizing Support, Legitimacy, and Coproduction" (particularly the case titled "David Sencer and the Threat of Swine Flu") and "Advocacy, Negotiation, and Leadership," in *Creating Public Value,* 105–192.

11. Accenture Institute for Public Service Value, "Managing Current and Future Performance: Striving to Create Public Value" (Chicago: Accenture, 2007).

12. John Dewey, *The Public and Its Problems* (New York: Henry Holt, 1927).

13. Ibid., 208.

14. Ibid., 219.

15. For a marketing view of public policy making in democracies, see Katherine E. Jocz and John A. Quelch, "An Exploration of Marketing's Impacts on Society: A Perspective Linked to Democracy," *Journal of Public Policy and Marketing* 27, no. 2 (2008): 202–206.

16. For an early critical account of how modern marketing techniques developed in the private sector were being used in democratic political processes, see Joe McGinniss, *The Selling of the President* (New York: Penguin Books, 1988).

17. John Kenneth Galbraith, *The Affluent Society* (New York: Mariner Books, 1998).

18. Allan J. Kimmel, "Deception in Marketing Research and Practice: An Introduction," *Psychology and Marketing* 18, no. 7 (2001): 657–661.

19. J. Michael Sproule, "Propaganda Studies in American Social Science," *Quarterly Journal of Speech* 73, no. 1 (1987): 60–78.

20. Axel Johne, "Listening to the Voice of the Market," *International Marketing Review* 11, no. 1 (1994): 47–59.

21. Archon Fung and Erik Olin Wright, eds., *Deepening Democracy: Institutional Innovations in Empowered Participatory Governance* (London: Verso, 2003).

22. Philip Kotler and Kevin Lane Keller, *A Framework for Marketing Management* (Englewood Cliffs, NJ: Prentice Hall, 2011). Also see Sally Dibb and Lyndon Simkin, *Market Segmentation Success: Making It Happen* (Philadelphia: Haworth Press, 2008).

23. Kotler and Keller, *Framework for Marketing Management*.

24. Ibid.

25. V. Kumar, "Customer Lifetime Value: The Path to Profitability," *Foundations and Trends in Marketing* 2, no. 1 (2008): 1–96.

26. Robert S. Kaplan and David P. Norton, "Customer Perspective," in *The Balanced Scorecard: Translating Strategy into Action* (Boston, MA: Harvard Business School Press, 1996), 63–91.

27. Alison Theaker, *The Public Relations Handbook* (New York: Routledge, 2008), 232–233.

28. Dennis L. Wilcox and Glen T. Cameron, *Public Relations: Strategies and Tactics* (Boston: Allyn and Bacon, 2011).

29. My friend and colleague Greg Parston from Accenture introduced me to the idea that businesses needed a tacit "license to operate" in the society that was created by the public's sense of good conduct on behalf of the firm. For further discussion, see Mark H. Moore, "On Creating Public Value: What Business (and Nonprofit) Managers Can Learn from Government Managers (unpublished mimeo, 2003).

30. Noel Capon, with James Mac Hulbert, *Managing Marketing in the 21st Century* (Bronxville, NY: Wessex, 2007), chap. 16.

31. Moore, "Mobilizing Support, Legitimacy, and Coproduction" and "Conclusion" in *Creating Public Value*, 105–134, 293–310. Also see Archon Fung and

Mark H. Moore, "Calling a Public into Existence," in *Ports in a Storm: Public Management in a Turbulent World,* ed. John D. Donahue and Mark H. Moore (Washington, DC: Brookings Institution Press, 2012).

32. Thomas C. Schelling, *Choice and Consequence* (Cambridge, MA: Harvard University Press, 1984), 57–83.

33. Tom R. Tyler, *Why People Obey the Law* (Princeton: Princeton University Press, 2006).

34. For a definition of a social norm, see Cass R. Sunstein, "Social Norms and Social Roles," *Columbia Law Review* 96, no. 4 (May 1996): 903–968. For their development and evolution, see Elinor Ostrom, "Collective Action and the Evolution of Social Norms," *Journal of Economic Perspectives* 14, no. 3 (Summer 2000): 137–158.

35. Brian Broughman and Robert Cooter, "Charity and Information: Correcting the Failure of a Disjunctive Social Norm," University of California at Berkeley Law School, Faculty Publications Paper 359, February 11, 2009, 4, 8. http://www.repository.law.indiana.edu/facpub/359.

36. H. Wesley Perkins, "Social Norms and the Prevention of Alcohol Misuse in Collegiate Contexts," *Journal of Studies on Alcohol,* supplement no. 14 (2002): 164–172.

6. Duncan Wyse, Jeff Tryens, and the Progress Board

1. This case is adapted from Pamela Varley and Steve Kelman, *The Oregon Benchmarks Program: The Challenge of Restoring Political Support,* Case Studies 1554.0 and 1554.1 (Cambridge, MA: Harvard University Kennedy School of Government, 1990). Quoted material in cases not cited otherwise in this chapter is from this source.

2. Oregon's citizen legislators did not work full time but met for six months every two years to enact legislation and to adopt a two-year budget.

3. Such cuts had not, in the end, been necessary in 1991, as the property tax rate limit had been offset by the rapid inflation of assessed home values.

4. About thirty agencies used the benchmarks in some fashion, according to a June 1997 Progress Board report, and a few agencies or smaller divisions did use the benchmarks for strategic planning. These included the Oregon State Police, the Department of Land Conservation and Development, the Health Division, the Board of Forestry, the Office of the Health Plan Administrator, and the Senior and Disabled Services Division, according to the report.

5. At the encouragement of Senator Bryant, the Progress Board later went a step farther. Tryens convinced the Department of Administrative Services to make sure that each benchmark relevant to state government operations had a "lead" agency with responsibility for coordinating the efforts of all state agencies in pursuing the benchmark goal. During 1998 interim budget hearings, Bryant also asked Tryens to lead off budget discussions for each of the state's

eighteen largest agencies with a report on the benchmarks for which they had signed up. These reports were intended to set a context for agency budget discussions. Tryens wanted to avoid the potential awkwardness of appearing to evaluate the performance of other state agencies on the basis of benchmark trends. He handled the dilemma by reporting neutrally on the benchmarks and their relationship to the agencies, without attempting to evaluate agency performance. In 1999, however, Tryens's role became more contentious. A group of Republican legislators sought to reorganize and reduce the scope of the Oregon Department of Transportation (ODOT), a move adamantly opposed by the administration. At the same time, a different legislative committee asked Tryens to report on ODOT's performance vis-à-vis the relevant benchmarks. The administration, meanwhile, did not want Tryens to criticize ODOT in any way, as this might provide the agency's opponents with further ammunition to dismantle it. Tryens walked a fine line, evaluating how ODOT was measuring its own performance with respect to the benchmarks but not evaluating its performance per se. In the heated political context, however, even this approach was regarded by some in the administration as providing too much ammunition for the department's enemies.

6. Tryens noted that these teams ultimately did not live up to their full potential because the staff at the governor's office did not seem to put much stock in them.

7. The Oregon Benchmarks have drawn a great deal of attention and comment, but they are reviewed in several different streams of scholarly work. On one hand, they are seen as an example of what is called "performance based budgeting." See, for example, Harry P. Hatry, John J. Kirlin, and Jeffrey Scott Luke, *An Assessment of the Oregon Benchmarks: A Report to the Oregon Progress Board* (Eugene, OR: University of Oregon, 1994); see also Julia Melkers and Katherine Willoughby, "The State of the States: Performance-Based Budgeting Requirements in 47 out of 50," *Public Administration Review* 58, no. 1 (1998): 66–73. On the other hand, they are seen as an effort to construct indicators of community well-being. See David Swain, "Measuring Progress: Community Indicators and the Quality of Life," *International Journal of Public Administration* 26, no. 7 (2003): 789–814. Finally, they are seen as instruments of public engagement and democratic accountability. See Alan A. Altshuler, "Bureaucratic Innovation, Democratic Accountability, and Political Incentives," in *Innovation in American Government: Challenges, Opportunities, and Dilemmas*, ed. Alan A. Altshuler and Robert D. Behn (Washington, DC: Brookings Institution Press, 1997), 38–67. The fact that this initiative fits into, and in important ways integrates, these different potential uses of a public value account for a state is what makes them so interesting.

8. As discussed in Chapter 1, the idea of an organization with a single mission that captures all its important effects is not quite right. Many public organizations produce results that register not only on the dimensions of value identified in their "core mission" but also on the mission performance of other

government organizations. For example, police have effects on the success of public schools and public health departments. It follows that any given public organization does not have the exclusive responsibility for achieving a particular desired social outcome. This is one of the reasons that dealing with important social problems nearly always invites an analysis of the contribution that is being made by several different public organizations. See Stephen Goldsmith and William D. Eggers, *Governing By Network: The New Shape of the Public Sector* (Washington, DC: Brookings Institution Press, 2004).

9. Examined closely, many of the other managers also should have measures focusing on citizen engagement, satisfaction, willingness to contribute tax dollars and volunteer effort, and so on. But Gale's case is certainly an extreme in the degree to which she is relying on a daily basis on the willingness of citizens to do their part in managing solid waste.

10. For a classic analysis of the limitations of the powers of elected chief executives in democratic societies, see Richard E. Neustadt, *Presidential Power: The Politics of Leadership* (New York: Wiley, 1960). He famously concluded that a president's power was little more than the "power to persuade."

11. This used to be a theme supported by one part of the Republican Party—progressives who believed in progress and science and believed that business corporations animated by these forces and commitments could be agents of positive social change. See Theodore Roosevelt, "The Presidency: Making an Old Party Progressive: From an Autobiography, Chapter 10," reprinted in *American Progressivism: A Reader*, ed. Ronald J. Pestritto and William J. Atto (Lanham, MD: Lexington Books, 2008), 175–191.

12. The Progress Board and its work has its own strategic triangle, even as it is trying to develop itself as part of the machinery that the Oregon citizens and Oregon government use to imagine and manage their value-creating potential.

13. This is the approach that is often taken by political administrations that use central staff agencies and budgeting processes for purposes of centralizing the management of the executive branches of government. Indeed, this is probably the most common approach. Recent versions have included planning, programming, and budgeting, zero-based budgeting, and management by objectives. For an encyclopedic review of this experience, see Albert C. Hyde, *Government Budgeting: Theory, Process and Politics* (Stamford, CT: Wadsworth/Thompson Learning, 2002).

14. The Congressional Budget Office has played a similar role in dealing with financial issues. See Philip G. Joyce, *The Congressional Budget Office: Honest Numbers, Policy, and Policymaking* (Washington, DC: Georgetown University Press, 2011). The Progress Board sought to play a similar role in constructing measures on the output side of government, and/or the difference between articulated aspirations, on one hand, and real material conditions in society, on the other.

15. By "aspirational goals" I mean goals that would be very hard for an organization to achieve in the short term but that reflected the ultimate goals of the society. By "realistic goals" I mean goals that were easier to imagine the organization achieving but that represented something less than what was ultimately desirable.

16. As Wyse acknowledged, "When you looked at any subject matter in any depth, almost anyone looking at it would conclude that we didn't have enough benchmarks to do justice."

17. John Kingdon has referred to these "policy windows," which show up for both large policy issues and small operational matters, in *Agendas, Alternatives, and Public Policies* (New York: Longman, 1995), 165–196.

18. Of course, there is always the risk that what seems like an urgent opportunity or threat is not, after all, so important to the long-term goals and becomes instead a welcome distraction from dealing with tougher problems. As such, the urgent can become the enemy of the important.

19. Richard Elmore, "Mapping Backward: Implementation Research and Policy Decisions," *Political Science Quarterly* 94, no. 4 (Winter 1979–1980): 601–616.

20. Mark H. Moore, "Creating Networks of Capacity: The Challenge of Managing Society's Response to Youth Violence," in *Securing Our Children's Future: New Approaches to Juvenile Justice and Youth Violence,* ed. Gary S. Katzmann (Washington, DC: Brookings Institution Press, 2002), 338–385.

21. Stephen Goldsmith and Donald F. Kettl, eds., *Unlocking the Power of Networks: Keys to High-Performance Government* (Washington, DC: Brookings Institution Press, 2009).

22. Ann Costello and Gregory A. Garrett, *Getting Results: The Six Disciplines of Performance-Based Project Management* (Riverwoods, IL: CCH/Wolters Kluwer, 2008), 103–142, 183–200.

23. This kind of work looks a great deal like project management, as it has been developed in both the private and the public sectors. The key difference is that in this case the projects are efforts that cross organizational boundaries so that there is no direct authority to draw upon in creating accountability and focus. For a discussion of project management in business, see Harvard Business School Press, "Project Management as a Process" in *Managing Projects Large and Small: The Fundamental Skills for Delivering on Budget and on Time* (Boston, MA: Harvard Business School Press, 2004), 1–12.

24. For a description of the kind of problems that such managers face, see John Buntin, *The General and the "War" on Drugs: Barry McCaffrey and the Office of National Drug Control Policy,* Case Study 1427.0 (Cambridge, MA: Harvard University Kennedy School of Government, 1998).

25. Robert Behn makes a useful distinction among performance measurement systems developed at the organizational or jurisdictional level, on one hand, and those that are focused on problems, on the other. He calls the latter

"problem-stat." See Robert D. Behn, "Designing PerformanceStat: Or What Are the Key Strategic Choices That a Jurisdiction or Agency Must Make When Adapting the CompStat/CitiStat Class of Performance Strategies?" *Public Performance and Management Review* 32, no. 2 (2008): 206–235.

26. There are important philosophical and ideological reasons that governments in liberal democracies tend to be reactive rather than preventative. The most important reason is that a liberal state does not want to intrude where it is not needed. Consequently, a liberal state often has to wait until a problem is objectively and visibly bad before entering into a situation. A liberal state is also notoriously stingy with public funds. Whether an ounce of prevention is actually worth a pound of cure turns out to be a tougher calculation than most people assume. For a superb analysis of how to make this difficult calculation, see Malcolm Sparrow, *The Character of Harms: Operational Challenges in Risk Control* (New York: Cambridge University Press, 2008).

27. Robert S. Gordon Jr., "An Operational Classification of Disease Prevention," *Public Health Reports* 98, no. 2 (1983): 107–109.

7. Harry Spence and the Massachusetts Department of Social Services

1. Adapted from the case "Harry Spence and the Massachusetts Department of Social Services" by Emily Kernan and Philip Heymann (unpublished, August 25, 2006).

2. James Sullivan, "Man in the Middle," *Boston Globe Magazine*, June 25, 2006.

3. Pam Belluck, "Harry Spence Clears Paths for the Schools Chancellor," *New York Times*, February 16, 1997.

4. Ibid.

5. Harry Spence (interview), "Close-Up with Harry Spence," *Voice* 7, no. 3 (2006): 8–10.

6. Massachusetts Department of Social Services (DSS), "A Three-Tiered Approach to Developing Family-Centered Child Welfare Practice" (Boston: Massachusetts Department of Social Services, 2002), 6–7.

7. Carlisle ran the DSS in the years just before the federal government moved from compliance-based evaluation to outcome-based evaluation for state-run child welfare services in 2000.

8. Doris Sue Wong, "House Review Finds DSS Rushes Its Investigations," *The Boston Globe*, October 9, 1998, B1 (Metro section).

9. Phil Primack, "Looking at DSS from the Perspective of the Front Line," *The Boston Globe*, January 16, 2000, C2 (Focus section).

10. Ibid.

11. Kernan and Heymann, "Harry Spence and the Massachusetts Department of Social Services," 34.

12. Massachusetts DSS, "Three-Tiered Approach," 1.

13. Ibid., 2.

14. Harry Spence, interview by Mark Moore, May 29, 2007. Quoted material not cited otherwise in this chapter is from this source.

15. A year later, in yet another statewide budget crunch, many senior staff members took an early retirement.

16. Kernan and Heymann, "Harry Spence and the Massachusetts Department of Social Services," 39.

17. Ibid.

18. Letter from Commissioner Harry Spence to the Massachusetts legislature, January 21, 2005.

19. Letter from Commissioner Harry Spence to the Massachusetts legislature, October 6, 2004.

20. Ibid., 4.

21. Letter from Commissioner Harry Spence to the Massachusetts legislature, April 24, 2002, 12.

22. Ibid., 3.

23. Letter from Harry Spence to the Massachusetts legislature, January 21, 2005, 2.

24. Ibid.

25. Kathleen Hennrikus, "Lewis 'Harry' Spence," *Boston Globe*, May 24, 2007.

26. Letter from Harry Spence to the Massachusetts legislature, October 6, 2004, 4.

27. Erwin C. Hargrove and John C. Glidewell, eds., *Impossible Jobs in Public Management* (Lawrence: University Press of Kansas, 1990); Horst W. J. Rittel and Melvin M. Webber, "Dilemmas in a General Theory of Planning," *Policy Sciences* 4 (Amsterdam: Elsevier Scientific Publishing Company, 1973): 155–169.

28. Josephine G. Pryce, Kimberly K. Shackelford, and David H. Pryce, *Secondary Traumatic Stress and the Child Welfare Professional* (Chicago: Lyceum Books, 2007).

29. This is a place where no small amount of political learning among those who want to call the agency to account would be very helpful.

30. This lag sometimes occurs because it takes time for a desired result to occur—we may not be sure that children who were reunited with their families after temporary foster care arrangements benefited until they grow up. Other times the lag occurs because the benefits accrue continuously and get larger as an early achievement is sustained—success in immediately reducing the threat of abuse and neglect to a child becomes larger and more valuable the longer the child remains risk free.

31. There is a background social context that profoundly shapes the conditions that a public manager is trying to alter, and that can be more or less easily engaged and mobilized by the manager.

32. Mark H. Moore, "Policing: De-Regulating or Re-Defining Accountability," in *De-Regulating the Public Service: Can Government Be Improved?* ed. John J. DiIulio Jr. (Washington, DC: Brookings Institution Press, 1994), 198–235.

33. Richard J. Light, "Abused and Neglected Children in America: A Study of Alternative Policies," *Harvard Educational Review* 43, no. 4 (1973): 556–598.

34. Mark H. Moore, "Invisible Offenses: A Challenge to Minimally Intrusive Law Enforcement," in *ABSCAM Ethics: Moral Issues and Deception in Law Enforcement*, ed. Gerald M. Caplan (Cambridge, MA: Ballinger, 1983), 17–18.

35. Spence points out that "conscientious error isn't 'error'; it's when the odds go against you" (personal communication).

36. Personal communication.

37. This movement to root professional practices in knowledge generated by experimental testing is called "Evidence-Based X." It appears in medicine, see D. L. Sackett et al., "Evidence Based Medicine: What It Is and What It Isn't," *BMJ* 312, no. 71 (1996): 312–371; in policing, see Lawrence W. Sherman, *Evidence Based Policing* (Washington, DC: Police Foundation, 1998); in education, see Philip Davies, "What Is Evidence Based Education?" *British Journal of Educational Studies* 47, no. 2 (1999): 108–121; in social work, see Brian Sheldon and Rupatharsini Chilvers, "Evidence Based Social Care: A Study of Prospects and Problems," *Journal of Social Work* 1, no. 3 (2001): 375–377.

38. See the discussion in Chapter 4 about the role of social research and development (R&D) in searching for production possibility frontiers in public management. For a more comprehensive treatment of why social R&D is important, see Geoff Mulgan, "The Process of Social Innovation," *Innovations* 1 no. 2 (2006): 145–162.

39. See the discussion about process values in Chapter 4.

40. Tom R. Tyler, *Why People Obey the Law* (Princeton: Princeton University Press, 2006).

41. This is essentially what Diana Gale succeeded in doing.

42. Thomas J. Peters and Robert H. Waterman Jr. described this as the "tight-loose" property of management control systems in successful companies. See their book *In Search of Excellence: Lessons from America's Best Companies* (New York: Warner Books, 1982).

43. The four characteristics of accountability systems enumerated in Chapter 3 described public agencies' political accountability to their authorizing environments and particularly to their key legislative overseers. The accountability systems we consider here are the much thicker and denser and more frequently used sinews of accountability that run from agency managers through their midlevel managers to the organization's line workers.

44. Obviously one could improve agency performance even more by working harder *and* working smarter. The Holy Grail in managing organizations is to find some kind of accountability system that can attract energetic, conscientious performance in doing what the organization already knows how

to do and developing the methods that would allow it to use its own operating experience to find new and better ways of performing existing or new tasks. Presumably the path here is one that moves along specific innovations and adaptations. Some of these can be big—whole new products or services being introduced with big strategic investment dollars behind them. Others can be much smaller productivity-gaining innovations. For a classic treatment of the requirements of an innovative organization, see Peter Senge, *The Fifth Discipline: The Art and Practice of the Learning Organization* (New York: Doubleday, 1990). For a compelling discussion of creating innovative health care organizations, see Richard M. J. Bohmer, *Designing Care: Aligning the Nature and Management of Health Care* (Cambridge, MA: Harvard Business School Press, 2009). For a discussion of the difference between managing for a few relatively large-scale innovations versus many small innovations, see Mark H. Moore and Jean M. Hartley, "Break-Through Innovations and Continuous Improvement: Two Different Models of Innovative Processes in the Public Sector," *Public Money & Management* 25, no. 1 (2005): 43–50.

45. For a comprehensive introduction to concepts of production and operations management, see S. Anil Kumar and N. Suresh, *Production and Operations Management* (New Delhi, India: New Age International Publishers, 2006), 1–17.

46. At the same time Burger King sought to customize its product by allowing customers to name the particular condiments they wanted to be applied to their (standard-width) burgers. See David C. Rikert and W. Earl Sasser, *McDonald's Corporation (Condensed)* (Cambridge, MA: Harvard Business School Case Services, Case no. 9-681-044, rev. 2/82); David C. Rikert and W. Earl Sasser, *Burger King Corporation* (Cambridge, MA: Harvard Business School Case Services, Case no. 9-681-045, rev. 6/81).

47. Moore and Hartley, "Break-Through Innovations and Continuous Improvement."

48. Sarita Chawla and John Renesch, *Learning Organizations: Developing Cultures for Tomorrow's Workplace* (New York: Productivity Press, 1995).

49. Thomas J. Peters and Robert H. Waterman, *In Search of Excellence: Lessons from America's Best Managed Companies* (New York: Warner Books, 1982).

50. Peter F. Drucker, *Innovation and Entrepreneurship: Practice and Principles* (New York: Harper & Row, 1985), 147–176.

51. David A. Garvin, *Learning in Action: A Guide to Putting the Learning Organization to Work* (Cambridge, MA: Harvard Business School Press, 2000).

52. David Ulrich, Steve Kerr, and Ronald N. Ashkenas, *The GE Work-Out: How to Implement GE's Revolutionary Method for Busting Bureaucracy and Attacking Organizational Problems Fast* (New York: McGraw-Hill, 2002).

53. Robert D. Behn, "Do Goals Help Create Innovative Organizations?" in *Public Management Reform and Innovation: Research, Theory, and Practice*, ed. H. George Frederickson and Jocelyn M. Johnston (Tuscaloosa: University of Alabama Press, 2000), 70–88.

54. Robert S. Kaplan and David P. Norton, *The Balanced Scorecard: Translating Strategy into Action* (Boston, MA: Harvard Business School Press, 1996).

55. Morton T. Hansen, Nitin Nohria, and Thomas Tierney, "What's Your Strategy for Managing Knowledge?" *Harvard Business Review* 7, no. 2 (1999) 106–116.

56. Kaplan and Norton, *The Balanced Scorecard.*

57. To see how a skillful manager faced a similar challenge in the private sector, see Mark H. Moore, *Vision and Strategy: Paul O'Neill at OMB and Alcoa,* Case Studies 1134.0–1134.2 (Cambridge, MA: Harvard University Kennedy School of Government).

58. Spence articulated a philosophy of casework that specified both the ends and the means. This could be seen as a violation of the principle that says the means should be left open. But the philosophy was sufficiently broad and abstract enough that it left a lot of room for invention in the means as well as the ends. As Chapter 4 indicates, the same property was characteristic of Toby Herr's approach to the management of the welfare-to-work process: a general philosophy caused frontline workers to do many different things. The philosophy of the means remained constant: the particular expressions of that philosophy in operations changed a great deal, depending on the circumstances.

59. Peter Busch, *Tacit Knowledge in Organizational Learning* (New York: IGI Publishing, 2008).

60. Howard Gardner, Mihaly Csikszentmihalyi, and William Damon, *Good Work: When Excellence and Ethics Meet* (New York: Basic Books, 2001).

Conclusion

1. James Q. Wilson and George L. Kelling, "Broken Windows: The Police and Neighborhood Safety," *Atlantic Monthly* (March 1982): 29–38.

2. *The Challenge of Crime in a Free Society,* Report by the President's Commission on Law Enforcement and Administration of Justice (New York: Dutton, 1968).

3. Ibid.

4. Mark H. Moore, Robert C. Trojanowicz, and George L. Kelling, "Policing and the Fear of Crime," *Perspectives on Policing* 3 (Washington, DC: National Institute of Justice, U.S. Department of Justice, and the Program in Criminal Justice Policy and Management, Kennedy School, Harvard University, June 1988).

5. Ibid.

6. George L. Kelling and William J. Bratton, "Declining Crime Rates: Insiders' Views of the New York City Story," *Journal of Criminal Law and Criminology* 88, no. 4 (1988): 1217–32.

7. Wilson and Kelling, "Broken Windows."

8. Kelling and Bratton, "Declining Crime Rates."

9. Lawrence W. Sherman, Patrick R. Gartin, and Michael E. Buerger, "Hot Spots of Predatory Crime: Routine Activities and the Criminology of Place," *Criminology* 27, no. 1 (February 1989): 27–56.

10. Herman Goldstein, *Problem Oriented Policing* (New York: McGraw-Hill, 1990).

11. James L. Heskett, *NYPD New* (Boston, MA: Harvard Business School Publishing, 1999), product no. 396293-PDF-ENG.

12. James W. Wilson, "Dilemmas of Police Administration," *Public Administration Review* 28, no. 5 (1968): 407–417.

13. *Report of the National Advisory Commission on Civil Disorders* (New York: E. P. Dutton, 1968).

14. David A. Garvin, *Learning in Action: A Guide to Putting the Learning Organization to Work* (Boston, MA: Harvard Business School Press, 2000).

15. David Ulrich, Steve Kerr, and Ronald N. Ashkenas, *The GE Work-Out: How to Implement GE's Revolutionary Method for Busting Bureaucracy and Attacking Organizational Problems Fast* (New York: McGraw-Hill, 2002).

16. Robert S. Kaplan and David P. Norton, *The Balanced Scorecard: Translating Strategy into Action* (Boston, MA: Harvard Business School Press, 1996), 126–146.

Acknowledgments

I'm not sure I have ever had a completely original thought. All the ideas I have written down, all the observations I have made, all the frameworks I have created have had their origins in something I learned from someone else—my teachers, my mentors, my colleagues, and perhaps most of all, the managers I have met in executive programs at the Kennedy School. They might not recognize their contribution; indeed, they might be anxious to disavow their influence! But I know the degree to which they have authored my work. This work is no exception. It is a simple accumulation of what I have learned from others.

While sifting through my recollections about how this book came to be, however, several particular contributions stand out. I think the book really began when Carol Weiss invited me to give a talk at a seminar she had been leading at Harvard on the evaluation of government policies and programs. In preparing for that talk, I had to confront the fact that despite my enormous enthusiasm for cost-benefit analysis and program evaluation—the methods I had been taught to use to recognize value creation in the public sector—those methods could not be used practically to manage organizations. Nor, it seemed, could budgeting techniques such as performance-based budgeting or zero-based budgeting be used, since they seemed to depend on the existence of a comprehensive set of program evaluations and/or cost-benefit analyses of all programs within a government agency. The idea of managing by objectives (MBO) seemed to have the most promise, since it was flexible and could cover all the activities of an organization, but at the time, MBO seemed to be focused on operational objectives that were poorly linked to valued outcomes. The challenge that Carol set for me in that talk was the germ of this book.

The book got another enormous push when Accenture created the Public Service Value Institute to support intellectual work on how to define and measure "public value." My friend and colleague, Greg Parston, was appointed to lead the Institute, and he challenged me to put my money where my mouth was.

I was always talking about "public value"; Greg challenged me to write a book that would advance the cause of defining and measuring it. It was hard to say no.

In working out the ideas in the book, I was fortunate to be able to work alongside some colleagues at the Kennedy School who were also working on performance measurement. Dutch Leonard, Christine Letts, and Jim Honan were working hard on Executive Programs in performance measurement for both government and nonprofit managers. Steve Kelman and Shelley Metzenbaum convened an Executive Session on performance measurement in government from which I benefited a great deal. Bob Behn developed first a course, then a strong research project on how the idea of Compstat spread throughout the public sector as a management technique, and more generally on how performance measurement could be joined to managerial systems to promote accountability, performance, and learning. At the Harvard Business School, I was inspired by Robert Kaplan, whose work had become very influential in both governmental and nonprofit organizations. In the world of public management and public administration, I followed the extraordinary path blazed by Harry Hatry of the Brookings Institute as he pushed the performance measurement agenda forward, documented what happened, and kept the flag held high.

I also owe a debt to Howard Husock and Carolyn Wood, whose leadership and protection of the Kennedy School case program in difficult times has preserved a wealth of information about how public leaders and managers address real problems. I am also grateful to Peter Holm for much-needed help translating complex ideas into comprehensible graphics, to Edward Wade at Westchester Book Services for copyediting services, and to Michael Aronson and Kathleen Drummy at Harvard University Press for their patience and support.

All of these intellectual sources and practical collaborators were hugely important in putting together this book. But it would never have seen the light of day were it not for the resourceful and indefatigable efforts of two young editors who took a lumpy manuscript and added whatever grace and coherence the book now has. One of these was Elizabeth Foz, a person I had first known as the childhood friend of my daughter, who had since become a formidable intellectual and editorial force. The other was my daughter, Gaylen Williams Moore. Gaylen and I had written a monograph on managing state arts organizations together, and that had been a good experience. But getting this book in shape turned out to be a challenge of a wholly different order. I am quite sure that I could not have gotten a stronger, more determined, or more talented editorial effort from anyone else on Earth. She put all of a daughter's love, and no small part of a daughter's delight in challenging her father's weaknesses, into the editorial effort that has made this book legible. I will be forever in her debt, and any reader who learns something useful from the book will be in her debt, too.

These folks tried their hardest to keep me from making errors. Those that remain are mine alone.

Index

accountability: in the private sector, 85, 149, 170, 387–388; demands for, 85–89, 96–97, 144, 150, 173–174; to elected officials, 86–87; and the media, 87–88; to the general public, 87–88, 278, 314–315 (*see also* grassroots public opinion); negotiating terms of, 91–92, 151–154, 163–164, 172–174, 392–395; resistance to, 96, 153; internal, 97–99, 199–200, 372–379 (*see also* performance management systems); and government performance, 97–99, 285, 315; and legitimacy and support, 114–116; forums for, 144–145, 155–156, 161, 376–377; to legislative overseers, 149–150, 153, 169, 353–355; mutual, 155, 159–161; principal-agent theory of, 156–160; for interagency cooperation, 338–339; peer-to-peer, 351–352, 382–385; "industrial" versus "professional" models, 380–381, 383, 390–392. *See also* legitimacy and support; oversight agencies
accountability relationships, 154–161, 265
accountability structure, 86–89, 93, 114–115, 149–153, 161, 164–167
account management systems, 275–276, 283–285
acute versus chronic conditions, 214–215
agency interdependence and coordination, 125. *See also* partners and coproducers

Anemone, Louis, 21, 25
appointed public executives, 95–96
arbiters of value, 32, 41, 58–61, 206–207, 221, 265
Armajani, Babak, 134, 136–138
auditing agencies, 86
authority of the state: just and fair use of, 32, 55, 219–221, 290, 371–372; costs of, 34, 54–56; efficient and effective use of, 290, 371–372. *See also* eligibility requirements; obligation encounters
authorizing environment: composition of, 114–115; empirical analysis of, 150–151, 161–167; conflicts within, 151; complexity of, 151, 164–165, 167–172; dynamism of, 151, 164–165, 172–174, 313; normative evaluation of, 162–163; and the quality of accountability structures, 162–163; legitimacy of, 163–164; individuals in, 265; political management of, 279. *See also* accountability; legitimacy and support

Balanced Scorecard, The (Kaplan and Norton), 84, 107
Barry, Marion, 73–74
bottom line, the, 38–39, 52, 109, 400
bottom-line management. *See* value-oriented public management
Bowsher, Charles, 209–210
Bratton, William, 19–38, 69–70, 99–100, 401
broken windows theory, 29, 402–403